Meditations on Christ

Other Books by Lee Irwin

The Dream Seekers: Native American Visionary Traditions of the Great Plains. OK: University of Oklahoma Press, 1994.

Visionary Worlds: The Making and Unmaking of Reality. NY: State University of New York Press, 1996.

The Gnostic Tarot: Mandalas for Spiritual Transformation. ME: Samuel Weiser, Inc., 1998.

Awakening to Spirit: On Life, Illumination and Being. NY: State University of New York Press, 1999.

Alchemy of Soul: The Art of Spiritual Transformation. WA: Lorian Press, 2007.

Coming Down From Above: Prophecy, Resistance, and Renewal in Native American Religions. OK: University of Oklahoma Press, 2008.

Meditations on Christ

Lee Irwin

Raa-Nub

Meditations on Christ

Copyright © 2016 by Lee Irwin

Lee Irwin has asserted his right to be identified as the Author of this Work. All rights are reserved, including the right to reproduce this book, or portions thereof, in any form. Reviewers may quote brief passages.

Book Design and Copy Editing
by Jeremy Berg

Published by Lorian Press
6592 Peninsula Dr
Traverse City MI 49686

ISBN: 978-0-936878-91-1

Irwin, Lee
Meditations on Christ/Lee Irwin

Library of Congress Control Number: 2016951905

First Edition: October 2016

Printed in the United States of America

0 9 8 7 6 5 4 3 2 1

www.lorian.org

Dedication

This book is dedicated to the sacred lineages of all past, present and future teachers and masters of the Hermetic path, to all Christ-Sophia seekers, and to the pure in heart, "for they shall see God."

Acknowledgments

My thanks and deep appreciation to the Lorian Association Board members and to Lorian Press owner Jeremy Berg for his willingness to graciously publish and to design the layout for this work.

Contents

Prologue I

Anastasis (Resurrection)
THE WAY: ONE CHRIST 1

    The Christ 2
    The Way 6
    Faith 11
    The Gate 14
    The Four Faces 18
    The Fifth Face 25
    The Church 29
    Authority 33
    Robes 38
    Diadems 42
    Grace 47
    Illumination 51

Apolutrósis (Redemption)
THE TRUTH: ONE SPIRIT 55

    Spirit 56
    Truth 59
    Below 63
    Resurrection 67
    Communion 73
    Devotion 76
    Blessings 80
    The Veils 85
    Gifts 89
    Humanity 94
    Comfort 98
    Divinity 103

Apokalupsis (Revelation)
THE LIGHT: ONE GOD 108

    God 109
    The Light 113
    Unknowing 118
    Prayer 123
    Attributes 129
    The Footstool 134

- Wisdom 139
- Mystery 143
- Unity 148
- Revelations 152
- Beyond 156
- The Return 161

Athanasia (Immortality)
THE ETERNAL: ONE TRUE LIFE 166

- The Eternal 167
- Unbound 172
- Salvation 176
- Redemption 181
- Virtues 185
- Vice 190
- Healing 195
- Peace 200
- The Waters 204
- Bread 209
- The Cup 213
- Reborn 217

Anabathmos (Ascension)
THE EVERLASTING: ONE RECITATION 222

- Everlasting 223
- Faith 227
- Education 232
- Good Thoughts 237
- Marriage 241
- Sexuality 246
- Children 251
- Work 256
- Play 260
- Old Age 265
- Death 269
- The World 273

The Sixty Aphorisms i
Bibliography vi
Author Biography vii

Prologue

This is a book about the Hermetic Christ, not the Christ of traditional Christianity, not the Christ of the Church, nor the Christ of the conventional faith of Catholic, Eastern Orthodox, or Protestant teachings. And yet, it is a book about a Christ of all those traditions and faiths; it is about an Inner Christ, the emblematic, alchemical Christ of the transfiguration, a mystical Christ of resurrection and rebirth. However, "new wine in old skins" cannot last, the skins weather and split, the seams break and the wine soaks into the ground or turns bitter. New wine is put into new skins and retains its liquid life in Spirit, mellowing with age, and yet sustaining its taste and quality. The Hermetic Christ is traceable to the very origins of Christianity and precedes those origins by many generations. It is a Christ reborn through a synthesis of multiple traditions, diverse ideas, and a mystical weaving of old patterns with new emergence spiritual realizations. The Hermetic Christ is not a remote or transcendent sign in any distant sense but lives vibrantly in the heart of the devotee and is a presence felt and known, experienced directly. This Christ resonates as a harbinger of Spirit, a sign pointing toward a mystical encounter, an image divested of exclusive ideas and opened to the energies of creative Light.

The Hermetic Christ is not an idea but an experience; not an abstraction but an encounter; not simply imagined, but a direct visionary knowing. And this knowing is deep and lasting, it opens the heart to the reality of Love, Spirit, and Mystery. In so doing, it transforms the initiate into a vessel of grace which radiates into the world as healing awareness. The wonder of the Hermetic Christ is that those who follow a Hermetic path, a heart-centered, transformative way, can become one with that Christ, one in Spirit, one in Mystery. It is not a Way based only in faith, but also in knowledge and a direct experiential truth that the Hermetic Christ dwells within. This knowledge, the degrees of knowing, is deepened as we pass through the Hermetic Christ, into the dynamic creativity of Spirit, and out into the Boundless Deep. This Limitless Deep has no boundary, no containment, no easy articulate summary or expression; all traditions are expressions of that Deep, all paths walk on the edge of that Abyss. And the Hermetic Christ is the emblematic Sign, the figure who walks on water, calling us toward the mystery and fulfillment of our own direct realizations in Spirit.

The origin of this book came in a visionary encounter, at a time when I least expected any such manifestation. It came unbidden and without forethought. At the time, I was in not inclined toward any form of Christian teachings. I was never a member of any church, nor was I motivated to become a member of any such community. While I was raised in a nominally Christian home, there was little or no actual practice or discussion of Christian traditions, other than a few holidays such as Christmas and Easter. On my own, I had repudiated much of Christianity because of its often violent, fanatical, and excessively aggressive, over-bearing history, feelings which troubled me for many years. I was deeply dismayed by the immense gap between Christian sentimental ideals and the actuality of practices which were rigid, intolerant, condemning, and unreceptive to other spiritual traditions. Many Christians seemed to have very little concern for spiritual self-development and seemed to promote only a small fraction of the greater teachings hidden behind often argumentative, inter-Christian conflicts. Many times, in speaking to Christians, I heard a denial of the revolutionary spiritual teachings inherent in the early Christian traditions as well as intolerant discourses with regard to non-Christian religions. Christians often seemed completely insular and incapable of truly learning from other spiritual traditions and then modifying and evolving their understanding of Christianity, understanding that these traditions might well challenge its most basic and supposedly fundamental ideas.

Preceding this experience, I worked for a campus ministry in a special position in which I organized discussion and study groups for students at the nearby University. My task was to develop a "spiritual search" program, directed at students who were not necessarily Christian or who were Christian but had strong interests in other religious traditions. I formed a bridge between Christian and non-Christian students who were seeking new directions in their own spiritual development. I ran mediation retreats, special workshops, growth groups, small evening discussion programs involving world religions and topical workshops in comparative spirituality and personal spiritual development. During the day I worked side by side with ministers from four different Protestant denominations, with whom I had cordial and positive relationships. However, after three full years of this work, I decided that I could not be content in campus ministry, even as an "alternative" group facilitator. So we parted amicably and I turned away altogether from Christianity, having seen it up close, with all its inner denominational workings, national meetings, competitions, and general secular concerns that left me having no desire at all to participate in Christian "professional" ministry. Overall, it was an experiment that convinced me that conventional Christianity did not provide the spiritual path I was seeking.

Thus, I was wholly unprepared for the visionary experience that came to me. This experience was by no means the first such experience of this type; proceeding this, I had many other visionary encounters. And I have continued to have them since this experience up to the present day. But none of them were so pointedly "Christian." Most other experiences were tied to traditions of India, Buddhism, or occasionally, Islam and Sufism. Other visions were linked to paranormal perceptions, out of body experiences, and lucid dreams and visionary encounters of many types. However, I also had experiences with a certain aura of Christian presence or ideas, for example, a vivid dream of being in a church and having some encounter or transformative experience. So there was a visionary thread woven through my awareness, but other traditions were far more present and vivid in my imagination. And I had certain experiences, of a very powerful and mystical sort, which had no connections at all to any "religious" tradition, even though they were profoundly spiritual. Then, one night, several years after leaving the ministry and having taken up the profession of carpentry, I had the following experience. I went to bed and slept for most of the night. Before dawn, I awoke in an altered state of awareness; at the foot of my bed stood a radiant figure, a Christ, who vividly appeared to me as a man dressed in a white robe, with dark hair, dark eyes, and an olive complexion emanating a lucid, intense source of love and healing. This love radiated from his heart with tremendous, profound power and radiated an overwhelming sense of spiritual presence; the love poured forth like a tangible light, vivid and utterly alive. It seemed to penetrate my whole body, mind and being, the entire room was filled with a gentle but invisible power and presence.

As I looked on in amazement, I saw that he had a book in his hand. He then looked at me, emanating invisible love, and said, "Why hast thou forsaken me?" And he leaned down and handed me the book, as it flew from his hand into my hand, saying, "This is the Raa-Nub." I took the book into my hands and looked at it. It was not a large book, and it had an engraved cover. I had no idea what the phrase "Raa-Nub" meant, though I recognized its Egyptian character. When he handed me the book, I saw that it was a mystical-hermetic teaching; a new interpretation of an ancient pathway. I took the book carefully and opened the cover and looked at the title page. It was titled, "Meditations on Christ" and consisted of a series of aphorisms, each with a commentary. At the bottom of the title page was an Egyptian symbol, an image which I did not recognize nor understand. The first aphorism was at the top of the first page and said, "There is only One Christ, eternal and everlasting; the same today, tomorrow and forever." I read through four more such aphorisms, repeated here in the Recitation, which were the core of the book and its structure. I looked up again at the figure at the foot of my bed, he seemed radiant, filled with sorrow and love, sober, serious, concerned for the suffering that all humanity felt. I felt dazed and overwhelmed. Then, he and the book disappeared, leaving me in a very deeply entranced state, vividly aware of his absence; for about ten minutes I could not move or even lift my arms.

This visionary experience occurred in October 1981, long before I would successfully publish any books. After I could move, I got up and rummaged through my bookcases and found an old Egyptian hieroglyphic dictionary (Budge) and I was able to look up the hieroglyphic image drawn on the front page of the book. After much searching I found the exact symbol with several variants; it was pronounced "Raa-Nub" (!) and meant "The Golden Raa" or "Golden Light of Divinity," a symbol that linked female sacred cow (earth) and the male sun (heaven). I had never seen this symbol before. I was astounded and could not forget this dream. Many years passed. I continued my study of world religions and world spirituality, going increasingly into the esoteric aspects of many traditions while also studying Native American and other indigenous religions. Several years later, I had a sudden, powerful inner inspiration to write down all the aphorisms for the Christ book; so I sat down and wrote out 60 of them in a single, brief evening. Then I began to think about writing a commentary for each aphorism and started by writing a little on a few of the early ones. I quickly realized that I was not ready, emotionally or spiritually, to write this book. I needed more life-experience, more integration, and a more genuine appreciation of the Christ-spirit in my own life. Many times I would return to this book, and then put it away realizing I was still not ready to write it.

After about ten years, having written several unpublished books, I gave up my construction business where I earned my master carpenter status, and returned to graduate school and earned a doctorate in comparative religion and folklore. I wrote a dissertation on Native American dreams and religions which was later published. I then began a college teaching career while continuing to write on native religions. At the same time, I also continued my explorations of world religions and the esoteric aspects of comparative and contemporary spirituality and, later, I successfully published several books on the subject. In this process of gradual development, I began to appreciate more and more the need for a spiritual rootedness within the "western" traditions that would encourage the same expansive freedom and openness I found in many of the "eastern" traditions. I delved more and more into western esoteric teachings and found, in particular, a fascination for the Gnostic and Hermetic philosophies. I traced the history of these writings into the present through the labyrinths of western alchemy, theosophy, kabbalah, magic, mysticism, occult philosophy and various esoteric movements and groups. Eventually I arrived full-circle, realizing that, after many other experiences had prepared the way, I was now back, 20 years later, to the visionary call of Christ. That visionary encounter beckoned once more, arousing within me a determination to meet that challenge and find the words to express my understanding of what I have called the Hermetic Christ. Even so, I was hesitant because of my lack of maturity. However, I wrote a draft of the book and then let it sit for another ten years, occasionally revisiting it and reflecting upon its contents.

In this reflective process, I came to realize that the Hermetic Christ is more than an idea or symbol; it is a reality born out of a vision that remains vital and vibrant within an esoteric search for spiritual truth. It is a relative truth, a personal truth, a meaningful spiritual path built on direct visionary experiences and intelligent reflections on those experiences tempered by many years of study, meditation, symbol making, and visionary transformations. The Hermetic Christ is not a sign of old order thinking, nor is it a repetition of older, archaic gnostic ideas, though it does resonate respectfully with some of those ideas. The work is Neo-Ontological insofar as it reflects visionary reality as the primary epistemological index for genuine spiritual knowledge. The vision is not secondary nor can its meaning and value be derived from some material or psycho-biological theoretical basis. The vision is a primary source of meaning, a communion with Spirit; it is a source of spiritual direction and guidance; it reflects a personalized ontology in which understanding is a direct function of illuminative experiences that result from an opening to new vistas of awareness.

These openings, and there are many different kinds, are facilitated by a special receptivity to altered states induced through the creativity activity of Spirit. The Hermetic Christ is a central visionary symbol of the creative foundations of human consciousness receptive to and enhanced by the inflow of mystical insights, illuminative states, and higher awareness. Christ, like many other great teachers, embodied, in specific and limiting historical circumstances, an actualization of that higher awareness. Other teachers, like the Buddha, the Bodhisattvas, the Rishis, Yogis, Taoist Immortals, the Saints, Mystics, Hasids, Sufis and Shamans have also embodied a wide range of variations of such awareness--each conditioned by place and historical circumstances. The birth of the Hermetic Christ is really a rebirth, it is nothing more than an ongoing affirmation of the capacity that all human beings have for higher awareness and illuminative states. We all participate in these states, through dreams, visions, sudden insights, bright moments of clarity, intuitive perceptions of certainty and lucid, clear understanding. The facilitation of those states is a matter of internal focus and shared communal relationships that act to enhance the spiritual intensity of those experiences.

The Hermetic Christ is a nodal point that, through internalization processes, becomes a bright spark capable of transforming the entire awareness of an individual or a community. And the Hermetic aspect is just that transformation: the art of spiritual awakening to new insights that lead to genuine illuminations and an altered understanding of life, being, and becoming. It is not a rational process, nor is it attainable through intellectual debate or abstract theories of mind, soul, or being. There is a Way, but it requires walking, not just thinking or debating. The Hermetic Way is a winding path, a labyrinth, a mythic journey into the soul's uncharted country, a path downward as well as upward, an integration of all below with all above. The Alpha-Omega of this path is the complete realization of the individual through awakened knowledge of the unbound Mystery that constitutes the true ultimacy of Being. And the Hermetic Christ is a beacon of that awakening, a bright radiance of Love so powerful and so intense that it leads to the Abyss where only the few may attain the higher realizations. For others, the Hermetic Christ is the sign of Presence that life as it appears is not the full depth, that life as it seems is far from complete.

As the years passed, I discovered that the original lack of Christian contexts in my visions was slowly enhanced by an increasing visionary call to acknowledge and embrace the "one true life" illustrated by more explicit Christian dreams and encounters. I have increasingly had more direct visionary experiences with a powerful Christian contents that have enhanced my sense of the Christ presence and how that presences infuses our humanity through the works of Spirit, supplementing and balancing the rich spiritual traditions of non-Christian religions. I would describe myself as a follower of the Hermetic Path, a seeker after a Grail whose vibrant presence is manifest in an Inner Christ, that is in an "anointing" that blesses and uplifts body, mind, heart, and soul. This blessing is best known in its impact on all our relationships, demonstrating how love, kindness, compassion and forgiveness are the foundations of enduring health and intelligent well-being. This matrix incorporates all beings, all species, all forms of conscious life into its fullness. The Indwelling Christ is this anointing presence, a seed that flowers into a fruitful matrix of generative creativity, wonder, humility and hope for human development and maturity.

The book is an inspirational work, arising spontaneously in its primary aphoristic form and then subject to many years of meditative reflection. In writing the book, I simply opened myself to an inner depth that was heart-centered and deeply connected to a series of mystical experiences, including encounters with a variety of spiritual teachers. The commentary on each aphorism has been slowly shaped and the themes repeat as new nuances manifest. It is a work not meant to be read in a rapid or swift skimming; it is meant to be read very slowly, one aphorism with commentary at a time as a source of reflection. The pace depends upon the receptivity and preparedness of the reader, more may be read at a sitting if the content resonates with the reader. There are teachings interwoven into the texts that creates spiritual themes related to a Hermetic spiritual perspective, centered on the Christ-spirit and the divine Sophia. It is a work that requires effort to assimilate and is a guide to a deep spiritual life in and through Christ. But this is a different Christ, one which must be adopted by the reader in his or her own fashion. It is a book of meditations meant to inspire a dedicated spiritual life in practice and in human relationships, grounded in love, respect, intelligent, creative thought, and a deep gratitude for the gift of life.

Finally, this work is only an introduction, not a summary conclusion. It is an exploration of a spiritual truth, a relative, non-absolute truth whose value only extends as far as the receptivity of the reader. To take away even a small part of what is written here as valuable makes the effort worthwhile; to take more only means greater efforts at sorting the differences and diversities toward which the Hermetic Christ points. There is no "one way" but a myriad of ways; the Hermetic Christ has multiple forms and many manifestations, some more powerful and valued than others. Each person has an obligation to discriminate between teachings, to weigh the worth of any one writing against the value of others, to internalize only those aspects which seem clear, positive, and luminous. Everything else can be set aside, until such time as the wheel turns and we find our self, once again returning to review past attitudes and insights, but then more aware and mature, more able to accept alternatives and new perspectives. Each person must walk his or her own path. Every person grows and develops in accordance with their inner clarity, in proportion to their receptivity to what they do not know, do not understand. It is there, on the edge of the Abyss that we learn most clearly our limits and it is there where we can surrender to a new insight that might, on the right occasion, transform our entire understanding. That limit is the province of the Hermetic Christ, watcher at the boundary, calling us out beyond those limits and into a new, vibrant, luminous world.

Lee Irwin
Johns Island, SC
July 2016

Anastasis

THE WAY: ONE CHRIST

"His eyes are like a flame of Fire and on his head are many diadems and he has a Name inscribed which no one knows but himself. He is clad in a robe dipped in blood and the name by which he is called is the Word of God."

Revelation 19:12-13

Lee Irwin

The Christ
There is One Christ, eternal and everlasting;
the same today, tomorrow and forever. (1:1)[1]

The Christ of faith is born, not by Mary, nor by water, nor by blood but through the struggles of the human heart seeking to overcome uncertainty. Divided, we dissect truth into divergent possibilities, often contradict our deepest needs and thus we suffer from the inconstancy of aspirations or desires. Too often, the mind divides and separates where the heart could unite and join. Mind contracts around shadows and magnifies its problems, counting angels on the head of a pin or numbering the golden bricks in the streets of Heaven. It unceasingly considers alternatives and options, and endlessly encircles its potential with skeptical constructions of uncertainty. Or, isolated, the heart lays hold of a sublime truth and contemplates every other path as partial and incomplete, and therefore, becomes itself incomplete. But spiritual truth is more powerful and more potent than the fears and anxieties of the uncertain heart or mind. For such truth, in manifestation and in Mystery, lies deep in the marrow of every living creature, hidden within the contradictions, in an energy of creative joy, in a deep stillness, in quiet light. Inwardly unified, the heart beholds this vitality as an infinite presence that is inseparable from all spiritual paths, a continual source of inspiration resonant with a similar joy within others. Where this truth is known, it transforms life and awareness into new modes of perception and where it is fully developed, it becomes a source of inspiration for renewed life and being with others.

From such truth is born the power and joy of Christ. For Christ is a mystery that each of us carries within us, often unknown and unseen. And how shall we attain a vantage point from which we can see through the contradictions and uncertainties that surround and encompass us? We must each look inward, past the emotional doubts and uncertainties, to a center, an inner vitality, where truth resonates within us as a luminous joy and teaches us to act from that center in order to transform confusion into peace and uncertainty into settled insights. By sensing and feeling that truth in others, through respect and reverence, we can learn from every heart, the path of heartfelt aspiration. By looking at what is above us and below us, within us and without us, we can learn the wisdom that supports the innocence of others, and heals their pain, sorrows, and unfulfilled desires. For each of us is a revelation, every being, a mystery of light and shadows mixed. These shadows are self-created or passed on to us by elder generations who did not accomplish the

---
1. Hebrew 13: 8, 15.

work of transformation, thus we are caught in old sorrows and unhappiness. The transition from childhood to adult, from adult to mature spiritual being, is a long and difficult journey in which we learn with increasing sensitivity the necessity of constant effort, distillation, and refinement. There is no end to such a path and every stage is followed by another; to learn this, we must give up our uncertainty and accept with humility our differences and divergences with others. When we do this, we begin to grow into a generation of worthy heirs, just as Christ was a worthy heir for those that came before him.

The Christ wisdom, the Sophianic source of illumination, is an image of our sorrows transformed into a joy and humility, a unity that transmits gifts of peace, healing, and an awakening of the heart to new life, new wine, new understanding. For this joy is not within time, neither this time nor any time, but is an intrinsic quality of our inmost being that truly opens the heart, heals divisions, and gives itself to the work of creation. It is a power filled with creative abundance, overflowing all vessels, and bringing life and renewed vision to the seeing and unseeing alike. It is overflowing because it cannot be contained in any tradition or teaching or translation, nor in any one being or bringer of light. Yet, it bursts forth in every eyelash, pore, and atom of Christ's smile; it is a luminous light in his tears and an infinite echo in his laughter. It is eternal and everlasting because it cannot be diminished or exhausted. It flows out of the springs of creation unstained by human folly or vice. Inexhaustible, this primal, pristine Wisdom pours itself out for the many, not for the few. It is an inheritance whose value cannot be measured in standards of material wealth nor validated by social success or popular recognition. It flows into the heart and out through the body's mind, instilling empathy and compassion in order to reach those whose thirst is real and whose needs are unsatisfied. It gives moisture to those who are parched and feeds the roots of those who might wither; it brings life to all without discrimination or reluctance. This Christ-wisdom, the holy Sophia, overflows and does not hold back from whoever may thirst.

The one Christ gives birth to infinite imagery, forms, and manifestations as every aspect and possibility is explored and expanded. And when it contracts and forms a seed around an impenetrable center, we call it religion or gospel or good news. But the good news is this: there is no end to the possibilities by which the Christ-wisdom can be known. Therefore see within your own heart, the point where all religion is born: in a desire for holy Presence, in an undivided aspiration, in the Mystery of Being and in the unending challenges of Becoming. For the "sameness" of Christ is the unending variety of all the Christ manifestations that express love and hope, pointing toward the as-yet unrealized potential hidden in co-created images of the heart. Today, a child is struck by a distraught mother; yesterday, a man was enchained for his murderous lusts; and tomorrow, a woman is denied her sense of autonomy and freedom. But the Christ-spirit is in them, in each and every one, in the blind, the suffering, and in their persecutors. Our prison is the prison of the heart that refuses to feel or sense another's pain, doubts, or limitations, that denies the possibilities of Spirit, that fails to recognize the inner presence within each of us. There is no one who lacks the Christ spark, the capacity for kindness and forgiveness, the inmost essential quality of Spirit that may become a river and source of purification. When we immerse ourselves in these waters, they bring living restoration, a holy baptism that nourishes our soulful need for guidance and direction.

The face of Christ can be seen in the face of every living creature, in the smile, the joys of that creature, and in the tears, the sorrows of that being. Not just human faces, but the non-human as well: the animals, the plants, the minerals, earth, water, air, and fire. All these beings, elementals, spirits, invisible powers, angels, and holy spirituals contain this spark of presence, this luminous eye of light in the face of Christ, however strange or uncanny. The Earth Itself manifests such life, as do the suns and stars, the many visionary worlds of others, all the realms and planes, all the beings throughout a multitude of dimensions and doorways, so that every mote of dust may be reverenced and every atom become a source of Infinite understanding. All that is created is created holy, everything that exists from the smallest sub-particle to the greatest stellar formation, from minute superstrings to trans-galactic megastructures, is permeated with Spirit and resonates with the vibrant energies and delights of eternal ongoing creation. Spirit is there, in the initial conditions of creation through every cycle of transformation and is an inseparable presence throughout the Whole. Thus the "sameness" of Christ is in the inner coherence and in the unending variety, always unfolding, always revealing greater possibility, a unique synthesis flowing back into itself, to rest, to dissolve its variety into inner Mystery and overflowing Holiness. And in the still depth of the heart lies the challenge to leave behind all forms, desires, or needs; to go into the Deep, into the endless seas of Spirit, Mystery, and Christ reborn. In that Mystery we discover the simplicity of our own individual life as also miraculous, profound, and blessed with the gifts of Spirit to live, perceive, feel and give thanks.

Today, the Christ-Light is rising above the horizon of codified doctrines and dogmas. It is shining as subtle energy, burnished as gold, yet reducible to powder; when cast to the winds, it settles into the deep veins of Earth. When it is dug, refined, and made into valued forms, it loses the luster of its holy character; but in the veins of Earth we see the secret. It shines as a natural abundance of precious, star-born ore that each of us must smelt in the Hermetic vessel of the heart, must heat to a pure liquid love, to infuse and transform our being, our relations, our community. We must learn to radiate that love out into the resonant harmonies of all embodied forms, share it with all living creatures, all animate nature, to behold it yet again permeating sky, space, and Infinity. This light is irreducible to one teaching, or one path; irreducible to a single doctrine or dogma, inconceivable in its all-embracing harmony. We recognize it in wonder, only asking that human minds and souls, however precious or insignificant, be opened, be awakened through the Christ-wisdom and be reborn for the joy of sharing in the Greater Life of Spirit. In our prayers, meditations, songs, celebrations and remembering that light is there, shining, luminous. To awaken to that presence is to celebrate with utmost joy, the wonder and miracle of life; to embrace that joy means to be embraced and to incarnate the physical, emotive, and mental dimensions of worldly life as a means for such a realization. I do not spurn the world but embrace its fullness as a creative expression of Most Holy Wisdom, as a place made to be a means for transformation, a place of utmost possibility and challenge.

This opening to the Christ-spirit has no fixed form, no predetermined steps or stages, only a genuineness of desire, a sincerity of intent, a sharing of ideals, an aspiration for true awakening. Ideals are born in the crucible of our sorrows transformed through suffering into joy and through pain renounced for hope and new knowledge. Such is the wisdom of Christ: to give love, to receive love, to be an instrument of divine energies for the healing and help of others. Such wisdom transforms each manifestation as an instrument, finely tuned, honed to an edge that cuts without hurt, that shaves away and sharpens without injury, that resonates with inner, harmonic joy. This is the image of the Hermetic Christ, a sacred emblem of awakened grace, a golden-white lotus come to life in the heart of the devotee, a seed pearl and luminous drop of wisdom filled with promise. It is an image of inner prompting that leads to new well-being born of spiritual dedication and a mastery of the arts of inner spiritual wisdom. It is an image of giving and gifting that has no strain, no false promises—a balanced center, free and fluid and well-grounded.[2] It is a deep calm and empathy that loves all created life. The Hermetic Christ is a way that cannot be measured or confined; it acts as a spiritual image for innumerable possible paths. It offers a way with a heart, a soulful inquiry into needs that thirst for love, and result in a holy marriage, the union of Christos-

---

2. Bhagavad Gita, 17: 20.

Sophia, filled with joyful calm and inner peace. It stands below and points to the union of all that is below with all that is above and beyond.[3]

The sameness of Christ is not found in just "one way" or in any predetermined path. Every image and idea is only a partial reflection of the deeper Mystery; every Truth, a partial light on Infinite Depths; every belief only a fraction of the Whole. All "ways" are Christ-ways when they are lived with love, compassion, forgiveness, kind words, caring thoughts, good deeds. The True Way is immeasurable, beyond the full grasp of any being, any small group, any large mass, beyond whole worlds, beyond the visible Creation. The Hermetic Christ is an image of divine possibility in the name of love and compassion, an Alpha-Omega, a new beginning, an ancient depth.[4] All images are only refracted images of an indivisible Whole whose Mystery is within us, in each blade of grass, in every molecule of sand. The "sameness" is the infinite and inexhaustible potential for expression and self-realization, the primal source of variety found and realized in particular form and specific manifestation. Today, tomorrow, and yesterday are an unbroken continuity, a Spiral or Cycle whose divisions are artificial and heavy with archaic memory. What remains unchanged is the desire in the human heart to be penetrated by the Mystery, to be One with the deepest sources of love, to be reborn in the image of Sophia-Christos, one whose smile is a union of female and male, young and old, before and after, and yet, immeasurably more. The Sophianic Christ is born of just this simple truth—the attainable desire for God. Such a desire is not only possible but actual and necessary; we are not separate from God but, as children of light, we rejoice in a gift we all share equally.

The Way
To seek Christ in both self and others as a source of guidance and inspiration, as a key to the deepest mysteries of the heart. (1:2)

The seeking of Christ is neither simple nor obvious.[5] Setting a foot on the path, we may soon discover that there is a deep and unfathomable Mystery at the vibrant center of our busy and confused lives. Each of us begins where we stand, in the present, at the moment when we receive a recognizable truth, acquire a spark of inspiration, however slight or distant it may seem. There is no unshaken ground upon which to rest, no calm moment but in the eye of the storm. But in a quiet moment, apart from the turbulence, we may open

---
3. Emerald Tablet, line 2 (http://www.sacred-texts.com/alc/emerald.htm).
4. Revelations 1: 8.
5. Proverbs 11: 14.

heart and mind to hear a word spoken of Christ. It is a word that gives birth, that creates and stirs desires, fosters insight, and raises aspirations.[6] This word arises in the heart, in deepest need, in a powerful longing. As the heart is veiled, so is the word you receive or reject. For such is the path: at every stage to unveil, to open, to overcome doubting and to discover, step by step, an Inner Light. Not because truth has a specific form or content or argument, but because it leads to deeper love and fulfillment, because it surpasses its own speaking and arrives at the Unspeakable. In the recesses of the heart, there is a most holy Mystery, a Presence, a Sophianic spark. A spark which ignites the soul, which burns the veils of unseeing and unknowing, clears the mind, and inspires a new confidence, a sense of liberation. This spark radiates wisdom outward into the world and transforms all those who receive it with genuine humility; it is not born of human aspiration or thought, but of a recognition of the unfathomable depth of its natal Source.

We must begin with the most basic of all concerns, to realize that truth is not outside of us but within us, waiting to reveal its reality and presence. All books, writings, and words are only a means to the direct discovery and experience of that Presence. In the light of that inner manifestation, the written word becomes straw, and speech, a disguise. Because we are limited, partial, finite and incomplete, it is necessary for us to find a way to sharpen and focus our attention and awareness. Therefore we may choose among many paths and diverse ways. Among these paths is the path of the Sophianic Christ, a way of wisdom, compassion, and understanding. Not all are called to this path, nor is it necessary in choosing Christ to renounce all other paths. Let each follow the teachings of his or her own heart. Let those come who feel so inclined, who desire to understand and to attain the reality of Christ, not for rewards, nor from anxiety and guilt, but from a desire for peace, who wish to walk a path of harmony and health. The way of Christ is broad, accepting, transformative, calling out of us the best that each may give. Few are those that walk the entire way, that arrive and see for themselves the full reality of Indwelling Light, dissolving all differences and merging in Spirit with All That Is.[7]

While we may be only mildly curious or interested, there is an inner awareness that what we presently know or understand is only a small expression of our true capacity. The fullness of the heart, its beliefs and passions, is rarely touched in the daily pattern of everyday life. In the manifestations of Spirit there is a desire to touch Spirit in every being, in every other person, in every living creature. We must not forget the reality of our potential and the inheritance of our capacity to think, feel, and act in accordance with our full

---

6. Qur'an 16: 102.
7. Corpus Hermeticum 1: 6.

spiritual potential. We do not live in a lifeless, uncaring world except insofar as we make the world lifeless and uncaring, insofar as we project diminished and contracted thought into the world we inhabit. Our alienation, unhappiness, indifference or forgetful pleasures, our constant reaching out for more, our restlessness, has allowed us to forget the inner presence that unites us. Indifference, fear and hate has allowed us to deny the meaningfulness of our inspired imaginings, our dreams, our deeper needs and sacred aspirations. Many have become alienated from inner life in the rush of outward events; they no longer sense that nurturing love of Spirit, the guiding reality of a compassionate and genuine kindness. Mystery has been reduced to darkness and God to a dim, distant and unfriendly, often alien light.

We must begin where we are, now, in the present. The unveiling of the heart cannot proceed in nostalgia for some past moment in life or history or in some speculative future when faith might be easier, more accessible. The time is Now, the question is Now—yet, it is not a matter of utter acceptance or denial. If we contract, we must expand; if we expand, we must contract. In this way each of us is capable of giving birth. The process of mutual expansion and contraction is part of the primary rhythms of spiritual life. The need to "press ahead," to hurry toward a poorly conceived and dimly seen end must be released. We need not delay out of fear or indifference; let each go forward at his or her own pace, questioning where necessary and giving up questions when no longer needed. When we honestly face the barriers of our fears, our poor mental and emotional habits, our doubts and denials, then we can move into a circle of mutual respect, self-realization, and spiritual trust. And there must be times of rest and renewal, when we lay down our books and ideas, our obligations and responsibilities, when we let go of half-formed attitudes, when we admire the beauty of a spring day or the wind in our hair.

The Way of Christ is not an obsession or an unbroken vow; it is charity, forgiveness, a guiltless love, joy and compassion. It is stable and calm, unshaken by storms and quiescent in the face of other worlds and realizations. It does not demand or insist on its own relative law; it creates as it unfolds the many reflected images of its Source. It manifests the beauty of Its inspirations in acts of peace and mutual support. Thus we begin without artificial restraints. Let each individual proceed according to the degree of their understanding to form and shape their higher potential. One image of that potential is the Hermetic image of the Sophianic Christ—a Christ transformed according to the understanding of the believer, but also a Christ manifesting within others. If we can see the reality of Christ within others, the Sophianic presence, in every other, then we have traveled half the way; the other half is to see the Mystery within All. Christ is many things to many persons, and there is no single face or image that can summarize the multiplicities of the Christ-spirit. Yet any image, inspired by devotion and filled through genuine compassion, can reveal the totality through which the Christ-spirit comes forth. It is a totality born of aspiration and fostered through understanding. It does not sit in judgment over us, but swells up from within us like an endless wave on a depthless Sea. Yet it is not a vague, diffuse loss of self, but a sharp, clear realization of the profound pulse at the heart of every living being that gives us a unique perspective and love of others. Through it we become conscious of the totality of many minds harmonized in an understanding of the fullness of the flower.

Why is Christ a key? Because Christ is a means, a way to unlock what is even now, at this very moment, living within and through us, an anointing presence. But for the lock to turn, it is necessary that we do not resist the feelings that arise within us, nor block the necessary turning over. The intuitions of the heart are crucial on the path at every stage. It is not only mind, which can divide and synthesize, but also the spiritual heart, unburden of its care for self-preservation, survival, or personal reward. A heart free of its restless, unquiet pride, a heart not broken in self-pity, a heart learning stillness, hearing, receptive, strong. A heart that senses the movements and rhythms of Spirit, both within itself and within others. An awakened heart is one inspired by a constancy of Presence. In that Presence, even Christ dissolves—there is only love, compassion, wisdom and an endless sea of potential Wonder. Or there is only God, Mystery, the Holy, and therefore, Peace. For the heart to open, there must be a means, one we accept and believe capable of teaching us and leading us beyond the barriers of our denials or fears. We must learn to focus our whole being into an image of love and compassionate strength that becomes a living flame, a fire that burns away the dross and materiality of our inherited disbelief, denial, and fear. The heart, opening to Mystery through the Christ-spirit, turns the key through deep acceptance of the loving grace we are each given, in every moment of our caring, and thus we burn away the accumulated layers, the rust of forgetfulness, and the restrictions resulting from a loss of center.

The Sophianic Christ is a sign that, once engraved on the heart, becomes an emblem of a true spiritual path. The deepest mysteries of the heart cannot be told, they must be known directly, with whatever aid is given, as a gift of love from those who care. We are not alone, we have companions and guides, guardians and teachers, workers in the way of light that encourage our awakening when we step fully into the Great Work, the full realizations of Spirit and Mystery. Christ is a sign like Jonah that we must go into the belly of the whale, descend into the deep, become knowers of shadows and darkness and sorrows, to be sea and earth lovers, in order to accept and fully realize our capacities in earthly life. To work the alchemical magic of transformation we must respect and love the Prime Material, the substance of our flesh and the joys of our incarnate life. Christ descends into matter and it is transformed through blood and sweat and tears into new life and the baptisms of flesh are awakened to inner capacities and spiritual vitality. The energized body, awakened and fully revered, becomes a temple of the Christ-spirit and thus, a sign of emergent wisdom, a connectedness with subtle spiritual worlds.[8] And it awakens to the pain, hunger, sorrows, and sufferings of others and seeks to work for the transformation of others, patiently, quietly, without self-glorification, in full acceptance of the value of every different path.

The mystery of Christ is like this: if you desire love, health, peace, and joy then it is only necessary to hold to those virtues as an offering, as something you are willing to surrender to, willing to give completely to another, so that the fruit of your desire will reflect that love, health, peace and joy. The Sophianic love is a mirror, its gives our actions reflected images that comes back to instruct us in ways leading to greater purity and grace. You may offer these acts to Christ, to Sophia, to the Holy Mother Spirit, who gives them back to you renewed and filled with wisdom's joys through the gift of your giving. What you give with sincerity, returns threefold; therefore you must choose wisely what you give when holding nothing back. In giving to Christ, you create a circle of energetic love and healing that flows back into every relation and interaction for its betterment. That love outlasts you, it travels within the spiritual worlds and circulates there its messages of awakened heart and mind; it is a stream within the greater ocean of Being and Becoming. On the Christ-path, this is both possible and actual. It is a matter of trust and surrender, of purity of intent. And Christ-Sophia stands below, ready to assist your uncertain heart, ready to inspire your formative will. Simply let go of your doubt, of your unstable resistance, and let what comes, come. In this way your yes will be yes and your no, no.[9]

---

8. I Corinthians 6: 19.
9. Matthew 5: 37.

Faith
**To distinguish the Christ of faith from the Christ of flesh,
to know that Christ is infinite in every manifestation. (1:3)**

As an image of the invisible God, the Christ of faith has no fixed form nor material counterpart; nor can that image be contained in only one created being.[10] The Christ of flesh, who wept from fear and cried to be released from his overpowering destiny, was a created being, born of the flesh of his mother and given life by Spirit. All creatures, however great or small, are given life by that same Spirit. Therefore the gift of life flows forth out of the mystery of a woman's body and out of the heart of the Invisible God. This is the common inheritance of all flesh. The Christ of flesh was called Yeshu'a ben Yosuf, born of a man little known to men, and Yeshu'a ben Miriam, son of a mysterious woman.[11] As the Christ of flesh grew, so grew the spirit within him, enhancing and unfolding his perceptions both inwardly and outwardly. And as his capacities and abilities grew, so also grew his understanding. Until finally, in a day unmarked in history, but knitted into the fabric of Mystery, Being and Becoming, he beheld the full reality of the Father. Thus Yeshu'a became a Christ, anointed, blessed, visible in flesh, sent forth to teach, to testify and bear witness through the reality of his gracious speech and remarkable powers.[12] But the Christ of faith cannot be contained by Yeshu'a ben Miriam, even at the moment of his transfiguration or in the mystery of his resurrection, the Christ of flesh is surpassed. And this is good, for the Christ of faith is the transforming Christ, in inner blessing and anointing of the heart, both an image and manifestation of the power within us. Not an image born of his mother's sorrow as Yeshu'a ben Miriam, but as an image which speaks and acts and guides us to the greater good, the deepest and most compassionate love.

The Christ of flesh was no ordinary man, for he came to embody a revelation of the reality of God within a living creature. And his power was the power to forgive and to heal; a power not his own but one given to him for the benefit of others. And his passion and his faith lifted him above those he loved, for his vision could not be contained by the beliefs of his day. Thus he rose to a height and a fullness commensurate with his willingness to embody the salvation of his people, therefore, he is called Yeshu'a ben David, son of a great King of Judah and Israel.[13] But the salvation of the Jews and the Gentiles was a work

---
10. Ephesians 3: 16-19; Galatians 2: 16.
11. Qur'an 2: 87; 5:116; 19: 15-34; 21: 91.
12. Luke 4: 22.
13. 2 Samuel 5: 3-5.

of many minds and wills sustained by accepted ideas and sought through worldly power. And men judged him harshly, this Christ of flesh, he who wept and prayed for his brethren, was crucified by the retribution and pride of the few, not the hopes of the many. His body ached and suffered while his soul went out into that greater Whole, embracing a world of suffering beings. The Christ of flesh was thus a nodal point, an embodiment broken by human ignorance in the face of indifference, but reborn in the minds and hearts of those who understood the gift of his suffering and the pain.

In resurrection, the Christ of faith was lifted beyond sorrow and embodied in belief that every human being may submit, through faith, to the power and potential of the Christ within, to be healed and to love and to compassionately forgive, and to thus rise above the violence of injustice and cruelty. And this power and capacity was given form by Yeshu'a ben Abba, faithful Son of the Father. Therefore, let us distinguish clearly between the Christ of flesh and the Christ of faith; let us understand that our faith must lead us from one to the other and then beyond. The image of Christ within us, even that image which has no face, is yet an image of faith—however simple or profound. And every image is partial, incomplete and finite as every image must be. The image of Christ is a Mystery manifesting as compassion, as a healer and teacher, as a transforming Presence shaped by the thoughts and beliefs of the beholder. These images are constructed out of the potential of our own inner nature—the Christ of faith is the Christ in which we believe. In the Christ of flesh, we encounter the historical manifestation and the breaking through of the embodiment of Mystery in one particular man. Not once and for all, but once and in all—for the Kingdom is within us and formed according to our own ideas and images.[14]

The Christ of faith is not static and unchanging, but grows or contracts according to the maturity and understanding of the believer. The faith of the believer stands on the direct encounter with the Christ as inwardly received. The Christ of the scriptures is not the only Christ; the Christ of the Church is not the only Christ. There is no "only" Christ but there is a Christ of the heart manifesting in our daily lives as a deep and resonant power of love, kindness, and joy, now, today. Therefore we must clarify what we believe and hope for and live according to—or we shall contract around the static and shrunken images of rigid interpretation, doubt, or pride. The Christ of faith is a power, a dynamic and transformative power, a power foretelling the inadequacies of a contracted state, forgiving and not condemning. It is an image of God within us that leads to our own greatest potential to heal, to create, and to serve. And

---

14. Luke 17: 21.

our service is not a slavish, self-denying servitude, but a joyful, willing affirmation of abundant power and fullness. The Christ of faith is a threshold, a door leading to an inner room where we may reverence the power of love as healing and transforming presence.

Every age has its interpreters, its images and ideas. When Yeshu'a lived, he embodied those ideas as they were revealed within him by Spirit. And the Mystery spoke and he attended to the Voice. So we too, in every age, must seek to hear that Voice, the response and inspirations that guides us toward light and health that calls and cries within us. In Christ, this means seeking to fully comprehend the reality of the Christ within, to find the healer that each of us is, to recognize the beauty and the power that gives freely and without grasping or expectations. The Christ of faith is the Christ we believe in, the Christ that inspires and gives us joy. This Christ does not condemn nor deny the possibilities of new interpretations but seeks to continuously refine and lift the interpretations to an ever higher, more comprehensive horizon. Therefore, we must distinguish between the Christ of flesh and the Christ of faith.

It is taught that the Christ of flesh lived and died for the salvation of many; this is true, not that all be saved according to the doctrines of the church, but that all be saved according to the intentions of the heart. And how shall we be saved but by throwing off every destructive, self-limiting, and coercive tendency, by freeing ourselves from an inflated sense of self-importance and by surrendering our tendencies to condemn, deny or destroy the beliefs of others. The Christ of faith flourishes in the atmosphere of receptive sympathy, sharing, love, communion in differences, in the diversity and fullness of individual integrity. The Christ of flesh embodies a power of real transformation in an encounter with limiting ideas, and every interpretation offers a new encounter with that same holy power. And the Christ of flesh bears witness to those limitations in his sacrifice and death. Therefore our own encounter must seek to realize the power that overcomes self-limiting ideas and gives us renewed hope and understanding, without censure, blame or condemnation.

It is not only interpretation but more importantly, embodiment, incarnation; the goal is to manifest, to substantiate, the reality of Christ. This manifestation is the essence of faith, and our interpretations are based in the reality of our manifesting that reality in our relations with others. It is not one Christ and one faith, but many faiths and many manifestations of Christ-like teachers and guides. Not one Christ eternally resplendent above us, an icon for adoration, but the reality of Christ within each person as love and as healing presence, however simple. It may manifest as a quiet voice or a gentle presence, a tranquil heart or a deeply felt sorrow; as a humility, a smile, or the willingness to give and to receive. It may be a vision of the whole, an intuition of truth, an inspiration, song or poem. The Christ of faith is not limited to death or life after death, but finds its most potent expression in this life, this present incarnation, with others. This Christ is infinite in every manifestation so that what is perceived is only the beginning of a great journey toward Light. The smallest intuition of Presence contains an infinite magnitude capable of opening the depths of the heart to an ever greater Deep. No revelation of Christ is complete or final. There is no final vision or end, only the necessary steps that each soul takes in its journey toward truth.

Therefore, you must believe in the Christ that is in you. You must cultivate your faith in such a way that the reality of Christ will begin to manifest. And if not Christ then the wisdom and love of Christ. In this way you will begin your journey not by clinging to a half-formed or narrow idea but by cultivating an actual presence within, a spark of divine possibility within every living being. In the Christ of flesh you have an example, a manifestation of the power of divinity raised according to the knowledge of those days. But in our own day, we must seek the inner Christ, not in the past but in the present. Seek not according to fixed ideas and images, but according to the reality of the present, through compassion and love that is a sign of the Christ-wisdom guiding you without possessive attachments or demands, gently, with peaceful intent. The spontaneity of love, as an opening of the heart, occurs naturally in the light of that Presence, unfolding the potential to share and to receive the joy and sorrow of others. Blessed are all those that love freely without attachment the weary and the sick; but more blessed are those in whom Christ loves eternally and forever. To love and to be loved, this is the essence of the Christ of faith.

The Gate
To know that Christ is the Gate by which we enter the depths of eternal Creation, a way without end, a light without limit. (1:4)

This does not mean that Christ is the only Gate. There are many gates and ways both known and unknown. There is no exclusivity in Christ. Many are the ways and many are the gates, and many are the names of the teachers that lay down a path. Through the gate of Christ pass all those who believe in the eternal reality of love, compassion, and healing. There are other ways and other gates equally as good and worthy as the gate called Christ. You have heard that the way of Christ is narrow and this is true to those who stand far off, looking on from a distance. But to those who stand before the threshold, it is very wide and to those who enter in, it is Infinite and Unending. This depth and fullness is born of Spirit and takes its life from the fullness of everything holy and profound. All realities may be known and discovered in Christ, but this knowledge leads us beyond images and ideas into the Holy City of Divine Presence. It is a journey of the soul, a journey in which the powers of reason and imagination must be surpassed. This power of the visionary Presence is not seen with physical eyes, but with the whole being of the seeker as the very basis of awareness. And such Presence cannot be measured or described according to fixed cannon or law.

In attaining to a realization of the Christ of faith, we free ourselves from the fixations of written history and begin our journey. It is a journey fraught with illusion, deception, and danger. Without guidance, we may blunder, lose our way, or be deceived by our own unhealthy attitudes, our instability or fear, our grasping after that which is above us or our rejection of that which we think is beneath us. Yet the needed guidance comes in many forms: through marriage and work, through child rearing and meaningful human relations, through study, self-reflection and meditation, through faith, prayer and humility. All these are valuable and important, for guidance is not a matter of a particular human relation, but of many years of effort, discipline, and the spontaneity of desire and exploration. We question, doubt, move away, come back with renewed questions, and continue our spiral journey toward the center. We must not imagine the future as a refuge from the errors of the past, rather we must learn to live authentically in the present and our faith must be present-centered; it must truly live and inspire us toward greater shared realizations and harmony.

Each of us, as individuals and as communities, must wrestle with the angels of faith and doubt to clarify the exact nature of what we believe. A naive faith is inflexible and incapable of growth and learning. A mature faith is receptive to other teachings and understands the complexity and multivocal speaking of many peoples in many lands. We must transform the unique center of our collective need for peace into actuality through compassion and mutual respect for the beliefs of others. Only in this way can we be worthy of true peace and harmony. The Christ of faith cannot be circumscribed by an exact doctrine or interpretation. Faith cannot be defined accurately as submission of the will to a collective dogma—that is obedience, not faith. Faith, to be made real and living must, like all living things, be capable of growth, change and flowering. And the fruit of this faith is peace, non-violence, and a just and balanced life. The Christ of faith is the Christ that lives in each of us. What we share in Christ is love, compassion, and the possibility of healing that is the true heart of Christ. The rest is only the necessary veils which make this love possible and tangible to our unclear apprehension, that makes it viable for our uncertain and not fully realized humanity.

Our task is a creative task. It is the task of the generations: to heal the wounds of the past, make straight the ways of the present, and to open the possibilities of the future to long enduring peace, understanding, and fulfillment. It is a search for wisdom and wholeness. A Sophianic illumination that leads us into the depth of everything Godly and Holy. And Christ is not the only way, the only gate—but Christ is a way and a gate. Therefore we begin with Christ of the flesh and reach the Christ of faith in order to discover within, the reality of Christ's love and power. And from the Christ of faith we reach the Christ of Spirit, the holy transformation of faith into direct knowledge (*gnosis*). In the Christ of Spirit we pass from belief directly into knowledge and new horizons of understanding. Faith without knowledge is a continual longing or it sinks to skepticism no longer capable of understanding. But faith realized in knowledge is its own affirmation and fulfillment. This knowledge arises from Christ and descends with the holy bride, the divine Sophia, as luminous wisdom.[15] It is the Marriage of the Lion and the Lamb, the union of the Above and the Below, a true Harmony of Spheres.

The gift of discernment is necessary. Not all visionary experience is comprehensible or positive in its immediacy. Spirit may leads us into the very darkness that must be transformed or presents us with the sickness that must be healed. But every gift of Spirit is a possibility for transformation, for that reason we hold to the Sophianic Christ. In Christ we find a norm, to love and to be loved, and this norm is trustworthy. Against it we may weigh every experience, every relation, every intuition. Does our experience teach us how to love more fully, more deeply, without possession or bitterness, without doubt, without sorrow? Are we loving to others, does it increase our compassion, our kindness, our willingness to give? Or does it draw out of us our own sorrow, bitterness and deceptions, feeding self-inflated ideas and aspirations? Does it liberate us from continual self-preoccupations, from endless self-concerns? Does it lead us away from vanity and error toward humility and the transparency of light? To be made whole, the imperfections must be known and transformed, not only individually but racially and collectively. Let us deal with those imperfections consciously and then let us release them so they have no hold on us. Then, may we be lifted in the joy of Christ to the higher union, to the sacred marriage; then, may we behold the infinite horizons of Spirit and Divinity within.

---

15. Corpus Hermeticum 13. 8.

Meditations on Christ

Beyond the Christ of faith, lies the Christ of Spirit. In the Christ of Spirit we pass beyond our ideas and into the living Presence. This encounter, this opening of the heart, this flowering of our faith brings us through the gate and into the City. And here we see the eternal foundations of creative life, the fountains that nourish the trees of paradise and the overwhelming beauty of its endless, creative play. For the power and complexity of creation continues unending, having never ceased, flourishing within the hearts of all living creatures. Who can grasp the vastness of its manifestations, of the many paths, ways, gates, teachings and traditions? For we only glimpse the far-reaching brightness of its Infinite possibilities, Its remarkable capacity for Newness. Today, tomorrow, and forever the creative life goes on manifesting in all its sublime, simple, and complex varieties, manifesting its innumerable joys and sorrows for the benefit of all beings. The whole of creation sings this song, a celebration of the eternal images of every species life, coming into Being.

Through Christ we may behold the mystery of this creation, of its continuous and myriad manifestations, its profound unending activity, and the vast silence of its overflowing perfection. The beholding of the Mystery is not attained in ideas or mental images, but through the living reality of Spirit, opening the heart, revealing the Infinite within. And in the Spirit of Christ we behold the lesser mystery of a compassionate, unbound love united with a higher, transcendent wisdom, Holy Sophia. This love is not bound by our individual or communal relations, it is a love which extends through the activities of Spirit and reaches every created being. It is a love which bears witness to the beauty and power of the entire Cosmos. Not a love confined by Christ but a love set free by manifesting the reality of Christ, within a loving heart, to teach the value and purposes of that love. This Higher Wisdom flows up and into the heart, or descends, illuminating our understanding and creating a gift of words, songs, and expressions. It flows out into the world as a creative resonance, an Orphic energy harmonized within a greater wholeness, as a resonant art of being. It is wisdom born of love to fulfill the purposes of co-creative, mutual life.

There is no end to the creative power of such love. Where there is love, deep and healthy, there is creativity and illumination. There is the gift most supreme, the power to heal, to make peace, to sustain life. That is why the ways of Christ and the ways of Spirit merge in the heart of an eternal weaving—to love, to create, to understand, to redeem all the ills of a distracted or denying life, to overcome suffering, to make new, to be transformed. What must end is the inflexible doctrines, the dogmas which blind that love and creative impulse and misshape it into images of authority, control, or obedience. We must end our attachments to traditions of authority and punishment, banish the darkness of oppression in the name of faith, the mockery that legislates a law with no heart. The greatest punishment is to be cast out from the joy of the creative life, to be bound by the inflexible authority of men under the power of their own shadows. A communal love is shared but not coercive; is mutual, but not authoritarian; is co-creative, not controlling. To love means to break through the barriers of our insufficiency, our impotence and to not oppress others with self-righteous proclamations of a limited and narrow particularism, a partisan view, an inflexible affirmation of a single hierarchy or position.

Every bond that is cut, frees us to participate more fully in the rightful inheritance of all beings—to create, think, and imagine according to inspirations that flow up through us into the healthy channels of artistic, intellectual, and social expression. Otherwise we shall only bind ourselves to ever increasing pain, sorrow and insufficiency. We are partners with all living beings in the way of creation and through love and humility, we find our place. Knowledge of the Christ-Spirit is an encounter with reality that shakes us out of the complacent strictures of our traditional, rational thoughts and beliefs. It challenges our ungrounded romantic ideals, confronts our unfulfilled aspirations, and resists unreflective beliefs. It is an opening of the heart in a desire for truth, through an encounter that takes us beyond the limits of faith or inherited ideas and into the direct experience with the bonds that must be cut. It is death and rebirth, painful but liberating, a suspended moment of what was and what is yet to come. And beyond the Christ of Spirit lies the Uncreated Light which transforms and utterly submerges individual differences into a pluralism of Divine Abundance through which even Christ cannot pass.

The Four Faces
To know the four faces of Christ: the literal, the metaphorical, the mythic, and the mystical: four cornerstones of mature faith. (1:5)

These faces of Christ, like the visionary faces of angels, express a multitude of ways by which Christ may be known.[16] Spirit is not bound by rigid laws or inflexible reasons, it arise as a visionary Presence constantly revealing new vistas of perception and fullness. And this Presence constantly transforms in accordance with the degree of receptivity of the heart and the maturity of a cultivated, sensitive mind and soul. It is not only mind, not only heart, but soulful being as well; desire and perception must open to the indelible touch

---
16. John 16: 13-14.

of this Presence, like an angel's touch hidden in the midst of our unseeing. The Gospel of Christ is the written record handed down through the generations, along with the letters of Paul and the early words of the first communities in Christ. We have no words written by Yeshu'a ben Miriam but only those spoken and remembered by others in the shadows of their first ecstasy and hope. And all these words are remembered in the light of a Promise, that is, in the coming of the Spirit of Truth (*Parakletos*). But the Promise was misconstrued, confused, and broken from the very beginning, for even the closest disciples could not clearly comprehend the words of their teacher and guide.[17] How then are we, distant and removed, to interpret these words and saying which from the beginning were obscure and difficult?

We must learn to trust the saying that the Spirit of Truth is within us. By this teaching we may recognize that the power and reality of Christ is manifest through the witness of Spirit. In the simplest form, it means simply to speak the truth with love. For this kind of speech heals and unites, resolves differences, that it might evolve its own relative understanding—for life is unity then division, division then unity. Nor does it present itself as law or doctrine committed to memory and then rehearsed in the presence of the unbelieving. It is not truth as it must be spoken to others but Truth as lived in purity of heart and in loving daily lives, in the openness of our unspoken actions. It is a living Truth, manifest in risks or inner challenges, in joys, doubts, or denials, in the intimacy of personal relations inspired by trust and hope. Truth is never "naked" for it is always clothed in our beliefs and needs. Therefore, let us put on garments unstained by falsehood, deception, seduction, or false exaggerations. Let us wash away the unhealthy stains of denial, jealousy, guilt, blame, or pretense. Let us clothe ourselves in the simplicity of direct speech, of heart-to-heart relations, with a willingness to forgive and to see beyond the tensions and false horizons of the present. For the Spirit of Truth is not bound by the present, nor the past, nor the future, but is rather an eternal expression of deep caring and love free of petty conflicts and self-obsessions.

There is no such thing as "literal truth," for such is the nature of every written and spoken word that no sooner does it enter the ear or mind of another than it takes on the forms and impressions of the mind that receives it. For if the very disciples of Christ could not agree, nor understand the words of their teacher and master, how can we say "I understand"? For the truth is, we do not understand, nor do we think clearly about these things. The glass through which we see darkly is the Mystery of Christ, and thus the Mystery of God. If the spirit of God cannot be contained in a temple built by human

---

17. John 8: 27.

hands,[18] neither can it be contained in a book written by human authors. The Mystery of the Words of Christ are clothed in the thoughts and ideas of those days; within those thoughts and ideas are contained the seeds of many more thoughts passed over the generations from one mind to another.[19] And it is within the mind and heart that the Mystery dwells. Therefore, the Christ words invoke the Mystery within us through the power of the inspirations that words give. But such a Mystery cannot be contained in words. And Yeshu'a ben 'Abba spoke many things mysterious and unclear, for such is the spirit of inspiration, to clothe in metaphor and signs the intangible essence of Mystery that remains to this day hidden in the heart of every living creature.[20]

Thus we ask, what is "literal truth"? Only through consensus can we agree on the meaning of even a single word, but our consensus is based on opinion, authority, and station. These are not the elements of the Spirit of Truth, but a reflection of hierarchical ranks so loved by those who seek power and position. Consensus is no safeguard against ignorance or error, for many falsehoods have been perpetuated by mass consent, by conformity to majority rule. The "literal truth" is never obvious or self-evident for it is always cloaked in the presuppositions of shared interpretations and beliefs. Every word has the power to evoke, through experience or imagination, the unique synthesis of those who hear or respond. It is not the words that are so easily rejected, but an inner pattern of interpretation arising out of an often unexamined prejudice—or out of knowledge and understanding. Thus whatever is consensual is literal only insofar as we make ever more rigid limitations on meaning and possibility, only insofar as we close our mind to new vistas of meaning and intimation. The literal meaning cannot be found simply in words but resides in the literal mindedness of the hearer.

When John writes, "Jesus wept,"[21] how are we to understand this simple human act? Can we say we understand why he wept? The written documents do not tells us why, it only says that he wept. Was it out of love for Lazarus, even though he raised him from the dead? Was it tears shed because of the pain and suffering of Mary and the other mourners? Was it tears of joy at the fulfillment of the promise and the testimony of Martha? Was it tears of sorrow that such an act was necessary for the unbelieving masses? Or were they tears of awe and love of God, tears sprung from the act that lay before him? Did Yeshu'a know why he wept or was it a spontaneous act of the heart, hard-pressed by the multitude in the face of the Mystery? Such acts have no single,

---

18. I Kings 8: 27.
19. Qur'an 37: 129.
20. Corpus Hermeticum 4. 4.
21. John 11: 35.

literal answer. We may agree he wept, but why is a matter of debate—and such it is for every action thus recorded—for the written word is only a small fragment of the life and mystery of Christ. And every word is a multitude of possibilities compressed into limited sound and form.

Even those who followed and believed in him could not agree, so that after his death there were immediately many interpretations and contradictions among his own disciples and followers. And here the Spirit of Truth guides us in seeing clearly the contradictions and confusions that result from every manifestation that is holy or divine. For if we cannot comprehend the tears of one we love, nor understand the needs of those for whom we care, how much more difficult to comprehend the Tears of Christ, the sorrows and joys of a man of mystery? In love, the impenetrable mystery is the depth and fullness, the richness of a growing and flowering life that sustains its vitality however simple or complex. It does not die and surrender itself to passivity, to the literal, to appearance or form that is fixed and frozen. For the literal meaning always dissolves into depth when we look long and deeper, without judgment, into the heart of another to behold there the same Mystery that gave Christ both life and power. Everything literal is only a surface waiting to be illumined from within so that it may become an interior image of the Mystery and like Christ, dissolve into the fathomless depth of Its unfolding manifestations and potency.

But what of the metaphorical nature of the teaching, the parables recorded, and the parable of the life of Yeshu'a? What is metaphor when every word proves to be an inadequate vessel of meaning and intent? For metaphor is like a man given a gold coin who buries that coin in hope of having some small riches in a future time when he may redeem himself from debt. So the words of the teaching are mined for specific meanings and hoarded up like small treasures according to the doctrines of believer to be used at some future time to justify the discipline of their own teachers. Like lean counting houses, those poor in metaphor claim to have found the inner meaning and the esoteric values, or rationalized the parable until it means only what is called for—a demonstration, a sophistry built on what has been left buried and unused in otherwise busy lives. Did Yeshu'a not say that this one coin should be taken and given to those who have ten?[22] For the richness of metaphor lies in its plurality of meanings, its multiplicity and multivocality, not in formulaic interpretations that serve a narrow doctrine or a single point of view. For metaphor serves to open and enrich our understanding, to provide new possibilities of awareness in which the inner reality which cannot be contained in words becomes visible

---

22. Matthew 25: 14-30.

and overflows the limitations of language and convention. Like seeds bursting into tendrils, roots, and stems, the words are nourishment for growth toward light.

When Yeshu'a says the kingdom of heaven is like a tiny mustard seed that grows into a sturdy tree and provides a resting place for all the winged creatures,[23] does such a statement have only one meaning? For this heavenly seed is like the love of Christ taking root in the soul and transforming body, mind, and heart into a resting place where visionary dreams may ascend and descend filled with the presences of Spirit. It is like an idea or belief that gains acceptance in the hearts of others and becomes a refuge from uncertainty and storms. It is like the first tentative steps toward maturity that brings firmness with age and a steady, well-grounded step. The mustard tree is a fragrant spice, pungent with delicacy, its four-pedaled yellow flower a medicine for healing, a sign of wholeness and integrity. Each petal is a synthesis of elements, an alchemical sign, whose luminous colors are an expression of a possible flowering of the heart. The meanings are endless and may be extrapolated to unfold many hidden vistas, the purpose to lead the heart and soul to new awakenings. Metaphor is not answered in simple analogy or in complex esoteric schemes, but overflows into a multitude of possible meanings, each opening a wider horizon on the whole.

Such metaphors and parables capture our attention and in some, give rise to reflection. These reflections are crucial, for it is not a matter of fixed interpretations but of the whole towards which the story points. For the story of his life, his teaching and death, are themselves a metaphor of the search for spiritual rebirth and renewal. It is story containing many other stories, an image filled with images until we arrive at the seed from which it springs, buried deep in Spirit and in holy aspiration. A beckoning light penetrates the deep and in that nourishing dark, conception and life flow into the matrix and are stimulated to thought and action. Each of us struggles, wrestles with indecision and doubt, and part of us must die that the whole of us can truly live. For each life is an allegory and metaphor to others; those lives well-lived, imbued with love, are a shining image of our own potential. To capture that potential, to compress it into a story, to an image, is the essence of all metaphor. Thus we see the image of Christ, the face of metaphor and allegory in the joys and sorrows of our transformation mirrored in every parable we apply to living with integrity and spiritual wholeness.

Deeper yet are the mythic strata, built one upon the other, like layered worlds, opening their horizons to the otherness of human aspirations. For

---

23. Matthew 13: 31-32.

Meditations on Christ

Yeshu'a spoke of the resurrection of the dead, of angels, of vengeance and judgment, of the final trumpet call and of the return of the Son of Man. Every image contains an infinity of forms, a possibility of worlds. Thus the story gives coherence and order, orients to a sense of place and time, to a present moment, to a visionary past, to a tentative future. To sit at the right hand of the throne of Majesty,[24] a ruler over the kingdom of the world, is an image insufficient to express the totality toward which it points. Such a world, of principalities and powers, ruled by authority and the dogmas of war and might, is only one image of the Whole, only one construction among many, neither true nor false, but a speaking in the name of faith, an image of a momentary world imbued with the authority of a particular time and place. Yet, the myth can never be reduced to history and the history can never be raised to the image of the myth without suffering loss to both. The image is a mythic world, a part containing the potential of the Whole, a unique configuration imaging the hidden power and beauty of Spirit manifest. And it is built with past imagery, as Yeshu'a built upon the foundations of Jewish faith in the midst of patriarchy and the ambiguities of the classic Mediterranean world.

The mythos contains the narratives and stories from which the world is made, the end toward which it moves; incorporating the literal and moving through metaphor, it unfolds a totality of visionary potential. The Bride of Christ and the New Jerusalem, Armageddon and the Seventh Angel of the tiny scroll, the scarlet beast and the pits of hell, all to be revealed in their day and time. This is mythos (and *telos*), the visionary end and conflagration of an ancient world and time. The mythic face of Christ is a speaking in the tongue of angels, a lion on the throne of justice and damnation, for the good of the few, not the many. Here all Christian dreams and visions, however small or vast find their place, as ladders and labyrinths in the depth of the aspiring, seeking heart. But the structures of world-inhabiting minds do not remain fixed, they change from year to year and from generation to generation. As the Christ of flesh transforms into the Christ of faith and the Christ of faith into the presence of the Christ-spirit, we see a corresponding transformations of mythic worlds. The images of Christ transform through art and literature, through film and fiction, according to the images of their day. But the storied mansions of heaven and hell, so well delimited in ages past, have fallen into disrepute, denied and disbelieved by many. Or in resurgence, they have been restored to a shadowy half-world barely seen but held onto with unquestioning loyalty born of an ancient desire for certitude and a predetermined end.

The Spirit of Truth is not contradicted in the formation of such mythic

---

24. Hebrews 8: 1.

worlds for this is truly the language and imagery of men. We have constructed and deconstructed our inner worlds, those embedded in the quick of our transforming selves, in our words and thoughts, where we seek to find what we may yet become. And we can surpass these worlds of condemnation, of heavens and hells, and a multitude can be uplifted through knowledge and wisdom beyond these early, limited dreams and visionary memories. For the mythos cannot contain but only image the potential of the Whole, only treat with disturbing discontinuity, the unrealized potential of the human capacity to suffer or to condemn others. Let us envision transformations through peace and non-violence, of a continual resurgence in Spirit, new life without denial or condemnation filled with joy and wisdom. In new visions, let us raise again the dead to life, open the doors of perception, perceive the world reborn through ecstasy and grace. The mythic face itself is surpassed, for beyond imagery and visionary dreams, beyond imagination and ecstasy, lies the dissolving of all images, ideas or words in the Source of all Imaginings.

This fourth face, Mystery Itself, cannot be revealed by thoughts, words or prayers. For this is the mystical face, imageless, a burning Light dissolving all veils and forms into its purifying flame, a flame dissolved in the ocean of the heart's light, into pure expanse and Presence. It is the action of Spirit on an image of the heart, through the Sophianic Christ, through the Regina Angelium, Queen of Heaven, through an angelic form that leads to true transformation, death, rebirth, and self-realizations beyond the imagery of faith or hope. For Christ cannot be contained in images or signs; the imagery must dissolve into its primary Source. This is the reality of Spirit, the holy actualizations of Presence, the manifesting of Mystery and the fulfillment of all that is yet to come. It is letting-go, a release of the past, an end to disquiet and turbulence. It is Christ dissolved into the being-so-ness of the present, into the fall of autumn leaves and the rising of a new day's sun. Thus Christ becomes a vessel and a means to attain to the Mystery, a spiritual power that no vessel can contain but into which every vessel must sink like ice into the warm oceans of Life.

This is Presence, Mystery, Spirit, and yet none of these. It is form and formlessness, love, knowledge and humility; pain, sorrow and regret; the touch of ecstasy and the deepest peace of understanding. To be filled, to overflow, submerge, dissolve and to be reconstituted according to our gifts, such is the mystical face of Christ. It is self-loss and true self-finding, an end of faith and the justification of faith, the presence of Divinity and the surpassing of Divinity. It is the absorption of all that is literal, metaphoric, and mythic into the great Ocean of Totality where no form, nor thought, nor feeling state can enter without profound transformation. It is the engendering of inner peace, expansive love, and outward calm. It establishes maturity and fulfills all claims of faith in surpassing joy. For maturity is a reconciliation of opposites, a dissolving of the conflictive world, an acceptance of what is yet unrealized in the human heart. These faces are the four cornerstones of the House of Prayer in which all may seek realization and stability. They are male and female, young and old, of every race, color or creed. They are part of the infinity of faces within each of us, without prejudice or denial. They are my faces, your faces, the faces of our shared and ennobled humanity, the faces of every life no matter how poor, how painful or how beneficent. Let us give thanks for those faces and seek them in every face we see.

The Fifth Face
To behold within one's self, the fifth face of Christ, resolved and reconciled in a healing love. (1:6)

The fifth face, like the sun, is your own face—your inheritance, your self-realized potential.[25] As a birth-right, you received this potential for the good of all beings, not just for personal adornment. It is your natural spiritual face, a Christ face unveiled in the innocence of a loving gaze, a clear and depthless vision. It is beauty on the face of the plain or disfigured, it is joy in the eye of the beholder, and delight in the elderly or old. It neither perishes nor is it born but surfaces to transform what is given, infusing light and peace. In woman, it is manifold in appearances and incapable of being named. In men, it is gentleness of spirit wedded to a sensitivity for all such manifestation. In children, it is joy, delight and energy channeled into activities of grace. In the old, it is deep calm, insight, and an oceanic loss of inhibition. In the sick, it is death, confusion and fulfillment. In the ignorant, it is denied, blocked and resisted. Yet, are we not all ignorant, all confused, all resistant to new horizons where even in blind anticipation, we find only old problems and old needs?

The appearances of this face depend on the maturity and health of the dedicated spiritual seeker. This is the face of Christ transforming both the individual and the communal life. In waking or in sleep, in activity or rest, it comes unbidden to the heart according to inner desires and aspirations, reflecting the state and station of the seeker. The fifth face, entirely personal and intimate, is perceived uniquely by each person as a transparent image of manifest eternity. For this reason we should not mock the visions and images of others—the blue-eyed, blond Christ or the black-skinned, dark-eyed Christ

---
25. 2 Corinthians 4: 6.

are images of the fifth face. Only the ignorant and unseeing say that "Christ was a Jew or Semite" for these have never beheld the fifth face of Christ within themselves. The adornment of Yeshu'a ben Miriam was the descent of Spirit transforming him within and without; so it is in every example of grace and blessing. The fifth face is the face uplifted in prayer receiving the deep infusions of Presence. The many visions of Christ, the multitude of forms, are incapable of expressing the magnitude of that Presence and thus each is a partial manifestation of the Whole.

Each of us must seek within the confines of our heart the purification of the images and appearances that arise. A child, young man, or woman, a saint or sage, an angelic presence, or any image of eternity—in whatsoever way Christ may appear, there is the message and meaning. But if we wish to surpass the literal, metaphoric, or mythic we must enter into the realm of the unlimited attributes, such as healing love or compassion. For the love of Christ, as a love for every living being, every aspect of life, is the source of the fifth face, a compassion for all that suffer or are abused, sick, lost, mistreated, or denied. Therefore the fifth face of Christ does not depend on fixed images, literal history, outward appearances or constrictive dreams. It is the face of the communicant transformed according to the presence and reality of Love, the compassionate Christ-face, the loving Sophianic heart. The face that is not afraid to look honestly into the face of another, in either suffering or joy, and to feel, heart-to-heart, the fullness, worth, value and desires of the other.

It is not a face of pride or arrogance; nor is it a face unmarked by error or mistaken loyalties. For the fifth face teaches us our limitations and boundaries, it lead us to see how and where we may help, both ourselves and others. It does not take upon itself more than it is capable of doing; it places itself last, not first. It is a face of love and inspiration that does not exalt in its power or magnify its capacity. It seeks to overcome its own inner boundaries, its own limited expectations. The Christ love does not desire self-denial but self-surpassing; a fullness gained without injury or harm. The inspiration takes us beyond our weariness and the love preserves us from our errors or mistaken perceptions. To increase our capacity to love we must not reach too far, too fast. Slowly, with patience, love may guide and purify, emptying us of our inmost fears or obsessions. To love simply, deeply, unpossessively with spontaneity freed from desire for gratification, to let that power flow through us to others without demand or expectation is a great gift. One requiring us to purify and unblock every pathway so we may apprehend the fullness of its presence.

The resolution of conflict is necessary, yet this does not mean the end to questioning. The fifth face, like every other face, does not give us answers and conclusions—it only opens us to deeper possibility through teaching us to accept with equanimity what is inconclusive, partial, and incomplete. The fifth face beholds the vastness of the Holy, the unending succession of numinous manifestations. The conflicts to be resolved are those that inhibit our trust and deaden our ability to love and to share. To open our heart to purity in love means to seek for deep, peaceful transformations among all other beings, to heal and to be healed. Let the joy of Christ that is in you, at this very moment, break through the burdens and confusions that binds you to a path of misfortune and sorrow. Rejoice that the fifth face is your own face realizing the power and presence of holy love! It is a power that heals every wound, trauma, and disturbed perception. And it will heal you slowly, patiently, time after time, drawing you to the fullness of your flower. First, the roots, then the plant, only after comes the healthy flower and then the fruit—a loving touch, a loving grace, a soothing and joyful presence.

As this face dawns, it soothes and releases the doubt or confusions, it heals the scars or wounds, it infuses the whole countenance with a softening of lines. The openness reflects a deep inner reality, the birth of joy so deep and powerful that it is beyond naming and yet, its mark is clearly seen. Prayer becomes a resonant ringing bell whose sounds and energies sing with echoed harmonies; meditation becomes a deep stillness within which a dawn light spreads a boundless reflection on all-embracing waters. In the fifth faces, the eyes are clear, certain, joyful, direct; the smile is contagious, the words are like a song, the energies bursting with a stern, loving glance that penetrates the great and small alike, making no distinction only seeing what is there to see. It is a face seen in a small child, in those whose burdens have been lifted, in the free spirit of the unconstricted and those whose love overpowers sorrows and loss. It is a face of one who has looked upon the Deep and seen all the images of his or her redemption from a lesser life.

The fifth face is a radiance that illumines the darkest fear, then heals it with compassion. It is a light that reveals enslavement to false ideals and purely self-interested goals, then draws us out beyond the narrow definitions of our justifications, beyond lovers, or families and friends, through affirmation, not through denial. Beyond the world of conflict and aggressive, selfish illusion, it draws us to a creative, caring, open world of health, love, and well-being. We must empty ourselves of illusion, our inner demons and illnesses, free ourselves from the dark side of our own collective preoccupations and racial histories. In the fifth face, the worth is found not in dogmas or eternal promises but in an immediate presence of health and serenity—for without these we only perpetuate the errors. We must release our hold on narrow laws, cease clinging to denials, and no longer ignore the necessity of inner work leading to more loving relations.

The reality of the fifth face awaits your commitment to a more dedicated spiritual life, it lies as a potential beneath the surface of your aging and all the marks written into the flesh as signs of how well you have lived. The fifth face of Christ was seen in his tears over the resurrection of Lazarus, in the joys of the transfiguration on the mountain with his chosen disciples, and on the cross when he cried, "Father, why have you forsaken me?". This is the face of humility, of surrender, of a cry that goes out from the heart and seeks its place in Spirit.[26] It is the cry within each of us that draws us to a spiritual path, that refuses to accept the limitations of a time or place and insists that we become more than we presently are. It is a cry that flows like tears out of the eyes of a lover who has lost a beloved partner and who longs for reunion and shared joys. It is a cry in the heart of the cosmos echoing through each of us, urging us toward the realization of our deeper needs, away from illness and neglect.

Every healing is a lesson in humility. It shows us the limits and extent of our illnesses; it teaches us about our gifts, and the limits of what we understand. To be healed through Christ means to be healed according to our capacity to love and to forgive. Not beyond our ability but with the hope of greater capacity beyond our present contractions as we let go of artifice and appearances. The fifth face dawns slowly, over years of inner and outer work in learning, giving, receiving and faithfully remembering the lessons learned. It is a face seen in both the young and old, radiating warmth and confidence, humility and joy, patience and peaceful intent. It is a face reconciled with the world, neither scorning nor condemning, seeking always the transformation of self and other in the context of honesty and trust. It is a face without pain or anxiety, that willingly gives the whole of itself for the benefit of others yet within the limits of a well-recognized natural capacity. It is calm, steady speech, bright awareness, illumination, laughter, and joyful wisdom. It is Christ manifesting, not as an individual being, but as a capacity for loving warmth, for giving comfort and for receiving the love and joy of others. It is within each of us, only awaiting our consent, our purity of heart, our nobility of spirit.

---

26. John 11: 35; Matthew 17: 2; Mark 15: 34.

The Church
To revere Christ and not the church in substitution to Christ; to follow the Inner Light beyond ideology, dogma or tradition. (1:7)

In the history and institutions of the church, both east and west, is the record and preservation of an error. This forceful claim, this dogmatic emphasis, serious and disturbing, has marked the history of Christianity with violence and discrimination. The error is this: the belief that there is only one Son of God, one true religion, and only one way to salvation. More than all else, these three beliefs have misled sincere seekers away from the center, toward the chaos of war, cultural and racial discrimination, and hatred in the name of a truth whose creation is a doctrine of men favoring their institutional values and worth above the values and beliefs of others.[27] It is an error rooted in human weaknesses of pride and conceit. It is an error found in every spiritual tradition that dogmatically claims the superiority of its own valued way of life over the spiritual ways of others. And many religious traditions make this claim, even though it is often denied by its more observant and caring members. How deeply rooted is the grasp of pride in the ways we follow, in the path best suited to our aspirations, in the chosen tradition we walk. When Christians are told, "Christ died for your sins," the claim is magnified to include every other human being. It is as though simple trust in a valued way of life were not enough but must include (or exclude) every other human being in a message given only to a minority once persecuted and then, inflated with its own collective self-importance, applied to all human beings. That claim is a narrow teaching; there are many paths and ways to salvation and none of them is supreme over other paths.

The dogmas of men have repeatedly confirmed the error of pride in following a chosen path, in thinking every other person must walk only their walk and talk only their talk. Because untold generations past and present have confirmed this error, because they have built great institutions and organizations, the error has become a doctrine repeated and often unthinkingly received by a majority. After two thousand years, such doctrines have become uncritically affirmed by elect members and by all those who silently accept the error. And often, it is the doctrines of the church which are worshiped, not Christ. It is the church which is served by the congregation and not Christ; it is the church which comes first, and not Christ. Constantly, the organization, the membership, the rules of order, the community and interests of the church, come first, not Christ, not the spiritual path of the individual, not the

---
27. Corpus Hermeticum 10: 14.

mutual awakening to shared spiritual concerns. And the errors abound as unexamined assumptions justifying the oppressions of others—in the name of ministry, conversion, and evangelism. Christ does not desire to be served by error but by the Spirit of Truth, to serve, not to justify or pronounce narrow laws or exclusive rules of faith.

And what is the Truth? For over two thousand years, followers of the church have exalted the majesty and glory of the Christ of their faith over all other human beings, traditions, or religions, exclaiming promises of salvation. The days of the formulations of their doctrines lie in two fundamental needs: first, to conceive in rationally comprehensible terms, the Mystery and ineffable depths to which Christ leads. Secondly, they express a need to affirm the totality of the vision of Christ in a totality of commitment for the realization of their potential as communal beings. The rationality of the form, in the beginning, was mythic, a cosmological drama fully attuned to the thought processes of those days, reflecting a certain mentality and spiritual vision. And that was natural and necessary. But as the institutions and structures of the early communities began to objectify themselves in relationship to a variety of political, economic, and cultural worldviews, the human desire for power, self-affirmation, and dominance became increasingly more central to institutional, patriarchal conceptualizations. The myth gradually became fixated into dogma, tradition into rigid affirmations, and community into a set of patterned relationships utterly excluding the non-conforming or unbelieving.

It has been the way of men, and men in particular, to exalt in the superiority of their beliefs and to perpetuate those beliefs as sacrosanct and holy. In the writings of Paul this error was first given sanction; and secondly, by the writings of the church fathers who followed Paul first, and Christ second.[28] In those writing, they have made a burden of the faith and beliefs of Paul and forgotten the sorrow and suffering of Christ. For the Christ of Spirit did not die for the condemnation and oppression of others, nor for the denial of their faith and hope, in his name or in the name of the Father, *Abba*. Rather, Christ lives for the affirmation of differences within Spirit and the fullness of its diversity in many branches, limbs, and leaves. Surely it is the sorrow of Christ that he was condemned by his own brothers, by the pride and hard-heartedness of his own people. How is it then that Christians believe in the superiority of their own teachings just as those who denied and condemned Christ? How is it they believe in only "one way" when that way denies the fullness of Spirit in all its manifestations, possibilities, and potential? For all these religions have come from a profound Source, TheaTheos, in whom all ways that lead to peace, wis-

---

28. 1 Corinthians 8: 6; Ephesians 4: 4-7.

dom, and love are good, valued and worthy of respect. Thus, blessed are all those revelations that have been poured out for the many in the name of the One, for the transformation of the many and not the few.

The totality of commitment in Christ asks that we fully affirm, accept, and believe in the worth, value, and holiness of all revelations and teachings that lead to peace and well-being. The days of the ancient mythos of Christ as supreme Lord and only revealer of truth are now passing away, soon to be no more. The Sophianic Christ descends out of the otherworldly heaven, out of magnitude and false glory, into the real world of everyday concerns, into the immediacy of our needs, and stands below, not above. Serving and not being served, let us not worship the church, nor its teachings, but following the path of the heart, let each person seek to embody Spirit with joyful devotion to fostering diversity and differences that all be enriched. Let us put ourselves in Christ and then, put Christ last, not first, a willing birth mother for the coming-into-being of others. Let us call Christ down out of the mythic heavens of patriarchy and into the world of our aspiring hearts, into partnership and shared respect. In the nearness of Christ, as brother and teacher, let us experience the shared joy of healing, our mutual capacities to love, and to reformulate our understanding that we compliment every tradition, in its goodness and positive values.

The power and reality of Christ is undeniable in those who open their hearts to Spirit and who act with sincerity, more real and more potent than any doctrine or dogma of men. The ineffable Mystery cannot be reduced to only one exclusive teaching, nor can it be sustained as a collective norm of maturity if it does not have the capacity to evolve, change, and radically transform our inner capacities to new expressions, insights, and realizations. Therefore, let us be wise in Christ; let us not construct fixed dogmas of faith; rather let us affirm the eternality of Christ in the simplicity of love and in the ineffable quality of our insight and illuminations. Let us find the courage to embrace a new path and new knowledge whose contents cannot be reduced to limited doctrines and restrictive dogmas. Now is the time to find the courage to affirm the Mystery of Christ through a free and creative recognition of a multitude of spiritual pathways, all of which can lead to new insights and spiritual attainments. What we seek is the suprasensual, the suprarational, the reality of direct seeing into the heart of Mystery and Spirit no longer constrained by the boundaries of exclusive community.

In our commitment to others, we may follow this truth: all beings can respond to genuine loving kindness, compassion, and forgiveness no matter how bruised or disfigured they are due to suffering, abuse, or lack of knowledge. All beings desire to live a creative, loving life of shared human relations based in respect, freedom, and valued differences, in peace and shared joys of community. However blind, every desire to see requires faith, then effort, and finally knowledge that is neither exclusive nor secret, but open, shared, and cultivated according to diverse talents and desires. This knowledge, as sacred *gnosis*, is not based in scriptures, nor churches, nor privileged orders, nor in monastic communities, but is freely given by Spirit through Christ-Sophia, Anointed-Wisdom, in many diverse ways, paths, teachers, manifestations and guides.[29] And many scriptures and teachings are worthy of study; there are many techniques never known or seen that can contribute to new unfolding and realizations. And how shall we know the greatness of the scriptures we read, or the promise we hold in our hands, if we are blinded by faith or dogmatic reason?

The greatest scripture is the one written on the heart by Spirit in the moment of realizing the teaching within, in the sanctity of a mind surrendered to Sophianic Illumination. It is an imperishable revelation awaiting our awakening to wisdom. On whatever path you walk, whatever teacher you follow, there is an inner wisdom awaiting your full consent to dawn, manifesting the fifth face, a ringing bell vibrant with love. Therefore, choose your path and walk it! If you choose Christ, know that it is a path of love, forgiveness, healing and wisdom—to put yourself below, not above. The light of Christ, through the illuminations of the heart, must reveal the errors, misjudgments, and false directions in order to lay down new pathways free of pride or fear. If we empty the heart of self, of preoccupations with our chosen way, and simply walk it generously, with love and care, causing no injury or harm to others, how can we not arrive at the goal? The light of Christ should be a guiding ray, a bright beacon to keep us from the shoals and hidden rocks of vanity, leading us to a safe harbor in which many ships may find shelter.

The true vicar of Christ is the voice of Spirit leading us to new wisdom through humility. Men, and men in particular, must tear down the scaffolding of their self-preoccupations and dissemble the rational fortifications and institutions that have barricaded them from the fullness of community in deep feelings of connection and relatedness. The voices of humanity, inspired by Spirit, speaks a multitude of languages and teaches a multitude of spiritual truths. Our ears must be opened to all these voices; we must listen with respect and appreciation for the directions they give. The revelations of Spirit are many and cannot be reduced to a single path or way; we must affirm all revelations and seek to reconcile them in the harmony and creative joy of our

---

29. Isaiah 11: 9; Luke 1: 77; Bhagavad Gita 10:9; Corpus Hermeticum 13: 8.

own path. And this revelation is continuous, not confined to the past nor to any one collection of writings; it is on-going, creative, emergent, in process, always unfolding and revealing. It is a way without end, and a content without boundaries. And in the joy and holiness of Christ, it is infinite, bursting forth in multiple forms, and flowering across a multitude of cultures, times, and places leading us far beyond the solemnity and silence of church or state or nation.

Authority
To invest no fixed authority in priest, minister, teacher, or guide; to follow the intuitions of the heart in devotion to Christ. (1:8)

There is no universal church other than the heart and no universal head of the church other than Christ. There is, however, universal love as exemplified by those who follow the inner teachings, and a universal wisdom for those who place themselves below. The true representative of Christ is the individual who demonstrates genuine care and concern for all living creatures. The broken branches of Christianity, its diverse and quarrelsome factions and divisions, must be healed and supported from the roots; the mother soil must be replenished in a new vision of unity and vitality. This Pan-Christian union cannot occur under the guidance or direction of a particular head or leader, not Protestant, or Catholic, or Eastern Orthodox, or any fractional head or charismatic leader. This inclusive union must occur through Spirit and the grace of multiple efforts by leaders concerned to preserve the good and yet willing to prune away withered, dead, and entangled limbs still snared in vines of exclusive, self-serving concern. The Christ of the flesh did not say: "Worship me as God," nor did he say, "Worship my representatives as God," nor "Worship the church and the priests or ministers as though they were me." He did say, "Love one another even as I have loved you," and "A servant is not greater than his master."[30] Therefore, if Christ is the head, the body must follow these words and stop inflicting wounds on its own members and on others.

It is the task of every follower of Christ to make peace with every other follower of Christ. If the fruits of faith and understanding are good works, love, kindness, and peace then we may be certain that we live as true sons and daughters of God. But if the fruit is hard and bitter with condemnation of others, with stones of denial and blame, with the broken teeth of those only concerned for the salvation of the few, then leave them to follow their path to

---

30. John 15: 12, 20-22.

the rewards they deserve. Those who stand in the Sanhedrin condemning an unknown Christ lash the body they claim to love; there is no peace in that love or healing in those denials. Therefore, let us not invest authority in any human being to the detriment of our freedom and personal responsibilities. The days of kings and autocrats have passed away into the shadows of their own created darkness and delusions; yet the blood of Christ still cries out from the damp earth of those slaughtered or condemned in his name. It is a mockery and inversion of Christ's passion to turn others into victims like Christ, to condemn where forgiveness and love are needed, to contract a holy teaching into the point of a nail used to crucify others. This blame is unacceptable in the Christ-Spirit, it is a denial of the passion for which he died and a perversion of that great love into an impoverished and empty shadow.

Let us remember the common ground of our trust, our own passion in Christ—to love, to heal, to remember and not to forget the circumstances of his condemnation, to stand outside the courts of the law, and to practice always a compassionate humility, a simplicity of concern for the well-being and survival of all. Let us worship God in a multitude of forms and possibilities within Spirit and rejoice in our shared union, our differences, our unique perspectives, and in the deep, abiding harmonies of genuine love and sparkling wisdom. Christ calls to us to actualize our deepest potential in sharing worlds with a multitude of others; to realize the inner resonance of souls, our self-surpassing capacities for spiritual realization through peace and shared insights. Every being, Christian or not, a follower of Christ or not, has such a capacity; it may be actualized in a multitude of forms, ways and paths. Another can only point to a possible realization, but we must individually actualize the capacity. The deepest guidance comes from within, from the in-swelling of Spirit, from the bright intensity of the inner light and presence. It is not created by another, nor does it justify another; it stems from the deepest root, an up-flowing energy of wisdom uncontainable in any one form. If another helps us to actualize that love and grace, we are thankful; but it is the same grace and love that gave that other his or her own understanding. In Christ, it is a loving heart, a heart that embraces all faiths, paths and ways, without denials or accusations.

The priest is a servant of God, not a representative of Christ; in Christ he or she is only a human being, nothing more, nothing less. Whatever station one may claim, we do not rise higher than our humanity in finding Spirit, we only actualize what is already in us. Priestliness, or priestesshood, comes after not before Christ, in the awakening of the heart and realizations of the soul, in the willingness to serve, not to lead. And it comes to many who will never be nor ever desire to be priests. The minister is a servant of Christ also, standing beneath the altar, both feet on the earth, both hands uplifted in prayer. But the minister is not the head of the church, nor an authority of the Word; for the Word is spoken unceasingly in the heart of every follower of Christ who, in Spirit, lifts the veil and listens closely to the quiet voice within. Both priest and minister come after the Word, not the Word of scripture selected, pruned, and edited by men, but the Word of Truth spoken in the living heart.[31] The Word is by no means confined to what men have called "the gospel" for the true gospel, the "good news", is this—every living creature is a Word of God, every soul, a breath of the divine Spirit, every life, a speaking, a song, a hymn of praise to the Creator. And every Word resonates within the Spirit of Truth given to it as it penetrates the heart and ears of those who hear in every Word, Spirit speaking.[32]

Words that heal, inspire, guide, give hope, console, support, uphold, encourage, nourish and show the way to wisdom and understanding are images of the true Word. The greatest teacher of the Word does not depend on scriptures approved by men, nor on sacred books, or hallowed writings, but lives in and through Spirit, the Word of the Holy Christ. This is the Word, the wisdom, that resounds within every being who loves without possessive tendencies, without clinging, without wounds, because that love, manifest in the *Regina Angelicum*, Holy Mother Wisdom, heals those wounds, restores dignity and embraces the rights of others to be different. Such is the Word that inspires and breathes life into us, flowing out of Spirit through Christ and the Sophia, into the children of light, into the spark that gives life. It is the same Word heard by Christ and resonant within each of us. It's authority is the way it guides and opens us to the suffering and hopes of others, the way it reveals the subtle worlds, the way it teaches us the path. For those whose ears are open, they hear this Word echoing over the whole world, as harmonic golden tones, resonating in the heart of every scripture, every word of life, every true teaching. No institution, office, sanctioned role or leadership can possess it; no instruction, teacher, or guide creates it. It simply flows out of the loving heart and resonates in the hearts of others.

All teachers, guides, ministers, priests and priestesses have a profound responsibility to demonstrate, not the authority of their office, but the intrinsic gift of the Word made real in their own lives. This is the gift of humility given to the faithful; it is the gift of worthiness, integrity, and goodness in Christ. Therefore they place themselves below, not above; last, not first.[33] And every

---
31. Corpus Hermeticum 1: 30; John 15: 3-4.
32. Corpus Hermeticum 13: 18.
33. Like 13: 29-30.

woman has a place among them, in the most honored ranks and stations, for women shall teach them a far better example than ever men attained. Masculine pride must be given up. Let monks marry and enter into the joys and sorrows of parenting, let them overcome their naiveté, that self-protected innocence that too easily miscomprehends the struggles of life, birth, and childrearing. As equals in every rank, women have their gifts as do men, let each determine for themselves, how best they may serve. The needs of others are only part of the path. There are needs for self-development, needs in co-related love, needs of understanding through differences, needs based in unique gifts, talents, and capacities that cannot be reduced to issues of gender or culture. What is not needed is wealth or power over others or false status or prestige; better to live without attachments to either wealth or poverty, free of prestige, understanding both and their limits.

Many have served only the church or community and the status and wealth it confers, missing the heart of the spiritual task, to transform self in relationship to others, all others, not just one community following where others have led. For many such teachers, Christ has become a comfort and shelter, an arena for indulging expressive passions, a goad urging consolidation though a joining that only obscures and hinders. Or Christ becomes a shield, a barrier against challenges to think and perceive differently, a wall that blocks out a larger and more complex world. The uncertainty of life, its demands and confusion, are dammed behind a simplicity of faith that no longer feels the passion for growth, but accepts a bound area as the only holy ground when all the earth is holy, free for all to walk. They take refuge in Christ, but to their shame, they are afraid to face the challenge of a more complex world, not separate from Christ but separate from the church. The way of the church is easy, but the way of Christ is hard. For each person bears the responsibility for their own soul, not the souls of others, though we may help where we can; yet, it is our task to one by one, awaken within us that resonant Word so we might hear the Word in others. Christ demands honesty, simplicity, a willingness to discard false ideals, fears, distortions and every unnecessary idea or institution that obscures the Truth. And the truth of Christ is this: love and forgive.

Where then shall we turn for guidance? We turn to the Christ within, to Spirit, to Mystery, to the holiness of the Word, to prayer that gives life and breath, to what is free from vanity and exclusivity. There are many souls longing for instruction, thirsty to drink from clear springs and new waters, to find untainted wells. And these wells abound! First in the pure of heart. Secondly, in all those who with sincerity and devotion seek to understand through prayer and meditation, the depths of Spirit. Third, from all those imbued with the joy and light of illumination, the healing grace, the touch of love that flows forth without limit. Such knowledge does not come from scriptures, or books, or written words; it comes from a depth of maturity found in inward devotion, luminous thought, serenity in realization. Fourth, it comes from those whose lives are dedicated to service, to sharing, giving and working for the health and well-being of others, be they learned or not. The way of Christ is not one of retirement from the world, for Christ did not retire. Rather is it found in commitment, engaged living, in the activities of wisdom tested in worldly life. Not only in action; there must be times of solitude, quiet, withdrawal, of being alone and apart. But also in action, involvement, in a willingness to share, engage, debate, reconsider, to occupy, work and transform.

There are many scriptures, works mystical and plain to study in the whole of all religious ways of life, in philosophies or sciences. And none need be held higher than others, for we have no need to judge the lives and concerns for those walking another path, another valid way. The Way of the Christ is open, sharing, interactive, in dialogue, seeking, questioning, exploring and creating. Guidance comes in many forms, from many paths, teachers, ways and instructions—who can name them all! It comes in thought, prayer, marriage, children, death, loss, illness, conflict, family, friendship, solitude, alienation and the joys of community. It comes through a continuous effort and willingness to learn, to grow, to share, to cast off, and to climb to new vistas with thankfulness to every teacher, friend, and guide. Through the Christ, these ways meet, meld, and dissolve in loving compassion and joyful, luminous, hermetic insights. And Spirit draws us above worldly learning and teaches us an inward grounding more secure and lasting than any institution, outer authority, or external guide. It is written, "the pure in heart shall see God" and does this not mean an inner purity of intent, a deep sincerity open to the suffering of others, valuing their differences, their sorrow, joys and hopes?[34]

We must learn to act according to our deepest intuitions, according to the Word that sings in our blood, according to Spirit overflowing. Spirit acts with power when we open ourselves and allow the blood to resonate, to feel the energies of Light. It carries us beyond the conventions of a socialized world that denies Spirit, that fears difference, that suppresses our freedom to find our deepest God-knowing. When Spirit manifests, it overflows the boundaries, cannot be confined to books, or offices, or roles defined outwardly. The power and capacity of Christ is uplifting, a swelling sense of harmony that bursts like a wave in a depthless sea.[35] In the pure of heart, it carries them to the other shore; to the place of peace, illumination and profound insight. In

---
34. Psalm 24: 4-5; Matthew 5: 8.
35. John 3: 6-7.

the restless, it carries them through the labyrinths of soul, beyond simplicity, into a diverse complex seeing, a many-branched universe of pathways turned back on themselves where they struggle to discover new visions of the Whole. The reconciliation of these two poles is to see them as one continuum, as part of a single harmony of possibility where simplicity and peace unite with complexity and creativity. And this reconciliation takes place in Christ, in having broken down every conflicting idea, resolved doubts, and reknit the whole in the image of a part that has definition without being too tightly bound. In the simplicity of the loving heart, this image is ignited and burns like a flame on the altars of peace; with fullness, a golden light that seeks only to light the flame in others.

Robes
To keep the robes and garments of Christ clean, pure, undefiled; to wash from them, all martyr's blood, all stains of sacrifice. (1:9)

How much suffering there has been in the name of Christ! So much sorrow, so much pain, blood, so many wounds, such an imitation of his suffering flesh and its painful burdens.[36] These wounds threaten to destroy us, to utterly exhaust us with the pain and the sorrow, to overwhelm even a life well-lived. But when I am burdened by this history of suffering, the wings of Spirit have enwrap me and spoken quietly in my heart with warmth and passion, saying "Their pain has gone into the earth, their blood is redeemed and forgiven, their sorrow and excess is no more, yet they live, continuing their journey." So must each of us, turning away from these paths of suffering, rejecting all forms of self-injury, walking the way between extremes, avoiding eroding, self-indulgent hard-heartedness. Our task is to seek truth without blood, without blame or guilt, without injury to self or others, without making a burden of our path or the practices we follow. To seek a path that is free of suffering, that has overcome the temptation toward self-inflicted pains and expectations of sorrow, this is the path of awakening to Christ, to the Christ of Spirit, not to the Christ of flesh.

There is a need for redemption, a redemption of the past, from all the excesses and extremes, from all the repetitions of abuse in the name of the Father. There must be a healing of memories, an inner forgiveness that moves beyond the old pain, beyond the wounds, beyond the tendency to resurrect the image of the harrowing of Christ as the model for a spiritual life. It is the life,

---
36. Revelations 6: 11.

not the death of Christ, that best exemplifies the Sophianic path: compassion, forgiveness, healing, redemption of pain, the removal of suffering, the opening of eyes, the straightening of bodies, the feeding of the hungry, the concern for those who have less or very little. The redemption of souls may call out of us a willingness to sacrifice, but sacrifice is not the path; our suffering is too often born of our incompleteness, our false hopes, our self-serving dreams, our tendency to deny, our lack of affirmation.[37] Suffering born from indifference, from denial, from careless attitudes and ill-defined, narrow goals shutting out the sorrows and hopes of others is what marks the death of Christ. But the living Christ, the affirmation of Spirit within, the life that sings in the blood, does not desire to create any stains of violence. In the name of Christ, there should be no violence, no oppression, no denial but rather affirmation, kindness, peace, and the freedom of Spirit leading to paths of well-being.

There has been too much oppression in the name of Christ, too much violence, too much condemnation of others, too much ignorance masquerading as holiness and too much self-inflicted sorrow. Such is not the path. The robes of Christ must be cleansed in purest water, with gentleness, with a thorough and patient scrubbing, with an honest, diligent care to preserve and reanimate a deeper spiritual radiance, to complete our collective healing. This healing, of body, of memory, of the past, of mind, heart and soul is a slow process, an alchemical work of generations, and the touchstone of that work is loving kindness, acceptance, humility. Who is really worthy of suffering? And what suffering is a genuine mark of Spirit and not misguided pride or deeply hidden fear? Only when we heal our own wounds, our inner pains and sorrows, only when we fully expiate our misguided past can we hope for a less painful future.[38] The Christ-Spirit can be that expiation, can open the heart to the mystery of love that heals deeply, that illumines the hidden fear, the sorrows, hates, and jealousies, the unbidden actions or words that diminish and contract our understanding until we see only the narrow circle of our own sorrows, wants, and needs. That love cannot be contained by pain, it penetrates to the very bone and marrow, seeks to heal the smallest trace of injury.

The heart, to be "pure and undefiled," must be animated with more than personal desire or a will toward conformity and obedience. It must be filled with an inner fire of transformation, it must be fully alive with the desire to heal, it must feel deeply the needs and hopes of others.[39] Expiation is found when we feel the hunger of those who have no food, the illness of those without healing, the homelessness of those without shelter, the confusion of those

---

37. Mark 12: 32-33.
38. Luke 4: 23.
39. Matthew 5: 9.

lost and misdirected, the helplessness of those beaten down and unable to rise or hope or dream or to thrive. Indifference is a stain on the robes of Christ; carelessness is a tear in the fabric; denial, a whip mark on the back. To truly feel the suffering of others is the beginning of the path, but not the end; we must also act, creatively, to counter that indifference and carelessness. We must seek ways to enact a greater awareness in response to the sorrows that already exist, so much in need of healing, so buried beneath the artifacts of an older, less mature world. Purifying the heart means to free it from the burdens of its suffering, to attain a stable, open, receptivity to deeper presence, to the unbidden freedom of inspiration and to a willingness not to cling or grasp onto that which passes beyond us.[40]

True healing is a spontaneous act of love, a sudden unhindered flow of energies moving in Spirit to result in an awakening of hidden potentials. Christ was an example of such healing and the Christ-presence remains a living channel for that love. Compassion is not an act of will; it comes spontaneously, even unbidden, in the face of those whose need is great and in search of new hope or direction. Compassion is an act of Spirit moving in us and through us, a channel of grace whose power and presence is a source of wonder, a source that claims our fullest attention and affirmation. Compassion is the source of the "joyful sorrow" that seeks the healing of others, for their good and fullness, and not for the sake of the healer. This sorrow is a passing moment in the flame, a purification that burns away the dross and leaves only the liquid intensities of love, formed according to the needs of those healed. That intensity flows through the currents of the entire world; it animates the cosmos and resonates with the deepest energies of creation. There is no sorrow in it and no pain or place where it stops and refuses to flow; what stops it is our unwillingness to receive, our resistance to being vessels, our clinging, our holding on too tightly. There are no martyrs in that love, no saints or sinners, no blindness or unseeing; there is only Spirit flowing, singing, being known, healing.

The blood of martyrs, and all those who die in wars or conflicts fought in Christ's name, are what has stained the robes. All those who have made claims for others in their own name, all those to have condemned unbelievers and stubbornly thrust up the barriers of their own shallow faith, these are the marks most difficult to remove. The ideal is to live, not to die; to become older, wiser, and more mature, not to wither on the vine while the fruit is still green and immature. We chose embodiment, life, existence, authentic and sincere engagement, incarnation through embodied knowing. Therefore we must follow a winding path, one suited to nature, one that moves with

---

40. Qur'an 31: 27.

the elements, not against them. The path of Christ is one that is natural, engaged, loving, able to direct the changes, inspired by Spirit and living to a mature age with loving family, friends, and companions. And what color are the robes we wear? They are not one color, but a multitude of colors, more hued and shaded than the eye can easily see, more diverse than any one color can equal. They reflect diversity, alterity, sobriety, joy and understanding, a range of moods, aspirations and realizations and not simply a code stamped by a restricted seeing. But nowhere among them is a stain based on a sacrifice through blood, through intentional harm to others, through a denial of the freedom to think or act differently. The song when they gather is one of enduring peace, creative, active, alive, vibrant in multiple harmonies, harming none and not requiring harm to self.

The path of non-violence does not mean that the violence of others can be accepted or judged unimportant; for what harms another harms me, harms all of us, impacts the whole. Therefore, without violence, resist violence and without injury or harm, resist injury or harm. Defend yourselves from injury! Do not think that not believing in violence is a path requiring you to sacrifice yourself to the violent. Violence must be met with strength, not weakness; with courage, not fear or passivity. The means require training, agility, a capacity to deflect and redirect in a non-harmful way the aggression and misdirected energy of others. In this struggle, love is the greatest resource for transformation and courage is the necessary inner strength to fully enact that love even when deflecting aggressive and harmful actions. Yeshu'a did not turn back from the Sanhedrin nor flee the judgment of those against him, yet, he harmed none, but only healed. This is the model: to courageously heal the sick and to face the denial of those more violently misled whose transformation is the deepest need of our shared humanity. The path we walk together is a path of individual choices; we must choose ways that seek to heal the injuries of the past and no longer enact the dramas of death or punishment.

Women have suffered much in their sacrifice and in placing themselves below in the name of the Father; but male expectations or demands for such sacrifice are false notions. What is hidden in this sacrifice is the expectations of the misguided, that women should serve and men, rule. Such martyrdoms must be repudiated; women must walk their own paths with full integrity, free and filled with Spirit. Placing themselves neither above nor below, they walk a path in sisterhood whose healing grace extends to all those willing to recognize the peacefulness and creativity of their gifts. Mutuality is the key, reciprocity the correct relationship, and conscious empathy the means to a more lasting truth. The gifts of Spirit are many, the Christ love is a river within Spirit flowing through us all, washing away the stains, purifying, healing, opening the heart to radiance. And woman's blood, her monthly flow, is holy, a source of life, a gift most sacred, a sign of life, of birth, of on-going, blessed creation. The blood that stains is blood shed through violence, not the blood of life nor that resulting from an illness or accident, but the unholy sacrifice of self or other demanded by those who remain blinded by pride and a tenacious ignorance.

The grace that washes away those stains is not found in baptism nor in rituals of cleansing, those these may help; but true purity comes from the heart inspired by Spirit and able to purge its hurt and anger and fear. In the calm of rebirth, in the joys of Spirit, in the intimations of the Christ presence, the fullness of that grace may flow forth without exhaustion, without end. It is not a path without sorrow or suffering, for in the suffering of others we have a world of woes in need of healing. The Christ-heart is not unaware of the hearts of others, however much sorrow they might carry. To live unstained in a stained world is not easy, it requires our greatest courage and determination, our inmost strength to actualize the highest ideal and model. Spontaneity that feels and desires the healing of others, without grasping, without denial, this is the first sign of awakening. The second is when that loves flows forth without effort and in a joyful, quiet surge, fills the world with its presence. The third when we no longer distinguish between our pain or that of another and remain stable, calm, and radiant with an unending healing love. It comes out of the depths of Spirit, flows forth, leaves no marks, no signs, no stains, and draws into its luminous circle those desiring new life, hope, and transformation. It is a circle open to every living creature, and its boundary cannot be seen or known by the worldly-minded.

Diadems

To know that the diadems of Christ are persons of humble faith who manifest Presence in a smile, in a touch, in a word, or caress. (1:10)

Walking a spiritual path is not a matter of leading, nor is it a matter of following. Such a path has to do with the double and simultaneous motions of an inward spiral and an outward expanse. We must each place ourselves at the center and then open our hearts to the authenticity of faith and to the fullness of knowledge. Whatever path we walk, it is the qualities we embody in everyday interactions that best indicate our depths and fullness. In Spirit, we start from where we are, simply, and then invoke the Christ presence within us, the Sophianic wisdom, as an agent of deepening awareness, as a catalyst for a more expansive knowing. Just as Christ has a Bride, so too do we have both the Bride and Bridegroom within us. Each of us must seek to balance and unite them through the *Hieros Gamos*, the Holy Marriage, in which an inner union creates an outward joy and through which male and female both attain to a fullness of mutual expression.[41] At first we are rough stones, unpolished, plain, unadorned and yet, containing within a promise of rare mineral, a gem-like spark of possibility. And Spirit washes us, tumbles us in the powerful currents and the turbulences of transformative experience, it washes away the surface and reveals an inner complexity of planes. In those planes we may see reflected a startling, infinite depth, an image of holiness in a piercing light that utterly unites us with our Beloved. This is the ring symbolizing the hermetic union, the Sacred Circle within which Spirit leads us to new wisdom and insight.

This does not happen suddenly and all at once, though we may experience sudden and unexpected breakthroughs, a momentary loss of self in the wholeness of creation. Yet we come back to the individual self, back to the ordinary mind and heart so often immersed in a world of cares and distracting concerns. So we turn again and again toward the center, cultivating those disciplines and practices which lead us to an on-going renewal of our deeper spiritual needs. And as we turn inward, we expand outward. Yes, sometimes we contract, even painfully so, and this is natural and expected. Sometimes we shed the world and all its harshness, indifference, and the painful infamies of our fellow worldly beings. We turn within so as not to bear the pain of collective immersion in disdain and denial. We turn inward in order to reclaim a deeper source of affirmation, not merely to find our unique abilities or talents, but to touch the source of Presence, the quiet play of Spirit inspiring us outward into the world as those bearing a gift. And our gift is perhaps very small, very simple, a flower, a stick of incense, a smile, a healing touch. And yet, its quiet radiance goes out into the world, like the sound of a temple bell in still air, a vibrant reminder to stop and to give thanks.

The beauty and power of the spiritual life is not only found in its most dramatic moments of personal revelation or in the mystic heights of experience. It is found also in the still moments of sunset, in the songs of dolphins at sea, in fog bound valleys of early morning, in the laughter of children and in the joy of friends meeting after long absence. It is found in those moments when the heart opens to the world, gives up its defensive fear and no longer shelters be-

---

41. Revelations 22: 17.

hind a belief or a spiritual practice. It occurs in a receptive heart that does not hide in guilt or anxiety, does not need to justify itself through the faith of others, no longer needs a complex of ideas or symbols to express its deepest concerns. That beauty and power is constantly with us, surrounding us, calling us out of our self-constricted mental and emotional entanglements, asking us to cut through the illusions and to let go of our unnecessary burdens. The Christ-spirit does not seek to imitate the sacrifice, the pain, the longing sorrows of earlier incarnations. What it asks, so quietly that we only hear it by stilling our inner thoughts and flights of imagination, is to learn to listen with our whole being to the vibrant singing of the world.[42] That song points to our individual capacity to join that song with a voice attuned to harmonize with others, or as occasion demands, to sing in solo for the joy of those who truly hear.

Such a song might be condensed to a single word of greeting, even to a glance that is clear and startling enough to reflect an inner resonance within Spirit. In the clearest sense, this requires nothing more than the ordinary exchange that nevertheless leaves a lasting impression. The nature of "depth" is a quality that opens a multitude of possibilities through an inner stimulation of concurrent depths in the other, a resonant harmony, a union of souls, a *Hieros Gamos* in a look, a dissolution of boundaries without dropping the veils. But there is no need to qualify it as anything special, rather we move ahead in being able to actualize it constantly as a natural gift we each have for truly touching others because we can be touched ourselves. The spiritual path is one that inevitably converges and crosses the spiritual paths of others; if it fails to do this, there is a deep and serious problem in the pathwork. The Christ walk should cross and converge with other paths, harmoniously, with sharing, joyful exchange and a vibrant communion within Spirit. The valley of such a walk is the ordinary world with all its beauty still vibrant and alive, and the peaks of that walk are the visionary horizons we attain to reveal our inmost potentials.

To be a "diadem" is no easy accomplishment; it requires a certain receptivity to the gifts of Spirit worked through a clear vibrancy of presence. The Christ walk should be simple, an affirmation of faith based in the positive example of a healing, committed life of love. It is not a walk that takes its model from the shadows of denial, suffering and pain that crossed the life of the Christ of flesh. Rather it takes example from the good of that life, the affirmations that led to the healing of others, from the miraculous gifts of Spirit infusing a world replete with violent affirmations of culture and the excessive "ways of the fathers." We no longer live is that age, nor do we accept

---

42. I Kings 19: 11-12

those standards, nor can we embrace the exclusive and closed byways of those who seek to impose their beliefs on others. To be a diadem means to shine inwardly, to graciously listen and to affirm the different paths we walk while yet walking a path each values dearly. It means to celebrate diversity while yet cultivating the unique means to a genuine awakening to Spirit. It means to follow Christ in joy, receiving those gifts given and seeing clearly the value and worth of the gifts of others, on every path, in every way that leads to healing and shared well-being. It means to embrace the good of every path and to distill that good into the vessel of our most faithful devotions.

The way of Christ is not narrow or closed to those who stand within it, but open to the gifts of Spirit and seeing beyond, the boundless expanse of Mystery. It is foolishness to imagine that any path is complete; all paths are reflections of processes that go far beyond the most exalted expressions or teachings of divinity. Yet, any path, when walked with Spirit can lead to a fullness and fulfillment that utterly dissolves doubts and uncertainties, reveals gifts of wisdom and illumination, and satisfies our deepest needs for an awakened understanding. We can pass beyond all concepts and experiences of "self" and into selfless, into unbound openness, into the very essence of Mystery where all essence is dissolved. We can embrace the forms and visions of our inner unveiling as signs and inspirations leading us to a union of Bride and Bridegroom. We can enter the ecstasy of that union, be merged in Spirit and reconstituted in the simple forms of humanity for the actualization of the Whole. We can walk in faith, love others as vessels of creation, and work for positive transformations at the most basic human levels. We can study the world, nature, the cosmos, the minute subparticle or the birth and death of the universe, and still walk a spiritual path with integrity, joy and simplicity.

We need not exalt in our faith or practice, there is no need to "convert" others; what is necessary is to exemplify the path we walk through the virtues we actually embody. The highest teachings are those that come without effort, spontaneously, revealing open vistas of awareness while simultaneously providing a deep, abiding ground wherein we can walk, and act, and live in the most normal circumstances. Yet, those circumstances can transformed, be inwardly opened and reveal Mystery and the presence of Spirit even in a smile. The spiral takes us inward toward awakenings that radiate outward into uncounted subtle worlds, planes, and dimensionalities while seeming to be the most ordinary, unexceptional events. The miraculous touch is one that dissolves the illness, soothes the fear, and points beyond itself to the radiant center of all becoming. The Hermetic Christ is an image of Spirit in that pointing, an Alpha-Omega impressed into the human heart as an alchemical sign of our capacity for joy and health. When we embody that image it acts to dissolve the hardness, the closure, the fearful resistance and opens to a vista whose horizon has no end, no boundary other than the one we draw as our limit. We all have limits, even the most profound manifestations of Spirit have limits and seeing these is a mark of integrity, a sign of humility in the face of endless Mystery.

In this process of awakening, we do not become the Christ or the Sophia Bride, the Bride or Groom becomes us, adorns us with the outward garments of the *Hieros Gamos* and leads us to the chamber of Union. Those garments are the virtues which we fully embody and manifest in daily life to others; they are not the signs and vision or mystical experiences but the grounded, vibrant radiance of a clear, loving concern for other supported through patience, kindness, integrity, wisdom, insight and care for this world and all the beings in it. The Hermetic Path is not one that takes us out of the world but deeper into it as caretakers, guardians, and faithful keepers of our own birthing ground. We embody the way we walk, we seek to transform ourselves into vessels of the Christ-Spirit so that we may preserve and value the world in sharing it creatively with others, with those from other paths and spirit walkways. In a Spirit-filled world we will discover hidden paths, texts and teachings, new manifestations, but what matters is the result, the fruit from the tree and not the esoteric materials that nurture its roots; not the structure of its branches, but the shade it provides for even the smallest sparrow. As spiritual guardians of earth, we must recognize the importance of the small and the value of the minute. Nothing is so insignificant that it can be lost or destroyed without consequences, therefore the Christ-Spirit values life in all forms, species, and manifestations, with love and genuine respect.

Spiritual presence is not unique to humanity nor is it a sign of unique capacity; such capacity is possible in all species and in all life-forms. The manifestations of Spirit are infinite and in the Christ form they become diverse and differentiated according to the inner capacities of the individual. But such manifestations can occur in other species, other beings, on this world and on other worlds. We are not the center of creation nor are we anything other than one species among a multitude of others. In the greater harmony of a vibrant and living Cosmos, all life in sacred and all species, a manifestation of divinity. Thus in the Christ-Spirit we value all life and we give it respect and recognition as shared among equals. We do not seek to dominate but to live in respectful appreciation of the gifts of each and every created being. We seek to be caretakers and keepers of the Eternal Flame, the spark of presence in every being however slight, great, or in-between. The Hermetic Christ celebrates the

Hieros Gamos as a celebration within all nature, vitalized in songs and celebrations, in the dancing of the world into new being. A touch or caress, a kiss, a smile, in the Christ-Spirit are all charged with the unpossessive joy of creative life directed to the preservation of species, toward a celebration of difference and variety. The Great Round is the dancing, expanding and contracting circle within which we each give birth to our inmost potential and in sharing it, contribute to a world emergent, more kind and complete. With humility, we make our offering, with humility, we receive the gifts of others, and in joy we join hands and dance.[43]

Grace
To open the heart in healing self and others; to give where there are wounds or sorrow; to share in Christ all joys and grace. (1: 11)

To follow the Christ-spirit does not mean to simply vocalize a teaching or to preach a set of fixed beliefs or practices. It does not mean to walk a path circumscribed by briars and thorns that cut against the spontaneity of shared beliefs and community with others. The Hermetic Way is one that stems from a world communion with the many faiths of others. Its bloom is in the face and heart of the transformed and awakened soul, those that have discovered a joy and grace beyond limited conformity to collective rule or law. To walk in the Christ-Spirit requires a loving heart that seeks to fully express and realize the inner bounty of Spirit in flowing forth into the world of human cares as a primal source of healing and goodwill, taking many forms and having many diverse means and paths. This love does not occur through self-promotion, nor in justifying a way of life as better than the ways of others. Such a justification is a fiction, a conceit based on illusions that cannot see beyond the narrow boundaries of a private and personal concern. In walking as Hermetic path, we set aside doctrinal differences, the disputes of the intellect, and the passions of unseeing commitment for a more self-reflective and receptive love based in maturity that goes far beyond the words and ideas of shared beliefs.

Having a path and following it is not the same as promoting it for the good of others. The greatest good of any spiritual path is found in the actualization of it followers to act with kindness, understanding, and sympathy for the suffering and struggles of others. We may disagree, we may defend our beliefs and commitments from the criticism of others, but the actual path has a far greater need for inner reform than outward witness to others. The real

---
43. Bhagavad Gita 9:26; Acts of John 94-95, 101 (Apocrypha).

witness is Spirit, the real test, a realization of Spirit in a mature and balanced life of loving wisdom and care for the preservation of the good in all teachings and paths. Our celebration is the intersection of Spirit with the joy of sharing with others, their paths, their walks, their visions and insights into the boundless abundance of Mystery. The Spirit of Truth in this process is speaking honestly with sincere conviction in sharing mutual beliefs, points of intersection, and participating in dialogues that fully value positive, non-coercive beliefs.[44] Where we resist is at the margins that impinge on the free realization of alternatives, that would use violence, oppression, or deny basic human rights. Where we converge is in the need for multiplicity of views that fully uncovers the depths and fullness of Spirit in manifesting wise and creative insights through a diversity of spiritual teachings.

Many are wounded and in sorrow, many suffer from injustice, abuse, and the dislocations of the oppressive interests and beliefs or others. Our world is far from enlightened and no country, nation, or political state has the necessary maturity to resolve the differences that continue to disrupt the emergence of an integrated world community. Such an integration must come from the realization of individual responsibility to live a mature, spiritual life dedicated to world peace, cooperation, and the emergence of a lasting and stable future. We are each a model; we are each a witness whose testimony must be grounded in a dedicated life of spiritual commitments. We must each put down roots, deep into the mother soil of our shared spiritual pathways for the purpose of creating an enduring world without the strife, pain and sorrow of ignorant greed, soulless confusion, or empty promises meant only to blind or pacify. The sorrows of many also are a witness; they testify to indifference, passive disregard, denial, and aggressive ambition; they ring with the empty phrases of self-justification that, in the end, result in death, destruction and multiple harms to others. Through the power and injustices of profit or fame or political self-assertion, a multitude suffers untold agony and sorrow. Through the propagation of rigid beliefs and doctrines, through imaginative acts of condemnation, whole peoples are denied the complexity of their actual pain and striving.

The miasma and confusion of so many, their ambiguous and unclear thinking coupled with fear and sorrow, can only be countered by the emergence of deep and sincere commitment to positive, exemplary spiritual values. This is a task for each individual, to act as a spark of inspiration, a source of actualization that seeks to fully realize the spiritual good of incarnate life. Through the Christ-Spirit, it is possible to embody, in the fullest sense, the joy and grace

---

44. Psalm 15: 2.

through which we can begin the deep healing of the earth, of all its diverse peoples, species, and individuals. To heal the wounds, we must also heal our own injuries, must release the inner pain, anger, and scars. In this, Spirit is the healing presence, the deep resonant wave that unties the knots, gently opens the wound and releases its harmful energies. The Christ-Presence is also a channel for healing, a medium that allows Spirit to follow its course through the energetic body, cleansing, healing and realigning the subtle centers. In this process, a deep opening of inward awareness requires letting go of old memories, impressions of sorrow, and all the echoes of earlier pain or injury. This gracious healing and cleansing, this letting go of old impressions, frees the heart of its burden in order to become a vessel for the healing of others.

Without this self-healing, without a piercing of old wounds and the release of static energies, the healing of others will remain bound by the inner conditionality of the healer. Opening the heart-center, in all its subtle channels and fullness of capacity, is a slow and progressive process of spiritual maturation. Even though such openings may occur in sudden experiences of spiritual ecstasy and *gnosis*, a sustained capacity to heal, openly and with utmost respect, requires a deep stability that may take many years to mature. Yet, in every act of love, there is healing. If we love others genuinely, without possessive grasping or clinging, with a sincere desire for their growth and healing, then we become agents of transformation. This is more than love rooted in sexual passions, though such passions can be healing and nurturing; it is love that flows out of our commitments to Spirit, our receptivity to Mystery in the depths of our humanity. In the Christ-Spirit it is an image of healing through our openness to an energizing presence that springs from the very wholeness of the creation, in every being, for their utmost good. It is a willingness to give, not of ourselves to our own diminishment, but of the gift of the Christ-Spirit given to us as an adornment of overflowing grace. Such grace is quiet and still, like a deep clear spring of healing water, it flows up and through all the channels and out into the hearts of others.

To "share in Christ" means to pass through the Alpha-Omega, through spiritual marriage, and to conceive inwardly, the fruit of that union in the form of a healed and healthy life.[45] Such a life is free from addictions, negative habits, self-destructive tendencies, free from petty bickering, aggressive self-assertion and insincerity that leads to harm for others. In the healthy life, there is a slow and natural ripening, a timely unfolding of potential no longer contracted by past experiences. There is an opening to new light and a receptivity to inspirations that guide and direct to the most fruitful outcomes. The

---

45 Revelations 21: 6.

voices of Spirit are many; the signs of maturity, clear manifestations of conscious choice and intimate surrender to inner light. The fusion of inner signs and outer events, their constellation within a complex world of suffering and desire, takes on greater and greater clarity leading to sustained actions for the healing and understanding of others. We do not decide, but are called; we do not choose, but we feel the wings of Spirit as they beat over us, fanning us toward actions in which Spirit breathes and inspires life. The Christ-spirit mediates, seeks a willing reciprocity between our limits and the needs of others. It does not demand or force us into action, but leads us by a simple proximity that gently presses us to act with concern for the developing good of others.

Our giving is a sharing, a communion that sanctifies a common hunger: to love and to be loved, to surrender our fear and uncertainty, and to find a secure, trustworthy path, one we can walk with our whole being. Whatever path we walk, we must walk it with our whole being, must seek to exemplify the good of what we are as spiritual beings, fully incarnate and living now, in this world. It is not a "transcendent reality" we are seeking but a full and complete embodiment, an incarnation of the Christ-Spirit in the flesh of each and every seeker. This is the alchemical marriage, the union of the soul with Spirit, of Loved and the Beloved, in order to give birth to a better, more mature world of equally embodied others. This union is complex, many-sided, and draws us to the deepest levels of Spirit in affirming an integration of multiple potentials. The realizations of this union will be many, with many forms and differences, but the consequence is a deep healing of soul, for self and others. This union touches the heart of the union in others, it is a marriage of mind, body, and spirit, a union of soul, aspiration, and the grace of healing. Spirit breathes into us, and our words become prayers for the healing of the world; Spirit infuses us, and our acts become mandalas of mutual insight and sharing. And deep in the center, the most holy Mysteries are unveiled that our eyes may see beyond the bound horizon and into the Infinite.

In healing the world, we must willingly accept the necessity of our own self-transformation. In seeking transformation, we must recognize the importance of the world in determining our place, time, and understanding. We must adapt, be willing to change, not petrify and not remain hidden or cloistered way from the demands of the turbulent multitudes. We must engage our full energy and yet, not over-extend and not diminish the precious substance of our incarnation through faulty choices or by taking on too many burdens. Each must find the balanced center between responsible commitments and self-healing; between helping and being helped; between finding rest and renewal and sacrificing it for others. There must be joy, deep and vibrant and free of grasping; there must be calm, inner peace, and a capacity for letting go. There must be a willingness to learn, to change, and yet, there must be a stable center, enduring values, dependable beliefs and developing, congruent thoughts. And there must be illuminations, visionary dreams that heal, a guiding presence, and a soft and receptive openness to inspiration. Everyone is capable of these manifestations, we need only to walk the path, one step at a time, to find where the work must be done. Let us each walk with courage the way that leads to renewal and new birth and let us each cast off the old skin that numbs us to the voices that everywhere cry out for healing.

Illumination
To seek full and complete knowledge through illumination and higher awareness; to see in Christ, the ascents and descents of Spirit. (1: 12)

Full and complete knowledge is relative and non-absolute; there is no "absolute" realization or illumination other than the fulfillment of soul capacity within each individual. This capacity is not all-knowing or omniscient, nor is it knowing "even as God's knows." It is a higher knowing, a series of spiritual awakenings leading to profound mystical insights.[46] It can be a fully illumined knowing, an enlightenment that exceeds words and concepts, that breaks into the free, open Infinite and experiences an abundant fullness overflowing without limits or bound forms, beyond measurable states and stations. It can be the soul's union with the Divine, an immersion and dissolution in Spirit, a complete transcendence of self, other, and of qualitative boundaries, a great vastening beyond all conceptual ideations, a complete mergence, dissolution and profound opening of the heart-mind. But this illumination is relative to the capacity, understanding, and fullness of soul that opens to an unbound cosmos of truly Infinite Being, Wholeness, and Light. No one being can actually Be that Fullness, that Infinite potential manifesting as the metacosmos; no matter how intelligent, mature, experienced, unique and capable of mystical realizations, no one being, not Christ, not Buddha, not Krishna, nor Lao-tzu nor any Sufi, Christian, Jewish sage or mystic, can know the fullness of God, know as knowing is within All Being, nor Be the utter fullness of the undying, eternal Mystery.

Always, there is more to learn, more to seek, a gleaning of wisdom that cannot be given simply as a gift of illumination but must be worked through

---
46. Lee Irwin, *Awakening to Spirit: On Life, Illumination, and Being*. NY: State University of New York Press, 1999. A book of ten principles based on the process of Awakening.

the fabric of creation for a fullness of manifold expressions. As relative, partial beings we may find our "relative absolute" that is, our unique fulfillment in which we discover a complete dissolution of self into the Selfless All and then bring that understanding back into the manifest world of incarnate life for the sharing and enrichment it offers. Such was the way of Christ, to walk a path to its highest end, to the cliff edge of possible temptations, to the high mountains of transfiguration, to the miraculous and profound, to death, resurrection and return.[47] It is one path among many, a path realized and then lived, bound by its own history, its reconstructed, relative truths, its magnified and infused promises, its shadows, discriminations and denials. But at the heart, there is life and hope for the realization of deeper truths, of on-going revelations and insights into the way, an embracing of illumined intuitions becoming new practices and reformulated beliefs. Illuminations of soul are the means by which Spirit manifests the Christ Wisdom and turns it into real being, into existential commitments, into desirable forms of Hermetic realization. Each of us is a path, a possible teaching, a manifestation of truth relative to our maturity and commitments to our chosen way.

We do seek a "full and complete knowledge"—that is, to the best of our capacities, to seek the highest realization of our individual potential in following our spiritual path. This knowledge is more than that learned in books or written words, more than oral teachings or rituals of empowerment, more than esoteric instructions and codes of conduct or philosophies of enlightenment. It's fullness and flower must spring from the individual, from the radiance of Mystery come to life in the living heart, from the Awakening of Spirit pressing us toward our fullest capacity. It is a gentle, constant emanation, a deep fullness that surrounds and opens us to the harmony and miracle of a living macrocosm. It is a surpassing moment of prayer in which the veil is lifted and we see clearly the reality of a vibrant Presence in all that lives and sings around us. It is an entry into the depths of Spirit where form vanishes, where energy is delight, and self is nothing more than a distant spark swallowed in a sea of holy, endless Being. It is a vanishing of Light into the vast Mystery of an all penetrating fullness beyond qualities and conceptions, beyond words and ideas, beyond the noetic intuitions of illumined soul and into the utter fullness of All-Conscious-Being. It is peace and realization, relative, promising, supporting life and being through a multitude of worlds, planes, dimensions and subtle realms, none of which captures or contains its overflowing fullness.

On the Christ path, it is a coming down of Spirit, a rising up of Spirit, a holy encounter transformative and radical in utterly exposing us to the full-

---

47. Matthew 17: 2, Mark 9: 2-3.

ness of its reciprocities and creations. And we become slight instruments of that creation in attuning ourselves to the fullness, in being able, however slightly, to share that inward unity that Spirit gives. Masked by the diversity of differences, by the dialectics of intellective doubt, ambiguity and a clinging resolve to hold to partial truths as though absolute, we know only a part of that Whole. But in the Wholeness, knowing it as such, we are beyond our individual depths, beyond our rational capacity and beyond all tentative instruments of constructive desire. In the coming down of Spirit, we must be prepared to surrender our cherished ideas and beliefs in order to see them reborn, Spirit given, as the constructs they are, relative and transitive, a means, not an end. In the rising up of Spirit, through the subtle centers of the body, in bodily sensation, in subtle pathways, through various centers and channels of body, soul is reborn, mind is transformed and life becomes an inseparable web of subtle relations vibrant with life in even the slightest touch, kiss, or gesture. Spirit takes us into the world, into the transformative depths of matter, into elemental being as agents of change and rebirth. In those depths, matter becomes energy empowered and alchemically awakened to new life—we experience directly the animation of every world, every stone, everything living.

This awakening is a holy Mystery, an act of illumination requiring necessary preparation and inner calm and stability to fathom. The Christ walk is a spiral path inward toward a realization that leads us out into the world for the benefit of those receptive to such a walk. We need only walk that path, to only be the manifest instruments of reborn life, to know the illumination as reality and to simply maintain that light in the everyday world of ordinary events. In that maintaining, all that is ordinary is transformed, is made remarkable, memorable, has impact and subtle influences that extend outward to the extent of its inner potential. The Christ of flesh embodied such a realization, made an impact through the fullness of being an instrument of Spirit, a man of Mystery, a emanation of human capacity transformed into holy being. The Christ of Spirit is the realization of that promise in the present, where the Spirit of Truth descends and ascends, in every human heart that seeks to embody the Christ walk as a way of love, inner clarity, and wisdom born of balanced illuminations. Small sparks of light or great, what matters is not the degree but the result; not the experience, but the outcome, the consequence in real life. All experience and knowing is secondary to the quality of life and the impact of the individual as imbued with Spirit—with the subtle grace and depths of illumined mind, heart and soul.

This "higher awareness" has many degrees, shades, subtle forms, diverse and different manifestations. There is no system that represents it well or completely and there is no need for ranking or comparing between systems. What matters is the manifestation in real relations, in the quality of life, in the capacity to love, heal, share, and to truly open to the depths. A mother's love for her child or a father's delight in a son are a means for Spirit rising; tears for a loved one or suffering for another, a means for Spirits descent. Solitude and prayer, meditation or chanting, communal celebration or ritual acts of worship may all heighten the process; but the deepest realization is a spontaneous opening of the heart, a recognition of limits in the midst of the Limitless, and a transparency of self that maintains a perfect balance in the pervasive All-Self of others. There is no need to absolutize the forms, degrees, stages, and so on, such efforts in the end only lead away from the inner diversity through which Spirit stimulates the enduring subtle change. The path does not have one form, but many; nor does it have one set of stages, but many, an innumerable, diverse and dense complexity of differences that cannot be solemnized in graspable ideas. There is something intrinsically ungraspable in the processes of Spirit manifesting in the evolutions of our creative self-becomings. The formal element is a dedication to the Christ path, the informal element is the way we walk that path and the transformal element is the realizations we actualize in everyday living.

The "full and complete knowledge" is the utmost extent of our capacity as spiritual, incarnate beings to realize a harmonious world of mutual, coexistent relations infused with grace and illumined awakenings. We must constantly strip away the layered world of inherited disbelief, of doubt, ambiguity and insincere application for a more committed, fully constant way of life that yet remains open, free, and creatively diverse. The Christ-spirit may be realized in many forms, but its heart is love, healing and a joyful sharing; at its periphery, we acknowledge the differences, yet embrace the intersections with other paths and seek to find a means for a shared understanding. But the center includes the boundary and the boundary reflects the limits of the center. Can you expand your center, make it more inclusive, loving, kind and yet, a source of integrity, purpose and clear commitment? This is the challenge: to open to Spirit thought Christ, to walk the Christ walk with dignity and compassion, and to realize the infinite capacity of the Christ heart to love profoundly the values and realizations that each seeker brings for the well-being of all, while yet walking your own path. To turn toward the other, not away, in seeking a reconciliation, a healing, a means for peace, enduring life, and inner calm. Christ is a model and example, but you are the realization and you, you and others, must make the necessary affirmation that makes it real, valuable, and worthy of remembrance. So it is, so it shall become.

Apolutrósis

THE TRUTH: ONE SPIRIT

Then I saw a new heaven and a new earth, for the first heaven and the first earth had passed away . . . and I saw the Holy City, the New Jerusalem, coming down out of heaven from God; prepared as a Bride adorned for her husband, and I heard a loud Voice from the throne saying, "Behold! The dwelling of God is with men."

Revelation 21:1-2

Spirit

There is only One Spirit, eternal and everlasting; the same today, tomorrow and forever. (2:1)[48]

Spirit is inclusive, encompassing past and future as well as the full density and complexity of the present. It's source is Mystery which is the endless depth of Being and Becoming, the sacred source of unfolding energies manifesting potential. Mystery and Spirit are inseparable from the initial conditions of the processes of creation, sustenance, and dissolution that reflect a multitude of natural cycles of manifestation. If the Hermetic Christ is the symbolic center of the path, then Holy Mother Spirit is the dynamic life-gift, the cyclical presence that enhances and fulfills the sacred potential within each being. In complement to Christ, Spirit is the radiant Bride that fulfills the creative potential for life and gives birth to a multitude of worlds, beings, and becomings. Spirit is the very *energia* of Mystery, its dynamic capacity to act, inspire, create, and transform. Spirit, inseparable from Mystery, draws out the inner capacity and potential of our awareness and our relationships to a multitude of other forms of awareness. In this process, names, forms, and ideas have all sought to identify that life-giving, dynamic presence and yet, always, Spirit cannot be bound by names, forms, or ideas; always, it is more than words and ideas can articulate.

The inner coherence of Spirit is found in Mystery, in the vastness of the potentials with which Spirit weaves the making and unmaking of reality in and through discreet, real beings.[49] Spirit, inseparable from the actuality of real beings, encompasses and surpasses those real beings, those instances of creative self-becoming, for a constant urgency that seeks to draw out of Mystery, All that Is and might Be. We, as limited human beings with our inherited views and subjective bias, must seek to recognize in Spirit the self-surpassing quality that inspires and leads us beyond our present state of knowing. Spirit not only sustains, but also draws us out of the bound circle of the present and opens us to an Unbound capacity to merge and to be one with Spirit. And this capacity is indeed great! The "gifts of Spirit" cannot be fully enumerated, they surpass all indexing, because those gifts are adapted and unique for each individual. Real beings, actualized and awaken individuals, know Spirit through those gifts, become instruments of a vital transformation that differentiates according to the predispositions and capacities of the instrument. We each

---

48. I Corinthians 12: 12-13.
49. Lee Irwin, *Visionary Worlds: The Making and Unmaking of Reality*. NY State University of New York Press, 1996. An exploration of our capacity for spiritual world-building and unbuilding.

receive the gifts of Spirit in accordance with our deepest capacities to actualize a pattern of Spirit-guided living. In the heart centered Christ path, this actualization includes a deep and abiding love for others that their gifts also be realized.

Spirit is not bound by beliefs or strategies of faith; it is we who are bound by our own convictions and ideations. Opening to Spirit is an act of overflowing that cannot be contained by simple convictions or by a path we walk; we bind Spirit by those very beliefs in not being able to let go fully, by not being able to let our convictions dissolve into Mystery in order to be reborn, through Spirit, as instruments of new understanding and insight. Thus we rise to a height commensurate with our inner development, and Spirit, infusing our whole being, flooding our vital-emotional, mental-imaginative, and intuitive-spiritual perceptions, is bound by the formative constructs, habits, and tendencies by which these various centers function. Water takes the shape of the cup into which it is poured; Spirit is able to open us only to the degree to which we can release our inner fears, resistance, and anxious boundaries. Yet Spirit can dissolve those very fears and anxieties, those bound habits, those reiterated patterns of emotional and mental reaction, if we open ourselves to the subtle inner working of its continuous presence. For Spirit is in us, about us, connecting us with a multitude of higher and lower worlds, an inner constant that requires only that we bring into focus our desire for transformation.

This is why we value Christ, because Christ is a focal image (among others) that may act to facilitate an inner awakening to Spirit. And the Bride of Christ is another such image, the feminized form of Spirit as a divine Sophia whose holy descent into this world is a fecund source of inspiration that stirs the sleeping soul with longing. This is the longing for union, for a oneness with Beloved Spirit that knows no boundary, that merges and rejoices in the interpenetrations of a profound *gnosis*, a true illumined knowing. I do not know Spirit, yet, Spirit knows me; I strive to actualize that divine presence, and that presence surpasses me, binds me, fulfills me and extends far beyond the limits of my individual knowing. I praise Spirit without reserve, and yet, always, Spirit points beyond self to the yet-unrealized capacities of the transforming soul. Blessed are those in whom Spirit manifests, but more blessed are those in whom Spirit has become the Bride of the *Hieros Gamos*. And most blessed are those in whom Holy Mother Spirit has become full Mystery, dissolving the boundaries and distinctions with perfect balance, grace, and realization. In the struggling world, we each must seek out the path that will lead to such a realization for the good of knowing our soul's true capacity. In such a realization, Spirit is the one true guide, the one true source.

There is "only one Spirit, eternal and everlasting" because Spirit cannot be bound to one form, one idea, one book, or one set of writings. A multitude of books, ideas, writings, and words cannot begin to exhaust Spirit, for the whole creation is the handiwork and inspiration of Spirit's Holy Mystery. Many are the forms, paths, ways, teachings and possible expressions and ideas in and through which Spirit manifests. Spirit is not bound by dogma or this or that doctrine; it is not the inheritance of one tradition or three, but the inherent, dynamically creative working of all creation. Nor is Spirit a simple essence or unity. Rather it is the sacred *energia*, a multitude of processes ever capable of division and combination, from the smallest to the greatest, leading to the woven, interdependent web of all living creatures, all life forms, in a sustained and living cosmos. Spirit is not simple but complex, not a single idea, but a manifest synthesis of dynamic processes, of a creative coming-into-being through many stages and transitions, inspired to give life its diversity, adaptability, and a sustained capacity to co-create. As long as there is life, there is Spirit; as long as there is a cosmos, Spirit acts and interacts; as long as living creature aspire, Spirit moves and gives life. Therefore, Spirit is eternal and everlasting; it is one in so far as we behold the unity of the creation, the inherent wholeness through which beings may grow, evolve, and comprehend their development. Spirit is a holy presence, a Mother weaving the world for the good of manifesting this entire universe, or multiverse, of longing, desiring beings.

And what is the "sameness" of Spirit? It is the inherent capacity to inspire, to conceive, emulate, transform and to realize a possibility or potential which enhances the whole and gives adornment to creation. Spirit is expansive in casting new being into the mold of already existing form and contractive in preparing to give birth. It may contract to the very depths of our most painful realization, our faults, short-comings, illnesses, and self-serving, unjust tendencies in order to open a doorway into a new recognition. It may expand into a vast horizon, into a transtemporal illumination beyond the normative contours of local space and time. It may become and unbecome, create and destroy, transform, awaken or put to sleep, as part of a far-seeing turbulence seeking to ensoul and adorn a world, a galaxy, or an entire universe. In this process, Spirit enlivens, enhances, draws out our capacities and points us toward the realization of our soul's purpose as co-creative beings charged with a responsibility to actualize our inmost potential, to inspire others, and to seek full and harmonious unity between beings, species, and kinds. Spirit offers us the gift of its constancy, it's ever-present inspiration, its enduring hope to create a fullness and to adorn ourselves with grace. Such is our challenge in

Christ, to attain to the holy marriage with Spirit, to receive inwardly the inspiration, and to give birth to a thousand worlds.

Truth
To know that truth is never too high nor too deep to be fathomed; beyond prejudice, perception and sense, in outflowing depths of Spirit. (2:2)

The nature of truth is vast and complex and interwoven into the very fabric of our becoming as limited human beings in search of illumination. What we know or believe as "truth" is a guideline to an ever-deepening synthesis of personal realizations bound by the natural limits of our individual and collective capacities. The truths we know are not final or absolute; they are relative to our maturity, experience, and social interactions. The spiritual path is a walk into a widening circle of insights whose contents are conditioned by a multitude of external and internal factors. And yet, we are seeking to fathom truth, that is, to dive ever more deeply into the full panorama of visionary experiences, insights, and illuminations that open the mind and heart to the full depths of spiritual life. In following the Hermetic Christ, we set a standard for this development that accepts the relativity of our individual experience while also believing in the validity of that experience as a basis for truth shared with others. We must learn to share our insights and realizations as part of many on-going dialogues meant to explore and actualize the unseen potential, the as-yet-unrealized aspects of truth that will help to create a more humane, loving world.

Therefore the truth we seek is a personal internalization of spiritual teachings that become a foundation for further developments that may well lead beyond those teachings into new, unexplored horizons of meaning. The truths we seek are not didactic, nor dogmatic, but relative and coherent within the context of following a Christ-inspired path. Other paths are equally valid and some paths may offer teachings or guidance that is more developed in certain esoteric areas. Other paths are a rich resource for continued development and can offer important resources or teachings complementary to the path of the Hermetic Christ. Truth is not reducible to a single path or teaching or tradition, but overflows the boundaries of every spiritual construction as a plenitude that cannot be contained by the debates and concerns of specific teachings. In this sense, truth is dynamic and intentional, it evolves in the processes of communal interaction as human maturity deepens and becomes more aware of the limits of human perception and insight. We are relative, conditioned beings; our ideas, beliefs, and understanding is also relative and bound by contracted attitudes, socially inherited bias, and the constructive *mythoi* of various spiritual worlds. Such worlds offer visionary teachings, but within Spirit those teachings are surpassed by the on-going, creative impetus of a latent developmental potential.

Truth is not static and spiritual truth is a relative horizon of meaning whose realization is inseparable from the individual capacity to embody and enact that truth as a witness to its depth and significance. This relativity is not arbitrary, nor is it simply "subjective" or reducible to a willful individual outlook. The spiritualization of truth is found in the capacity of the individual to surrender, in a deep inward sense, to renounce the tendency toward grasping and controlling. This means moving beyond the manipulation of ideas as an act of sheer intellectual construction and learning to open to illumined states of awareness, to genuine *gnosis* and truthful spiritual insight. The path of the Hermetic Christ is based in a truth-context of personal realizations balanced by a broad and deep familiarity with many spiritual traditions and teachings. The discipline of the Hermetic path is a constant effort to refine, distill, and transform the immature self into a more soulful, aware being whose inner realizations are harmonized with compassionate, loving ethical concerns and a broad spectrum of teachings that emphasize the mutuality and independence of each spiritual seeker. In this process, Spirit acts as the primary life source of inspiration and guidance toward a faithful realization of shared truths and committed actions.

Spirit is the guide, the primary source for the self-surpassing, creative energies that act to inspire transformations toward greater maturity and awareness. The creative energies of Spirit are interconnected through processes of on-going thought and action that seek to realize some unique combination of those energies in an inspired state of full, individual realization. This is a profound and sacred process. In its depth it is primordially Hermetic, that is, an inner urgency toward an actualization of potential in the heart of each being. In awakening to that inner presence, to Spirit within, we discover the primal source for all truth, the mystical, energetic, subtle brilliance of an inner light whose radiance is a gift that transforms individual awareness. In Yeshu'a, this working of Spirit reveals an example of an awakened soul whose capacity to share that illumination was manifested in miraculous abilities to heal and awaken others. Yet, this same working of Spirit is possible within each of us as vessels of illumination set on a path of kindness, respect, and love for others. We must each move through and beyond the prejudices that would bind and limit our beliefs in such healing love; the truth of this teaching is that every individual has a capacity for healing if she or he overcome their own inner resistance and self-doubts. The light of this healing presence is a gift of Spirit that dwells now, in each of us, if only we open our hearts fully to the inflowing inspirations.

In such an opening, we move beyond "sense and perception" into the deeper dynamics that connect us with a larger, more alive cosmos of loving, illumined others. The veils fall away and we behold an expanding horizon of inwardness that opens out into a fully animate intersection of multiple worlds and subtle realms of being. In this visionary context, truth is relative to the magnitude of the vision, its boundaries, its qualitative insights, its capacity to comprehend a horizon that truly surpasses and transcends individual understanding. Yet, Spirit calls us to understand, to seek a wisdom that surpasses reason, imagination, intuition, and even mystical states of unity and absorption. The "truth" in this context becomes a distillation of experience that cannot be fully transferred into discreet words, thoughts, or adequate descriptions. What remains is a relative *theo-mythos*, a holy story of absorption in Spirit and Mystery where words, thoughts and noetic contents dissolve and remain only outward expressions of boundless inner unity in an infinite universe of holy creations. In this process, the Christ becomes an additional sign, a sacred symbol pointing toward a path, a way toward truth, a process of awakening that is, in the knowing, surpassed and transcended. Such is the spiritual path, leading to plateaus and vistas that beckon the seeker onto new horizons of insight and understanding.

The saying that truth is "never to high nor too deep to be fathomed" means that in following Spirit, we can be led to those horizons of meaning that will yet offer new direction and possibility within the confines of natural, spiritual, evolution. What evolves is not Spirit, but humanity. Spirit is an abundance of "uncreated grace" that proceeds out of Mystery as an internal dynamic through which innumerable actual beings seek to realize specific manifestations of potential. We are constantly seeking to actualize our own individual realization of "truth" and in following a spiritual path, we seek to surpass the norms and conventions of constricted thought by cultivating a living relationship to Spirit as a primordial source of inspiration and guidance. We can do this through an assimilation of teachings that provide guidelines, instructions and practices to enhance our inner awareness but the goal is to open the heart to the Holy Mother Spirit as a primary source of inspiration and illumination.[50] In Christ, the model is given through prayer, healing, communion, and teach-

---

50. John 3:21.

ings that provide direction as well as a living example of potential actualized through Spirit. But we must accept responsibility for the on-going processes of spiritual discovery by which we seek to validate just those teachings most primordial for the development of diverse global communities of faith, for a co-existence in peaceful, creative relationships.

The truths being fathomed are truths relative to the context of an emergent world of diverse spiritual beings. The spiritual adherents of every faith are being called beyond the exclusive claims of their original foundations to a new, co-creative existence within an emergent spiritual pluralism whose roots connect to an ancient wisdom that values the contributions of every distinctive community and whose limbs reveal new fruit from new approaches to Spirit. No community need to abandon its heritage or history, but only to open to the emergent energies of creative relationships within Spirit for the maintenance of peace, global harmony, and well-being. The ethical ground of this emergence is a distinctive commitment to non-violence, cooperation, respect for differences, and a deeply tolerant attitude toward cultural and spiritual differences. Teachings that would deny or castigate the religious beliefs of others must be discarded; beliefs that magnify the relative importance of one faith (or its practices and rites) over another only act to retard the spiritual processes of creative emergence. The "relative truth" of any tradition or teaching is not found in the goals or aspirations of its ideals as much as in the ways in which those truths are lived in order to foster spiritual tolerance and diversity. The point of "hard contact" is the boundary where exclusive claims deny the value or significance of other traditions. In the Way of the Hermetic Christ, there are no hard boundaries or exclusive claims to truth, only relative claims whose boundaries are dissolved in Spirit for the good of mutual coexistence.

The outflowing depths of Spirit, the gracious creative energies, born out of Mystery, are inexhaustible and ever-active in seeking to inspire the followers of every spiritual path. The intensity of the inspiration springs from an inner correspondence with the deepest resolve within Spirit to create a wholesome, integrated world of diverse, creative individuals. Such individuals will inevitably form a multitude of communities, each a living microcosm that reflect a wholesome balance in support of a wide range of spiritual teachings. The goal is not to find a path that excludes the paths of others, but to walk a path that joins and corresponds with those others. In the process, the path gives grounding and direction, it orients and teaches necessary attitudes, beliefs, and practices. It sets up a condition for mutual sharing and exchange; it provides a meaningful context and a sense of community with like-minded others. It teaches truths that can be shared and discussed as resources for deeper awakening; it offers a more spiritually complete way of life by affirming the value of different ways of peaceful coexistence. And it need not claim any exclusive truth. In the Hermetic Christ, the way is to link with other paths, to establish communion, and to share insights as a natural outcome of exploration and global coexistence. In Spirit, these truths are always deepening, leading beyond boundaries into potential creative depths where inner light and illumination reveals the expansive circles of interconnection and mutual well-being.

Below

To learn from all teachings, not to worship Christ above others; to know a Way within Spirit that puts self below, not above. (2:3)

For two thousand years, Christians have placed Christ above, in the hierarchic heavens of the *Mundus Imaginalis*, the visionary realm, as a supreme ruler and lord. The image of the heavenly, patriarch king is an inheritance from an even earlier age when indeed, kings ruled, blood determined social position, and war was fought to enforce a king's will. Those days of blood and fire are still casting shadows and outlines in the present etched in violent shades of aggressive dominion and fearful submission. The image of the Throne, symbol of patriarchal rule, resonates with all the terrors of men at war, asserting a will to power in defense of the violent use of destructive weapons in the name of partial truths taken to be inflexible mandates meant to empower conquest. In the shadows of that Throne huddle the impoverished, starving, beaten, and oppressed, the immigrant victims of all the stark ideologies of rule and lordship. This Throne of Judgment, this shadowed symbol of patriarchal rule, this seat of divine dominion, can only be a place of holy wisdom when men have ceased to oppress others in the name of any inherited teachings that demand the submission, conversion, or damnation of others. Only when we renounce the kingly glory of the Throne, can we discover a deeper, more mature wisdom that resonates with the creative truths of others. When we discover the deeper Wisdom, the inclusive signs of Isis, Mary, Sophia, and the many feminine teachers and guides, as diverse nurturers of multiple pathways, will we begin to understand the inner teachings of the Hermetic Way.

According to a sacred parable, the Divine Sophia, holy wisdom, intuitive illumination, spontaneous birth-mother of the gnostic, visionary Aeons (Sacred Principles), sought her origins in the Deep, in Bythos, forefather of silent-mind, in the endless expanse of the Infinite.[51] In the uncreated Mystery and

---

51. Lee Irwin, *Awakening to Spirit*, 355-358.

Immeasurable holy vastness of primal creation, she found a Depth beyond her capacity to know and, thus, having discovered limits within herself, she became reconciled to the Pleroma, the Divine Fullness. In the Hermetic archetypal heavens of the *Mundus Imaginalis*, she resides as a holy sign of Spiritual Wisdom whose judgments reflect an understanding of limits, a recognition of the relative boundaries of human intelligence and the partiality of all visionary attainments among the illumined or enlightened. In this imaged, radiant Wisdom, the thorny, woven crown of Christ becomes a silver filigree, a luminous diadem of transformed individuals whose beaming subtle rays transmit acceptance, love, and support for all those who walk in peace, the stony roads of incarnation. This Holy Mother Wisdom, as the bride of the *Hieros Gamos*, gives full depth and wholeness to her Beloved as a profound gift of Spirit, uniting the Christ with new wisdom, new outpourings of the precious waters of life.[52] In this blessing, Christ descends into the world of human care and places himself in the midst of turmoil for the healing of the World. And Wisdom resonates a deep compassion for the suffering of all those bound by the dark laws of ignorance and denial.

Not to worship "Christ above others" means not to hold a view that the primal Alpha-Omega can be reduced to a single human-divine manifestation or to only one form. There are a multitude of forms and manifestations of the creation renewal and of its end, but what matters more is the cohesive, impassioned, and committed life of an enduring present. The present is a timeless moment capable of great expansion that incorporates the visionary into a profound knowledge where the signs of Spirit manifest a plurality of forms, similar to the great classic, archetypal vision of Arjuna revealed to him by Krishna.[53] In this vast panorama of god-forms, of holy incarnations, avatars, and mystic Saints, Sufis, Hasids, Rishis, Immortals, Bodhisattvas, and realized beings of a multitude of races, genders, ages and religious orientations, none is supreme. Like a great galactic mandala that turns and realigns, the patterns shift, some elements drop out and others are added, a new emphasis or nuance is revealed, alternatives form appear, new centric catalysts emerge, submerge, and reemerge in the on-going revolutions of human spiritual development. And each realization is a gift of Spirit, a concatenation of creative energies alchemically purified in the prayerful realizations of the soul desiring illumination and wisdom.

We must learn to desire wisdom that is inclusive, visionary, interactive; we must take up the challenge to evolve beyond the view that claims an exclusive boundary as the only measure of truth. The emergent visionary beauty of

---
52. Revelation 22: 17.
53. Bhagavad Gita, 11: 5.

an illumined soul is one of the most precious manifestation of Holy Wisdom. But such manifestations are relative to the scope and fullness of our inward receptivity to diverse and multiple worlds of spiritual seekers. In this pattern, Christ is an image of illumination, a true Alpha-Omega, a radiant archetype beckoning toward the fullness of an ultimately transformed human soul. In soulful awakening, we strip away the clinging garments of inherited belief, the rag and tatters of exclusive isolation, for the naked beauty of a soul surrendered to radiance beyond form, imagination, and absolutes, to a soul given over in inward purity to the manifold baptisms of Spirit. And this baptism, this spiritual descent of grace, this warming of the heart in Christ, this burning of the holy ember, this celebration of the holy marriage and the Bride, is a joy so profound that words cannot contain it. It leads us over the threshold, into the waters of life, immerses us in the holy illuminations, washes us in the stream of creative becoming, and blesses us with the oceanic joys of a multitude of shared truths.

Among those truths the Hermetic Christ is an alternate sign, an emergent truth with a relativity that gives a radiance to endure and to be an offering to the paths of others. And this Christ descends, a redemptive presence offering a pathway toward a radical affirmation of incarnate being as inseparable from the creative processes of continuing emergence. This Christ stands below, not above; he surrenders his throne to the Bride, to the awakened wisdom of a loving and compassionate companion, to the Holy Mother Spirit, whose excellence in understanding is born out of the unity of Mystery and Deepest Being. This creative process of descent is a prelude to a new redemption whose goal is non-condemnatory, an inclusive teaching, rooted in non-violence and propagated in the healthy soil of a garden rich with a multitude of spiritual teachings. It is selective and values all teachings that promote life, peace, and co-creative love. It understands and accepts competition as a creative tension seeking to maximize an inherent capacity but balances that acceptance with an ethic of deep respect, kindness, and a recognition of limits as natural within every striving. We must learn to seek our boundaries without violating the boundaries of others; we must reach out to fulfill our potential based on the rights of others (human, animal, plant) to live alternative, peaceful paths.

We may choose non-striving, non-competition, the quiet ways of an inner creative realization, a natural inward opening of heart over years of life lived with quiet, compassionate conviction. As Christ descends into the world of human cares, becomes an integral part of the living world, we begin to realize that the magnitude of Spirit transforms the image into a vivid presence. It may take the form of the Christ child, the healing Christ, the suffering Christ, the Christ of the transformation, Christ the teacher and poet, the theophanic Christ, the resurrected Christ. Or it may take the form of the Bride, the potent, radiant virgin Queen of Angels, the Mother of the Holy Child, the blessed Woman of Healing, the visionary Keeper of Sacred Traditions, the Guardian of the Threshold, the Most Holy Mother Wisdom. In whatever form Spirit arises, the Hermetic intention is to embody the teaching simply, with humility, with kindness foremost and without attachments to stages, attainments, or personal visions. Such visions are only transient thresholds, moments of illumination, dreams or powers playing themselves out in the *Mundus Imaginalis*, none of which are final or absolute, but which can offers guidance and insight. We can move beyond form, beyond the contents into the energies and through the energies into Being and Mystery as instruments of a greater transformation than our individual realizations. We value individual realizations and visions but we know them as relative forms that point beyond.

In Christ we find a new example, he descends out of the patriarchal heavens of old and becomes a fertile presence inspiring new birth and conceptions within Wisdom, as a guiding image stimulating new potentials. We must open our hearts to the inner illumination, through a multitude of creative forms no longer bound by creed or institutional doctrine. We are free to choose and in our freedom we face the responsibilities of co-creative newness, of the efforts to bring into actualization, the unrealized capacity that remains yet buried in Christ. Not all of Christ is resurrected; not all of the capacity is known or realized until we reach the full spiritualization of our inmost gifts and abilities. We are each potential healers, capable of deep, impartial love, able to move beyond our inner barriers, able to remove the numbing pains of past habit, past mistakes, past illusions for a renewing flow of creative energy. We need only open our hearts to Spirit, placing ourselves within the creative matrix of life unbound by narrow doctrines and denials. We can learn from all teachings and still follow Christ; be companions with members of every spiritual walk and still be faithful to the Hermetic pathways. We may distill from the wisdom of the ages a multitude of teachings which act to amplify our communion with a diversity of paths rich in dialogue and shared insights. Thus we place ourselves below, with the Christ who walked among others after the resurrection and we seek in that walking, new images and understanding of our goal.

But when I write "we place ourselves below" I do not mean that we surrender integrity or abandon our responsibility to choose, act, decide with commitment, the path we follow. The path of humility is not easy, and it does not involve allowing others to choose for you! To honor Christ, the descent of Spirit in the Christ form or in the Bride or *Hieros Gamos*, means to live with more integrity than simple conformity to collective norms. It means to open the heart to the deepest truths you can bear and then, to bring them forth as signs of a growing wisdom meant to carry us past the inadequacies or boundaries that still inhibit mutual growth. It is not a matter of either enacted self-concerns, nor of the eccentric differences that mark us as individuals, but of the deep renewal of the community, an over-turning of the soil that honors the labor of others but offers new seeds, new variants, new properties and forms for creative transformation. If we stimulate growth, this is Spirit acting; if the people say, "We did this!" then we have become instruments of transformation; if personal identity is erased, yet, nothing is lost, then Spirit sustains us. In placing self below, we become a holding ground for manifest alternatives, an actualized moment of spiritual gifting, a means for the *Hieros Gamos*, the Sacred Soul Marriage, to manifest new birth. In that gifting moment, we receive all that is necessary and in sharing it with others, we become a luminous sign for the advance of others. Such is the way that has no end, the path of the Hermes-Christ, messenger, guardian of boundaries, teacher, guide of souls, master of dreams and visions.

Resurrection
To rejoice in resurrection and new life; to seek the manifestations of Christ in the gifts of Spirit, celebrating life, not death, nor the cross, nor crucifixion. (2:4)

When Yeshu'a was arrested and taken before the Sanhedrin, before the high priests, elders, judges, leaders and scribes of Jerusalem, they spoke to him saying, "Unless you believe as we believe, you shall be condemned!".[54] And Yeshu'a was hung on the cross because he made claims that challenged the way of their fathers; he did not believe all that they believed. In this example, we have a teaching: that whoever condemns the faith of another stands in the Sanhedrin, condemning Christ. And whoever condemns other followers of Christ also stands calling for crucifixion. The sign of this condemnation is the cross, and this sign is worshiped by many as the symbol of the story and death of Christ. But Christ grieves to hear it said that the instrument of his death and torture is the symbol of his teaching; for as he lives in the heart of the faithful, it is to celebrate his teachings and resurrection, not his death.[55] Therefore, let us not worship the cross. On the path of the Hermetic Christ, the cross is a sign of violence, of inflexible and intolerant attitudes toward the

---
54. Mark 14: 63-64.
55. Qur'an 4: 157-158.

faiths of others, and a symbol of human ignorance. Of all signs, the cross is the sign of oppression, an alien construct having no part in the teaching or new life in Spirit other than as a shadow that falls over the innocent who walk in peace, a way of non-violence, tolerance, and acceptance of diversity. Let us not image the cross of the crucifixion or wear it other than as a sign of what it truly is: an instrument of torture used by those who would oppress differences.

Acts of the condemnation and crucifixion are acts of ignorance masquerading as piety, an aggressive defense of guarded truths that have no tolerance for the full diversity within Spirit, in all the many revelations superseding the teachings of any one path. Always, Spirit urges us to move beyond the narrow boundary, beyond the self-serving laws of closed community, beyond the high walls and locked gates of exclusive human truths. Acts of condemnation, sanctioned by laws, or customs, or mythic imagination, result in a tearing and disturbance of the fabrics of creation; life is given to us to revere and to love, not to condemn or deny. The power of Spirit within is a reverence for the life-gift, a deep appreciation of the creative energies of inner exploration, a guide to act in ways that preserve life, maintain its goodness, and foster its inner wealth and luster. The emergence of spiritual life is the greatest gift, rare, fragile, hopeful, an immanent potential whose seeds are Spirit given for the benefit of the whole and not for the magnification of only one path. The sign of the cross is not a reconciliation, not an integration of what is above with what is below, but a sign of humiliation and defeat, a sign that tradition may dominate over emergent wisdom and that acts of healing are subordinate to acts of law or the invested interests of socially established powers. Thus the cross of the crucifixion is only another sign of the impediments that keep us from realizing the greater potentials of Spirit.

And how is Christ resurrected? Is it a secret lineage, a mysterious tradition of holy blood, of the Magdalene, the black Madonna, and the esoteric teachings of Languedoc, or northern India, or some other recreated, underground teaching?[56] Or is it a world transcending, visionary ascent into heavenly realms guarded by the doctrines and institutions of an authoritarian church? There are followers of both of these, the lesser known traditions of the esoteric teachings and the exoteric teachings of rationalized theology. But I say, the resurrection of Christ occurs in the heart of the faithful who, receptive to Spirit, experience directly the affirmation of the Christ-presence. Whatever insights may be gleaned from the esoteric and exoteric teachings, well and good, as long as seekers remain open to the creative horizons of direct experience tem-

---

56. Laurence Gardner, *Bloodline of the Holy Grail: The Hidden Lineage of Jesus Revealed.* NY: Barnes and Noble Books, 1997. Traces the historical lineages of Jesus and Mary Magdalene.

pered by humility and patience. Resurrection is new life, a rebirth in Spirit, Spirit-guided, and in that rebirth, we become healers and take to heart, our calling as Christ inspired individuals. It is not that Christ was resurrected in the past, but that we resurrect Christ in our own hearts, now, in the present, in part, for not all of Christ is yet resurrected. Only when we can know directly the working of Spirit within, its call and grace, its profound affirmations of life, diversity and difference, can we know what yet remains concealed in the heart of Christ.

To love as Christ loved, is to love beyond what is written or remembered, to love beyond the narrow parameters of faith, and to enter into the ocean of the all-loving Mystery. This living Mystery, the utterly alive, life-giving, inspired breath of life, is transmitted by Spirit and birthed from the Christ ember buried deep in the heart and devotion of the soul. And soulful being cries out for that Christ touch, for the hand of divine ecstasy to awaken our deepest potential to be instruments of a joyful wisdom, inheritors of spiritual truth, in communion with the faiths of others. Our truths are relative to our maturity and experience, relative to the depths of the Christ-presence, relative to the full scope of our limited understanding. That love, the life-gift, flows out into the world of manifest relationships and supports the beauty and harmony of soul's awakening to the truths of others. Let us rejoice in sharing those truths! Let us turn our face away from condemnation and celebrate the common good that pushes us toward a new horizon of insight and clarity. There are many paths we can walk to reach this horizon and Christ is only one of these pathway teachers, only one emblem of the Alpha-Omega that exceeds all individual forms or teachings. Let us not worship the symbol of Christ's mutilation but seek to transform the elemental energies of soul into a creative, harmonious, reborn spiritual joy.

In following the path of the Hermetic Christ, we open ourselves to an emergent visionary world whose paths do not always lead to the same mountain top. Some paths are bound by the laws and traditions of many generations of seekers, some have their inner way and spiritual techniques for attaining rebirth and higher *gnosis*. Some deny such illumination, others proclaim fixed hierarchies of faith, and others, an exclusive world of fixed assumptions closed to outsiders and intruders. This is only natural and part of the working of Spirit through evolving humanity to reveal a multitude of ways for a multitude of beings. In the Hermetic Christ, we have another sign, a teaching that is not bound by the laws of others who follow a different Christ path. Every path has its own visionary worlds, its own ways of seeing the fullness of the whole, its angle of vision refracted through the teachings of its illumined practitioners and refined through diverse interpretations. And these visionary worlds are not identical nor do they fully correspond; where they intersect, there is joyful sharing and where they diverge there is inner acceptance of difference. Our paths are many, our truths are relative, and our goals are to learn from each other, the values that sustain positive differences.

We must allow Spirit to instrumentalize the capacity of the soul in accordance with a developed, high standard of ethical concerns directed toward preservation and respect for life in all beings, all visionary horizons that lead us to peace and creative sharing. Let us throw wide the gates of peace and trust that many may enter the holy city without fear of violence and chaos because our path is grounded in non-violence, love and acceptance of diversity. How simple it is, but how difficult to enact! The resurrected Christ in the heart of the faithful does not demand either death or sacrifice or denials but calls out for life, rebirth, new sharing and deep compassion for all living creatures. In this resurrection, the gifts of Spirit may flow forth unencumbered, manifesting Christ-presence through the subtle energies of our gifting to others, even in a smile or gentle touch. The drama of this resurrection is its global manifestations, the ways in which Spirit acts to awaken a sleeping humanity to a deeper, more profound potential. As this awakening spreads out, intersects with the energetic and creative actions of other paths, waves are formed that will increasingly wash the entire world. These waves will lift the veils that conceal a vaster drama of soul's becoming in a complex, living cosmos of multiple worlds, beings, and dimensions.

On the Hermetic path, we prepare for this awakening as a necessary stage in the full realization of human capacity as a fully resurrected manifestation of world-awakening. The fully awakened horizon of illumined seeing cannot be contained in a single pathway, but as a visionary teaching, the Hermetic Christ points to an awakened humanity no longer bound by constrictive traditions or harmful laws. In walking the path, we seek to realize the exact nature of our individual capacity to contribute to this world-awakening and to exercise an illumined concern for the well-being of all humanity, for all species. But we do this without false exaggeration, without any need for exclusivity, without denying the paths of others, placing ourselves below, not above. In this surrender to Spirit, we become instruments of new life; we become caretakers and mother-fathers whose task is to preserve, nurture, protect, and to create those circumstances that lead to peace and intersected understanding. Beyond world-awakening, the task is even more urgent to foster an enduring foundation of transformative values that promote peaceful global communities for all generations.

Meditations on Christ

Multiple communities for the development of soulful being can only form through a creative, shared desire for a higher quality of life no longer limited by harsh laws and dogmatized values. Creative tensions are part of that process by which we discover the nature and boundaries of personal understanding and the limits within communal life that must be reshaped and transformed for further growth. In Spirit, we celebrate life; in Christ, we have a non-exclusive, hermetic model of illumined concern for the well-being of others. In Mystery, we have the unbound universe of all spiritual paths whose heights stand far below the potential that gives birth to a multitude of universes but whose visions may extend to the highest degree of human capacity for wisdom and spiritual realization. I celebrate this unity, I rejoice in this sharing of views, and I call out to all my brothers and sisters to awaken to the holy depths of illumination that lifts us to resurrected life. To be reborn in Spirit means to attain the vision that leads to awakening, to receive the baptism of Spirit as the gift of the Christ-presence, and in higher illuminations to surpass all constricted visions for a perfect, sustained, clear unity-with-all that comes as a gift of Spirit.

Yet it is not the experiences or illuminations that matter, not the ecstasy or visionary immersion, rather it is the consequences of the seeing that result in visible deeds and acts of love. Faith can lead to these acts, even without seeing, and seeing can mislead. Always we are challenged to discriminate between the inner reality and the outward work or effort. There is a reciprocity between what we know and how we act, and in the end, we must each decide how to best contribute to the spiritual well-being of the whole. Whatever the choice, however inward or outward, let us act with integrity and not deny others who make a different choice to actualize the capacity. What we share is an ethic of non-violence, creativity, and heart-centered dialogue based in a strong determination to live lives of integrity as an example of what can be in becoming fully human. The Christ-spirit is even now vibrant in the heart of creation, calling out to every seeker on the path to choose a way that endures, that results in illumination, that becomes a testament to new wisdom and insight. In that path, we set aside the symbols of death for new signs of creation and rebirth, for an inner baptism in Spirit as a sign of resurrection, for an awakening to Spirit that leads us beyond suffering and into a joyful wisdom.[57] May the sacred angels of light illumine our pathways, may they leads us to Spirit's gifts, and may the most holy Wisdom teach us the roads that lead to peace and shared understanding. So be it now, in all that has passed and yet to come, Amen.

---

57. Acts 15: 8-9; Psalm 51: 10.

Communion
To join in communion of Spirit with all faiths, all ways; to not deny differences, to value diversity, to share and celebrate, to see the Christ of others. (2:5)

Can we say there are others Christs, other than Yeshu'a ben Miriam, son of Mary Theotokos? Yes, the Christ-spirit has inspired many to be vessels for the gracious awakening to healing, love, and compassion for all. And each Christ-like manifestation is unique and subtle in difference and degree and no two are identical. Just as the sages of India would claim the Buddha as one of the incarnations of Vishnu, so too followers of the Hermetic Christ see the Christ-spirit in the followers of Buddhism, in all those teaching love, compassion, and non-violence. Just as the teachers of India affirm the incarnation of divinity in multiple forms, so too, the followers of the Hermetic Christ see that divinity may manifest in a plurality of holy men, women, and children who each become instruments of Spirit in the healing of the world. The way of the Christ is non-exclusive and receptive to the faiths and teachings of others, the "imitation" of Christ is not simply backward-looking ideal, but a present-centered, future understanding of the Christ-spirit infused into every teaching that values life, diversity, and a loving, healing way of life. From such a perspective, the Buddha remains the model of Buddhism and the Avatars of India find their center in the life-streams of Hinduism. But there is correspondence, there is a touching of the heart that opens to Mystery, the deep vibrancy of shared love and wisdom.

To love and to be loved, to heal and to be healed, to give graciously and to receive with humility, to teach and to learn. Such are the ideals of awakened teachers whose messages are for all humanity and not simply reducible to one culture, or one time, or one person. Yet, each has integrity and uniqueness, a center from which she or he speaks, and each shares in a spiritual kinship with the teachings of others. On the Hermetic pathways, there is no need for a forced comparison; a gentle recognition of similarity is all that is necessary, a seeing of the subtle lines that intersect and animate diversity in the World-Soul. This World-Soul (*Anima Mundi*) is not a creation of any one pathway, but is the collective resonance and creative power of all pathways, the spiritual matrix that sustains our mental, spiritual and emotional well-being on a global scale.[58] In that creative milieu, the Christ-spirit is a symbol of convergent wisdom whose goals seek to evolve a more loving, caring humanity dedicated to the preservation of life in all its diverse complexities. The many pathways may

---
58. URL: http://hermetic.com/moorish/mundus-imaginalis.html by Henri Corbin gives an overview of the Mundus Imaginalis concept.

be imaged in a panorama of spiritual teachings as a Greater Mandala whose intent is to bring all beings into harmony and correspondence, without force or coercion. The spiritual kinship of this Mandala is to recognize the affinity and relationships between teachings and teachers, to see the Christ-spirit manifest in multiple forms, not all reducible to any one archetype or model.

The heart of the Hermetic Christ is as vast as Spirit and as deep as deepest Mystery and without doubt, there comes a boundary that once crossed leads to an infinity of divine forms, faces, and images. In the Greater Mandala, there are many ways to the center, many paths with a unique teachings that lead to illumination and spiritual knowledge. Arriving at the center, the form dissolves, the Mandala vanishes, the pathways become multiple weavings in the World-Soul whose forms are beckoning to self-realization and self-transcendence. Those threads of light and dark, gray, dawn, noon, and twilight shades of silver and red-gold illumined insight, dissolve into the pervasive energies of Spirit as soul is uplifted, transformed and awakened to the vaster living harmony of All-Conscious-Being, the great Sat-Chit-Ananda whose contents are formless and whose depth is manifest in an immeasurable wave of Oneness. Yet, the creative play of Spirit, her energies and creative weavings, lead us back into form, back into the play of creation for the purpose of fully manifesting all possible shades in the painting and singing of human dramas, desires and aspirations. Like a vast mural whose diverse forms tell a great story, so too the weavings of Holy Mother Spirit tell the story of the human search and struggle, on this one world, for true wisdom and understanding. On the Hermetic pathway, our walk leads us to many other stories, traditions, and paths where we may hear the underlying harmony of intentions.

The weaving of the World Mandala is a sacred activity within Spirit that acts through the heart-centers of diverse beings to create a reciprocal understanding of unity-in-diversity. We are each a node in that Greater Mandala and what we place at the center solicits Spirit as a sign or emblem of the path we follow. On the path of the Hermetic Christ, the central symbol is a Cup of Offering, the Marriage Cup, a silver-white moon-cup with a golden edge, filled with purest water and wild mint and inscribed with a sacred verse: "Let those who desire take the Waters of Life freely."[59] The script is graceful, subtle, written in Koiné Greek, beneath the golden rim, followed by the same verse in the language of the community who use it. And on the side of the Cup held outward to the next communicant, is a larger inscribed image of the Egyptian Ankh (*Crux Ansara*), sign of Life, Peace, and Health. The Ankh is a true Hermetic sign and its symbolism has many diverse interpretations, primarily as

---

59. Revelation 22: 17.

a radiant symbol of healing and the enduring powers of divinity and wholeness. As a conjoint symbol, the Ankh is a union of the ancient sign of the Sun disk (*Raa*), joined with the sign for lasting protection and many years (*Shen*, a circle with a line at its base), and united with the *Djed* sign (an upright pillar or handle) as the base, signifying stability, the backbone, and regeneration. When not in use the Cup is covered with a silk scarf, a sign of the veiled condition in which we too easily forget our spiritual vows.

The Ankh symbol, a union of female and male, represents the life-breath supporting incarnate life, a celebration of sexual harmony, the *Hieros Gamos*, and the inward birth of Spirit through an arising of illumined awareness. Alternatively, the Ankh symbolizes a hand held mirror, revealing a reflective self that sees Spirit within the contours of self-other relations. It is also a sign of life as the Fire-Rose representing continued soul-life beyond death and an on-going resurrection in a multitude of new lives and incarnations. Inscribed on the Cup of Offering, these meanings infuse the cup, transforming it into a *Vas Hermeticum*, a vessel of Spirit charged with potency and healing. The waters represent the subtle energies of Spirit in liquid form mixed with the fresh mint symbolizing regenerated, healing life. Holding the Cup aloft, we gather in communion and offer this recitation: "In sharing this Cup, we make an inward sacrifice, we offer our failings and weaknesses up to Spirit and we pray for renewal, strength, and courage. We open our hearts to the Christ-spirit, to the Mother Wisdom, and accept full responsibility for our words, thoughts, deeds and desires. We surrender our pride in accomplishments, rewards, and attainments. We accept with humility our limitations, our ignorance and sorrows; we strive to move beyond those limits through the guidance and inspirations of Spirit. We open our hearts to that guidance and with deepest love, we receive the grace and blessings given to us, as a testament of enduring faith and devotion. May Spirit guide us, keep us whole, and show the path best suited to our needs. So be it, now and always, Amen."

To "share and celebrate" means to join together with others whose path may differ but whose hopes and aspirations harmonize with the pathways of the Hermetic Christ. Such communion is not exclusive, but inclusive, not a wall or division, but a doorway and sharing. And that doorway stands open to all those who would share the vision of the Great Mandala of all faiths co-existing in harmony, without striving for dominance or mastery of one over others. What we celebrate is the reality and presence of Spirit, what we share is the hope in peace, loving, honest relations, and a co-creative world of gifted others who also work for the well-being of those seeking self-knowledge, open communion, and shared understanding. In reaching out, what we offer is not a teaching but a valued way of life that seeks to enhance a more spiritual vision of the Whole. This greater vision is not found in eclipsing the teachings of others, but in their mutual intersected light, in points of harmony and positive resonance that fully recognizes the value and beauty of other spiritual paths. The heart of the Hermetic Christ is open, inscribed with the love of Spirit, his arms are extend, offering the Cup as a sign of sharing, healing, and peaceful intent. This love, born of Spirit and Mystery, flows out into the world through the communicant; the Bride resonates with that same love, animating all who surround Her with joy and blessing as she too offers the Cup.

Spirit sings in the blood, in the very bone and muscle, through the neural pathways, transmitting a holy presence whose subtle energies pervade and flow outward into the subtle etheric worlds of astral and noetic consciousness. This gifting of Spirit in communion with the visionary worlds of others is an essential process of subtle interaction by which the Whole is transformed into the ever-evolving Greater Mandala of cosmic creation. This Mandala has no one form, no particular fixed structures other than those we choose as adequate for our own needs as spiritual beings seeking further guidance in attaining enlightenment and higher realizations. The microcosm of that Great Mandala is found in the incarnation of an individual soul into bodied form. We are each an intersection within that Mandala, a jewel in the jewel web, a nexus that resonates within Spirit, the holy form is our own incarnate life. The luster of our awareness, its lucidity, depth, color, and intensity is strengthen by every act of kindness, non-possessive giving, ungrasped sharing, loving joyful concern, and bright gift of clarity we bring to our human relationships. We are each a holy Cup inscribed with sacred verses and filled with the waters of life, pure to the degree we live purely and able to heal to the degree we are healed. As vessels of communion, we must each seek to transmit the pure elemental currents of healing and well-being. And we find that fullness in Spirit, through Christ, or through other teachers and paths, leading us to spiritual community and shared embrace.

Not only do we see the Christ-of-others, but we also see the Christ-in-others. Yet we must always take care not to allow a vision of Christ to blur or impose itself on the inner structure of other pathways. Every pathway has its own integrity, its own inner structure and meaning, its own special character and vital life. What we seek is a resonance, a shared harmony of meanings that allows the full integrity of one to stand in mutual respect with the full integrity of the other. We do not seek to eliminate or mask the other, but to enhance, to compliment, not to deny, but to affirm, to see the glass as full, not half empty. We are all vessels, and we are all carrying Spirit to some degree and what we seek is a vision that illuminates the fullness of each, the degree of their offering, not their lack or inadequacy. We all lack, we are all limited in some ways, even the most enlightened and illumined are still relative, partial and in-process. Let us seek to find the complimentary addition that each offers, the good that is in each, no matter how distorted, ill-intended, or confused, for we too are in some ways ignorant and incomplete. Rather, let the goodness and fullness of Spirit flow forth out of a heart-centered, Christ-centered, Spirit-centered love that gives itself fully without sacrificing integrity or diminishing the luster of deeply held values. To love with integrity mean to love fully in Spirit wisely guided by clear intentions and values long practiced in daily life. Only when we love in this way can we hope for true communion with like-minded others whose paths may differ, sometimes radically, with our own but whose goals resonate with shared, creative, mutually loving energies.

Devotion
To love as the Bride loves, purely, with deep devotion, without attachment or sentimentality; calmly, in Spirit's deep Wisdom, forgiving, open, full of good fruits. (2:6)

The devotion of the Bride is to the Spirit of Truth, Illumination, and heartfelt conceptions that unite the soul of Lover and Beloved in a joyful birthing of mutual concerns. It is a relationship of equality in which Lover and Beloved share the fullness of the Cup of Communion, drink deeply the purest waters, and receive in confidence, the grace of life-long commitment. The soul's union with the Beloved is joy, awakening, and transformation; the gift of the Beloved is wisdom, a knowledge of limits, and a recognition of shared capacities for the higher awakening to Spirit. In that awakening, we pass through all the layers and veils that keep us from seeing clearly the deep potential and inner beauty of the Beloved. To love as the bride loves is to love unpossessively, to love kindly, generously, with a deep caring for the other that seeks to support growth, health and well-being. Yet the basis of such a love lies in Spirit, in purity of intent, in mutuality, in the heart of life in which everything lives and is deeply revered and shared. It is a love that overflows the Cup and spreads into the world as a subtle, expansive wave of unifying, creative energies seeking a correspondent sympathy through which we know and love others.

In this love, devotion is a commitment to the reciprocities through which the undercurrents of the wave return to gather together spiritual seekers on the pathways of communal self-realization. It is not an isolated love, nor a love confined or burdened by a closed dyad; it is a love open to loving others, strengthened by the dyad. This dyad, the couple, love shared by two as a spiritual relationship, seeks the correspondent sympathies through which it enhances and is enhanced by others. This enhancement flows forth out of the heart as an inspiration of Spirit seeking correspondent joy and gladness of soul-emergence through a multitude of spiritual relationships. Every relationship may enhance our understanding and act as an agent of change and self-other awakening. We need only to open our heart to Spirit, to the life-principle, to the deep reverence that recognizes the gift and joy of life as shared by all alike. In Christ, that sharing is found in a love for others that seeks optimum health, depth of spiritual commitment, fullness of concern for others, and a lasting celebration and thankfulness in and through Spirit and Mystery. The reciprocities of such love cannot be enumerated, they extend far into the future, incorporate the past, and resonate through a multitude of subtle spiritual worlds in the present.

Yet, this love is not sentimental nor clinging nor is it a matter simply of feelings or emotional infatuation. Sophianic love flows forth from deep devotion to the creative intentionalities within Spirit. These intentions are born through collective (and individual) energies that seek to manifest a variety of spiritual philosophies, pathways, and worlds. This seeking, this spiritual play, this exploration of possible constructions, acts to give increasing depth and nuance to immeasurable capacities for creation and enactment. What focalizes this inner capacity for expression is an intentional preservation of species, a willing commitment to variety that provides opportunities for enhanced life. The focal heart of that intention is a loving concern for the preservation of higher values, through honesty and directness, as manifest in each and every living relationship. It is not simply to love and value species existence, but to nurture within each species a perception of spiritual qualities that contributes to a positive diversity within the Whole. Such perception is reflexive, we see ourselves in others and others see themselves in us. We are not the same, we may differ radically but we all live and have our being within the Whole and we all share a cosmos of complex interactions, relations, and a variety of densities within Spirit.

As such, we are co-creators. Our preservation of others is a form of self-preservation in a cosmos of rich and complex interactions that call upon us to act with charity, compassion, and concern for the well-being of others. This is a matter of spiritual principles, of a pathway approach to correct living within a world of differences often charged with powerful and conflictive values. We must love as the Holy Bride loves, with purity of intent, not selfishly, not possessively, not with aggressive, unrespecting passions, but with a deep wisdom that seeks to preserve and value the full correspondence between beings. We must not love passively, closed off to the passions of others, but must instead open deeply to the guiding energies of Spirit. In this love, Spirit inspires, gives direction and empowers the soul to act with respectful passion in love regardless of difference or disagreement. This requires a mastery of passion that does not deny passion's strength or expression but which seeks to find its most sublime manifestations in deep and powerful, heart-centered mutual concern. Such love overflows the personal boundaries of known relation and calls us out into a more expansive care for all being, all species, all life wherever found.

The Bride loves purely. This means that the loving concern we express, the Cup we offer to others, is one which has the purest water, unstained by inner turbulence that seeks only its own rewards often at the expense of others, unpolluted by a grasping mentality that no longer heeds the undeveloped aspirations of those we claim to love. It is not a purity of attachment, a devotion to one other, but having devotion to another; such love is capable of ungrasping relations that seek to enhance the quality, worth, and value that the other might contribute to the Hermetic Circle. In the Christ-spirit, this love flows into a multitude of relations seeking to enhance our interconnectedness and thereby affirming a more essential view of human (and non-human) spirituality. It is not the path we walk, not the spiritual teachings we follow, nor the disciplines we practice, but the love and wisdom we share with other beings that marks our spiritual maturity. The love of the Bride flows out of Spirit, into the world for the enhancement and evolution of every being, however different their spiritual paths. Hermetic Circles intersect through a multitude of spiritual paths, many diverse, intelligent, creatively formed teachings, and yet remains open to new expression in relations with all species.

Such loving wisdom flows forth through appreciation and inner integrity that does not violate its own centered values and commitments. The marriage of the Bride and Groom, the *Hieros Gamos*, the holy union, is a soulful awakening to responsibility. It moves beyond an affirmation of the dyad (or individual family) and seeks to encompass a world, even a multitude of worlds, without trampling on the rights, integrity, differences, needs and struggles of others. The responsibility of love is to remain open to those who think and believe differently, to listen with ears receptive to points of soulful contact that affirm shared values and does not prioritize our values over others. It means to explore alternatives and to make necessary compromises without surrendering integrity. Yet, one of those values, one of those Christ-centered beliefs, is the crucial importance of heart-centered dialogue, listening, hearing, and responding with love. The Bride is forgiving, not unforgiving; she is capable of seeing beyond the limits that keep love bound to narrow demands; she is capable of acting with integrity to move others into an intersected circle where Spirit enhances all. It is not a forgiveness that takes on the weaknesses or failings of others, but that seeks to transform those others modestly that they may break through limitations and attain a more loving spiritual awareness.

This is forgiveness that values the necessity of limitation as a means toward self-knowledge; a knowing that is capable of crossing boundaries through respectful inquiry and self-scrutiny. The dialogical relation is built up through receptive hearing, reflection, and a keen awareness of inner values capable of adaptation, not a rigid adherence to unbending principles. We are required, though love, to take in the concerns of others, our children, friends, acquaintances, strangers, as unconditioned by our own needs or ideals. In order to instrumentalize Spirit, we must learn to calmly, purposefully, provide a context for learning that moves beyond the immediate circle of our more passionately held beliefs. We can love fully, with deep integrity, even while we search for a means to overcome a boundary that divides us from others. We do this not by pushing to the front, but by sitting calmly in our circle, near the boundary where we intersect with the circles of others. We can also sit in the circles of others in order to learn from them, and with them, the truths they hold as passionately, peacefully real. The greater circle of shared wisdom, the Great Mandala of socio-cosmic spirituality, requires us to contribute receptive energy to the emergent intersections between circles and traditions and not simply to barricade ourselves behind the tenets of a particular faith or tradition. As emergent, loving beings we are co-creating that Great Mandala every time we interact respectfully with the teachings of others.

The good fruits of Wisdom are many, some sweet and some bitter, as we see where we can and cannot impact the well-being of others, where we can and cannot change our own contracted disposition. Self-knowledge is a combined knowledge of possibility, actuality, and limits. In Christ, we can see that very example, as a man limited by his time, place and predispositions; as an ideal, manifesting greater possibility; as an illumined teacher, revealing particularity in a valued way of life. The Hermetic Christ is not all-knowing nor all-powerful, nor an ultimate end for humanity, nor is he a ruling autocrat in the mythic structures of a projected male heaven. He is rather the Groom who taking Wisdom to himself with deepest love and respect, discovers her gifts for far reaching tolerance, equality in justice, and in deep concerns for the marginal, liminal, downtrodden, and lost. The Hermetic Christ is filled with Spirit's love, with the deepest Mystery of an outpouring that cannot be contained, with an intensity of concern that cannot be buried by collective indifference nor self-serving norms. The relative Wisdom of higher illuminations reflect brightly on his forehead and in the eyes of the Beloved he sees a self-surpassing depth, not meant to be mastered or controlled. This is the supernal beauty of Spirit, her gift of grace to those able to receive her Wisdom, the burning luster of Her presence within that teaches us to walk humbly in the relative inspirations we share.

Our love is not perfect. We struggle to make it real and vital and filled with higher visions that we may act with more effective impact and concern for others. Even an infused spiritual love, one that pours itself out of the very heart of the cosmos as pure Spirit, burning away dross, ignorance, indifference, and apathy, lighting the higher worlds with luminous rays, can only be effective to the degree that it is received willingly by others. The higher Wisdom is capable of complete self-surpassing, a deep mergence and union that leaves the soul shimmering with infinite reflections of grace and hope. But the human incarnate entity, and the incarnate creatures of a created world, can only receive that Wisdom through their receptivity to a complete opening of soul. And love is the way, love is the path by which we learn to truly open our hearts to the wonder and joy of a living cosmos utterly permeated by holy depths of Spirit. And in receiving that love, we become, over time and through efforts and careful reflections, wiser, more mature, more thoughtful, caring, concerned instruments of creative, positive change. Such love is a wondrous gift, a blessing of the highest sort, and it pours down on us, through us, continually as an inner, subtle radiance penetrating all living creatures. We need only to awaken to it, only feel within the full intensity of its life-force to realize that love is a carrier of a profound wisdom that once known, will transform us deeply.

Blessings

To know the union of the Bride and Bridegroom through the blessings of Spirit; to behold the New Heaven and the New Earth, the unity of all Above with all Below. (2: 7)

The manifestations of Spirit are beyond counting, they permeate the world and animate the living cosmos with instances of beauty, power, and grace. One of these manifestations is the union of the *Hieros Gamos*, the sacred marriage as a sign of the soul's attaining awakened and illumined insight. It may be a profound ecstasy of interpenetration, a joy so intense that it radically exceeds and surpasses the boundaries of normal self-awareness. It may open a vista of boundless energies unified in a series of vast waves or it may simply blossom like a fire rose, lustrous with intensity, color, and vibrant, radiant beauty. It may be a simple, deep intuition that confirms in an unshakeable way, the sacred character of all creatures and creations. It may be the smile of the beloved lighting a way into the future as an enduring soul-mate whose presence is a source of inspiration and guidance. As we remove the veils, lay bare the soul and stand naked in that light, we are transformed, penetrated from within; the body as temple becomes a living affirmation of illuminations permeating every layer and contour of physical, emotive, imaginative, and noetic life. This union is holy; it is a confirmation that the capacity of every individual far exceeds the limited threshold of current awareness. In this process we must find the courage to lay bare the inner reality of our aspirations and dreams in order that they may be transformed into actual attainments, neither inflated nor diminished in relationships with others.

The *Hieros Gamos*, as a union of Christ and Sophia, of love and wisdom, is an interpenetration of the soul by Spirit's grace, an awakening to mystical depths within the actuality of immediate participatory experience. It is a union of the male and female, the masculine and feminine, the twin poles of soul's life balanced and harmonized by the energies of creation and delight. In this union, neither pole is lost nor diminished in the other. Both retain unique aspects of their various manifestations and in that process, they give birth to a third identity: the awakened soul. In the beginning this awakened soul is like a child who sees the world with newness and wonder, whose psychic and spiritual wakening is absorbed in the magnitude and intensity of a living cosmos. At later stages, the child grows toward maturity, learns separation, and becomes a vessel for the transformation of others, a *Vas Hermeticum* in whose crucible the purification of soul radiates forth into the world as a source of healing and joyful grace. An image of the awakened soul is like this: a polished stone carving of a youthful androgyny, seated on heels with knees on the ground, palms together before the chest, head bowed. This image is buried in the central chamber of the temple altar (the heart) as a sign of an inner potential of the soul's capacity for illumination; underneath it is inscribed, within a triangle, the alchemical symbol of the union of gold (Sun) and silver (Moon). This triangle is the sign of Mystery, Spirit, and Humanity; it is a symbol of the thrice-great transformation and of the three roses of rebirth.

In awakening to the true depths and capacity of soul, the individual dissolves the barriers that bind him or her to a lesser understanding. This unbinding, this release from the fetters of habit and unseeing doubt, leads to a new understanding. We are not simply physical beings, not simply a product of biochemical neurology and psychic energy, not simply a construct of a collective template nor a product of socially induced values or beliefs. We are much, much more. We are shaped within the creative processes of a holy Biocosm in which the creative ability of the individual is a dynamic channel for the manifestation of Spirit. This manifestation is capable, in the receptive individual, of breaking the bonds of collective mentality for the emergence of a more illumined seeing. In this process of awakening, the soulful being becomes increasingly aware of living nature, of biocosmic animation, replete with the living energies of Spirit. This awakening, through the inner marriage of Soul and Spirit, Christ-Sophia, emerges out of the cocoon of inherited beliefs and spreads wings of new color and intensity in the supernal light of a living, boundless Immensity. The gold-white radiance of that light dissolves all thought, all feeling, all individual awareness, and absorbs the individual into an rainbow embrace that no longer distinguishes either heaven or earth. In that joyful union, Christ and Sophia become one with the larger Whole, the All-One-Ocean; they merge into the limitless, multispectral aura and become inseparable from the Mystery that gave them both life and intention.

All that is above is also all that is below because every atom and subparticle of creation is permeated with Spirit from the most minute to the most vast horizon.[60] In the creative processes of human development, many events, great and small, are linked and penetrated by the creative energies of Spirit. All of these energies together surpass and surround the human evolutes with an intensity of spiritual capacity far greater than the realization of any one individual. Yet, as followers of a spiritual path, those energies act upon us to inspired within our hearts and minds a complex series of images, teachings, and ideals that move us toward spiritual fulfillment. The union of all that is above with all that is below is a spiritual realization that places the individual at the center of the Great Mandala for the actualization of deep potential. The degree of spiritual realization is a relative attainment within the total dynamics of a profound creative process. We each seek to find our place. There is no absolute scale; such an idea is only a creation of imaginative rationality. The true scale of the "above and below" is a freely interpreted range in which we each find the appropriate embodiment that images the interactive process. Our measure is a reflection of the attainments of the human species as a whole; our place is an image of a part within that whole.

In finding our place, we are linked to the attainments of others and co-create the very scales by which we can value and understand our accomplish-

---

60. Emerald Tablet, http://www.sacred-texts.com/alc/emerald.htm (Diverse translations).

ments. As followers of a spiritual path, we may look to Christ as an example of the illumined Soul, we may regard the Sophia as an image of Spirit descending into the heart of the cosmos through Soul for the purpose of awakening us to an ever-living presence. What we attain is a relative spiritual awakening, a discovery of individual depths measured against the depths of others within a depthless cosmos of multiple species, races, worlds, dimensions, and living spheres of beings of many types and kinds, some far beyond ordinary perception. The blessings of Spirit, for which we give thanks in the depths of soul, heart, mind and being, is held back for none. But it is our task to prepare the vessel and to perfect the instrument in order that the realization of potential attain to its highest degree of expression, coherence, and meaningfulness. We are blessed in accordance with our inmost attitudes of heart and mind, in correspondence with our capacity to receive, in harmony with our preparedness to instrumentalize the gifts we are given. This is a matter of humility and self-knowledge, of simplicity in desire and willingness to accept the limits we each carry as part of our conditioned search for wisdom.

These conditioned limits are natural and part of the very processes by which species evolve and become something more. And Spirit, in blessing us with graceful awakenings to potential, shows us the way to move beyond limits into a wider, more aware activity. The "new heaven and new earth" symbolizes the awakened, illumined incarnate alchemical life whose purpose is to continue the events of human spiritual development.[61] This development is not simply a world-transcending development, but a world-transforming encounter whose visionary horizons far-exceed present conditional awareness. The creative events of this self-surpassing spirituality lead us full circle to embrace a new heaven and earth with a passionate concern to preserve and enhance creative life for all species, to find the means by which we may all peacefully coexist. In this marriage, this soulful union that results in a more illumined, expressive instrumentality of potential, we must seek to create conditions of sanctity in order to preserve the lives of every seeker. It may require a journey that goes beyond a known or recognized boundary; it will require courage and determination to break the conditional bonds that inhibit us. It may be necessary to construct and build sacred community in a context of discovery, even uncertainty. Yet, such realization is based in the necessity of maintaining loving and trusting relationships, in meeting the responsibilities of those relations with genuine, attentive concern. Every spiritual seeker faces this challenge: to move forward toward greater awareness and to meet our responsibilities in relating, loving, and working with others.

---

61. 2 Peter 3: 11-13; Corpus Hermeticum 9: 6.

Such is the context for a genuine preservation of species, the key is cooperation; we must not sacrifice others to our own search for illumination and we must not allow others to inhibit our growth. Individual autonomy and freedom must be balanced with loving relations and necessary compromise. We cannot impose spirituality on others. We can encourage others, love them, hope for their spiritual growth, but the greatest impact comes from example. We must exemplify the spiritual path we each follow; we must seek to fulfill its challenges and highest ideals in order to manifest in our own way the potential which the path teaches. We are each known by the fruits of our labors and the luminous character of our daily life, by responsible commitment to spiritual goals that truly exemplify the path we walk.[62] In following Christ, we seek to manifest the Hermetic pathways, to attain the marriage, to unite Bride and Groom, inner and outer, to give birth in daily life to the luminous child of awakened heart and mind, to become, through dedicated practice, mature and responsible adults whose wisdom is valued because we have each found our place within the Whole. The moon, the sun, the stars are the adornments on the sacred garments of the bride and groom, but beneath is the sacred heart of naked love uniting to create an illumined third. Within that love all the energies of Spirit flow forth to bring into awareness the full depths of soul's capacity for wisdom and illumination. The Cup is offered, the liquid life is pure, fresh, sparkling, vivifying, uplifting, shared with grace and genuine love.

The unity of the above and below cannot be truly known as a mental or imaginative image; it must be experienced and known directly, in the depths of the heart as a visionary illumination, in mind as true *gnosis*. The path we walk is a path leading into the mountains, into the heart of communities dedicated to spiritual transformation as actual awakening. The Christ-spirit is an emblem of that process. The journey into the desert is a grappling with temptation and a rejection of self-serving desires; the transformation is on Mount Tabor, in the moment of the lucid spiritual illumination made real.[63] The grace of Spirit is the joyful sanctity by which the path is confirmed; the union of heaven and earth, male and female, groom and bride, sun and moon, gold and silver are all images of the cosmic, alchemical processes by which we find our place. Not the place we are given at birth, but the place we attain to in rebirth; not the limited conditions of social or mass existence, but the attainment of the limitless horizon of spiritual awakening. Christ is the exemplar who also walked this path, who struggled, attained, and gave himself to the awakening of others. And Spirit is the *electrum*, the alchemical amalgam through which this awakening is possible, that adorns the altar with presence before which

---
62. Matthew 7: 16.
63. Matthew 17: 2; Luke 9: 29.

we kneel offering our prayers and thanks. In prayer we ask that Spirit guide us, show us the path, open our soul, and keep us from ignorance, illusion, and self-deceptions. May that light illumine our pathways, make us whole, unite us with the Beloved, and fill our hearts with the fullness of creation. May it be so, now and always.

The Veils
To know Spirit as the Mother of many Mysteries; that the heart is veiled, to remove the veils, gently, with loving care, to see the Child reborn. (2:8)

Spirit as Mother refers not only to the Divine Sophia but also to the spiritual aspects of motherhood and child-bearing, the love a mother feels for her child. The image of this love is seen in the Theotokos, the mother of divinity, of Mary with Child, or in an earlier period, the child falcon Horus (*Har-Si-Ese*) held in the arms of his loving mother Isis-Hathor. This mother-child image as a symbol of love and connection, as a sign of holy birth and rebirth, is a powerful affirmation of the central place of woman, life-giver, birth-mother, bride, teacher, and vessel of the Holy Spirit.[64] Spirit as Holy Mother Spirit, is imaged as a primal source of life and soul-birthing that passes each of us through necessary contractions into the world of embodied, incarnate perception. She is also Eros Mother Logos, primal matrix of contemplative silence and stillness of mind, inspired by the harmonies of light, energy, and a multitude of seed-syllables, each with the power to give birth in sound, word, and song. As the mother of all divinities, Holy Spirit abides in every manifest god-form as indwelling presence, as a creative mix of power and potential sustaining and nurturing the life-process. She gives birth to every world-ruler, every maker of creation, every goddess and godling, however great or small. Spirit as the Divine Feminine Creatrix, Supreme Matrix, nourishes all life, in this world and in the worlds of the disincarnate, humans, animals, insects, birds of the air, fish of the sea, all the visible and invisible creatures.

Spirit abides from the very beginning, as the implicit creative energies divinely concealed in the most minute particles and sub-particles of creation. In the "initial conditions" of creation, she is there, fully present with inexhaustible potential, the Creatix of Mystery, her ancient ever-active energies weaving worlds-within-worlds. Spirit singing within the harmonies of creation in the making and unmaking of worlds subtle and gross, imaginary and actual, envisioned and attained, remembered or forgotten. Spirit preserves and sustains

---
64. John 19: 26-27.

the most archaic happenings, allows every act, thought, and desire to impress its energies into the subtle weaving of what is past but not lost, to become an energy of soul still knowable from first creation. In giving birth, Spirit sustains the inner qualities that make each person unique, however subtle the differences, in order to fully express the potential yet concealed within Mystery. At death, Spirit preserves the on-going soul in its journey through multiple worlds, each adapted to the predispositions of the inmost energies, through cycles of incarnation, in order to continue the processes of often eons-long development and maturation.[65] Spirit is the protecting matrix that values all life and encourages continual growth toward full awakening. We reverence her divinity, we submit to her guidance willingly without sacrificing the gifts she gives us.

Because Spirit is the "mother of many mysteries," we cannot know Spirit in all the potential and possibilities inherent to Her creative manifestations. But this does not mean that we cannot know Spirit in the reality of a lucid seeing, in illumined states of clarity and wonder. We can and must seek that clarity, must be willing to offer our deepest desires as capable of transformation to a more mature seeing. It is not perfection that we seek, but wisdom and maturity; a more mature seeing is still relative, still limited by the actuality of desires, thoughts, and beliefs. And yet, Spirit urges us to transform our inner capacities, to awaken the sleeping potential for visionary knowledge, to move beyond the immediate perceptual world and into the greater matrix of creation. Spirit nurtures this process of awakening in every soul that desires to be transformed through surrender to the purifying states of illumination and rebirth. Death of the "old way" is there, death of the "old soul" is part of the process by which the soul is made new; we die to the "old self" that the reborn self may be manifest. We proceed step by step, we plunge in and then draw back, immerse ourselves in practices, and then reform our understanding, study the teachings, and then find the interpretations that best fit a present stage of realization.

The heart is veiled. This means that it is not simply a matter of desire or aspiration, though aspiration and desire are crucial in motivating the soul toward rebirth. Yet, it is often the very nature of our desires that limits us and binds us to a lesser way of seeing. We must be willing to surrender unto Spirit our inmost aspirations that they be transformed, purified, intrinsically reborn as part of the process by which we come to know that which we did not know, and to see that which we did not see. Our eyes are not fully open, they see only into the dream world we have collectively created as a normative boundary

---

65. John, 3: 7-8; Bhagavad Gita 6: 41-43.

that confines our impulses toward doubt or self-destruction or toward harm and indifference to others. But we may see those collective laws as necessary inhibitions only insofar as we have not done the work required to purify our spiritual aspirations.[66] Attaining that purification, we are incapable of violating the free expression of positive, loving relations, we are no longer fighting against a lesser self to maintain the integrity of realized spiritual goals. We become those goals; in doing so, we move far beyond the collective norms into a more grounded, sincere, loving atmosphere of care, trust, and loyalty to ideals that we each embody.

Tolerance, compassion, clear thinking, dedication to the well-being of others, humility, service, solitude and prayer—each is a veil that conceals an even greater capacity for rebirth. Each is a virtue that may be actualized in Spirit as a path, a spiritual condition far exceeding the complacent norms of collective behavior. But these veils must be removed carefully, respectfully, in a manner that preserves within Spirit, the utmost capacity of the naked soul.[67] We cannot go directly to the full realization of spiritual virtues because we must grow into them through a sustained transformation of the collective. This is the Great Work, not simply to seek spiritual fulfillment, but to seek a collective transformation that will resonate with others in lifting humanity toward a higher value life. Spirit urges us toward that commitment, toward the interconnected affirmation of differences that preserve life, value diverse paths, and act to exemplify the highest quality, the greatest purity, the fullest presence of which we are each capable. Because we cannot remove these veils except through dedicated efforts of self-transformation, we must each open our hearts to Spirit, on the paths we follow, to inward guidance and direction.

Each must follow the inspirations he or she receives, each must weigh those inspirations against the inspirations of others as a corrective against imbalance and extremes of many kinds. The purification of desires proceeds through inward relation to Spirit and through our loving relations with others. Both are necessary aspects of collective transformation; the full circle of spiritual relations invokes the full capacity to love and be loved as well as to know and be known. This is a spiritual mystery of the highest kind and can only be realized in actual loving and knowing. The veils that are removed are those that keep us from fully actualizing our species capacity for loving, concerned, shared responsibilities imbued with a genuine spiritual illumination. The deep capacities of every virtue is charged with the creative energies of Spirit, we need only open the heart to each virtue by enacting it with full commitment to our spiritual ideals. To do this, we need to enact and embody those

---

66. Bhagavad Gita 2: 48.
67. 2 Corinthian 3: 16-18.

virtues we hold as valuable in order to receive the inspirations of Spirit for their fulfillment. The more we can act with sincerity and commitment, open to response and correction, the more we are able to receive inspiration that will empower further acts of love and concern. Inspiration is an opening of the heart to the felt reality of Spirit leading beyond inspiration to illumination and higher spiritual knowledge. But first we must be well-grounded in living an ethical, non-violent, loving, compassionate life.

To see the "child reborn" means that the *Hieros Gamos* has occurred within the soul of the aspirant and led to death and rebirth. This death can be very gentle and hardly visible, a passage into more subtle worlds each more subtle than the last. Or it may be a struggle, a passionate inner battle against ingrained beliefs, early attitudes no longer viable, or habits of mind and body that obscure the full potential. Or it may be a struggle with madness, illness, denial, deep resistance, and a constant return to old boundaries that refuse to fall. But in all cases Spirit is there, a guardian who awaits the soul's call, a presence whose wings hover over and around us waiting for an inward assent to rebirth.[68] This affirmation must come from deep within to effect true awakening, but even if the affirmation is veiled, even at the outset as a tentative request, a small tingling along the nerves, a thought that seeks inspiration, Spirit responds. The child lies hidden in the soul, an image of rebirth, a sleeping child awaiting the kiss of love and devotion to live more fully in the incarnate world of veiled and partially veiled others. The image of the Christ-child is that image within each person that represents the inner capacity for full spiritual awakening; a child of the union of the male and female, of the integration of the masculine and feminine, of a sincere love shared between responsible partners, parents and children, teachers and students, friends and strangers.

The image of the Christ-child is an image of capacity for spiritual maturation under the loving guidance of Spirit. The mothering of the soul is found in a capacity to embrace the positive value of being incarnate, to celebrate the joy of inspired living, to value fully the beauty, power, and wonder of a created world. Like Horus at the breast of Isis-Hathor or the Christ-child at the breast of Mary, we each may drink the milk of life as given by Spirit in accordance with our thirst. Even when weaned, we do not cease thirsting; the pure waters of life, also Spirit born, continue to flow in our tears, blood, and in liquid life of all kinds as signs of spiritual presence. The very air we breathe is Spirit laden, subtle with the energies of sun and moon, vibrant with planetary and astral influences, shimmering with elemental powers, radiant with lucid spiritual waves. We can drink all this, we can absorb these various "subtle fluids" as

---

68. Titus 3: 5 *paliggenesia*, "Rebirth".

part of the awakening to Spirit whose unending energies sustain the worlds and all beings within them. But we do so gently, respectfully, without grasping, without tantrums, demands, aggressive inclinations or sullen withdrawals which in the end only result in a loss of spiritual nourishment.

We need not be greedy but only take in what we can fully digest, what nourishes us to greater health and not simply because we have an insatiable appetite or refuse to moderate our habits. The child must grow up, must become in turn, a parent and an example to others for their children. The Christ-child is not an emblem of perpetual infancy, but a sign that points toward the necessity of growth and independence. The Christ-child becomes the Christ-man or Christ-woman, the mature adult that has transformed natural appetites into intrinsically informed spiritual attitudes and practices. The Christ-man or Christ-woman are not children, but mothers and fathers, adult harbingers of spiritual potential actualized in everyday living. To become the embodiment of the Christ-spirit means to overcome the habits and veils of childhood without sacrificing the joy, inspiration, and clarity of childhood. It means to retain the good and to transform it through education, learning, practice, and moral life, into a radiant example of mature spiritual well-being. Spirit as the mother of many mysteries, leads us in this process, weans us from early dependency, and shows us the path to shared autonomy, responsible commitments, and unveils as we purify, the holiness within all. May we attain to that revelation, now and in the future. So be it.

Gifts
To know the City of Peace as Spirit dwelling within all humanity; to enter the Gates of the City with gifts of thanksgiving. (2:9)

It is a spiritual calling to recognize and affirm peace as an indwelling presence in all humanity. This calling is based in a positive vision of the sanctifying power of Spirit as a primal source of healing and reconciliation. What men divide, Spirit unites, and in the play of its creative energies Spirit creates and recreates the basis for a higher and more complete harmony, diversity, and co-relation. This understanding of peace requires us to look beyond the fractal differences of personal attachments and into the very heart of creation. Inherited beliefs are only a preliminary basis for such understanding, often, they can impede and misdirect perceptions and substitute mental habits for living insights. Sometimes, such beliefs can create a context for better understanding, but even the rightly-guided must be willing to surrender outward forms of belief in order to follow the currents of Spirit into the creative depths of Mystery. In those depths, peace is a viable, living presence, a pervasive current within all that teaches us a common truth—that all life is sacred and worthy of reverence. The reality of this truth can only be known fully when it is experienced directly in a Christ-heart as a reflected image of love, a love of all creation, of all beings.

There is a thread of harmony that permeates the creation, a song whose variations are infinite and whose melody cannot be reduced to any inscribed forms. It flows like a current of light and fire mingled with shadow and sorrow, like a joy that longs for peace and a fear that such peace will be long in coming. It has primal resonance within prayers, chants, canticles, and hymns; it is heard in the various sacred music of the world and echoed in the very sounds of nature. It is heard in sea waves beating the sands of every continent and in winds through wooden chimes and hollow bamboos, echoing the inner melodies of harmonious life. In the human heart, this sound is an emotional bond to a vibratory world sometimes transmitted and felt in mythic words or poems or oracular speech. It can be heard in words of love spoken softly in private and in the cadences of a passionate declaration in support of a human need for health, well-being, and fair treatment. It can be heard in the timbre of the voice of each individual, in the quality of the sound of their words. This holy song sings in the blood and creates a tempest in the heart seeking to know truth through thanksgiving for each and every gift given to us. It is a quiet presence permeating the World-Soul and giving inner resilience to all living creatures.

The spiritual call to the perception of a shared inner peace, to this inner harmony of co-relation, cannot be reduced to any one doctrine, religion, philosophy, science, art or general teaching. Such a call exceeds all the forms of specific manifestation, goes beyond the words, ideas, or ethics and touches the heart center with a poignancy that cannot be reduced to a simple feeling or thought. This living fire burns away doubts, purifies perceptions, and leads us to a new threshold of understanding. We see and behold the peace that dwells within us as an enduring presence, as an illumined horizon of Spirit embracing the hearts, minds, souls of all living creatures. Each seeks to rise to an inner realization in accordance with their gifts and abilities, as inherited, learned, or as a free flowing grace of Spirit. The aspirant hears the song, knows the heart's cry as one's own, attunes the soul in accordance with an inner dedication to Spirit and realizes the presence as a sign of growing maturity. This peace passes understanding, it is not a product of external agreement or accord in carrying out the instrumental life of polity and organization. This peace is holy and resides within the heart as a collective desire to live peacefully and cooperatively as an expression of shared ethical values.[69]

In the life of Spirit, peace is an enduring inner condition born out of commitment, devotion, inner determination and gradual awakening to deep empathy and love. I do not say that love is the inmost condition of Spirit, I say rather that the task, as incarnate beings, is to choose love as the primal basis for our mutual spiritual development. The inmost condition of Spirit is Mystery, and Mystery in unfathomable in its depths and possibilities; its inmost reflected intentions are only knowable by the attributes we choose to manifest in our own lives. The Christ-path is one that calls us to manifest the positive virtues of loving kindness and graciousness in human relationships for the well-being and healing of all. In that process we are given the task of revealing the "Christ-nature" in the very acts, thoughts, feelings, and intuitions of daily living. To see peace, to know it, we must live in a full and complete way, without ambiguity or doubt, with deep conviction in the truthfulness of a chosen path. Many are the paths and many the diverse ways of Spirit and no person knows all these ways but through the path they follow. Therefore choose wisely your path and do not wander from place to place and from condition to condition constantly justifying your ambiguity. On the path of the Hermetic Christ, we embrace love as a primal condition necessary for the flourishing of all beings, whatever their paths or ambiguity. And we chose peace as the manifest condition for the unveiling of a deeper, shared understanding.

The City of Peace, the New Jerusalem, is an inhabitation of many paths; not one way, but many, not one truth, but many. The truths of Spirit cannot be contained in one path and the paths of Spirit are beyond counting, like the stars, beyond full knowing. What we know we know in part, not in the whole of Spirit, not in the fullness of Mystery, not in the utmost degree of the Christ-presence. But the part is also a whole, this is the paradox of Spirit, to make the part whole, a reflection of the fullness, and yet, still a part. This is because the fullness of Spirit, of all the creative energies, is constantly bringing into being a nuance, an attribute, a set of qualities not yet fully manifest in created others.[70] This is one of the great inner secrets of the Hermetic Christ. We do not know Christ, nor have we ever, not fully in the fullness of Being, in the fullness of Spirit, in the actuality of Mystery and holiness in the deepest and most profound aspects of his manifestations. This is because the manifestations of the Christ-Spirit are ongoing, emergent, engaged in becoming more fully manifested. Why? Because the Christ-Spirit is a vessel of revelation, an image within the world soul that seeks to make more complete, the understanding

---
69. Philippians 4: 7.
70. I Corinthians 2: 10

and wisdom of humanity. Spirit has poured its luminous energies into Christ forms, Christ beings, as a means for capturing the attention of those seeking to be more perfect vessels of love.

There are many Christ-beings as images or manifestations and each serves as a vessel for the maturation of human souls. They are seen in the multiplicities of the City of Peace, in its gates, its altars, its collective differences manifest in a variety of forms. Each form leads to its own realizations within Spirit, each opens a doorway and creates a condition for the soul's growth toward new horizons of experience and learning. Not all images lead to the same realizations, nor do they produce a similar consequence; each offers the gifts and realizations of its past and present becoming. No one image incorporates the inner realizations of other images, each must stand as it is, a testimony of Mystery transmitted through the variable and conditioned vehicles of tentative human forms. The evolution of humanity is itself a necessary condition for the arising of multiple forms, each with its own history, origins, interactions and influences. Universal claims within spiritual paths are all relative to this process of multiple generations manifesting gradual realizations of potential. The gifts of peace are many and so are its pathways; we must each chose our path and make it viable in teachings we transmit through daily example. Even the "evolution of species" will be surpassed; how much more so, the examples that gave it form and content.

Gifts of thanksgiving are: healing, generosity, purity of concern, honesty in love, compassion for suffering, and a deep determination to actualize inmost potential for the well- being of the whole. These are only a few of the gifts; their full catalogue surpasses easy summary.[71] What matters is our ability to offer our gifts as resources for the rebirth and rediscovery of deep and enduring human spirituality. Every generation is the time of awakening, every era is the time of challenge to overcome the perceptible norms and to see beyond the boundaries of simple belief or convention. A path is an aid to the discovery of our gifts, and each path offers its own rewards for the faithful seeker. On the path of the Hermetic Christ we do not deny the miraculous, but seek to transform the soul of every aspirant into a vehicle for the miracles of Spirit as given in specific abilities of each soul. The transformation is an awakening to Spirit that allows the soul to discover its deeper potential in illuminable depths that carry perceptions beyond the visible and material into the subtle, energetic, and psychic dimensional complexity of a fractal universe of multiple beings, forms, and planes of co-existence.[72]

The path of the Hermetic Christ leads indirectly into the density at the

---
71. 1 Corinthian 12: 4-11.
72. Lee Irwin, *Awakening to Spirit*, 217-220.

heart of creation, into the alchemical fire of Spirit that awakens the soul to its potential for rebirth as a vehicle of peaceful, joyful wisdom.[73] It does not lead directly due to the limitations of individual perception and emotional unpreparedness; only through inner transformations can the goal be reached. This means that the inner work must be done; faith or beliefs is by no means an adequate basis for this transformation, though faith may support the entire work. The gifts of Spirit must be discovered in awakening to a quality of life necessary for their manifestations. This quality of life must then be actualized as intrinsic to following a spiritual path; to believe is only the outer most shell. To actually walk the path mean finding the inner strength, courage, and surrender to actualize the hidden potential, to awaken the sleeping dragon of our innate potential, to master its manifestations and to make it a source of utmost transformation. The Christ-Spirit is not fragile or weak, nor is it over-aggressive or demanding; it flows through the awakened heart as inspirations of profound love and healing energy in a balanced, stable, grounded way of life. The awakened energies can overwhelm and mislead, can cause confusion and disturbances of many kinds. Therefore, seek those gifts that are constant in your own nature, those ways of peace and kindness that are deep planted and root well in common, shared life.

To live peacefully, non-violently, with kindness directed toward the well-being of others is central and of far greater importance than critical detachment and intellectual austerity. The path of Christ is a path of the heart, of the soul, not simply one of intellect or ideas detached from actual explorations in courageous and compassionate living. The gift of peace is not an idea, it is a way of living that calls forth a deep alliance between ethical values, actualized virtues, and inner luster of soul. This inner luster cannot be fully realized without the qualitative actualization of a virtuous way of life, dedicated to the well-being of others without compromising deep held values. What gives luster to the soul is its inner illuminations when Spirit rises spontaneously to bless the formations of qualitative life with new adornments in emergent abilities, insights, mental clarity and greater connectedness within the World Soul. For these gifts we offer thanksgiving. Knowing the heart is an altar, we strive to make it pure to manifest Spirit's gifts without attachment to their recognition by others nor to possessing them for our own benefits. As we are freely given, we freely give back to Spirit every offering as a testament to Spirit's grace. We stand firm on the basis of peace and respectful reverence for all creative gifts and we ask, in the name of Spirit, that those gifts flourish in all beings for the good of the whole. May it be so, now and always.

---

73. Romans 14: 17.

Humanity

To receive the gifts of Spirit in a fullness of humanity; to live in harmony with all species, to reverence all life, to serve rather than to be served. (2:10)

The primal gift of Spirit, the most essential gift, is the gift of life. To be alive and to have awareness is foundational for the development of our full humanity. This gift, to be a living being, means to feel, sense, and experience the world as a consequence of eons long development. We find ourselves immersed in a world inhabited by a vast number of other species, surrounded by a multitude of living creatures, a world teeming with life, in the seas, in the air, beneath the ground. All these creatures, great and small, share this most basic of all conditions, they are alive, they interact, procreate, live a life span, die, and their progenies continue the cycle. We all live through Spirit, all sustain life as a gift, Spirit-given, to be a multitude, an interrelated web of incarnate beings whose fragile awareness is open to the impact and influence of a dense world of others. In this condition of immersion, we seek to understand, to develop awareness of the lives of others, of the human and non-human, the plant and animal worlds, the ways of the creatures of the deep from the most hidden to the most microscopic. Spiritual understanding also leads beyond the visible and into the invisible worlds of dreams, visions, the afterlife, into the subtle planes, dimensions, and into the great Ur-Space of the all-containing worlds of the *Mundus Imaginalis*, into all the subtle, imaginary, and psychic dimensions. And throughout all, Spirit abides as the mother source whose creative energies act to sustain the wonder and magic of creation.

Our place in this great web, this evolving Great Mandala of living beings, is to cultivate a deep sense of reverence for all life and to act with appreciation for the life gift. The basis for this reverence is a felt sense, a heart-centered openness, to the beauty, power, and creative differences in other living creatures. On the Hermetic path, the gift of life is a manifest sign of co-relation, a sign of responsibility to live with thankfulness for the richness and rarity of such abundance. What gifts we have been given! To live on a world so filled with beauty, so abundant with life, so diverse and multispecied, so layered with exquisite, diverse ecologies from jungle to desert, from forest to tundra, from river valley to mountaintop. All abounding with life, all heavy with the fruit of flora and fauna, all nestled into the dynamic conditions of local ecological life-webs. Our human role in the midst of this abundance, this remarkable living world, is to open our hearts to its richness, its wonder, its fullness of natural beauty and to revere the diversity, complexity, and the wonder of each and every living creature. To walk as caretakers and guardians of the holiness of creation and to lay down forever, our swords, shields, guns, and weapons of self-destruction, this is the task, in this generation and in every generation to come.

To reverence life means not to manipulate it for pragmatic and self-serving ends; it means to value the intrinsic worth of the lion and mountain goat, the night moth and the spider, as signs of Spirit manifesting. Life, as the most supreme gift, is to be valued, sheltered, preserved, and a true knowledge of these many life forms, passed on to future generations. As an Hermetic sign, all of nature is a great teaching, the signature of divinity is inscribed in the heart of each living creature, human, animal or plant. Reading that signature takes us deeper into the mystery of creation, into the heart of reality, where each letter and each sound of that signature becomes an echo of the signatures also inscribed in the hearts of others. Each signature has its unique meaning and each resonates within the whole as a pattern whose value is inseparable from the full panorama of all created beings. We are not unique as a human species. Our gifts are no greater than the gifts of other species on other worlds in an inhabited universe of vast creation. On this world the task is to preserve and revere, not to dominate and control, to sustain and not to destroy life in all its unique and varied manifest forms. On the path of the Hermetic Christ, we do not place ourselves above creatures nor do we see ourselves as superior to other creatures. We repudiate the teaching that humanity has dominion over all creatures of earth[74] and say instead, let us choose to preserve, to honor, and to coexist in harmony with reverence for all creatures.

We know that the rattlesnake is poisonous, we know that the tiger has claws that rend and tear, we know that the bear is stronger, the horse faster, that the shark may be dangerous and microbes can carry illnesses. We are fragile, capable of dying through inattentive co-relation, and as a species we must find our niche in relating to others safely. But knowing our vulnerability does not sanction aggression and control of other species simply because we have the power to enact our most violent fears and desires. In a mature species, one that has moved beyond adolescent manipulation and self-aggrandizing, life becomes more precious, calling forth the utmost in cooperation to preserve and sustain all its variety and diversity. And the basis of that cooperation is reverence for life, itself a gift of Spirit. From the Hermetic perspective, life in not an accident, but an intentional creative evolution whose initial conditions were imbued with the life presence at the very moment of first creation, at the very micro-instant of flashing forth in fire or in the long-sustained and co-

---

74. Genesis 1: 27.

evolved condensations that led to a particular world of life-sustaining forms. Born out of Mystery, Spirit is the source of life, the inner continuity, whose creative energies have been there from the beginning, are sustaining us now, and will be there at the dissolution of every world. All creatures are valuable in this process and reflect in multiple ways, the diversity and difference that makes incarnate life so valuable and worthy of respect.

Spirit is the all-containing matrix of creation and Her energies are complex beyond comprehension; slowly we learn to revere the gifts given to us as a world and slowly, we become co-creators. To live in harmony it is necessary to thoroughly understand each and every species and its place and contribution to the whole. Therefore we are obligated to study life in order to fully preserve its unique manifestations, not as cold-hearted and detached observers, but as sensitive, empathic, loving co-creators. The Hermetic path is a spiritual path and requires that we cultivate deep reverence in order to fully behold the fullness of the harmony that sustains the World Soul. All creatures are part of that greater soul-life that constitutes the Gaia principle, the sustained, interactive web of planetary life whose psychic constitution is inseparable from our own well-being. The signature of divinity written within all natural life forms also inscribes a sacred teaching: all life is sacred, all creatures worthy of respect, all living forms worthy of preservation. The Christ-Spirit in this process is a rediscovery of the ancient teaching of the sacredness of life embodied in the sacrifice of our species arrogance that would dominate where it must learn to love and to preserve. The task of the Hermetic seeker is to transform, through Spirit, the heart and mind of humanity by being a living example of one who loves, cares and seeks to preserve life. Therefore we reverence all creatures, the harmless and the dangerous, and seek to live in balance with all.

In caring for others, we learn a lesson. The health and well-being of the world depends on a strong intentional concern for inter-species relations that honors the needs and rights of all animate life, not just humanity. Human health is inseparable from the health of all species; recognition of interdependence is a sign of maturity. Positive loving concern is not stagnant nor does it simply seek its own benefit. By seeking to promote the health and well-being of the whole, we come to recognize our place as inseparable from Spirit-inspired relations. The creative energies of Spirit are best actualized through loving kindness but these energies are blocked by self-interest or by a closing of the heart. When the heart opens and compassionately seeks understanding, acquires wisdom through receptivity to others, then Spirit flourished and we awaken to the fullness of our human potential. That fullness can only be known through a deep and penetrating awareness of the complexity of life and all species relations; our human capacities are far greater through our relationships with other life forms, through an extended kinship metaphor, than through a defensive isolation or denial of others. We discover our full humanity in opening to others as part of an extensive caring including all species, as brother, sister, relative. Just as Christ opened through Spirit to a compassionate healing of the unseeing and injured, so too do must we open to healing and sustaining a multitude of diverse beings, all worthy of preservation and respect.

Our deeper humanity extends beyond the limited horizon of self-concern and immediate family and friends. It extends into the very heart of creation because it is a gift of Spirit. Spirit gives us our humanity, ennobles it with the luster of good thoughts, good words, good deeds, adorns us with positive virtues and acts to maximize our awareness. It does this by drawing our attention to each living creature as a spiritual sign of the beauty and power concealed behind the facade of preoccupied, distracted living. It calls on us to reverence the creation, to see Spirit in every life form, to know that the beetle and dung ball is just as precious as the lotus and the water lily. We must allow our senses to open to the inner reality, the hidden miracles of life that support and nourish our species maturations and awakenings. As we open, Spirit enhances awareness, opens our inner capacity for seeing, and awakens the sleeping soul to the incredible intensity, energies, and subtle etheric being through which we all coexist. These creative energies permeate the world, are embodied within us in psychic forms, and express hidden psychic capacities to energize and awaken the fullness of our humanity. In that awakening, we open to the etheric and subtle life, to other life forms, and we see that all life is imbued as we are, all are living signs of Spirit. On the Hermetic path, we walk in awe of this beauty, this holiness which is a sign of inmost being, and we seek to live in balance with all creation and to attain a full realization of that beauty.

As Christ descends out of the higher heavens, he returns to the world, not as ruler and king, but as a servant washing the feet of the poor and far traveled.[75] His coming is an act of love and compassion tempered by long years of waiting for the arrival of those whose understanding would reach beyond self-serving law and obedience. He kneels as a sign of the words written on his heart by Spirit, "love and be loved" and "heal and be healed." There is no glory, no self-aggrandizing, only humility, surrender to Mystery, and a willingness to learn, to exemplify, to be an example of what we would value in others—their love, their concern, their honesty, clarity, and integrity of purpose.

---

75. John 13: 5.

In serving each other, we set the example, not by surrendering integrity, but by serving the highest standards of compassionate concern. Placing ourselves below, we have a willingness not to perpetuate the folly of unreflective living; the challenge is to exemplify the spiritual path, to walk it with conviction and clarity of mind and heart. To serve where best we can means not to sacrifice spiritual intent to the expectations of others nor to abandon principles to the unfair or unjust demands of unreflective social collective. We must each walk with integrity, exemplifying the path, and seek to honor others in celebrating the co-creative harmony within which Spirit acts to inspire all beings. The challenge is to become the path we walk, to embody the Hermetic Christ, the Holy Spirit, the Sophianic Bride, and through loving grace to serve the needs of those who also seek to actualize the fullness of their gifts.

Comfort

To give comfort to those in need without distinctions of class, position, race, color, gender, or age; trusting the power and humility of Spirit, of Christ. (2:11)

Our responsibilities on the spiritual path include both self and others, both the search for personal transformation and for collective transformation. Such transformations can only come about because we cultivate a deep and genuine concern for the well-being of others, on whom our own well-being depends. The work of Spirit is not a selective work for a chosen few, but a universal work for the good of all. This good is a great abundance that overflows into creative loves and relationships that sustain and support the weft and warp of mutually interwoven lives. Feelings of fear, alienation, loneliness, and isolation are symptoms of severing the warp and weft, indications that one has lost the feeling of human connectedness and the patterns and forms of communal life. Too many are wrapped in social dislocations of class and privilege that perpetuate a private concern for personal fulfillment disconnected from the greater needs of those who often lack even the most basic support for a healthy life. Our spiritual awakenings are linked to the health and wholeness of the world; we are part of a greater wholeness in which the internal beauty of the world is visible only to those whose concerns are world embracing.

Every path that teaches human health and loving communal relations is a testimony to Spirit insofar as it promotes a genuine concern for others beyond the members of the community. Love is not bound by communal rules nor is membership in community a requirement for the works and benefits of

Spirit. From the beginning, Spirit overflows, pours itself into all created beings as vessels of transformation and draws out the hidden potential for greater awareness and awakening. Love, desire, passion are all part of this process; family, friends and community extend it into a matrix of relations that can foster or inhibit growth. Through spiritual work, we shed immature attitudes and habits, awaken to the task of supporting a greater network of relations and finally, open our eyes and heart to the needs of all being, human, animal and other, as part of our own awakening to Spirit. The call is for a deep honesty and integrity of action that is also fully respectful of the paths and ways of loving others.

In the path of the Hermetic Christ, we seek an inner spiritual awakening that opens us to the presence and reality of Spirit in others. Every living being embodies Spirit, every creature is a sign and signature of divinity whose radiance and luminosity is there, now, awaiting the call to transform the vessel of the heart into a living presence, a Cup of Offering, a chalice of Spirit. The divinity in every being is in you, in me, in every creature; it is immanent, awaiting only the correct actions, inner intent, and devotion to attain a more radiant manifestation. Insofar as we care only for personal growth and development, Spirit gives us only the dreams, visions and illumination necessary for personal awakening; but insofar as our concern is for the health and well-being of each and every creature, Spirit teaches us to behold the divinity in all. That presence is embodied in the Christ-Spirit, in the *Hieros Gamos*, in the spiritual union of the soul with divine illuminations. And it spreads out, like waves, from the hearts of other creatures, as each awakens, each sees the presence in the other. This interreflected light is a sign of the depth and fullness by which Spirit sustains life in all creatures. The Christ heart emulates this depth and fullness, it radiates with the inwardness that is in all and in so doing, it opens the hearts of others to their own hidden potentials.

To "comfort those in need" means simply to love them, to give them whatever aid can be offered, and to do so as an act of reverence to Spirit, who gives us all life.[76] Comfort is more than a nodding recognition of the needs of others; it is an active participation in assisting those in need. It means sharing with others, giving to those who have less or little, and establishing the means by which others can be sustained and uplifted. It means not simply to alleviate an immediate crises, but to provide the means by which such crisis can be avoided and eliminated. It means establishing a lasting and healthy sense of world-concern that embraces the full humanity of each and every person, that seeks to sustain a co-equal world free of excess and extremes. We do not all

---

76. 2 Corinthian 1: 3-5.

live in a balanced world. There is great imbalance in wealthy, poverty, having and not having, exulting and denying the needs of others, and often, a blind celebration of consumption, acquisition, and excess. We need a far greater and deeper simplicity, a voluntary simplicity that seeks to shed the externals of acquired wealth and to live simply and modestly.

Imbalance stems from the excess of having and the lack of giving. It grows with preoccupations for only personal survival, and thrives on greed and material wealth. We must shed excess, live more simply, be willing to share with those in need, and not become caught in shallow self-preoccupation with only individual development or personal spiritual practice. Hermetic spiritual practices also involve others, also tests our abilities to live with an open concern for the welfare of those who suffer, lack, have less, are sick, confused, lost, disturbed, or broken by the indifferent impact of material excess or lack. The health and growth of community depends on its ability to take in and to support others; a centered giving is a gift of Spirit that embraces the differences that might divide and uses them as a means to heal. This is a gift of rare and unusual potency—to take in the other and to find the gifts of the other that can build a better understanding. We are not required to save others, nor to induce them to believe in only one spiritual path; but we are required to love others in Spirit and to work for their good as well as our own. The balance is in finding loving ways to instill the inspirations of Spirit that motivates the transformation to spiritual life and yet, to maintain the integrity and values of each path. Every path has its challenges and on the path of the Hermetic Christ, we seek to actualize an enduring reciprocity with all other paths, with all those in need.

To give comfort without distinction for class or position means not to place those with more, above nor those with less, below. What is above is also below and what is below is also above. This ancient Hermetic teaching means that we are mirrors to the souls of others; that we are each a microcosm of all that others might also be. The Hermetic path has followed innumerable world lines into the present and, under other circumstance, we might be the very one who seeks and needs help. The face of the other is my face and the need of the other is my need; and yet, I am not that other nor is he or she, me. We are each unique and yet, related; individuals, and yet, part of a collective; single and yet, plural. In this condition, "class and position" are only external reminders of separation, an indication of the distance we have yet to travel toward a goal of genuinely shared benefits. Our mutual well-being requires us to attain to the fullness of our potential in ways that will benefit others. On the Hermetic path, we seek to do this without resort to force, violence, or aggressive, covert coercion; we seek instead to model a desirable goal, to be living examples of the truths of the path, to be rich in virtues and to live simply without excess. Class and position are only for those who have not yet found the inner fellowship and harmony of Spirit that overflows in the hearts of all created beings.

The attributes of race, color, gender or age are each significant because they mark pathways, traditions, customary attitudes, folkways and beliefs, and unique stages of life experience and emotional relationships with others. But they are not a basis upon which to determine gifts of Spirit because those gifts are given to all without qualifications. Race and color are prejudicial mental barriers for a majority of those identified with their own race and color; but in Spirit, such distinctions are only subtle signs of difference. Yet beings suffer and have undergone woeful excess and terrible persecutions for this most destructive phantom from the undercurrents of the human soul, a phantom in search of justifications for enslavement, persecution, and extreme denial of the rights of others. In Spirit, such ignorance is a shroud over the soul and it creates a world of shadowed relations in which immature beings have exercised excess in a multitude of violent, repressive actions. Women and children alike have suffered similar persecution and denial as have the aged, infirm, feeble, and all those limited in abilities. Arrogant prejudice has marked every tradition, every nation, every country with the scars of injustice, with the whips and chains of enfeeble maturity unable to rise above its own limited, truncated horizon of self-celebration.

Such ignorance is the bitter, hard fruit of a self-enamored majority whose inner thoughts, however justified in religious teachings, emanate from a closed mind and a soul in captivity to its own self-justifications. These are the chains we must break, these are the mental and emotional conditions which challenge us to awaken to a more integral vision, a more comprehensive understanding in which each and every person can live without fear of prejudice or persecution, without anxiety about difference. In Spirit we are each free, not determined or defined by others, and in that freedom our task is to exemplify the potency of an inner vision to heal and transform ignorance into a new, joyful wisdom.[77] If we must confront ignorance, then we must learn to do it with courage by holding firmly to spiritual values that provide the guidelines for creative social action. It is not enough to simply protest, we must do far more, we must seek to emulate the vibrancy of Spirit in all our actions, thoughts, deeds, and desires. We must become vessels of Spirit that overflow, not contracted souls in protest. We must open the heart center and allow the natural currents of Spirit to act on all those around us to inspire a more graceful way

---

77. John 8: 31-32.

of life.

The impact of Spirit depends on the clarity and purity of life we live, on the inner work we do to clear out all the old angers, fears, anxieties, shallow prejudices, pride and resistance to change that inhibits growth. Purity of example can do far more to change others than any teaching or philosophy of life. It is not simply what we say or believe, but what we do, how we act and where we resist in order to transform the intolerable actions and insensitivities of others. Spirit is there, both in us and in others, whatever the divide, the gap between perceptions and beliefs, Spirit dwells in all and gives life and potential to every soul. Spirit is the support, foundation, life source and deep spring from which we can draw the most healing waters, the most soothing grace, the purest and most subtle influence. We must learn to trust the power and grace of Spirit to give us the inner strength and inspirations to guide our actions in working with others. The Hermetic Christ is a sign of dedicated actions, of commitment to carry through a vision, not to death or through suffering, but to life and rebirth. The burden is to bear the full weight of fractured humanity, our conflicted history, wars, persecutions, hatreds, and to seek transformation of them through inspired living. To rise above petty cynicism and nihilism, to see beyond the narrow horizon of the present, and to seek a realization that will nourish the inward life of all.

In Spirit, we find the source and in Christ, a model to give all that we can to the well-being and becoming of others, on whatever path they walk. We are not required to confront the ignorance of others who live in the shadows and prejudice of their own hatreds other than through the inspirations of Spirit. Where Spirit leads, there we follow; but we must test the inspiration against the qualities of our own personal life. Can we see the mote in the eye of the other but not in our own eye? Can we criticize lack or ignorance and not see it within our own life?[78] The test of spiritual integrity is to purify the soul of its deepest and most burdensome bias, to free the heart of all acquired prejudice, to release all the old pain, sorrow and inner dread in order to become a clear vessel for the overflowing fullness of Spirit. Until this inner work is done, we will be poorly effective in seeking to help others. And others can teach us more, shows what is still hidden from our own view, reveal a contour of soul that still needs refinement. This is why we must value relationships, seek to develop long term intimacy and to listen to the words of those we love. And when this inner work is done correctly, the burden passes away, the weight is lifted, and Spirit swells up to act through the purified soul. We become an illumined vessel who needs live only with humility in the face of Spirit's inner

---

78. Matthew 7: 3-5.

power, for in that power, all healing occurs, all grace flows forth, and all tasks are lightened.

Divinity
To see and honor the divinity of others as they are honored in Spirit; to let go, to not cling nor build barriers, but to open a Way and make it a guided path. (2:12)

To see and honor the divinity within others, each person must see and honor that same divinity within self.[79] The divinity within me is also in you and the divinity in you is also in me. Like the two master whose paths crossed while walking in the cool of the evening, each saw the bright spirit within the other, and when they met, each exclaimed in joy about the holiness that shone from the other and yet embraced them both. Such is Spirit, a presence that enlivens the world, gives it soul, and transforms awareness into the soft illuminations of creative love and compassion. If we cannot see the light within us, it is difficult to see it in others, even when we meet a soul whose grace and beauty flows out into the world with perfect clarity. We may be inspired, we may be moved beyond words, beyond descriptions, into a sense of empathy with the most creative energies of becoming. But that moment will pass when the luminous soul passes, what remains is the hidden light, concealed beneath doubt and distraction. To honor the divinity in others, we must honor the divinity in every soul and not deny its presence or power in our own soul. We are each a vessel of grace and each a grounding rod for Spirit; the energies of creation flow through the inmost soul, the soul no longer afraid or in doubt, a soul free of pride, pure, clear, open.

The path of the Hermetic Christ is to walk in just this way, with a deep and profound recognition of the holiness immanent within others. To fully honor that divinity with each person, both in the forms of its manifestations and in its formless presence. Like a well-guarded light within a lamp of clear glass or a blue-white flame burning on the wick of inspired wisdom, like a pale luminescence of moon in a vast and empty sky, Spirit beams forth its creative energies within the heart of every living creature.[80] When Christ stilled the waters of the lake of Galilee, when the storm abated and the wind suspended into timeless silence, he walked in the power of Spirit. The waves were stilled, the turbulent energies soothed by an up-swelling of great faith, a holy *gnosis* of luminous joy spreading its calm to others, touching them, showing them

---
79. Bhagavad Gita 2: 29-30.
80. Matthew 6: 22-23.

the Mystery.[81] We must learn to walk as though we would walk on water, with deep abiding faith in the divinity within that gives life and breath for all we think, feel, and desire. We walk in Mystery, surrounded by Spirit which gives us the gifts of knowledge from the slightest physical impression to the most profound mystical insight. And Spirit penetrates us to the very quick of the soul, flows through soul's inmost depths seeking to recognize its source and origins within the Deep.

The limit is knowing where we cannot see even when we see deeply, knowing when we must return to the center and let the boundary remain undefined. The web of creative energies is a boundless activity uncontainable in form such that every creature is a weaving whose fullness surpasses the visible limit. Each weaving is part of a greater whole through which a multitude of spirit worlds come to be, each interpenetrated by the other in a Mystery so vast and deep that no one soul comprehends its fullness, its delicacy, its immense powers and alternatives. Yet, those great creative energies are what makes us unique individuals. In the heart, as a spark of undying illumination, Spirit resides, awaiting our awakenings. If we honor that presence in others, we honor it in self; and if they honor that presence within us, they honor it within them. What matters is not the form or the path or the practices or promises; what matters is the realization, the awakening to Spirit, the direct seeing within self and others. If we cannot see, then we must believe in the possibility of seeing and we must strive to see! We must open our eyes, remove skeptical denials, doubts, hesitations, strip away indifference, distraction, fear; we must live with the courage necessary to be overflowing vessels of Spirit.

Thus we begin with a twofold commitment. First we make a solemn vow to seek the presence of Spirit in each and every being, without exception or qualification. Then we must seek that same presence within self through a process of purification, dedicated living, and the actualization of deeply held values that will weather all storms, all turbulence, all upheaval, stillness, and passivity. We must arouse within the pattern of our chosen path, a way that has no end, only a determined, considerate, compassionate movement away from ignorance and toward wisdom.[82] It is ignorance to condemn others, ignorance to deny the divinity within all, ignorance to promote one path over others, ignorance to call your way supreme. Every soul must awaken to its own limitation, even as we comes to know its true nature within divinity. Spirit surpasses every realization, every spiritual teaching, every soul and enlightened, illumined being, from the most angelic through the most mystic to the most common and ordinary—yet each is a miracle, each a testimony

---
81. Matthew 8: 23-27; Mark 4: 38-39
82. Acts 2: 28.

of Spirit's grace. This is the wonder of Spirit, it gives us illumination, sacred transformation, holy realizations of the inmost divinity, unity, and light and yet, surpasses all with infinite, abundant capacities nurtured in Mystery.

To "open the way" means to live a life worth honoring, to live as the highest example of the path we walk. On the path of the Hermetic Christ, on the path of peace, we seek to live illumined lives by honoring others, by living honestly, compassionately, as healers, teachers, workers in the garden whose labors are for the fruits of the earth, not heavenly rewards.[83] To "open the way" means to attend to your dreams, visions, inspired revelations and illuminations but not to raise them as a standard by which others must measure their worth. If a plant produces less than others, we do not tear it out by the roots but give it the extra attention it needs to be healthy. If a branch is too heavy, we prune it; if a thicket is too choked, we thin it in the most minimal way, perhaps to cut a path without doing violence to the wildness and natural growth. To make a path, we do not cut a straight road over the bones of our ancestors or through the beauty of the world for pragmatic gains. Instead, we adapt to the contours of the land, fit our walk to the curve of the hill and preserve wherever possible the reverent traditions of others. And we walk softly without a sword or weapon as peace-makers seeking to instill values of non-violence by example and by courageous actions dedicated to the preservation of the good.

We must let go of the ancient dualities, the metaphysics of absolutes, the old ways that would deny or divide according to narrow law, limited visions, and the bound artifacts of dialectic thought. We must open the world to the vaster whole within which Spirit cannot be reduced to an either-or, cannot be contained in black and white or contracted into simple polarities of have and have-not, of belonging or not-belonging. In Spirit there are no oppositions, only points on a circle whose circumference is vast beyond measuring. At the center is love, patience, and wisdom; in the heart, compassion, faith and a willing surrender to Mystery. What is necessary is to live with integrity, to have clear values, and to follow the path into the dense heart of creation by honoring all life and all teachings that promote growth and mutual diversity. If they raise a standard of absolutes, shake off the dust from your feet and do not promote your own view as superior. Your greatest testimony is the quality of life you live, not your arguments or philosophical ideas. It is not a polished intellect that determines the spirituality of a life, but a will attuned to wholesome values enacted with integrity, compassion, and inward humility. We must not cling to abstract defenses nor to visionary inspiration as the source of genuine

---

83. Luke 1: 79.

spiritual attainment. Real attainment is visible on the face of the devotee, it is a light that permeates into the hearts of others, makes them more aware and transmits its quality in subtle ways.

To "make a guided path" means to live in such a way that Spirit is evident in the choices you make, the words you speak, the aspirations you attain, and the quality of all your human relationships. There is no master and there is no student because we are all masters and all students. We each contain within us a plurality, an inner wisdom and innocence that reveals quality of soul and opens us to play many roles. The freedom in Spirit is to follow its fluid grace, to play different roles without clinging to either mastery or fear. In life, we each play many roles, some more difficult than others, and true mastery is to play them all well, with integrity, and with an inner awareness of Spirit that allows us to learn from each role. Are you a master? Then learn to be a student. Are you a mother? Then learn to be a child, or daughter, or son. Are you a man? Then learn to be a woman, one in childbirth or one giving aid to the sick and dying. Are you a scientist? Then learn to be an artist, a musician, a singer whose words are written in Spirit. Our capacities are inseparable from the creative energies of Spirit and the "guided path" is one whose diverse, imaginative expressions cannot be limited to doctrines or fixed rules and techniques. The real master gives up mastery and the real student seeks to never cease learning. In Spirit it is not the role you play but how you fill the possibility with a new magnitude of inner illumination.

To "let go" means not to cling to what was once a necessity but is now a barrier for new understanding. When you see the limitation, it is a sign that the time is fast approaching to let go of that limit. But first you must truly see it in all its ramifications, how it inhibits your growth, how you cling to it as a refuge against greater risk or greater responsibilities. Before letting go, there must be understanding. If you throw something away and have not healed the cause of its manifestation, it will return sevenfold. So first there must be a clear and vivid seeing that strips away the comforting illusion and removes the barriers that reinforce an unnecessary habit, attitude, behavior, way of thought or feeling. Then plunging into Spirit, we let go, drop the pattern, open to the inflow of new direction and inspiration. And that habit, that tendency comes back, reasserts itself, and must be resisted sometimes many times over. Such struggles are not won by will alone, understanding that sees the limit supports the transformation; and Spirit, when sought in prayer and inner calling, swells up to give the inspiration, courage, and direction for sustained growth and change. The talent that is not buried but brought into light, is drawn out, encouraged by love and affirmation, made to multiply; but the talent that is buried lies fallow and, eventually, is lost.[84]

Spirit seeks to maximize human talents, to foster growth and to encourage the development of an inner sense of deep responsibility to others. This is the path, to live creatively, by example, in Spirit as a model of what might be. To "open the way" means to live with heart and soul dedicated to the inner guidance of Spirit in order to foster positive human relations and to encourage that same growth in others. On the path of the Hermetic Christ, it means to practice the inner alchemy by which soul attains true illumination and then to live simply, in the world, as an example of the way that has no end. We are not seeking some imagined, predetermined goal, but a way of life that will endure, as exemplary amidst the paths of others. So we seek to educate ourselves, to learn to play many roles, each a spiritual challenge, and to find the mastery that moves beyond mastery. In this process, Spirit is the source of endless potential for growth and change. We need only live according to those higher values that fully embodies our capacities as creative, loving beings. We need only honor the divinity within every living creature to see the magnitude and wonder of the unfolding creation constantly at work around us. In the subtle world as in the bodied life, this creative activity goes on, further subtilizing, evolving, developing on a scale beyond comprehension. Yet, magically, each life contributes to the whole; thus, we seek to live fully, inspired by Spirit that our contributions be a testimony to that wonder, that holy, unending, ever-becoming.

---

84. Matthew 25: 14-29.

Apokalupsis

THE LIGHT: ONE GOD

"And He who sat on the Throne said: "Behold! I make all things anew. Write this for it is trustworthy and true. It is done! I am the Alpha and the Omega, the first and the last. To the thirsty I will give freely from the fountain of the Waters of Life."

Revelations 21: 6

God
There is only One God, eternal and everlasting; the same today, tomorrow and forever. (3: 1)[85]

The word "God" is a written sign for the greatest of all Mysteries and the One God is an emblem of that sign that can never be compressed into words. All our words throughout all generations, in all languages, in all mental images and visions, in all sculptures, paintings, poems, songs, hymns, and celebrations, only point beyond themselves to an Undefinable All.[86] Yet every sign and image is a coalescence of creative energies, a weaving of intangible potentials with tangible forms, seeking to embody a radiance, a splendor that continually surpasses its visible manifestations. Of all creative signs and wonders imbued with radiance, it is the natural world that best exemplifies that sacred, hidden power. Every living creature is a manifestation of that Mystery, from the microbe to humanity, from the World Soul to stellar and astral radiance, from the sun to the galactic swirls of the most ancient creation of days. In this wondrous universe of creative, profound, far-reaching energies, where creatures beyond measure inhabit a cosmos of multiple planes, dimensions, and psychic worlds of struggle, hope, and self-becoming, that Mystery we call "God" is there, omnipresent, the basis for all self-knowledge.[87] Embedded in a world so rich with sacred energies, so powerful with creative actions that we can barely comprehend them, we must learn to live with our eyes open and our hearts ready to receive the hidden inspirations of that Presence.[88] We must learn to live within that Mystery as a known and welcome foreground that makes us what we are—loving, creative, inspired beings.

The Mystery cannot be reduced to a single name or word; many such words are adventitious, added, secondary, non-essential. In the scriptures there are holy names, in oral traditions, there are sacred mantras, holy hymns, praise songs whose words reflect the mental radiance of an inward illumination. In such a context, the word "God" cannot equal the fullness of the reality towards which it points, it can only represent in relative truths a certain linguistic history, certain peoples, times, cultures, and places. But that word cannot equal or contain the fullness of the Mystery within which it reverberates as an echo of identifiable spiritual life. We may also designate that Mystery as Abba or "Father", the Father of Lights "within whom there is no variation."[89] This is a true inscription, meaning there is no addition and no

---
85. Inayati Order, Ten Sufi Thoughts, 1: 1-3 (http://www.sufiorder.org/Sufi_Thoughts.html).
86. Mark 12: 29; 1 Corinthians 8: 4.
87. Corpus Hermeticum 1: 31, 2: 16, 9: 9; Bhagavad Gita 9: 17-18; 11: 5-13.
88. Mark 4: 11.
89. Mark 14: 36; Galatians 4: 6; James 1: 17.

subtraction, no change that is not part of the fullness within which all change occurs. What changes is form, manifestation, understanding, maturity, and wisdom. What remains unchanged is the overflowing potential, the capacity for infinite births and rebirths, the radiance of the many lights whose fullness lives in stellar brilliance and is then reabsorbed into that depthless Deep. For God is the constant within which all change occurs and without whom there would be only an unknown nothing. In the All that is divinity, change is internal, inclusive, not bound at the edge nor incapable of growth. Mystery overflows, manifest forms, and in the Great Work, creates continual rebirths to new, more expansive awareness.

We may also designate that Mystery as 'Imah, "Mother," the measure of all things, who was once in slavery with her children but who is now free.[90] In that name, the foremothers are liberated from bondage and servitude to male divinity and by that name, we invoke the Mystery of the *Hieros Gamos*. In the holy city, this marriage is a supreme union manifest in the soul's realization of the sacred Mystery embodied in woman as the Divine Sophia (and Holy Isis). As with the Hermetic Christ, this union reflects the deep structures of our tripart nature: distinctive bodies, distinctive souls, distinctive minds. Unified in mutual interpenetration of body-soul-mind, the creative differences of gender, whose roots draw life from most sacred sources, act to enhance our mutual self-becoming in God, in Spirit, in holy Mystery. The Mother of Lights is the primal, creative matrix within which and through which all beings are birthed, given awareness, and sustained, made conscious of our obligations through spiritual rebirth. In all ways that God is called Father, so also we can use the name Mother; yet, there is a difference, for in the name of the Mother, we may include all paths, all ways, all revelations whose goals lead to peace, wisdom, and mutual respect for life, for children, for the family of humanity in a non-conflictive, creative world. In the name of the Father, we may see the structures and forms by which a path is made straight, cleared of obstacles in laying out guidelines and directions for the needful soul. Yet neither of these names, neither Mother nor Father, can equal in full capacity the Mystery which surpasses all names, all gender, and all form forever.

Together these names and forms can be invoked as TheaTheos, the great Mother-Father union within whose divinity a holy child, male or female, is conceived through love and given human form. Many are the forms that result from this union, some far removed from the human scale and others, closer in kind and degree. But all are sacred, for all life is sacred; the birthing of a child is one of the great miracles of Mystery. Life comes forth from life in all multitude

---

90. Galatians 4: 24-26.

of forms, and in being alive, we celebrate and revere that source from which we each come. We are born of Spirit and Mystery, not just flesh and blood; we are born of into the matrix of the World-Soul and our awakening is an act of reverence to the primal ground of all-becoming. We give thanks to our parents, but they are not the source, only the vessels through which Spirit and Mystery work to co-create the marvelous radiance of a newly born soul. In TheaTheos, Spirit and Mystery act as a unified Hermetic sign to represent a deeper truth that beyond all creation, there is unity that can never be dissolved nor distilled to engendered beings in all fullness and capacity. Likewise, the *Hieros Gamos* is a sacred paradigm, an archetypal union meant to channel the energies of creation into new life, not a final stage or condition. Inspired, we cultivate inner maturity; attaining maturity, we give birth; giving birth, we must parent our creations, then, releasing them, we continue to seek inspiration. In this process, both male and female unite and separate, join and act independently, share, and yet each retains a unique authority.

Thus we are each "stewards of the mysteries of God"[91] and as such, we each have responsibilities to move beyond the formal signs, words, names, and attributes that reduce the irreducible to a recognizable set of qualities. In passing beyond qualitative attributes, we do not deny their necessity or usefulness in creating ways that have names and forms. But that which is "eternal and ever-lasting" has no qualities that can be adequately enumerated as final or definitive. All such designations only point beyond themselves into the indefinite Immensity that can be known in a single flash of light and yet cannot be contained within the entirely of the visible cosmos. In the "godhead," the *theiotes*, the "invisible in the visible" is an irreducible feminine inwardness of divinity, an inexhaustible and limitless potential, only superficially visible in the astral, lunar, and planetary fullness of uncountable worlds and stars.[92] This inward capacity impregnates Spirit with all the energies of creation and nurtures her children through the inseparable processes of co-evolutionary transformation. Like the virgin birth of Christ within Spirit, Mystery acts to make fecund the diverse possibility and Spirit acts to give it form through soulful embodiment. Mystery surrounds, penetrates, and contains within an immeasurable capacity for actual "creative occasions" and Spirit, as birth Mother, is the interactive matrix through which those occasions are dynamically embodied.[93]

This Mystery is "the same today, tomorrow and forever" because there is no temporal boundary, no limited frame of particular space-time by which to

---
91. I Corinthians 4: 1.
92. Romans 1: 20-21.
93. Lee Irwin, *Awakening to Spirit*, pp. 161-165, 256-260.

delimit either past or present except by appeal to relative embodiments. The "eternal now" is that creative potential acting to bring into forms the gross, subtle, and transcendent, the fullness that IS at this very moment the utmost expression of the present. What is past is inseparable from what IS and what will become; what will become cannot be reduced to non-existence, but swells up within Mystery as what has always been possible. What passes away is transformed, not lost; and what comes to be, is only a temporal manifestation seeking new embodiment. And this process is creative, on-going, non-static, non-repetitive, non-reductive. It spirals inward toward perfection of expression and spirals outward to intersect with all other worlds, creations, dimensions, and forms of self-becoming. In that process, Spirit acts to weave and unweave and Mystery is the inexhaustible reservoir within Spirit that gives inspiration, direction, and guidance. The Mystery of the One God is the intentional heart of creation embodied in living creatures of all species, types, and kinds. Within each of us is that Divine Presence, that spark, that deep source of illumination that acts to provoke, promise, draw, and guide us to the fullness within Spirit by which we reach our utmost in enlightened, loving co-existence.

In the super-essential life, in the Light of the illumined soul, that intention becomes a profound harmony whose overtones extend into uncountable dimensions, worlds, and planes of creative activity. Yet, those same worlds, planes, and dimensions can dissolve into a vast, shoreless noetic Spirit-Light whose waves wash away all sense of diversity and difference. In that living Mystery of wholeness and unity, the Light itself is supernal, transparent, luminous and filled with utmost holy Presence.[94] This is reality, truth, the way that holds all ways and the end that has only a vast promise of continued life, being, and illumination. In this Light, "God" becomes a word indicating contracted moments in time, perspectives articulate from the limited horizon of particular beings embodied in particular places and in manifest, worldly conditions. Language, words, written signs, utterances, cannot do more than vocalize a desire for that transparent Light within which all words dissolve and through which the deeper vision is born. What we call God is partially knowable through scriptures, writings, words of holy men and women, teachings and traditions, through master and guides that appeal to our limited mental-emotive capacities. But the full reality must dissolve those words, teachings, and signs and give birth to an inner illumination of soul that carries the aspirant beyond language, normative space-time, culture and conditionality and into Mystery, into the most holy arena of spiritual awakening where, as souls, we are tested and tested again.

---

94. Bhagavad Gita 13: 17.

The perfection of soul that illumination implies can only come because we learn the necessary lessons, because we undergo the testing of Spirit that allows us to plunge into the dissolving reality and to re-emerge with a balanced, centered vision of potential and capacity.[95] Many have suffered inflation, imbalance, and an excessive celebration of their attainments and realizations. What is important is not the experience, not the illumination, but the quality of life that demonstrates a spiritual path as actual in everyday words to others, in responsible living, in care-taking, and love for the well-being of all. The Mystery is for all, Spirit works for all, even in blessing one soul, the emanations are for the many, for every other soul touched by that one. Mother, how can I express the holiness of Thy gifts? Father, how can I live to bear witness to Thy presence? In the Christ-spirit, these questions arise deep in soul's awakening and press the heart for affirmations made in the ways we each choose to live and in the values we espouse. In holy marriage TheaTheos, imaged in the Christos-Sophia, enwraps the soulful being and makes him or her a vessel of an infinite concern for all creation, inexhaustible in hope and determination. The challenge is not to reduce the Mystery to words known or thought, not to delimit the mind by clinging to concepts inadequate to carry the actual reality toward which they point. Best is to cultivate an inward presence and to actualize it as a modest example of how one may truly be "a steward of the mysteries of God."

The Light
To seek with humility, patience, devotion, and courage, the Mysteries of Light; a knowledge that surpasses ideas, images, and intuitions. (3:2)

This is the "light that passes understanding" and that cannot not be thought or understood simply as an idea. But it can be experienced and known directly as a gift of illumined grace and peace, for the knowing of that light extinguishes all sorrow and uncertainty of soul.[96] Many times I have seen and known this light, and every time it has been a moment of profound affirmation and renewal. This light is not an expression of solar or astral lights but far exceeds even the brightest sun or star. Yet this light is inseparable from the "light that lights the world" and makes us self-aware beings.[97] Christ is not that light but as an emissary of the Father of Lights that light is in him, as when he

---
95. Qur'an 3:29.
96. Psalm 119: 130; Philippians 4: 7.
97. John 3: 19-21.

stood with blazing garments and a "face that shone like the sun" on the mount of transfiguration.[98] This light is holy and has no boundaries within space or time and its contents are utterly transformative as it lifts the soul and breathes into it a radiance surpassing mind and all individual limits. Inseparable from the Mystery, this light extends through all created realms and beings and is known in its most minute expression as an inner spark, a sacred source of soul's awakening. It is capable of dissolving all awareness of the body, all awareness of soul, all awareness other than its own infinite extension and at the same time, it gives ecstatic affirmation of Spirit's loving presence. I have been dissolved and reknit; blessed is the soul of one who returns and gives that light to others freely, without demands or expectations.

This light is a primal source of illumination, enlightenment, and mystical union and has innumerable forms of expression and manifestation. In its most accessible form it is a flash of intuition, a bright flare of mental insight, a sudden rush of energy and illumination that is as quick as the blink of an eye. It gives the mind a sudden, very brief sense of its hidden capacity for illumination, as an unexpected insight into problems or challenges whose solutions are found without effort or strain. It is a spontaneous arising, natural, capable of opening the mind to inner depths of awareness through focused attention. The mind must be clear, not anxious — relaxed, open, receptive and lucid with regard to inner currents of awareness. Then, in a moment of insight, we can see within that clarifying thought a presence that gives it form and shape and light. This is the Uncreated Light, the light that is not simply mental or emotive, a light that is inseparable from Spirit, a Holy Source, that works through mind and soul as an agent of transformation within all beings, great and small. In the heart this light is a spark of divine presence, a Christ ember, a hidden node within the divine Mystery that reverberates with all the life-gifts of a soul empowered by grace and the dedications of love. In compassionate living that light is present as an invisible radiance of kindness, as a harmony of touching and being touched, as loving warmth flowing out to others.

In this light we know and experience Mystery and its multitude of forms and expressions, for in that light there are many mysteries, lesser and greater. The greatest of these mysteries is the translumination of soul into perfect grace, accord, and unending abundance with qualities of spiritual wisdom. The least of these mysteries is the presence of Spirit manifesting in everyday life. Yet these two are simultaneous expressions within a round dance of possibilities whose manifestations are beyond counting and whose activities are a call to see all that is inward balanced with all that is outward. In Mystery, there is

---

98. Matthew 17: 2.

no "inner and outer" because that light is the source of all conscious, creative being throughout all worlds, now and always. We are "in" the Mystery and the Mystery is "in" each of us; and the light of that presence shines everywhere without exception, even in the utmost darkness of a denying, contracted soul. The visible sun is a sign of that light of Mystery; it gives us life and sustains us in the rhythms of transforming day and night. It shines as an enigmatic sign, an emblem of the tremendous creative power and intensity of all that is and is yet residual within us. Without that light, this world would be no more and so it is with the inner light, the light that gives wisdom and understanding. Without that light, we would not be, not see, not manifest as part of an evolving World-Soul whose inhabitations are prized for their diversity, beauty, and expression of mind and heart.

We are each a vessel of light transformed into a holiness of evolutionary forms whose embodiments reflect the qualities of our inner awareness and illumination. In seeking light we begin with humility because our knowledge is relative, partial, in process, reaching up from the roots of embodied life toward the light that sustains and nurtures our growth. Those roots are sunk deep into species history, into the rocky soil of Gaia whose fertility is threatened by living only external, outer lives unaware of the mysteries which give us life. And that soil is saturated with the blood of all those who suffer for this ignorance, just as Christ suffered, and the pain and sorrow is felt in the body of earth and in the World Soul, crying for an end to the violent, trampling, disregard for the precious life gift. In shadows of sorrow, that light is there, but buried beneath the burden and anguish of multigenerational ignorance, disdain, and self-exaltations. We must not flee our embodied life, must not turn away toward light as an escape from the responsibilities of creation. Our task is to embody light in living fully as incarnate beings whose gifts and graces are for the benefit and adornment of the World Soul. We must accept in all humility the task of living exemplary lives that demonstrate the gifts of Spirit through fully valuing bodied life in all its various forms and expressions.

The very purpose of the creation is such embodiment, to demonstrate clearly the fullness of the Mystery as a godly-minded, spirit-inspired, living being whose life, like the Christ-life, shines forth clearly. We are each capable of becoming illumined beings but only if we make the necessary commitments, the inner changes, respond to the call to awaken from sleep and to open our hearts in a most loving way. We do this with humility and patience. That is, we need not strive to reach beyond our capacities as much as strive to fulfill those we have already received. We need only to give our full attention to the gifts we have, to the full realization of what we already embody. This is not a transcendent task, nor is it a call to renounce life as we now live it. Instead, let us accept the gifts and limits we have and let us realize that we are limited and partial beings whose abilities are not yet fully realized. Let us dive deeply into the challenges that we each face and transform ourselves through those challenges into more aware beings whose understanding and love is a testimony to Spirit and a hallowing of Mystery.[99] The light that illumines this transformation is already present, already at work stimulating an inner desire, already acting as an inner pressure toward growth. Like the yeast in new made bread, it causes an inner expansion, its arises and ebbs in accordance with our intentions, following the contours of mind's preoccupations, but always present, always active, always pressing for a more aware state.

In patience we learn to accept the rhythms and processes of the heart contractions and expansions. We are not always aware, not always attentive to Spirit's call, not always able to hear the "still quiet voice." We learn patience because this process is not a matter of willful exertion, or self-determined effort. Awakening to inner light, to Mystery, is a subtle process bound with many causes and consequence, some more distant than others, and all woven into a pattern that must be lived and realized strand by strand. Sometimes we must unweave a pattern in order to reknit anew a direction better taken, a past better left behind. We hold a pattern as a sign of our present orientation, our present circumstances, but we must not allow our self to be bound by that pattern, because as vessels of light, we are always capable of surpassing what we have already become, always able to overflow if only we have the courage and devotion. We make necessary efforts and we practice inner disciplines, act with responsibility, and make sacrifices and compromise to live well with others. But these efforts are not made without inner support. When we chose well, with spiritual intentions, with clear mindedness motivated by positive, loving values, Spirit is there, acting to support and enhance those efforts. But when we choose badly, self-indulgently, without regard for consequences, with inattention to the needs of others, then we are diminished in our efforts. We must learn to balance inner needs and outer demands and without abandoning integrity or higher purposes, learn to act with Spirit, with light as our inner guide.

This take courage. Following a spiritual path does not mean abandoning our relationships with others, even when those others do not comprehend nor grasp the truths that guide us. The key is transformation; without transformation there is only a static repetition of habit and a clinging to ways less aware. There must also be transformations within relationships, an inner

---

99. Qur'an 2: 269.

development that leads to new insights and a shared vision of the whole. Thus, we must each learn to exemplify the path by the way we live, with compassion in search of wisdom. We cannot sacrifice the search for wisdom to the stubborn, closed mindedness of others, even those we love sincerely. We must find the courage to act in accordance with our spiritual path, to live with humility and patience, enacting on a daily basis the way we have chosen. Christ did not turn away from others; he was a healer, a compassionate, living spirit of kindness and caring. Yet he did not abandon his path for others, but lived with dedication to his own inner vision for the realization of his way. Guided by Spirit, imbued with Mystery, he acted to heal and transform; so must we, each as a testimony to the values we hold as true and worthy of realization. We do this not at the cost of others, not as a consequence of their suffering, but as compassionate, creative seekers after truth. In loving others, we must not hold back our deepest love but we must also not let that love bind us to a lesser way, to a less realized life of committed seeking. Love is a challenge that balances between giving and receiving, between pouring out and taking in, between two hearts capable of melting into a higher third.

We must love courageously and with all our being the Mystery that gives us the capacity to love others. In that love is light, the light of Spirit, the deeper radiance of Mystery imbuing the heart with profound joy in loving every other being. Such love is not bound by individual relations, but overflows through those relations into an ever-widening circle of loved and loving others. Such love is itself a light, a flame transmitted from one candle to many, a pure love that lights up the world. In courageous, humble love, we can see God; we can see the divine face in the eyes of the other, see the Beloved in the face of all humanity. Such love is a radiance that surpasses normal human affection and transforms it into a wave that has an endless Source.[100] In mind, this light is a brilliant, all-pervasive visionary presence of vast dimensions and incalculable depths but in the heart, this light is a gentler, loving embrace that includes the soulful well-being of others. This love, this Christ-Love-Spirit-Mystery, flows out into the world as a tremendous gift and grace, and it resides as a radiant fire in the heart of every living creature. The "sacred heart" is the heart inflamed by love and calmly centered in humble and patient awareness of its profound and holy mysteries. It is beyond mere intuition, beyond ecstatic feeling, beyond images and forms, and flows out of the heart of creation as all-embracing waves of deepest concern for the well-being of all. I offer my prayers to that Holy One, that divine fire that burns away inadequacy, dissolves all doubts, and vanishes spectral form for the pure immanence of light. Blessed

---

100. Corpus Hermeticum 11: 15.

is the one who beholds that light, but more blessed is he or she who shares it with others. May that light burn brightly in our hearts, our thoughts, prayers, and intuitions leading us to its ever-luminous presence. Selah.

Unknowing
To seek God in Mystery, in all stages, in the depths of Unknowing; to discern that all stations are Christ created and all stages, Spirit born. (3: 3)

Why do I use the word "Mystery" when referring to the greater and greatest realities of Spirit? Because that which we call "God" is so often reduced to simple thoughts or beliefs far removed from the fullness toward which the word "God" points. The All that God Is cannot be fully compressed into words or beliefs or ideas based in faithful adherence to doctrines or ideas created by men for the satisfaction of their intellectual passions. Nor is it simply a question of truth and falsehood, nor a matter of faith anchored in a valued way of life, nor commitment to virtues we take to be foundational in shaping our shared communal lives. All of these are important concerns, but the fullness of Mystery encompasses them and surpasses them by an immeasurable horizon of becoming far beyond the understanding of ordinary humanity. Our humanity is not mature nor is it yet prepared to fully bear the depths and heights of a God-filled universe of infinite creative potential. Instead, we create local doctrines, enclosed teachings based on circumscribed knowledge, and cut pathways meant to appeal to the mental horizons of a certain stage of maturity. To enter the Mystery, to open to the fullness within Its vast Being, is to prepare the soul for transformation through dedicated surrender to that which cannot be contained in simple ideas and beliefs. Simple ideas can be used, they can be like steps on a stairway which lead up a mountain side suddenly opening on a vista that extends understanding far beyond the making of the stairway.[101]

The Mystery of God is holy, not to be profaned by an excess of rationalism nor reduced to dogmas supporting exclusive claims of faith or narrow pathways for only the elect. There are no elect. We are all, each and every one of us, a soul in progress, a becoming seeking absolution for the pains and sorrows of others, a feeling, creative intelligence in search of illumination and insight. For some, it is easier because of the pathways they have walked previously, because of the earlier transformations of their suffering or because of the innocence

---
101. Qur'an 70: 3-7, *Al-Ma'ārij*.

and purity of their creative realizations. For others, it is harder because of the shadows through which they come to light and because of the marks of their own indulgent habits, strengthened by the oppressions of others, leading back to shadows and sorrow. It is said that "the pure in heart will see God," and this is true.[102] Those whose lives are dedicated to the ways of compassion, wisdom, and visionary truth, to the relief of the suffering of other, and to the healing of the world, will see God, through the illumination of their soul, and through the purity of their intentions. What we must cultivate is not ideas about God but a pure and dedicated life in which Spirit acts to inspire us toward a realization of our inmost potential.[103] If we think intelligently about divinity and holiness, if we approach such a topic with a reverent concern for the purity of mind and heart, then realizations will flow forth.

But if we cling to dogmatic beliefs, to mythic forms as unbreakable templates, to emotive states of ecstasy, then we will rise no higher than the limits of our attachments. We are not really wise beings, nor are even the most enlightened guides able to lift us out of our ignorance unless the will is truly able to surrender attachments to rudimentary thoughts and narrow beliefs. The Mystery is far greater and more boundless than even our most mystical traditions. It is an illumination that overflows the lesser vehicles of mental form, dissolves them, and transforms awareness into a wave that has no beginning and no end. Such a wave flows outward in all directions and is depthless within; it has no boundaries other than the vast multitude of life forms that give it expression in limited instances of creative realization. Surrender your ideas of God and plunge in, you will be transformed; your mind will no longer be a mere reflection of the world, your soul will no longer be a contracted image of the past, you will open, flower, extend into the holiness that cannot be spoken and be absorbed into the radiance that has no name. You will be reborn through Mystery and become a vessel for the transformative energies of Spirit. Blessed are all those who see God, but more blessed are those whose full surrender leads them to peace, healing, and the awakening of others. In that peace there is an undying illumination whose depths can never be exhausted and whose fullness is immeasurable.

The depths of Unknowing are the very depths of illumination, the inflowing intensity of infinite Light, the baptism of the soul through an awakening whose confirmation is love, compassion, and understanding. It is the in-flooding of substantial life with the very energies of creation, awakening inherent potential. But even as those energies are awakening, the very boundaries of personal identity are dissolving, sloughing off the mental habits

---
102. Matthew 5: 8; 1 John 3: 2-3.
103. Psalm 139: 1-18.

and attitudes of indiscriminant immersion in embodied existence. Out of that dissolution, the soul expands to merge and inflow into Mystery without the bound conditionality of narrow mental or emotive sensations. All is preserved and all is transformed, this is the great miracle of spiritual illumination. The awakening of soul to its own limits is simultaneously a surpassing of those limits for direct perceptions of the qualitative holiness of the Infinite.[104] And this holiness is qualitative, that is, it is a fullness of possibility unified through an intense, overwhelming display of inner qualities consistent with the highest ideals of human evolution and spiritual development. The realization of those qualities must, however, become embodied through actual human beings who choose to enact those qualities in a genuine spiritual life. They are there—love, compassion, kindness, warmth, intelligence, wisdom; a creative, aesthetic, visionary understanding and a profound insight into the very structure and fabric of being—yet, these qualities remain dormant within Spirit awaiting the appropriate medium for full expressive realization.

The Unknowing is a transpersonal horizon of utmost dimensions and verticality, from the most subtle to the most manifest, spread out through the entire matrix of cosmic life as a foreground for evolution and spiritual becoming. The Light that surpasses understanding is the subtle radiance within which the works of Spirit are differentiated through diverse energies into a vast spectrum of observable events. The background is the qualitative potential, the capacity for manifestations that actualize the most virtuous qualities in a free, non-harmful, creative way of life. The Unknowing may be known through these qualities, but in themselves, these qualities are capable of infinite variation and embodiments. Always, the manifestations are a vessel overflowing while the observable forms are only the emergent edge of an Infinite capacity. The words are a song and the song is a calling, and it hovers just on the threshold of the Unknowing drawing our attention away from the manifest sound and contents, toward the Source. And the Source is infinite, beyond description, surpassing thoughts, words, ideas, and beliefs. Such is the Mystery, always present, always active through Spirit, always rich, full, inexhaustible, yet hidden and concealed in the ordinary everyday mind, shimmering in prayer, rising in dreams, manifesting through illumination, and dissolving the knower and the known. In that union of dissolution, there is rebirth, on-going awakened seeing, and a stability born over time that shapes a spiritual way of life.

In this process, the Hermetic Christ is an emblem of the soul's successful awakening and illumination. And we see in that awakening of the Christ path

---

104. Qur'an 2: 286.

that every station is "Christ created" as manifest in the actualizing of the Word, as a rightly guided path of love, healing and courage. The stations are not fixed; there is no certain number nor any division of steps that must be taken as authoritative. Each station is divisible into others, some stations are not yet known, and others, too static and rudimentary. A "station" is only a resting place, a stop or state on a much longer journey that leaves all stations and states behind and does not cling to them as markers on a way that is Infinite and without boundaries. The Christ created stations only mark a process of suffering and transformation that leads beyond suffering and transformation into illumination and resurrection. Such stations are memorable as a part of the path that has been, but not necessarily of the path that will be, or is now coming into being. A path may have innumerable stations, and each soul, struggles, suffering, challenges, sorrows, joys, and attainments. On that path, there are indeed stations marked as places and times of transition, insight, realization, and a recollection of the journey. But then, we move on, following that pathway toward a more distant horizon where pathways dissolve, journeys vanish, becoming transforms into Being, and seeking results in finding.

The Christ created stations are emblematic signs engraved in time that resonate with the collective meditations of diverse peoples over many eras of spiritual seeking. They are adaptable to the circumstances of the individual but they are also a ground for contemplation on the suffering, trials, and commitments we each face in living an authentic spiritual life. There is no spiritual path that lacks suffering or awareness of suffering; to imagine such is to live in an ungrounded world of imagination. If the suffering is not our own, then we need only open our eyes and hearts to the suffering of others to see its manifest reality. And the suffering of others is our suffering as well; the hurt of every child, is our hurt; the pain of loss and separation, our pain; the struggle against ignorance, our struggle; the feeling of loss in death, our loss. The path of the Hermetic Christ takes us through each station into the sorrow and pain of the world, for it is that sorrow and pain we must heal for each of us to be whole. The Christ path is not one of detachment, it is not based in transcendence and disdain for the world; rather it takes suffering as the very ground of our utmost challenge, to make the world into a place of healing, joy, and creative beauty. The stations are those very places where we stop and seek the healing of others in the face of injustice, violence, irrational upheaval and all the pain and trauma of oppression, doubt, and shame. This is a path of courage, determination, a willingness to go into the heart of the world and to redeem its fall from grace through love, intelligence, humility, and a committed peace-inspired spiritual life.

All stages are Spirit-born because these stages must unfold in accordance with the needs, capacities, and specific abilities of the individual. There are no fixed states, just as there are no fixed stations. All is fluid, flexible, adaptive, flowing with the energies and transforming the bound places into a more free, playful expression of inward intent. Spiritual development is not a lineal progression and rarely does it proceed in irreversible stages. More often, there is a sliding back, a retrogression that rediscovers lost ground, a return to what once was for a better understanding, a recovery of the past for greater maturity in the present. The pattern is cyclical and, over time, expansive. As the cycles turn, we in-gather the learning of the previous cycles and move beyond mere repetition into greater maturity of insight and a refining and transformation of habits and mental-emotive reactions. Always, we are conditioning the soul toward light, seeking deeper illuminations, following the visionary dream to its utmost horizon in order to dissolve our own ignorance. Stages may be mapped, but no map is equal to the experience, no scheme, adequate as first hand encounter. Guides and teachers may help, provide directions, give encouragement, but the greatest teacher is Spirit and the greatest promise, fulfilled in Mystery. Stages are Spirit-born because, for each individual, Spirit gives us the grace and bounty of Mystery in just that measure best suited to our needs and abilities.

In whatever stage, at whatever station, we find our self, it is just there at that point that we seek God, in Mystery, as guide, teacher, and inspiring presence. Every point, every moment is a stage, every stopping place for reflection, a station. In that moment of stopping, we stop within Mystery; in the moment of going forward, we go forward in Mystery. There is no place, no time, in waking or in sleep or imagination, that we are not cradled in Mystery and supported by Spirit. We need only open our hearts to that presence, know that it is the All-Containing; we accept its working in the depth of our being, receive gently that spark that gives hope, that light that illumines the soul. Everywhere we go, in everything we do, in every thought, we act as though it were an offering; we give of ourselves, and in the Christ way, we are transformed, becoming vessels for the instrumentality of Spirit, becoming a manifestation of capacity for world healing, world awakening, soulful co-creations. Whatever action we take in the name of Spirit we ground in compassion, non-harming, consideration, and thoughtful sensitivity. This way, Spirit leads us to Mystery in the doing of our everyday work, in the carrying out of normal actions made into a path through clear intention and surrender to Mystery. The gifts of Spirit flow throughout the entire world constantly seeking vessels of expression; we need only attune our lives to those energies to make them real. In doing so, we follow the Christ path and take one more step toward healing our self, others, and even in small ways, the world.

Prayer
To know that prayer is a ladder and meditation an Infinite well; to draw deeply, to extend fully without fears, attachments, or sorrows. (3: 4)

The knowledge of God does not come simply through reading books, though the study of theologies or written texts and scriptures, may help give guidance. True knowledge comes directly through medi ated experience and through a prayerful, meditative practices. It comes also in dreams, visions, spontaneous experiences, and unbidden at times even to the most worldly minded. There is no set formula nor structured path that can guarantee such knowledge and no techniques in either prayer or meditation that unfailing produce the necessary insights and illuminations for all practitioners. We are each a story, each a pattern made over multiple generations of incarnate existence, each a consequence of many past actions and each a weaving of multiple causes. For each of us, there is a way that works best and finding that way is part of the pattern of seeking and following a spiritual path. Guidelines can be laid down, techniques and visualizations taught, prayers learned and practiced, but the actual realization of light comes through Spirit as a gift built on inmost intention, strengthened by effort, enhanced by sincere practice and discipline and actualized through the inflowing grace of spiritual realizations. There is both self-effort and grace; both holding on and letting go; both clinging to the tiger and letting the tiger carry you where he or she will. Knowing how to ride the tiger is a matter of experience, letting the tiger carry you is a matter of courage and inner surrender, without experience and inward surrender, books, texts, and ideas only keep us on the surface, unable to grasp or be grasped.

Learning surrender is not easy, it requires something more than simply letting go. What we surrender is not our aspirations or the desire for light and illumination but the self-preoccupations that motivate the search. Letting go is part of the Hermetic process by which transformation penetrates the very heart of self-awareness. That penetration comes from within and opens a vista that no longer clings to the bound circumstances of a single lifetime, no longer seeks to evaluate life from the isle of isolated seeing. We are each part of a greater reality, one that encompasses all of our daily concerns and all the concerns of those we love, a reality that expands those concerns into an entire cosmos of interrelated beings. In Spirit and Mystery, these concerns reflect processes of gradual transformation whose intentions correspond to our deepest desires, needs, hopes, and dreams. Expanding outward from the heart-centered opening, the Hermetic circle embraces all living beings, incarnate, disincarnate, and never-incarnate, as co-participant seekers whose spiritual paths all contribute to an expansive network of related teachings. Surrendering our attachments to one path is an initial step to understanding the interconnectedness of all spiritual teachings; surrendering a belief in the exclusive value of one path only opens the heart to the value of other paths. Surrendering our attachments to a chosen way only allows us to sense more fully, the ways of others.

Surrender moves forward in concert with inward integrity and purposeful commitment to higher values. When the tiger carries you, you must let go and allow it to take you where she must because you have given yourself into her care. The tiger is the manifest, creative energy of Spirit, a spontaneous inward response to a prayerful surrender that draws the seeker into a sacred embrace. We ride the tiger when we do not lose our balance, when we are not flung aside by the energies, not confused or disoriented, not mislead into extravagance or excess. This requires an active will that lets the tiger lead us without force or compulsion and that allows the seeker to arrive at the goal fully alert and luminously aware. Riding the tiger requires an inward sense of balance, harmony of action, concentrated attention that is yet free and flowing. Learning to ride with grace teaches us to surrender to the motion and to willingly act in concert with the manifest energies of developing awareness, without any special claims, without proudly shouting from the tiger's back. In visionary ecstasy we may stand silent on the tiger's back, suspended by creative energies in an act of reverence and soulful union with Spirit.[105] There is music in that ride if you listen carefully; there is beauty, art, science, and a profound harmony whose waves cannot be measured in the degrees of their penetration. In riding the tiger you may exert some degree of direction, some intentional construction of goals and aspirations. This is an advanced practice; the earlier practice is to let the tiger carry you, to let go altogether without restraint to those inner energies and to follow where they lead.

Letting go altogether is often chaotic because the inner work of preparation rarely equals the depths of inmost penetration. In some rare cases, the purity of a life, the inner innocence of a soul or its many purifying incarnations, may make it an instrument of a full, spontaneous realization of potential.

---

105. In Hindu religion, the Supreme Goddess, Durga Maa, dressed in red, rides the tiger representing courage, wisdom, power and ecstasy.

Otherwise, it is a matter of degrees of preparedness or the degree to which the aspirant is able to do the necessary inner work in clearing away inherited bias or contracted understanding. Social conditioning, time, place, parents, friends, teachers, lovers, children, and historic communal events all act to shape and influence development. Biology, inherent capacities, talents, skills, coordination, intelligence, emotional maturity, psychic sensitivity, and inner motivations combine with soulful evolution and pre-incarnational cycles to create mental and spiritual horizons for possible growth. Inevitably there is resistance, habit energies, attitudes, and beliefs that act to inhibit or induce growth. Letting go is chaotic in this process when inhibitions are suddenly released and Spirit initiates profound physical, emotional, psychomental and spiritual transformations. When the tiger pounces and carries you away, it may well leap to a new horizon of awareness that utterly overcomes the lesser circle of former perception. This may be initially confusing and disorienting, but as one is carried from place to place, from perception to perception, if mind and heart are steady, there is continual learning, merging and integration of experiences.

Meditation is a means for making the heart and mind steady, for learning stability, inward calm, poise, and balance. A deepening meditation is a process of settling into utter stillness, receptive to the swelling of light but resistant to the chattering of mental habit or intellectual conditioning. This stilling process, of learning to breathe deeply in the lower stomach, of settling the mind into stillness, of watching the flights of thought like honking, distant geese in a winter sky, leads to deep concentration.[106] Such concentration arises without effort or force, without control, in simply allowing the mind to enter creative stillness, to abide in lucid calm, to rest in quietude without worry or concern. At depth, meditation is nothing other than a natural, relaxed, deep concentration fully aware, focused in a single point of attention spread out through and beyond the entire body.[107] It is entry into a vaster field of elemental constructions in subtle energies that permeate body-soul-mind within the more comprehensive energies of Spirit. These creative energies are intrinsic to the transformative processes by which the meditative mind merges into harmonious synchronization with the all-pervasive contents of illumined insight and higher awareness. Stillness and tranquility become a context within which many spontaneous, luminous insights first create flashes of understanding and later, a luminous abiding at the heart of creation. Further, the meditator is then completely dissolved into the energies where Spirit and Mystery continue to enact the dramatic processes of preservation, destruction

---

106. Psalm 46: 10, "Be still and know that I am God."
107. Bhagavad Gita 6: 25-27, Brahmabhūtam, "tranquility . . . to become one with God."

and recreation on a cosmic scale.

The goal of meditation is a deep mergence with the processes of creation, an inner awakening to the subtle energies that extend throughout the created realms, and an affirmation of Spirit as the mother source of all becoming. In companion with that meditative practice is the active direction of attention through prayerful surrender to that mother Spirit source. We may call on a variety of forms, images, manifestations, or created icons to focus the meditative or prayerful process. Yet, in prayer, there must also be naked attention that affirms the soul's aspiration toward union and mergence with the Beloved. We call out to that holy source, to the Father of Lights, to the Mother of Illuminations, to TheaTheos, to the receptive understanding of Spirit, to the full depths of Mystery. Beyond the images, there is only the naked intuitions of prayer that arise from the heart as pure intention, free of the heaviness of self-preoccupation, lightened by surrender, and guided by pure aspirations. Focused in the heart, prayer is a calling, a song, a quiet speech meant only for the Beloved; it is a call for guidance, a celebration of holy desire, a reverent seeking after direction for the soul's growth, a call for peace, healing, and union. This calling, this inner longing merged with thought, is a medium for reciprocal intuitions; it is part of a process by which soulful longing finds intuitive direction and spontaneous guidance.[108] In Spirit, prayer is a medium of inspired awareness whose inmost contents can actually facilitate profound transformations in self and in others.

It is said that prayer is a means for the creation of angels and there is a truth in this saying insofar as the intentions of prayer become actuators of change. Whatever the form of these actualizations, their angelic-etheric contents act to create circumstances and events whose empowerment resides in the purity of the prayerful soul. Not in purity alone, certainly not in outward disciplines or ascetic practices, but in a purity of intent within Spirit free from self-serving concerns and fully energized by compassion and care for others. The "prayers of the saints" are forms of actualization because the ministering angels they create are an outflow of Spirit working through the vessel of profound inner union and surrender. Prayer in this condition becomes an active presence in the world, an angel of grace acting to bring about a soulful call energized by Spirit and sustained in Mystery by principles of love.[109] Think of your prayers as the creation of angels and then ask yourself, what angels do you create when you pray? Are they worthy of creation and do they reflect the divine source of their ultimate origins? Or are they only shadows dressed in light, serving to

---

108. Psalms 141: 1-2; Matthew 21: 22; Corpus Hermeticum 5: 2; Qur'an 2: 186; Bhagavad Gita 11: 44.
109. Luke 1: 13.

enhance your own self concerns and frustrated desires? Every prayer has the potential to become an active presence in the world, therefore we must take responsibility for the dream work that supports those prayers and learn to purify their deep intentionalities. The ground of creation is sustained through the visionary worlds we inhabit and in prayer, those worlds take form through angelic inspirations, requiring us to pray with utmost love and concern.

Every angel ascending the stairway carries a message of the soul and an energy of actualization; but every angel descending the stairway carries with it the inspirations of Spirit. Inspired prayer is the greater actualization and descending angels seek our affirmations to fully actualize our potential, as when Jesus prayer in the garden and an angel appeared to strengthen him.[110] Therefore in prayer, we become a ground for the transformation of human suffering, pain, ignorance and illusions if we can strengthen those same angels by sending back prayers to renew and enhance their inspired energies. Prayers for peace, healing, or creative understanding builds this creative circle, this Hermetic interaction or reciprocity between heaven and earth, because it seeks to enhance the well-being of all. When inspired prayer comes, we need only affirm its goodness, its value, to strengthen its effects; we need only receive it with humility and pass it on according to its inmost intention. A higher manifestation of this inspired prayer leads to visionary encounters with the angelic forms; in those encounters it is possible to see into the creative heart of world transformation, to see the actual energies of Spirit manifest as visionary reality.[111] The vibrancy and power of such manifestations is a matter of the capacity and strength of the evolved soul, the inner purity, surrender, openness, and receptivity to holy works that cut through ordinary appearances and swell up to confront the prayerful heart. This is a matter of maturity, many transformations, and a gradual awakening to the fullness and holiness of creation.

When we pray or meditate, we must give up fear, attachments, and inner sorrows that inhibit and keep us from the full bounty of prayerful awakening. This is why meditation is valuable, for in meditation we may confront our inmost inhibitions, fears, and sorrows, our fanciful imaginings, our self-preoccupations, in order to clear away the deadwood, painful incidents, inherited trauma and confusion, transmitted through endless cycles of intergenerational relations. Transformation means letting go, surrender means no longer clinging to wounds, awakening means moving beyond fears, giving up old personality traits that limit and inhibit change and maturity. True spiritual growth means moving past the normative barriers of inherited

---
110. Luke 22: 41-44 (43 is often omitted in translations).
111. Revelations 10: 1.

grief, imbalanced relations, painful childhood experience, and old ways that reinforce a more limited understanding. It means breaking the mold of habit, living with a freer and more expressive energy that facilitates change and energizes new awareness in a loving and compassionate pathway. One sign of the Hermetic Christ is as an angel of healing, an angel of awakening whose resurrection in the heart of the seeker is a rebirth leading to profound love, healing, and illumined prayer and meditation. The Christ Angel is a visionary sign that fills the world without limiting its expression to any one path; it is a meditative image of Mystery, an energetic light within Spirit, a creative form whose complement is the divine mother, the holy bride, the Regina Angelicum, Queen of Angels, like the Virgin Mary, whose light and smile is a soulful joy and whose presence is an unending source of inspirations.

Prayer is a form of healing and meditation a source of inner stability in the face of dawning transformations and a multitude of spiritual awakenings. Many pathways are laid down in prayer and many techniques advanced through meditative practice. In the heart, both may merge and become an infused intention, a meditative prayer of contemplation, an inner stillness speaking in quiet tones, an inmost calling of holy names. The many mantras, chants, songs, recitation, and holy names are each a means to solicit the grace and presence of Spirit. Active prayer is a calling and receptive prayer is a listening and hearing; active meditation is focused attention and receptive meditation is a receiving of ever-expansive horizons of soulful being. On the Christ-path, the Hermetic union of prayer and meditation is of utmost importance as the primary means for awakening to Spirit. Regular meditation-prayer, on a daily or twice daily basis, is a foundation of soulful recollection necessary to bring the wandering mind and heart back to its primal center. In that prayerful practice, we enter into communion with the angels of creation, harbingers of spiritual awakening, that reflects the maturity of our inner attainments. In that inner silence, we may hear the "still small voice" of wisdom,[112] inspired guidance that leads to new awareness, a turning of the soul toward light, an inner illumination purifying all past suffering and sorrow. On that path, the Christ Angel stands, arms outstretched, ever ready to receive the faithful and to embrace the pure in heart.

---

112. 1 Kings 19: 11-12.

Attributes

To know God as veiled in attributes, images, forms, qualities, inwardly, outwardly and in Christ; to pass beyond and yet, to honor each manifestation. (3: 5)

There is no end to godly manifestations, no end to the possibilities within Spirit for creative expression and realization in human form. Every creature is an expression of divine energies woven through processes of interaction according to place, time, and inner capacities. As creative beings, we too are able to create images and forms that reflect our inner aspirations, hopes, dreams, and fears. These images and forms are also manifestations, refractions of greater creative processes in which all beings participate. Manifestations are embedded forms of energy that coalesce around numerous focal points forming a matrix whose intentions are multiple and not singular. As such, manifestations rarely represent just one thing, or just one idea or intention; normally they are complex expressions that act to synthesize diverse possibilities into common concerns. On the spiritual path, on the Christ path, these manifestations act to form our internal images of divinity, of truth, of holiness. If we bracket out a certain set of such manifestations as "sacred" it is only a convention that helps us to focus our attention. When we say Christ manifests Spirit, Christ is an image of divinity, of God, we are affirming that some manifestations epitomize a certain path, a certain way to live, or a certain spiritual ideal. But if we regard that manifestation as an exclusive expression of divinity, then we lose the Mystery, we lose our capacity to appreciate the richness, diversity, and inner fullness yet concealed in other manifestations.

Every created being is a manifestation of divinity, therefore, every created being is a wonder, a marvel, an astonishing work of patient, endless evolutions that unite the most subtle with the most material. Our failure to see this, our incapacity to experience wonder is a mark of our closed perceptions, of our bound horizons curtained over with skeptical doubts or dramatized self-concerns. Every creature calls us to regard with reverence the holiness of the processes by which we and all creatures have attained awareness and identity. This is true for every plant, animal, sea creature, those of the air, the earth, those visible and invisible, those whose trace is only an impression in ancient stone, archaic bones, or even a chemical-molecular pattern reconstituted. The wonder in this process lies in the depths of celestial matter whose energetic properties are manifestations of Spirit and whose forms are a mask concealing the hidden potentials of Mystery. We tend to reduce spiritual manifestations to human individuals or ideal images but the primal manifestation is the entire creation, the entire structure and contents of an expanding human awareness that beholds the magnificence, the wonder, the awe-filled immensity of a limitless cosmos continually eluding our comprehension. In the process of awakening to Spirit we discover the inner connectedness, the increasing correspondence, between ourselves, other manifestations, and the whole of creation.

As the ancient Hermetic teaching expresses it, we are each a cosmos, each an image manifesting the Whole; a wonder, a holy becoming in the midst of eternal revelations.[113] To behold this, we must open our hearts, minds, and inmost capacity to the fullness of creation and celebrate all manifestations as sacred, worthy of preservation, as primary sources of co-evolution and mutual becoming. If we choose to note among all these many manifestations, a particular form or image as representing a spiritual path or a spiritual teaching, as a source of revelation, we must learn to do so non-exclusively. We must learn not to extol the virtues and teachings of one manifestation above manifestations sacred to others in a world filled with manifestations. The same is true for all our thinking about God or Spirit or Mystery; attributes such as love, power, compassion, forgiveness, are all worthy, noble, and luminous. But no list of attributes, be they ten or ninety-nine or ten thousand and one, can fully describe the reality toward which they point. This is because all manifestations are a mask and all attributes an abstraction that leaves unspoken, the overflowing heart that dissolves words and attributes into boundless illumination and knowing. Yet even this illumination is a manifestation, a particular awakening to infinite expression, of an endlessness that has no full definition and a union whose contents are beyond description.

Thus we live embedded within a series of manifestations, interrelated through various attributes, acting to veil our understanding but capable of being lifted for even more profound awareness. We select a manifestation, a form, an image of divinity, a messenger, a carrier of teachings, as a guide or primal source of spiritual guidance, an ideal image. This is natural and good. But no manifestation can represent all the teachings, no manifestation can image all the possibilities within divinity. Teachings given to particular peoples at particular times are relative to their maturity, their needs, and their limits. All teachings are relative to the capacity of the members of a believing community to pass through the external forms into living Spirit, to a *gnosis* that reveals new depths, new dimensions and possibilities for positive spiritual growth. Thus we can honor every manifestation, reverence each teacher, each guide, each vessel, each holy word and yet know that what we reverence

---

113. Hermetic Definitions 1: 4-5.

surpasses the manifestation, surpasses the word, the image, and leads us to the very heart of transformation. In that fire, in that liquid illumination of awakened seeing, everything flows from multiple centers through currents of lucid seeing, into a great reservoir of infinite capacity and world-embracing potential. From that potential, each and every one of us is given the gift of life, the most profound of all manifestations. From that potential we seek to manifest in our own lives the sacred character, the attributes and qualities of divinity, that best represent our unique contributions.

Yet, we are thickly veiled, layered in the mental-emotive conditioning of family life, social obligations, communal relations, religious beliefs, and the historic context of our place and time. From this veiled condition, we see God, the most holy Mystery, also heavily veiled, hidden behind the illusions, ideas, and sanctioned teachings of a particular path or spiritual perspective. No path is completely free of illusion and no path is complete in what it teaches; always there is need for refinement, new thoughts, creative reinterpretation, and thus, new manifestations. The healthy tree is one that can branch, divide peacefully, and yet retain its roots, its sense of relation to all its branches, divisions, and fruit. From its fruit, new trees are born. Knowing there are other trees whose fruit is different and yet, just as sweet, only makes the value of the differences that much more worthy of preservation. We cannot cut at the roots of other trees and expect the differences to endure; therefore, we act to preserve differences and come to love the variety and diversity, appreciating the worth of each as each contributes, however little or much, to the diversity of the Whole. Thus we do not deny the value of the veils, the necessity of progressive learning, or the timely revealing of new perspectives. Each has its place and none represents an end, only an on-going growth toward greater wisdom.

It is said that the angels once asked to see the holy Mystery without veils, but the voice of the Throne replied that the 70,000 veils were necessary, for those even among the highest angels who sought to behold the full glory of the Throne would surely be consumed long before all the veils were lifted.[114] Our ears should be open to this teaching. As mortal, incarnate beings, the attributes, names, and manifestations are themselves guides and paths to higher knowledge, and beyond them lies an immensity and holiness far surpassing even the most enlightened being. Our search for enlightenment and illumination follows a multitude of pathways that seek to lead us to a lifting of veils, where we may behold the unsurpassing glory of primal creation in all its limitless possibilities and potential. In that glory we are dissolved, ourselves surpassed, our individual knowledge becomes only a resonance, a song sung

---

114. Quran 2:255, Sufi teaching.

in harmony, variation, or occasional dissonance, with the greater energies and music of creation, sustenance, dissolution. Even in the still center, the vast primordial Ur-Space, the substantial and insubstantial Metacosm, continues to harbor infinite resonant harmonies whose manifestations are found even in the fall of snow, the patterns of waves on the beach, or in the nuclear density of a drop of spring rain. In the eye of Christ, we see the same sparkle, the same enlightenment and illumination, reflecting in transfiguration, the luminous glory concealed in the heart of every creature.

We see that sparkle in the eye of the Buddha, in the celestial Bodhisattvas, in the dance of Krishna with the Gopis, in the soft and hard movements of illumined dance, in the T'ai Chi of the four seasons and the rooted overflowing abundance of the Dao. We see it in the Buddhist Taras and Dakinis, the images of mother wisdom and power, the feminine divinity of the Prajñaparamita or in the holy Virgin with Child, in Horus and Isis. We see it in the images of Saints, Yogis, Sufis, Hasids, Daoist immortals, Christian mystics, enlightened Buddhist masters, and in spiritual teachers of all kinds, as male, as female, as child. All are visionary images, manifestations, attributes of divinity in the existential sense of their capacity to facilitate inner growth, transformation, and an awakening to illumined insight. In the Christ image we see the work of Spirit manifesting as healer, teacher, transfigured angel, master, guide and son or daughter of the Most Holy Light. Outwardly, this image may be characterized in forms and icons reflecting a variety of teachings, patterned after diverse ethnic, cultural, or historic conditions. Inwardly, it is an "image of the maker" whose contents and form are individualized according to the importance of various spiritual influences. There is no one correct image, every image reflects the capacity within Spirit to manifest a possible new form or representation whose impact and value lies in its capacity to lead the heart toward greater spiritual awakening and responsive care. The multiple intentions at work are part of a process that exceeds the individual need or temperament, that points beyond itself to a new horizon of understanding.

Each Christ image, each image of the Bride, through generations of prayerful intent, becomes a means for carrying the mind and heart beyond the image and into an awakened seeing, into the light where images dissolve and new birth occurs. Through meditation on the image, we can pass through the image into a deeper and more luminous source in which the image is only a prism through which multi-spectral light can be refracted into visible form while yet concealing a far vaster spectrum of radiances. We must learn to unveil the image, the Christ form, the Virgin, Bride, or Child, as a Raa-Nub, a synthesis of energies whose full contents cannot be contained in any form or image. As these energies are released, they swell up into the neural psychic network, expanding outward toward unknown cosmic horizons and, dissolving inwardly, they leave only the tenuous membrane of "self" as a focal intersection of all that is within with all that is without, with all that is above united with all that is below. The image is a catalyst, a guide whose Hermetic energies reflect the energies of Spirit and which acts to awaken the dormant potentials of the sleeping soul. As the soul awakens, it penetrates through the images, is guided by Spirit to ascend through the unfolding of the image into its multiple intentionalities, awakening various inward centers and expanding outward to embrace and to be embraced by the Mystery. The veils are lifted, perhaps only a few, but enough for an illumined seeing, enough to break through the opaque images to the transparent source, to the luminous expanse of an imageless horizon.

Thus we honor all manifestations, all holy images, that seek to promote the spiritual well-being, health and mutuality of compassionate and loving co-existence. The Christ image, the Christ being, as a holy means to illumination and awakening, is one among many; other images emphasize other teachings, all of which contribute to the richness of our species understanding. But none of these images, attributes, or manifestations is supreme; no teacher is greater than all others, no teaching all comprehensive. Each is relative to its origins, its unique spiritual history, its conditioned arising from unconditionality. It is that unconditionality that we seek in the heart of the Hermetic circle where the path of the Hermetic Christ leads us to an inner dissolution and spiritual awakening that unites us with the round dance of all creation, all paths. We celebrate that dance with other images, teachers, guides, and spiritual manifestations; and yet we seek to move beyond the images, attributes, and forms into the formless, imageless, pure intentionality of luminous awakening. We seek, "to know God" in the direct, simple, unequivocal way of direct personal *gnosis*, knowing that this journey is relative to our capacities as human beings and knowing that the Throne is veiled and unapproachable beyond the point where no individual, self, or realized being can be found.[115] Dissolved in that Light, only light abides, itself a veil over veils, concealing the most holy of holy densities whose creative potential far surpasses the works, wisdom, or collective understanding of any race, species, world or written work. Even Light is a veil and in the Face of Mystery we can only bow and give thanks for the gifts of life we have each been given.

---

115. I Corinthians 3: 16; Hermetic Definitions 9: 3.

The Footstool

To know that the Footstool of the Throne is in your own heart; may you be strong enough to receive It, even an atom of Its dust! (3: 6)

The magnitude of the holy Mystery is beyond description, and its depths and heights are immeasurable. By what means could we measure that depthless source other than through the lens of our own experience and encounters? When the forms dissolve and the structures of self-awareness melt, then the radiance of a hidden inner light begins to absorb all the tangible memories of self-constructed knowing. That radiance penetrates the very bones of the body, shines forth from the heart, surrounds, permeates, and absorbs the lesser identity leading it to utmost splendor. Yet, nothing is lost, there is no destruction or denial, only a deep and profound joy that the basis of all awareness is this holy, sacred, and all-pervading Presence.[116] The preservation of self is the manifest creative work of Spirit weaving intangible, subtle energies into a hundred billion forms, like animate images on a vast tapestry, while also maintaining the hidden unity of the constructive warp and weft, the interconnected plasmic bonds of the jewel net creation.[117] Each of us is a knot, a particular complex center of woven fibers whose strands link us through body, heart, and mind to the hearts, minds and aspirations of others. Yet, this tapestry once dissolved into its inner creative energies, dissolved into the primordial Mystery, into unity and inner harmonic resonance, leads to a profound insight—all beings are one in Mystery, one in Spirit, one in creative value, worth, and importance.[118] Each of us is a gemstone whose value lies in our the capacity to reflect clearly inner light and to embody outwardly, a unique and valuable form.

When we think of Mystery, of God, we can only project images and abstractions which contract the Mystery into a graspable form or construction. This mental and imaginative reduction is a reflection of our limitations, creative when infused with a reverence sense of presence, stale when reiterated as a unreflective, dogmatic norm, and simplistic when made comfortable and predictable. The overflowing energies of Spirit are constantly drawing us toward a renewal of perception and an awakening of awareness as our images become increasingly unsatisfactory, trivial, or stereotyped through lack of reflective concentration. What we must learn is to penetrate the image to its

---

116. Corpus Hermeticum 5: 5; Luke 2: 9 (Glory = Indwelling Shekinah); II Corinthians 6: 16; Revelation 21: 3-4.
117. Indra's Jewel Net as in Hua Yen Buddhism.
118. I Corinthians 12: 12.

inner reality, to cut through the form to its inner living presence. Every image of mind is a potential teaching, its content concealed by an outward form, but its inner potential charged with the deep and subtle vibrancy of Spirit. Holy images are a means for awakening the mind, for stirring the soul by allowing the inner light of those images to act as a goad moving us toward creative, hidden depths. The compelling quality of sacred images is found in their capacity to stir the soul, to open us to depths felt but unseen, to draw attention toward the inner illumination of mind and heart. This is also true for sacred music, dance, and other artful expressions of communion with Spirit. What makes those expressions sacred is their capacity to awaken in us, a felt sense of presence, of shared love, of a penetration of the sound, the image, the expression with an inner current that carries us beyond form and outward appearance.

At the heart of this process, the image becomes a means for the invocation of genuine reverence because in its contemplation, we can experience directly the reality toward which the image points. Consider the image of the Throne of the Regina Angelium, the Queen of Heaven, the Divine Sophia, Holy Wisdom, holding on Her lap the Christ-child as Isis, Goddess of the Throne, held the child sun god Horus. This pure white translucent Throne, carved with the invisible symbols of sacred invocation, sits on a raised, square, stepped platform of white crystalline allotrope diamond. At each corner of this raised platform stands one of the great winged archangels: Michael, Gabriel, Raphael and Uriel, each veiled by a multilayered garment of radiant multicolored light. Each holds the appropriate symbol (sword, staff, cup, and stone) and each bears witness to their assigned tasks: herald of life and death, messenger of revelation, healer and protector, teacher of divine mysteries. The hem of their garments are rimmed in gold whose brightness burns away human ignorance, the straps of their sandals are plaited from hairs taken, one from the head of each of those whose life was sacrificed for love, and the belts of their robes are dyed by the tears of those who most long for God. The magnitude of their power is like a thousand suns condensed to a drop of dew that falls from a single feather of a wing into an ocean of love. Each archangel has ten thousand invisible feathers and each drop of dew renews itself constantly through the bliss and joy bestowed in standing on the threshold of the Throne. Beyond this threshold, no mortal or angel passes, each is dissolved in the intensity of its radiance and in the celestial consummation of its holy energies.

On the great Throne sits the Holy Mother Spirit, the Regina Angelicum, the divine image of the eternal creator-creatress whose form is concealed beneath the 70,000 veils of layered, alternating luminous light and all-encompassing void dark. The outer most veils are embroidered with essential ideas and the inner most are purest radiant being-light whose magnitude ignites all the stars and suns of all known and unknown galaxies, born and unborn, now, in the past, and forever, amen. We are ourselves veiled in similar ways, concealing within our mortal frame and feelings, within our thoughts and beliefs, a deeper, more profound holiness that emanates directly from this Throne. On the subtle blue-white of Her outermost veil, embroidered in visionary images of gold-white weaving, are lotus images of the Hermetic aspirant, each accorded its time and place in revelatory manifestation. From the lowest hem of that outermost veil, there is a silken fringe made of the most subtle, sacred substance. This fringe contains uncountable threads and each thread connects invisibly to each living being, incarnate or disincarnate, human, angelic, or trans-angelic. And every thought, feeling, impression, or sensation is transmitted by this thread to the hem of the holy garment and on to the very heart of the Throne. This hem conceals the holy feet of the Mother as She sits in perfect awareness of all that transpires through the pure *gnosis* transmitted through Spirit to Her inmost heart. Every offering made to the feet of the divine mother, in human form as avatar or saint, ascends directly to the Throne and is made known in all its sincerity to the heart of creation.

On Her head is a luminous crown of purest crystalline diamond, a single spark of which provides the highest dissolution of self. The radiance of this spark, a Christ ember, leads to pure annihilation in which self-awareness is dissolved and we are veiled from our human attributes to enter momentarily into the vast presence of Mystery, for this crown is Mystery, concealed in a revelatory form. If we seek to see the holy Face of this Mystery as imaged in the revelatory form of the Regina Angelicum, we cannot hope to behold it as a sufficient visualization of the full reality which it represents. The reality of the holy Mystery is subtle and penetrating beyond imagination and that Mystery veils itself through Itself and we, as selves, are already inseparable from that veil. Every vision is a veil and every illumination is a lifting of the veil for a revelation of what remains still hidden. We are each a sacred nexus, an intersection of spiritual potentials given life and breath for free self-expression and each a dissolving drop in a sea of limitless joy. True knowledge requires a long journey that takes each of us in his or her own way to the very threshold of the Throne, to the Footstool, where we may each bow and surrender all concepts, attributes, and mental forms. We accept there the baptism of Spirit, the cleansing of self, the purification of all wounds, regrets, doubts, fears, angers, lusts and desires for the pure influx of a luminous healing whose depths dissolve all self-abiding and offers the infinite grace of profound transformation.

The spark of that luminous crown lies in your own heart, in the depths of your soul, in the inmost center of your most passionate being. You must breath on that ember, cultivate the flame, arouse the inner intensity of your deep soul desire, nourish the warmth and deep feelings of love that spread from that center to envelop your whole being. Through visionary flights, following the thread to the hem of Her skirt, we arrive at the threshold of the Throne and we bow before the Footstool offering our whole being to the Mystery that sits radiantly enthroned. And from her lap, the Christ-child images that union of soul as a radiant child-being born of the *Hieros Gamos*. We are each this Christ-child, each in the moment of illumination, a child of the Mother-Father union that represents the evolutions of consciousness balanced and rebirthed in new visionary forms. The Father is the invisible Mystery that lies hidden in the encircling, creative energies of the Holy Mother Spirit. She is the worker who weaves those energies into actual, visible forms; He is the source for the stimulus of conception. She plants a seed of the invisible and unknown Father in the depths of every soul; She weaves, with an atom of dust taken from the Footstool, the sacred pattern of new emergence.[119] That atom, that sacred pollen, is nourished by angelic presences, by the devas, angels, and asuras of the subtle realms, for the purpose of awakening each soul to its inmost destiny. We need only arouse that spark, that seed, for it to open us to the Throne where we may behold through direct illumination the inmost reality of the divine Mystery. The smile of the Christ-child is like that of Gopala, the baby Krishna, whose incarnation is a profound source of spiritual realization for innumerable devotees.

The ascent to the Throne requires a willingness to purify the heart, to strip away self-obsessions, to heal all wounds, to give up the circulatory patterns of trauma, to overcome the lassitude of passive habit energies that support less aware actions. The trumpet call of the Throne is a sound that cuts through all self-loathing, all self-doubt, all insecurities and imbalanced inflations. That call knocks down every soul to the level of its actual attainments, strips away all self-concealing accretions, and lays bare the naked immaturities of soul life. To rise from that paralysis, to ascend from the massive collective bonds of cynicism or denial or fear requires an inner courage, an inner determination that allows no outward relation to impede or deny soul life and no inner attitude to blind the soul to its inmost desire. What every soul desires in an inward depth of self existence is to know the source and support of its individual being; the joy comes in realizing that it is a shared, mutual reality whose foundations

---

119. Lee Irwin, *Awakening to Spirit*, Appendix: The Divine Sophia, 355-358.

are woven in love, trust, and deep compassion. All the threads ascend to the fringe of the outermost veil where they are each differentiated according to the state, motives, dreams and desires that lead to spiritual awakening. And the world is woven in such a way that we are each led to meet and encounter those who will most benefit that awakening. In this way, spiritual communities are formed and act as a focal center of emergent wisdom and illumination. And in each of them, the Holy Mother is present and the Invisible Father offers the gift of utmost illumination. And on the path of the Hermetic Christ, in the image of the Christ-child, sends his radiant smile into the round dance of holy worshipers.

Not only strength, courage, and purity of intent but also humility, patience, and inner surrender are necessary for the unveiling of the heart. To bear consciously even an atom of divine Mystery requires an inward willingness to accept the guidance of Spirit, in all its demands, forms, and multiple applications. There is no one path, only a variety of individuals who must each walk in ways consistent with their gifts. There is no one illumination, the variety and variations in awakening are beyond calculation and the evolution of spiritual gifts take many diverse forms. No forms are intrinsically better or higher, no formless realizations are superior, no visions a necessary sign of illumination. Let each seek to maximize the potential that leads to peace, loving relations, wise insights, compassionate healing, and creative, aesthetic expression for the betterment of soul life. In whatever way we walk, let us each value honesty, patience, courage in confronting ignorance and self-aggrandizement, and let each resist destructive habits, arrogant self-assertion, and the denial of the rights of others to live according to non-violent, non-destructive ways of life. In Spirit, all is a weaving of potential whose utmost source of inner unity and wholeness allows for the utmost expression of outward diversity. What binds us is the common visions we share, the spiritual practices we undertake, and the values we promote as necessary and good for human development. On the path of the Hermetic Christ, the ways are many, the means are many, but the intent is to awaken inner potential and to find within, the luminous spark that leads to visionary transformation.

Wisdom

To be utterly One in the Mystery, with God, in essence and manifestations; by Wisdom inspired, by Light uplifted, illumined, fully alive. (3: 7)

The most important aspect of this saying is to realize that we are already one with the Mystery, inseparably so, and regardless of our personal history, we can never be separated from that primal unity. This unity underlies all existent manifestations, known and unknown, seen and unseen. It reflects itself within the essences of the creative energies of Spirit and is the inner coherent source of all evolutionary changes. It is not simply a oneness or a unity, it is the inner living reality of Mystery that permeates all beings, all conditional life, and all cosmic forms, gross and subtle, with potential fullness and abundance beyond description. It is seen in the energies at the heart of an atom and as a divine spark in the heart of every human being; it's wonder is its undiminished brightness, unstained by human folly, greed, vice or ignorance. In the Christ, this inner unity is a living testimony to the illumined presence of Spirit removing the outer veils and revealing the inmost presence of the Father, Abba.[120] Just as Christ opened his heart to the Father and discovered the limitless vision of the inner unity of Spirit, for the good of others and not just for himself, so too, may each of us awaken to the Mystery and find within, that dissolving presence. The gift of this inner union is already given, already present in the human heart, already pressing against us with each heartbeat, with every breath we take. It is there, waiting to be found and shared. All we need do is open our hearts, assent to the inflowing radiance of the Mystery, and accept the responsibility of that radiance as a healing presence whose expression is one of the foremost concerns of Spirit.

To be "one in essence" is not the same as being omniscient or all-knowing or enlightened in an abstract or intellectual sense. It means to enter the light and be reborn; it means to open the heart in humility, devotion, and surrender. It means to find the center and to hold to it in the face of all turbulence, upheaval, and confusion. It means to have deep roots, planted in soil that cannot be exhausted and with limbs that give shelter to those without roots or branches, to be a resting place for many living creatures. And where is the earth, the soil that cannot be exhausted? It is in Spirit, in the Father, in Wisdom with all Her graces, and deep in the Mystery of the all-containing One. This One is manifest throughout the fullness, the height and depths of primal Ur-Space that makes up the multi-layered, multi-temporal, multi-dimensional cosmos

---

120. John 17: 20-22.

we inhabit. Ur-Space is inseparable from mind and psyche; it is both the womb within which all ideas, images, visions, and imaginings are conceived and nourished and it is the boundless arena within which all human dramas, in joy or sorrow, are enacted. It is the All-Containing space of the Holy Metacosm, holding and sustaining created forms from the most dense to the most subtle and it is activated by the creative energies of Spirit through the evolutions of each and every individual. Because of its greatness, we must approach it with deep reverence and humility; because of its power and potential, we must be willing to accept radical inner transformations. This is not a matter of only thinking, but of a direct visionary plunge into the heart of creation, without losing the center, without suffering imbalance or excess.

Holding to the center means that we are able to fully release our inner barriers, let go of fears and uncertainties, and allow the creative energies of Spirit of act on us a guiding presence. This presence draws us, each in our own way, toward the heart of creation where we shed the outer, inherited forms of acquired learning and old emotive-intellectual patterns for a rebirth in Spirit and Wisdom. This is the mystical baptism of light which floods the heart and soul with a deep and profound union, symbolized in the *Hieros Gamos*, as the union of the Lover and Beloved, of the soul and God. This union is not simply a state of ecstasy, but a fruition of soul that impregnates the psychic-self with new life, a life whose birth and development is seen in the attainment of qualities of beauty and grace. These are soul qualities, the inner power and luster of soul-light breaking through the form and revealing the subtle, pervasive reality of Spirit. On the path of the Hermetic Christ, this illumination leads to a more loving, impartial, and compassionate way of living, the heart becomes a source of radiance whose subtle energies act to open the hearts of others. Over time, the heart is transformed into the Christ-heart, that is, into a center whose depths are inseparable from the Father of Lights, the Mother of Life. This opening is revelatory and prophetic as it removes the veils of ordinary perception and uncovers a vast panorama of spiritual transformations.

The Father of Lights is the sign of the creative, evolutionary potential revealing itself through cosmic processes of expansion, balanced by a necessary inward contraction meant to draw on inner resources for further expansion.[121] The balance in this process is found in a non-attachment to form while using form as a creative medium for instruction. The entire cosmos is a teaching and Ur-Space is a relative designation whose contents are beyond full description. The loving Christ of the Father is a teacher of inner truths whose outward manifestations are healing, community, and genuine loving relations between

---

121. James 1: 17.

men, women, and children. The developmental potential finds its basis in the unity of the Metacosm, in the fractal patterns, in the intrinsic beauty of proportional form, in harmony, music, in all sacred sciences, and in the manifest arts of spiritual transformation. The celestial image of the Father of Lights is seen in all the stars together, and in the illumined history of human evolution towards a more integrated, mature diversity in spirituality, as seen in the lives of saintly human beings. We are each a manifestation, each a participant in essence, each a relative expression of divinity whose capacities are yet, unknown and by no means fully explored or actualized. The task of the Christ-heart is to open to the inner capacity that leads to transformation in the creation of a non-violent, peaceful world of spiritually linked others. Each must seek to be a light within the Father, to find the dissolving power of light as a reflection of love within the Mother, as an illumined presence that dissolves all self-centered concern and opens on to a vista that has no boundaries.

In that light, we discover a boundless love whose bounty is measured by a capacity to embody ever fuller and more complete expressions of loving kindness in all our relations.[122] To be utterly one in the manifestation means to act as a fully sentient, aware being whose heart is open to the suffering and turbulence of the world and whose will is directed toward the healing of all the wounds and blind habits that make life so difficult for so many. But not just love, also there must be wisdom and in the Way of the Hermetic Christ this wisdom is imaged as the Holy Mother Spirit, Divine Sophia, whose active, engaged manifestations work to awaken the sleeping souls of the forgetful through multiple expressions in art, music, dance, and poetry; in social relations and communal constructions; in sacred teachings applied to every walk of life in preservation, reverence, and respect for the integrity and healthy needs of others. The manifestations of Wisdom are found in holy women, in embodied incarnations of female teachers whose spontaneous realizations have led them to become vessels of light for the awakening of the World-Soul.[123] These holy women come from many diverse traditions, particularly from India, but also from other spiritual traditions. Their presence is a Hermetic sign that the transformation of the World-Soul requires and fully supports the realization of a multitude of female avatars whose work is the rebalancing and harmonizing of spiritual diversities into a pluralism of interconnected spiritual paths.

On the path of the Hermetic Christ, these women deserve the utmost respect and reverence as embodiments of the Divine Sophia, the incarnations of the Regina Angelicum, and as Brides of Christ whose manifest teachings

---
122. Matthew 5: 14-16.
123. 1 Corinthians 2: 7.

intersect and weave together the alienated strands of male spirituality. The Christ-hearted man, the embodiment of a reborn Hermetic spirituality, honors all such manifestations knowing that the heart of creation is inseparable from the nourishing, necessary presence of loving feminine spiritual expression. All religious pathways can learn and be instructed by this emergent feminization as an necessary healing for all masculine spiritual teachings and traditions. There is no path that cannot benefit from the deep integration of the feminine; the Christ-hearted man, following Wisdom, seeks to encourage and nurture the full expression of female spirituality in all aspects of the path. Many will be the female teachers and guides in the times to come, and many of the truly great teachers will be women. This truth is so apparent, so vivid, that the enlightened heart can only celebrate with joy the many manifestations to come. I honor you all, with utmost love, and I celebrate within my heart, the beauty and fullness of your being. In this arising, the presence of the Divine Sophia shines like a beacon, no longer fallen into the world, but reborn as a necessary light and guide, fully empowered and in every way a truly luminous source of wisdom and insight. May the days of your presence be long, and depths of your wisdom immeasurable.

In essence, we all share the same love, the same inner unity of awakened concern, an intimacy without inner barriers whose intention is the healing of the world. In the heart of creation, there burns a great, pervasive light whose radiance is found in every created being, in every living thing, in all manifest forms however great or small. Wisdom, embodied through the divinization of the feminine, gives us a multitude of examples of how we should live and how we should honor and revere all living creatures. Love, embodied through the divinization of the masculine in the Christ-heart, gives us also a multitude of examples of how to honor, support, and seek the healing of others. We must learn to do this without discrimination against the state or circumstances of those whose wounds, habits, or ignorance only reflects the painful state of their conditionality. Breaking through the conditionality of our own states is a major task at every stage of the spiritual journey, even for the most illumined. To heal others, we must be healed; to give, we must receive; to love, we must be loved. Therefore, we turn to Spirit, to the depths of Mystery, to the indwelling presence, to the upsurge and overflowing of the heart cultivated through spiritual disciplines, heart-felt prayer, and inner devotions. And in this process, we find inspiration! In the examples of others, in the grace and shared empowerments of spiritual community, in the still, quiet dawn, in the depths of night dedicated to inner reflection and deep breathing that nourishes an inner flame.

To be fully alive means to be in the living presence of Spirit, with the outer veils lifted, that we may gaze on sublime truth while standing naked to the light. It is our own veils that are removed, our own limitations that are overcome, by grace, by efforts, by a concatenation of diverse causes and effects, we stand at the threshold of the inner temple and in that moment of openness, we receive the necessary gifts. Then we are uplifted, then we are illumined and inspired. And the gifts are a responsibility, an instrumentalization of individual potential for the purpose of sustaining the highest qualities of spiritual life. To be living examples of the path, not merely walking in its shadow, but living fully in its light. This means we are each fully capable of mystical transformation, fully able to cross the threshold and to surrender inwardly to Spirit. You will know them by their fruit, the healthy, realized soul does not seek its own glory nor does it seek to be reverenced but to reverence others. She stands below, not above, and he stands below her; in this way, it is possible to honor every manifestation and to hold none as superior but each as living the relative truth of their honest experience. In their hearts, they are all one, not in their teachings or lifeway, but in the dissolutions of light, they are no longer distinct. Thus the spiritual path has an end, it leads to the limits of our individual capacity while simultaneously showing us the depthless ocean of creation. In that inner oneness, we are awakened to the relative limits of embodied life and realize that every spiritual path is a boundary and every teaching, incomplete.

Mystery

To enter the Mystery of God with an empty heart; in unity and accord, to surrender to fullness without measure, immersed, overflowing, utterly dissolved. (3:8)

How difficult it is to be an empty vessel! Always we are overflowing with thoughts, feelings, ideas, desires, aspirations, fears, anxieties, and uncertain longings. Our minds are rarely at peace, rarely quiet, rarely able to reflect the immeasurable depth. One of the many veils that must be lifted is that of self-preoccupation, of a constant dwelling on personal concerns, ambitions, needs or desires. To lift that veil, there must be an inner sensitivity to the presence of Spirit, a receptivity to a deeper, hidden truth. This truth, which dwells in each person, like a divine atom in the heart, has no fixed content or mental-emotive structure. It is an absorbing fire that reduces all thought and belief to a single flame whose purity dissolves all mental turmoil, all emotional flux and mood. In the beginning, this flame must be protected and sheltered against the constant turbulence of inner storms and outer pressure. In the middle, it becomes a constant state of luminous presence, and in the end it becomes an ocean of infinite mercy whose horizon has no boundary or limit. But first you must empty the heart, still the ever active mind, focus attention, breathe slowly, deeply, and allow yourself to open inwardly. This opening is a gradual process of growth and increasing sensitivity to the subtle worlds, to the creative energies of Spirit, and to the wholeness which supports all spiritual evolution and development. Opening is partly a matter of surrender, but also, it requires a wisdom that sees the real nature of self and others within the world-soul.

Our relationships to each other establishes a ground for the unfolding of soul qualities if those relations are built on respect, love, and living a life of committed dedication to spiritual values. It is not simply a matter of following a path, having a spiritual philosophy, or practicing specific meditative techniques. We must also work diligently on our human relationships, to such a degree that individual spiritual qualities are inseparable from each and every relationship we develop with others. And we must not isolate ourselves in closed communities or cloak our incapacities by denying the world or the more worldly minded. The path of the Hermetic Christ leads us into the world, not away from it; to the sick, blind, and deaf, to the aspiring, seeking, and hopeful, to all those in need of healing and compassion. Every human relationship presents opportunities to practice the spiritual virtues that exemplify the path we each follow. If these relationships are difficult, demanding, or challenging, the ability to rise to that challenge is a mark of the depth and commitment we have to fully actualize the presence of Mystery in our lives. Do we seek the Mystery for self alone? No! We seek illumination as a means for the healing of the World-Soul and this means through the love and compassion that we bring into every human relationship. The Christ-heart is not closed within divine glory but open, loving, sharing the virtues of wisdom and heart-felt concern in all human relationships.

We empty the heart so that Spirit may fill it and Mystery may act upon each of us in distinctive ways that will best heal the sorrow and suffering of others. Suffering can be found among the poorest and the most wealthy, among those who have and those who have not, among the elite and among the most common. No one is exempt from the suffering that comes from living a closed, bound life of painful struggle, whatever the context; we all suffer from past errors, poor judgments, and limited horizons of thought or belief. But love flowing from the Christ heart, open to all paths as a spark of transformative presence, can act as a primal source of healing and rebirth. Like the Christ-child on the lap of Wisdom, like Horus with Isis, the soul is born through the earth-energies of the Mother Spirit and lifts its wings to light. This light comes to us through a spiritual center located in the depths of the heart, a heart that is earth-made, a material form whose symbolic action is to continuously circulate the energies of Spirit. As a psychic center, the heart is a focal point of sacred *energia* (or *prana*), the cosmic, subtle radiance that penetrates all solar space and gives its life-energies to sustain awareness. The union of all that is above with all that is below occurs through the spiritually illumined heart; this union is a sign of a profound interaction between the most material and the most subtle. The eye of the heart, like the eye of Horus, must be opened in order for the soul to perceive its actual nature and its inseparable connection with Spirit. When opened, that eye reflects a light whose presence dissolves all doubt and all resistant ideas and attitudes.

To empty the heart means to give up striving after spiritual attainments and psychic abilities; it means to let go of mastery, to no longer need signs, to be free from grasping spiritual needs. It requires no teacher, no master, no initiation, and no adherence to the closed rules of any one community. An aspirant may have teachers, may receive initiations, live in community with others, but these things do not guarantee illumination, nor do they necessarily result in positive attainments. What must happen is an inward surrender, a letting go of externals, and a willingness to dissolve all aspects of self into a greater wholeness whose boundless expanse fills the heart-mind with a true sense of individual limits while also drawing on individual ability to fulfill potential. You cannot measure this potential because it is the potential of creation; you cannot contain it because we are each a relative being whose capacity is dependent and conditional. Therefore, let go of your aspirations for mastery and surrender to the vastness of the limitless, boundless immensity whose creative energies surpass all human manifestations. The great storehouse of wisdom contains an abundance of treasures far beyond the capacity of any one individual to fully value in all its worth and diversity. Even the most enlightened soul, the most divine avatar or holy manifestation, is still only a part, a relative condensation, of a greater reality whose horizons cannot be expressed through one individual, one community, one world, or one great union of worlds.

Always, Mystery exceeds our relative boundaries and Spirit acts to weave its multiple dimensions and emergent horizons of transformation. We may embody the truth that is revealed to and through us, we may each become a manifest sign of higher agency and revelation. But realizations will lead, again and again, into a dissolving horizon of Spirit where no individual attainment can fully express what lies within that light, that most holy Mystery. Behind the 70,000 veils where even the archangels cannot ascend, lies a brilliance and intensity that utterly dissolves all individual awareness and absorbs the individual into a unity and joy that is the greatest of all gifts. Therefore, create an attitude of longing and adoration, inwardly sustained, outwardly kind and compassionate. Returning from that embrace, we can only celebrate its magnitude and potential, we can only be vessels of its transformative power, only act within the limits of our individual capacities. Mystery cannot be fully rationalized nor can it be grasped by the limited mental horizon of an illumined, awakened soul. But it can be experienced directly, can act to absorb the individual and transform awareness and understanding to the most intimate degree possible. Such *gnosis* is a profound and holy event unlike any other; in that event we overflow, dissolve, merge, and become consciously participant in the very creation of life. We become the handmaidens of the holy marriage, those whose lamps are lit and whose oil is fragrant and luminous.[124]

Being utterly dissolved does not mean having no self, it does not mean striving to overcome ego-awareness. This dissolving is a positive, creative experience that results in a vastly expanded vision of human capacity in the midst of a great and holy cosmos. Spirit constantly works to energize the human soul with transformative visions whose contents lead toward an ever expanding horizon of spiritual potentials. In that process, the everyday identity is constantly challenged to release its narrow perspectives, its clinging to old thought forms, its unnecessary dependence on habit, unexamined attitudes, or recurrent anxieties. The deep *gnosis* is an on-going process of transformation that reveals the expansive contours of life within divinity. It is an awakening and opening of the heart to the direct flow of Spirit, through prayer, meditation, breath, visualization, and musical, artful forms whose contents stimulate the desire for soulful union and illumination. Dissolving into that light is not a death but a true coming into life, a true revelation of the magnitude and wholeness that permeates all aspects of creation. This illumination is an enhancement, an added horizon of bounty and abundance that places all self-awareness into a relative context of value. On the Hermetic path, there is no need to devalue self-awareness nor to celebrate its relative perspectives; we are each a focal matrix, a relative manifestation of awareness whose perceptions are concurrent with the perceptions of others.

Through love, simplicity, honest relations, sympathy, sharing, and compassionate dedication to truth, we each contribute our unique perceptions to the growth of others. To live in unity and accord means to value the self

---

124. Matthew 25: 1-3.

in a relative sense, as we each make our contribution to developing species maturity, we each exemplify the path we walk. To attain the illumination of self is only part of that process, for the self is never truly dissolved, but it is transformed, purified, made transparent and liberated step-by-step from its obscuring tendencies through illumination. Yet even after such experiences, we are required to continue the alchemical process, to refine, subtilize, and draw the self to its most complete maturity. This takes a life time of effort and consistent, long term practice and dedication to spiritual values and ideals. It is not a matter of diving into the luminous ocean of light but of emerging from it with a new understanding that permeates and inspires all your human relationships. Such inspiration is a direct gift of Spirit, a manifestation of the Christ-heart through the abiding presence of Holy Wisdom and all her handmaidens, the virtues of a spiritual way of life. We surrender to beauty, to love, to the path of the heart, as an act of dedication to truth that leads us gently to the very precipice of self-annihilation that we may understand the immensity within which we dwell. We returned humbled, not exalted, inwardly surrendered, truly initiated, with our foot set on the path of our true spiritual work. To act as living examples of the illumined, to make no self-glorifying claims, and to serve all those who also seek to overcome their suffering and disconnected sorrows.

The joy in this process is threefold: first, in the personal awakening to Spirit, to the Christ-heart, to the mother of Wisdom, the Divine Sophia, the Regina Angelicum, the Hieros Gamos, following a chosen path. Second, in attaining actual illumination through spiritual discipline, communal practices, or the spontaneous gifts of Spirit, we are instilled with deep reverence and hope. Third, by bringing that illumination into every aspect of our daily life, into every relationship and into the very heart of our practice as an ongoing presence, we discover the spiritual currents that flow continuously drawing us deeper into the creative energies of Spirit as agents of change and transformation. In learning to share that inspiration non-aggressively, calmly, potently through dedicated commitment to spiritual values whose qualities illumine our relationships, we learn that we are not perfect, that we have limits, and that spiritual attainments do not equal perfection. At times the heart contracts, we draw inward, we seek solitude or feel the burden of our spiritual responsibilities. This is natural and often signifies a need for rest and renewal which is also an intrinsic part of the path. We must learn to let go, release expectations and seek to live in a natural rhythm that celebrates cycles of rest and renewal as well as cycles of creative effort and striving. Thus, we do not seek perfection, only the human norm that best exemplifies our full potential; we seek illumination in Spirit, the Christ-heart, but as limited, relative, fully human beings.

Unity
To maintain the unity of Spirit in the bonds of peace; to diversify, individuate, recombine, create, explore and expand with ever greater honor to the Whole. (3:9)

Giving honor to the Whole is accomplished by living in an exemplary manner, by embodying the principles of Spirit in a dedicated life of seeking, realization, and sharing with others. What becomes "ever greater" in this process is not the reality of Spirit but its active presence in the mind and heart of the seeker. That presence, that reality, is already fully present, at this very moment, fully actual, fully abundant with the grace of an overflowing plenitude whose creative energies are boundless. In honoring the wholeness, the fullness of all interactive relation between beings, our knowledge must continually expand by throwing off its limited preconditions, by releasing attachments, and by opening to an inner horizon of expanding awareness. This can only be accomplished in a mature, lasting sense through a full embodiment of that inner horizon as incarnate in an actual way of life, in a path that leads to spiritual realizations of the greater, expanding cosmos. It is said that the universe is expanding and this is true because inwardly we are opening to the fullness of all possible spiritual worlds. We are not collapsing into one-dimensional, exclusive ways of thinking but opening continually to increasingly diverse horizons, to the inter-dimensional relations between subtle planes and worlds. We embody those subtle planes and those alternative worlds are not in conflict when we open the spiritual centers of our awareness with love, valuing everything that contributes to a preservation of life, diversity, and meaningful, respectful human relations.

In this process, Spirit acts to enliven our understanding and our awareness becomes deeply rooted in the rich, abundant, earthy soil of bodily life. We are each a temple and this means that we honor the body, fully, and respect deeply the female capacity to embody the life-gift in the incarnation of soul within her womb. Her blood is sacred, her nurturing capacities, a profound and holy gift. The body, male or female, is a relative image of divine creation whose elemental components are all worthy of study, respect, and understanding.[125] There is no need to reject, abandon, or deny the body in the processes of spiritual

---
125. Hermetic Definitions 2: 1-6.

awakening. The gift of the body is a wonder; its complexity a reflection of stellar energies and earthborn evolutions. The expansion of awareness through the processes of spiritual development is incorporative, it takes into its own evolutions all the preformed stages of previous growth and honors every stage, every step of maturation. But we do not cling to that process, to the steps and stages, as though they were each the goal. We do not carry the ladder around on our backs or use it as a measure of the accomplishments of others or as means for climbing over the walls that others may built. Having walked the steps and having reached the higher platform on which we discover the temple that is our own body, we then enter the temple and worship the inner divine presence that gives the temple its luster and illumination.[126] The steps and stages are no longer the issue, what matters is an attitude of reverence, one that causes the fire of the heart to shine forth and merge with a higher light. Thus the body is revered as an image of divinity through which we may honor the very processes of life and creation.

In exploring the heights and depths of our multidimensional awareness, we come to a threshold, a liminal boundary, where inspired words, sacred symbols, certain musical sounds, celestial images, creative forms, and various relationships between astral and terrestrial events become charged with profound significance. It is as though everything were suddenly lifted to a new level of intensity where even slight events, a feather from a bird's wing, a drop of dew, a grain of sand, takes on whole new dimensions of meaning and signification. This is because awareness pervades all aspects of life and divinity is written into the very heart of every existent thing. Spirit surrounds and penetrates us, sustains our individual identity, and acts on our awareness to urge us to new degrees of insight and participation in Mystery. The Heart of Mystery in an inner unity that fully embraces all emergent forms from the most ancient and subtle to the most contemporary and material. The means for the perception of this unity is the heart-integrated-mind, the soulful being, open to a living cosmos of conscious, active, intentional others beyond counting or imagination. And this self-revealing cosmos contains powerful, tremendous beings whose elemental formations are of the most holy construction including the very soul of the planet we inhabit. As we move through the body into the various centers of awareness, we also open to a variety of worlds and beings whose coexistence reveals whole orders of evolution intimately connected to our own and yet, in many ways, autonomous and independent. There is unity in this diversity and emergent diversity in this unity.

In great Ur-Space of all possible worlds, in the primal architectonics

---

126. John 2: 21; 1 Corinthians 6: 19-20; Luke 11: 34-35.

of eternal creation, there is no limit to the ways in which worlds can be reconfigured. We are not bound by material form but material form is a reservoir of possible transformations. Primal matter is not a formless substance, but a conditioned and relative formation concealing an immense potential for energetic change. Like minute particles or multidimensional superstrings containing vast reservoirs of potential energy, it is only a matter of directing and focusing that energy for the purpose of species transformation. Just as the body is an energetic vehicle for increasing individual awareness, so too the earth is an energetic body for increasing collective awareness. This includes all interspecies relations and the emergence of subtle realms whose elemental forms are inseparable from the very fabric of cosmic existence. Like a butterfly that emerges from the cocoon spun by a wingless larva, so too humanity can transform into a far more spiritual creature whose body and home are barely recognizable by its larval form. These are the very transformations of the Hermetic path, symbolized by the Christ-heart opened to the New Jerusalem, a city of Peace, within which the sacred marriage is consummated, celebrated, and becomes the basis for a new holy child.[127] Every child participates in this rebirth of the soul as a vehicle for the evolution of new understanding and world insight. Every soul is a possible means for the awakening of the world and its transformation; every soul carries the very spark of creation within as a primal, creative energy of divine presence.

Our task is to diversify, combine, articulate in words, forms, songs, or in the metaphors and mathematics of science our individual insights, our creative exploration into the possibilities of alchemical change. In this process of expansion and contraction, in all the necessary stages and steps of awakening to Spirit, we become the makers of our own destiny. In maturity we become responsible for the future evolutions, for the consequences of our actions, for the fateful result of our doings and undoings.[128] There is no master plan, no inescapable result, no "father" who takes our responsibilities from us. In our collective becoming, we must choose among many paths which goals to pursue and if we will act with or without reverence for the tremendous gifts we have each been given. Following a spiritual path is a choice made to live according to the highest values that you would choose for future generations on this (or any) world. No one person can take responsibility for the consequences of all human decision making (or lack of same) and no one individual can represent the complexity of the whole. It is a species task to transform species awareness. It is a necessary collective activity of tens of thousands, of hundreds of thousands, choosing to enact and live according to patterns that will enable

---

127. Revelations 21: 2-4.
128. Lee Irwin, *Visionary Worlds* 168-176.

the birth of a new shared awareness less bound by individual eccentricity and more supportive of a healthy diversity of interests, skills, and contributions. We must each choose. We are on the cusp of a creative collective awakening, on the threshold of a magnitude, of a leap into a far more spiritualized world that can only be sustained by the conscious choice to live a more loving, wise, and interconnected life.

In this process of collective spiritual awakening, the bonds of peace are crucial. In order for there to be an intersection of worlds, or multiple dimensions of creative relations, there must also be a ground of peace that supports the emergence of new life in all its fragile, exploratory forms. Otherwise, even the collective awakening will be lost in the shadows of repressive fear, hate, bias and willful, stubborn prejudice. The old way was to fight in the name of one exclusive truth but the new way is to honor diversity, plurality, difference while making and creating peace. This peace springs from the deep wells of an inner unity that dissolves all form, all outer veils, all individuals, all collectivities into the dense heart of divine life that spills out of the illumined center of creation. A center that is everywhere, in every path, in every teaching that seeks to preserve life, uplift understanding, and to create a way that can be walked with joy in the company of loving others. Brothers and sisters, mothers and fathers, children of all ages, adults young and old, this is the time, now is the moment when we must choose to live according to our highest ideals. The Christ-heart is sounding its rhythms, the most Holy Wisdom is smiling her smile, the golden child has raised a finger that points at you. You are the center, you are the creator of life that seeks to reach beyond present fear and uncertainty, it is your heart that is a vessel of overflowing love. Open to your inner capacity to feel that love, to be a channel for healing, and to live an exemplary life.

You are not alone but in the company of a vast multitude of others who all want that love to overflow its bounds and pour itself like a living fire into the matter of creation that we may all be reborn in clarity and wisdom. We open to the inner unity whose diversity is infinite and whose pathways are like water poured down a mountain into uncountable streams, falls, and rivers nourishing a dry and thirsty multitude who all desire the freshest, purest water. Such are the waters of life, where we immerse our self in the pure presence of Spirit, lose ourselves in the currents of a greater ocean, and surrender to a vast plenitude that only asks us to honor fully the wholeness that guides us to actualize our inner potentials.[129] That water, that pure lustrous shimmer of Spirit's presence, baptizes us by lifting the veils and teaching us the path

---

129. Revelations 21: 6; 22: 17.

we may walk to fully honor the beauty of creation. The thirst for illumination is a guide, the waters of life are the living presence of Mystery satisfying the deepest of all desires, our seeking spiritual guidance, direction, and fulfillment. Each of us is a path, each of us a way that leads to possible enlightenment and spiritual awakening; we need only open our hearts with sincerity and passionate longing, to taste that most delightful joy, the kiss of the Beloved that opens before us an unimaginable intensity of desire whose fulfillment is complete union, a dissolving into an infinite embrace. May we find the means and ways to celebrate with others all the diversities of such awakening and in that process to honor always the greater fullness of the Whole. Sēlah!

Revelations
To seek revelations in what is small as well as what is large, in the subtle, correspondent, above, below, and in-between; in what gives life and in what takes it away. (3: 10)

Science is a creative process of revelation as well as art, music, poetry and social revolution when it is cultivated as intrinsic to a spiritual worldview. There is a scale to revelation that begins with a brief and poignant insight, a flash of intuition, or a hard sought realization and leads to higher order perceptions in which the very nature of our lived reality is transformed. There is no revelation without transformation. Revelations passed on in the form of sacred texts are only meaningful insofar as they provide guidelines and directions for transformation. Revelations are a basis for confirming a valued way of life at the same time as they are a challenge to that life to grow toward greater maturity and understanding. Revelations are circles connecting with other circles, forming new complex intersections of meaning and placing us on the cusp of emergent insights. They are rooted in the evolution of species, branch into many diverse limbs, and result in the emergence of whole new ways of thinking and acting. There is a profound difference between revelation and tradition; revelation is the emergence of new understanding based in experiential, psychic encounter. Tradition is the pattern and practice that is established to preserve that understanding in viable social forms. Revelations are part of the unfolding of human self-knowledge and discovery of the sacred; traditions are habitual codes which attempt to sustain primary values. Both are necessary and formative in the collective sense insofar as they promote peace and cooperation between traditions.

The primary energies of revelation are directed to the awakening of potential, in Spirit, for the preservation of the highest qualities of life, of ways to live that fully embody spiritual principles. The preservation of these qualities extends all the way down to the most minute life forms, to the very most microscopic, infinitesimal, minute particle of life, into its most subtle, energetic sub-processes of primal sentience. Everything that lives is valuable, everything that manifests life is an expression of the sacred origins of creation. The vast energies of creation, in Spirit, are the basis for the emergence of all that was, is, or will be, and this emergence is ongoing, periodic, cyclical, rhythmic, pulsating with all the phases and variances, the inherent chaos, natural to emergent life forms. And the study of these processes, of the most minute life forms to the greatest, is a revelatory exploration, a challenging journey into the unknown, unrecognized, unappreciated complexity of the Whole. Revelations, as spiritual intuitions that arise from concentrated regard on the most subtle aspects of creation, are the primary means by which we attain to a more mature view of the cosmos. But those revelations also reflect the emergent states of our shared consciousness, a partial light mixed with all the bias and sometimes fearful ignorance that keeps many bound to lesser visions and less mature knowing. In this circumstance, it is necessary to constantly reflect on our individual and shared state of development, seeking ways to move beyond the bound prejudices of inherited beliefs.

Revelation is not free, not unmixed with the biases of even the most receptive heart-mind; the soul is the medium of the influx of light whose colors reflect the health and well-being of inner life. The most lucid colors, the most translucent emanations, proceed from those whose soul is deeply rooted in a positive, loving concern and respect for the inherent value of every living being. It may be for animals, plants, marine life, winged creatures, microbes, or etheric formations larger than a galaxy; whatever harbors life, deserves our utmost respect, our deepest concern to understand. We do not stand in the path of a charging elephant, nor casually handle what is poisonous or dangerous; when we fully recognize the limits and vulnerability of our own boundaries, we take necessary precautions. Yet, in an emergent, revelatory cosmos of multiple beings, worlds, planes, and subtle forms, the Hermetic way is to seek empathic understanding (*verstehen*), to investigate the nature and origins, the worldliness and evolutionary directions, of all life forms. It is not the calling of every individual, but certainly it is a spiritual calling.[130] The investigations of all sciences, when carried out in the most humane and sensitive way, with utmost respect for life, can be a sacred path. What makes it sacred is that the seeker moves beyond their prejudice and bias into the

---

130. Ephesians 1: 17.

living heart of divinity and comes to see the interconnected wholeness, the Mystery of the entire creation in whatever is being studied. The revelatory process opens the mind to the inner reality of the subject under study because study is carried out in rightly-guided ethical and spiritual actions.

Revelation is an inward opening, an inner realization that connects to a larger cosmos, sometimes constructed by mythic beliefs or mental structures that seeks a context for understanding. Some revelations are deconstructive, they dismantle a previous worldview or belief; some are reconstructive, they reveal an unknown or unseen horizon of meaning. Most reflect the subtle and pervasive presence of the Mundus Imaginalis, the celestial world of visionary forms. In fewer instances, revelations may dissolve all form into the formless, creative energies of pure Spirit, in the inherent unity beyond visionary forms that pervades all awareness. Many sacred texts carry the imagery of the Mundus Imaginalis, the stark, potent, awesome forms of revelatory, visionary manifestations, be they angels, archangels, devas, asuras, celestial bodhisattvas, Taoist *hsien*, Japanese *kami*, or any of a host of profound, etheric beings. Or, on the Hermetic Christian path, the beloved Mother and Child, the Regina Angelicum, the Holy Wisdom, the Shekinah, the Seraphim and Cherubim, the Christ and Mary Magdalene as ancient, archetypal visionary forms of the multilayered heavenly realms. Also there are all the intermediary beings, the earth and water spirits, the elementals, the Sidhe, the little people, the night riders, the animal familiars, the spirits of the land, the sacred powers of the directions, of the mountains, the plains, the forests, the lakes, rivers, seas, skies, and winds which may become means for spiritual opening to the Visionary Realms. These visionary worlds open into the Mundus Imaginalis through the explicit media of each spiritual tradition as a revelatory basis for the awakening of inner potential.

The land, the earth herself, is also a basis for such revelation. What is above is also below and what is without is also within. The World-Soul is the emerging, soulful, collective identity of all the species of this planetary home, united through a transpersonal horizon of profound spiritual magnitude. The true emergence of the World-Soul as a conscious reflection of collective self-awareness, denying no species its place, reverencing all life, is a human spiritual event of greatest importance. It is the opening of the wisdom eye to the value and significance of all created life, to the wonder and beauty of an inherited world shared with a vast diversity of living creatures. It is also an opening into the cosmos, an awakening to a diversity of other worlds and life forms, a realization of a vast interconnected network of spiritual relations in which visionary forms provide significant intentionality for transformation. In this awakening, it becomes clear that the interconnected net of relations extends far beyond the visible, material world into the most subtle realms, into far distant places whose familiarity is part of much greater evolutionary patterns. The In-Between becomes filled with a plenitude of cosmic imagery and subtle planes born and sustained in Ur-Space through the energetic media of Spirit and Mystery. The meaning and purpose of this imagery is the awakening of souls, the perpetuation of emergent consciousness, and the expressive continuation of creation as ongoing and infinite. In-Between becomes the vast network of relationships that extends to the primal beginnings of multiple worlds and reaches to the most emergent forms of new life even now awakening on the most distant proto-world.

Revelation is not simply from Above, but also from Below; it is the marriage of Earth with Heaven, the creative balance of dark and light, the union of the sacred marriage that fully respects the material media of creation as a necessary means for emergence.[131] We do not seek to abandon our incarnate state, but to fulfill the incarnation with the joy of illumined understanding as co-creators. In-Between is a constant ferment as Spirit weaves uncountable energies into creative, visionary intersections of the Below and Above, in the correspondent matrix of unending transformations. And each of us is a center in this process, a living being whose intentional concerns, dreams, hopes, and desires act to direct the creative energies through spiritual commitments, through dedication to a valued, harmonious way of life. On the Hermetic path, we walk with an inner concern to truly know Spirit, to be one with the creative process, to become vessels for the expression of illumined understanding.

The Christ-heart is a source of strength, love, and healing and these three potencies act as a magnetic center for a creative transformation of human relations. As a center of awareness, the Christ-heart is at the intersection of life and death, at the balance point where opposites meet and dissolve in the potent energies of love. This love is not created but given by Spirit as a primal media of new awakenings, of entering into the shared world of courageous actions, of measures taken to restore balance and integrity. The intersection of the Above and Below is found in the human heart, on the spiritual path, where inspiration leads to creative action and commitment leads to exemplary living.

What gives life, is a deep respect and reverence for Spirit as the creative source of inspired living; what take life away, is living in a contracted, cynical, fearful state of non-belief. Every person is capable of revelation, it is not simply for the elite nor is it circumscribed by fixed conditions or

---

131. Corpus Hermeticum 1: 14-15.

requirements. Revelations come through a soulful way of life that opens the heart to the Whole, that seeks sacred knowledge in living a dedicated life of spiritual commitment. The positive values, the ideals of spiritual life, must be embodied, become evident in a way of life that proceeds in accordance with the strengths and gifts of the individual. It is not simply a matter of conformity to collective ethics or norms, but an inner awakening that leads the heart and mind to truly reverence life, others, nature, creation, and the cosmos as media for spiritual illumination. On the Hermetic path, we cultivate mind and heart in order to open to Spirit, to creative revelations that confirm a principled, balanced way of life. The responsibility of the Hermetic path lies in the heart of each individual, to fathom the way, to live according to its highest standards, and to act with love and courage in all circumstances. The Christ-heart does not turn back and it does not push ahead; it centers on Spirit, on Mystery, on the illumined presence that guides, on inner revelations meant to heal and bring peace. We are each a source of revelation when we live truly, according to our highest spiritual values. And when we slip or fall, we do not linger on failure or wounds. We get up and walk forward in humility, taking to heart the lessons learned, and accepting our imperfections without denying our potential for growth and maturity.

Beyond

To never say "I am God" for God's Mystery is within every being and comes on "clouds of glory" infinite with beauty, grace, and that which is Beyond knowing. (3:11)

We are all children of God, without exception. Every living creature is a work of Spirit woven out of creative energies whose manifestations are billions and millions of human years in the making. This making and unmaking works through the porous materiality of form in processes of evolutionary transformation, including our own bodies, minds, hearts, and souls. We are inseparable from the Mystery, from the inherent god-nature that enlivens and infuses the entire multicosmos. Yet, that god-nature exceeds the immediacy of our perceptions, transcends our limited physical-mental horizons, and harbors within Itself uncountable other life forms whose history and evolutionary cycles far surpass our present human conditions. We may, through the right application of spiritual principles in the shaping and living of our lives, open our horizons to a greater fullness of understanding. We may attain to illumination and a true *gnosis* through which we can perceive directly the holiness and sacred dimensions of Spirit. We may receive the gifts of Spirit with humility as vessels for the pouring forth of many teachings and directions for the self-development of others. We may receive in the depths of being, a true acknowledgement of the inseparability of God-soul-Spirit as a divine trinity in which the Christ-heart resonates within us the presence of sacred love and healing joy. We may be extinguished in ecstasy, be one with the One, annihilated in divinity as a drop of water in the oceans of energetic creation. But we are not gods, we do not become god, and we are no more than vessels for the creative expressions of Spirit.

You have heard it said that there are "manifestations" whose task it is to reveal teachings; but I say, every teacher is a student, and every teaching is a stage toward direct knowledge of the heart. In this process, teachers are like stones in a river, one crosses over by stepping lightly on each stone that leads to the other side. We do not carry the stones with us but leave them as markers for the stepping of others. All these stone are necessary, each has a place that leads yet another step closer to the other side on which teachers are no longer necessary, for there Spirit becomes your guide and Mystery your soulful ground. People fear taking responsibility for their own spiritual development, they prefer all too often, to give over their thoughts and beliefs to the rule of the Other. But Spirit calls you back to your own inmost self and seeks to revive in your inmost will a desire for full responsibility in all your actions, thoughts, words, and dreams. Teachers are not absolute nor omnipotent, that is an imagining of less mature thought in which power is construed as a sign of dominion, lordship, not by wisdom or compassion or love. In love, in the Christ-heart, there is no need for dominion, no need for an absolute and inflexible standard by which others are either elected or condemned. On the path of the Hermetic Christ, we do not seek lordship nor absolute teachers, but a compassionate, mature heart that understands the relative value of every teacher, teaching, and path. In this path, Christ becomes a vessel of Spirit, a means for the transformation of others, and an example of suffering, determination, and hope.

Christ is not absolute and his teachings are not absolute; they are relative to the awakened heart in which Mystery and Spirit act to inspire a deep and abiding wisdom. In the Christ-heart, in the anointed soul, there is no condemnation, no judgment that determines forever, the soul-life of those dedicated to alternative spiritual paths. In the Christ-spirit, we rejoice in the multitude of teachings, in the diversity of paths and in the promise that Spirit is the highest guide. We recognize the pathways leading to illumined seeing as reflections of an archetypal, visionary process of spiritual awakening whose intentions are peaceable, communally healthy, diverse in individual application, and a support for a multitude of others. The way of the Hermetic Christ is wide, multilayered, diverse in application and yet, demanding and disciplined in determining a specific practice. The Cup of Offering is held out to all those who seek illumination, whatever path they follow, whatever tradition they honor. The doors of the temple are not closed but open to all spiritual seekers, the altar is adorned in the symbols of the *Heiros Gamos*, of the spiritual union of male and female, and the Divine Sophia and Father of Lights bless that altar through the angels, archangels, powers and presences of all creation. And Mystery abides beyond form and imagery as the primal source for all of Spirit's weaving. But no teacher is God, and no teaching, final or complete. Yeshu'a, as the son of god, is a living memory and a living presence, an actualized being of higher magnitude who manifest the Christ-spirit principle. But we are all sons and daughters of God.

As an avatar or incarnation of Mystery and Spirit, the Christ-spirit lives on in a multitude of world lines expressing creative evolution in and through the transparent spheres of the Mundus Imaginalis. And that Christ-presence has been embodied many times in the spiritual history of humanity through incarnations in the great saints, martyrs, mystics, spiritual revolutionaries, male and female, and in a diversity of spiritual teachers in all branches of the history of the Christian faith, as well as in certain teachers more marginal to institutional communities. These incarnations of the Christ-spirit, in the forms of actual historical individuals, include many esoteric schools whose followers embraced the Christ as a central presence in their spiritual teachings. The "true" teachings are not a codified body of institutional norms and required beliefs, but the living reality of Christ in the loving heart. And this reality has no boundaries determined by external norms of conformity or obedience to human authority or by the pressures and obligations of communal membership. The incarnation of the Christ-spirit occurs in every act of love, in giving to others without thoughts of reward, in sharing and honoring the struggles, sorrows, pains, and joys of those immersed in worldly cares and concerns. The incarnations of the Christ-spirit are many, not few, found on the margins of human life as well as at the center. We are all sons and daughters of God and we are all seeking guidance and inner direction for drawing forth the beauty and holiness of Spirit that dwells within us.

The coming of Spirit is like the "clouds of glory" promised in the return of Christ and these clouds have come, like those of the transfiguration, descending on each person in the form of visionary gifts of Spirit.[132] This

---

132. Mark 13: 26.

"coming" is part of the promise of the manifestations of Spirit in the hearts of those who cultivate loving kindness and seek the healing and well-being of others. Whoever hears the knock at the door, receiving the Groom with welcome and greetings of joy, opens the heart to his coming, enters that glory as a gift of Spirit.[133] Such is the baptism of Spirit, a beauty and grace to all those who receive it without shame or guilt, opening the heart to a cleansing rebirth. The beauty is in its immeasurable depth, the grace, its giving each heart the appropriate measure of its depth. As vessels, we can be filled to overflowing; we can receive inwardly the full content of our worth, the true capacity of our soul's attainments and be adorned in that process. In that overflowing presence we discover the relative measure of our wisdom, our capacities, our limits and boundaries, even as Spirit carries us across to the other side. The Mystery surrounds us with its fullness and boundless expanse, penetrates our soulful heart and lifts the mind to a vast horizon of possible becomings. In returning from this visionary presence to the living moment of embodied life, we see clearly the unknowability of the Source. We see how vastly we are transcended in that presence even while we participate fully in its embodied forms. We feel the nurturance, the abiding guardianship of Spirit, as it hovers over us, wings sheltering us from the permeable limits of our human understanding.

What is beyond knowing is the fullness and activity of Spirit as it acts to transcribe the visionary worlds of embodied life into the potential manifestations of Mystery. What is beyond knowing is the fullness of Mystery as it abides in the infinite expanse of all created worlds, as it sustains the reservoir of its inner potentials, and as it overflows in the massive architectures of all space-time and becoming. In the vastness of Mystery, in the holy depthless potential for life and creation, the actions of humanity reflect only one small world among uncountable others. In our species maturation we will come to the realization that all life is holy and that we are only one participant in a much greater pattern of on-going evolution and cosmic transformation. Like the Divine Sophia who sought her own origins in the depths of the Forefather, and who was restrained by limits, so too are we restrained, not by outward force or control, but through an inner realization of the depthless Mystery intrinsic to our relative and limited wisdom and abilities. Yet we may know God, may enter the Mystery, be blessed by Spirit, behold the visionary gifts, receive the blessings of a multitude of souls, and attain to a lasting illumination. Our path is not limited by the relative maturity of our soul, but by the simple fact of our conditional, embodied life as discrete, individual beings. As the soul opens, expands into the Mystery, receives the blessing accorded by Spirit, and acts

---

133. Revelations 3: 20.

with integrity and love in all human relations, then we may see clearly the vaster whole in which all paths unite.

There are many "sons and daughters" of God, of Mystery and Spirit, who have acquired their realizations through dedicated lives of inner discipline and healing works. They follow many diverse paths and their teachers are well loved and honored; this is appropriate and correct. But the greatest teacher is Spirit and the Christ-heart manifests as a gift of Spirit working through a diversity of circumstances and individuals to make us ever more keenly aware of that bright, inward presence. Even the most enlightened teacher cannot walk your path for you nor give you the gifts that Spirit pours out freely to all who seek Her guidance. As the Mother of Lights, Spirit burns with all the primordial brilliance of the first creation and like a flame carried to a candle, provides the spark that lights the marrow of the soul from within. Teachers may come and go, but Spirit abides, enduring and eternal, now and always. We do not become gods in awakening to Spirit, in becoming instruments of transformation, nor do we need to claim any title or rank or mark of attainment. In the lifetime of any teacher, they need be nothing more than a channel for the instrumental awakening of others through any multitude of skillful means. This is true for Christ and all his followers; what matters is a loving heart, a mature, insightful wisdom, and a willingness to abide in Spirit as the means for co-creation and communal peace.

What is beyond knowing is the Mystery of what each of us has to offer through the gifts of Spirit; we discover these gifts by throwing off constrictions of the heart. In opening our heart to Spirit, we become participant in Mystery and thereby, manifest those qualities best suited to our individual nature. We must desire that transformation without imbalance or excess and without fearful clinging to older ways of thought or belief. We must embrace courage and inner determination as guidelines to authentic living in Spirit. We must open inwardly to inspirations and the up-flowing presence that will open the horizons of intuition and insight. We must live simply, without pretenses; calmly centered in the subtle, transparent veils of Spirit's making. In prayerful, meditative reflections, we need only recognize the temple of the body and honor the heart's place as a containing the ember of a divine fire. We breathe deeply and the embers ignite, we sing or chant, and they burst into flame, we love others with mature joy and the light of that flame sheds a holy radiance. We become sons and daughters of the presence, we become children of the Holy Mother, communally linked by a shared wealth of practices and disciplines. We become inheritors of a higher wisdom within the Father whose teachings bless us with visionary participation in the celestial dance of immortal spirits.

In this way, we each become teachers and students; in this way, we each receive appropriate guidance. May Spirit bless our seeking and help us to attain the fulfillment of our potential, now and in every life to come. So it is and so it will become. Amen.

The Return

To know God-in-Christ is a great gift and grace; but only if that knowledge returns to the world sure, serene, dedicated to lasting harmony and peace. (3:12)

Entering into Spirit, into Mystery, is a journey that brings us into ever deeper connection and relationship with others. This connection is not based on social forms, customs, or outward appearances. It is based on an inner awakening that results in a direct perception of psychic and soulful relations with others — human, animal, plant, the very stones and minerals whose elemental structures all resonate with the vibrant harmonies of Spirit. In a "living cosmos" the presence and actions of Spirit, through the mutual penetration of uncountable creative energies, result in a deep and abiding expression of the sentience and fullness of Mystery. In Mystery, there are unfathomable depths whose actualization of potential proceeds through the manifesting of uncountable beings, worlds, and subtle planes. As we journey into these depths, we become ever-more aware of the inseparability of the individual from the Whole and the actualization of the Whole through the individual. The part does not equal the Whole, but the part gives the Whole its nuances, diversity, and differentiations. And individuals join together in the formation of community and communities form positive connections, webs of potential relations, for the evolution of higher species awareness. Every individual who dedicates him or herself to the embodiment of Spirit through the actualization of higher values contributes to the evolution of species, and every soulful illumination lights the world through a vast network of spiritual relations. The illumined heart is such a beacon, a radiant clarity of light carried within a spreading wave of love whose origin is Spirit.

When I speak of "knowing" God-in-Christ, I am speaking not of faith, or belief, or intellectual knowledge; I am speaking of the illuminations of heart and mind found through direct *gnosis*. This "knowledge" proceeds from Spirit as a gift responsive to human efforts, to a dedicated heart that seeks to know the inmost living presence.[134] This knowing is an illumination because it opens

---

134. 1 Corinthians 12: 8-11.

us to the magnitude and fullness of the Mystery, in degrees according to our abilities and capacity, and results in a transformation of our understanding. This awakening is deep and carries the balanced and healthy soul to its utmost origins in Spirit. It can carry us far beyond the everyday persona, into the vastness of the Highest Self, to the Para-Atman, to the *Paramaartha-satya*, the ultimate enlightened realization wherein no individual can be found and which no written words adequately express. Between this highest transpersonal realization and the ordinary persona, there exists innumerable degrees of subtle realizations, ranging through a plurality of visionary worlds and resulting in a diversity of spiritual teachings. The goal is not "ultimate enlightened realization" because we must each rise to that potential that best reflects our inner capacity, our contribution to the emergence of divine potential. The "ultimate enlightened realization" is really only a unique attainment that dissolves the world into its primal unitary fullness; it is a relative contribution, not the goal of the path, not a true absolute as much as an ultimate experience.

The world is not *maya* or illusion; it is not a trap or a descent; it is not a prison, a carnal house, nor a lower order of existence, nor is it strictly, a realm of suffering. This world is a manifestation of Spirit, a place of holy creation, like all worlds and places, and we as human beings are an embodiment of Spirit, down to the most minute, subtle particle of our being. In a "living cosmos" we live as a manifestation of the long, immeasurable cycles of creation, in the patient, careful, delicate weaving meant to sustain and promote life in all its variety and differences. On the path of the Hermetic Christ, we celebrate creation as the greater good, as the primal activity of Spirit, drawing forth the inner capacities of Mystery to create and sustain a world with all its multitude of species, soulful life-forms, and spirit energies beyond measure. Life, all life, is holy. The earth, the moon, the planets, the suns, stars, galaxies, and all the macroforms of heaven, are holy. Life is precious, incarnating in human form, a sacred event, nourishing and protecting others life forms, a spiritual calling. The world is a place of great beauty, of wonder and power and magnificent creatures; it is a joyful garden that we have not valued because of our own species arrogance. And the highest form of this arrogance is to reject the world, to see as entrapment, to refuse to open the heart to the responsibilities of creation and becoming. Human insights are relative to this embodiment process; ultimate, transpersonal immersions are not the basis by which the value of the incarnate world is determined. The great creative value of incarnation is the necessary creative process of manifestation, actualization, and existential realization of possibility.

Meditations on Christ

The greatest calling is to reverence life in all its forms and to value above personal existence, the processes of on-going creation. In order to truly accomplish this reverence, it is necessary to open the heart to the primal sources of life, to the spiritual wells from which we draw forth the gift of the pure life waters of Spirit. Whatever path you walk, let it be one that honors life, accepts responsibility for its preservation, and teaches you to live respectfully, with reverence for the gifts of life in each being. The body is the altar and the world is a temple; the body is the tongue and the world is the bell. Let that tongue speak with the inspiration of Spirit, resounding in the world as a harmonious, clarion call to love, honor, and coexist in peace. Let it not be a clanging of absolutes, a cacophony of competitive claims, a boastful denial of the world or a proud disavowal of the value of suffering and sacrifice. Do not harp on the denial of the world or body; celebrate instead, its beauty, complexity, and interrelated connectivity to the living, breathing Whole. Spirit is breath; Mystery is life; incarnation, a tremendous gift. Do not let the poverty of your imagination bind you to a narrow material world of ascetic denials; seek instead, an inner gratitude for this opportunity to live, breathe, feel and sense the living energies of creation from top to bottom, in all their beauties, mysteries, and far-reaching connections.

To live in harmony and peace means to embody in the depths of your being, that peace that passes understanding, that harmony that rises from a heart dedicated to deep and powerful loving relations.[135] To know God-in-Christ means to have received the "anointment" of Spirit, to have awakened the Christ-heart, the heart bathed in Spirit and fully appreciative of the gift of life and all its wonders and shared relations. It means to honor woman with all your being as the mother of life, as the vessel of living Spirit whose children are her exemplary teachings, to honor her innumerable ways of living, her psychic gifts, her visionary embodiment and creative inspirational, higher wisdom.[136] It means to honor all children as the blossoming of soul-life in the garden of the world and to give them the love, care, and guidance that will best preserve their reverence and respect for the world and all its living creatures. It means to honor the man, his strengths and weaknesses as expressions of his gradual coming-into-being, his intellectual capacities, his creative genius as expressions of Spirit, his loving concerns as an embodiment of the Christ-heart. Serenity and dedication are marks of a disciplined soul, male and female; joy and love signs of an illumined heart; ecstasy and transcendence, a mark of Mystery; humility, patience, and wisdom, a consequence of maturity. We must seek maturity, though our chosen pathways, for the sake of all children, all creatures, all life

---
135. Philippians 4: 7.
136. James 3: 17-18; 2 John 1-2.

in order to act with intelligence and foresight for its preservation.

In dedication to harmony, by living peacefully with great integrity and creative purpose, we create the foundation for future well-being. To know God-in-Christ is only one way, one path, one possible teaching resonant with a multitude of other paths and teachings. There is no exclusivity in Spirit because Spirit pours itself out into the heart and soul of every life, into the recesses of all creative expressions and acts to amplify those conditions that best promote a reverent, energized, affirmation of life. Every path that honors life and reverences its diversity and differences, is a source of teaching. The Christ-heart has many forms and the "anointments" of Spirit flow through all races, cultures, times, and peoples, Christian or not. The gift and grace of the knowledge of God-in-Christ carries us beyond Christ, beyond the anointments of Spirit and into the very heart of Mystery, to the God-Presence indwelling in every soul, every life form. Such knowledge is a direct seeing, without intermediaries, beyond all visionary forms, beyond angels, archangels, spirit-guides, teachers, and illumined or enlightened others. It is a direct entry into Mystery that dissolves all external forms, dissipates all visionary appearances, and results in the unveiling of the inmost essence of divinity. In this Unity, there is no second, no other, no distinctions, no individual self; there is only the Mystery, the holy, vast, all-expanse of an unending depth of luminous, living potential whose fullness is the source of all creation.

We return from such knowing, this deep *gnosis*, with a burning reverence for all-that-is, with a profound gratitude for the gift of life, and with a will to honor the creation as a holy act of love. We come wearing the robes of our own history and past as outer garments, as external signs of a particular time, place, incarnation. But inwardly, we have walked in the Greater Mystery, we have seen how easily our outer robes are dissolved, how the naked soul stands in lesser light and how it becomes transparent, translucent, transcended in that greater Light whose bounty has no end. How holy this creation! How profound and deep! How wonderful the gift of life! We return humbled by this knowledge, seeing how much it outstrips the lesser configurations of incarnate life while simultaneously acting in every way to preserve and nourish those incarnations. I praise Thee from the depths of my heart, most Holy Spirit, most high Mystery, most unknown, awesome God. My words are like doves released from the captivity of my ignorance, and I beg them to fly upward to Thee, that you may hear even the slightest cry for all those who suffer and grant them healing, illumination, and light. How mysterious are Your ways, how unfathomable and deep, the depths from which we come, how wondrous the infinite oceans of creation. Show us the pathways that lead to honor in all the ways of this holy creation; show us the songs and dances, the celebrations that will demonstrate our devotion and reverence for life. Grant us the inward peace and serenity to live without harming others, to love without possessiveness, and to release into Spirit's care, the fullness of our future becoming. Praise be to Thee, Oh Mystery, Oh Life! Amen.

Athanasia

THE ETERNAL: ONE TRUE LIFE

"Then he showed me the river of the Waters of Life, bright as crystal, flowing from the Throne of God . . . also on either side of the river, the Tree of Life, with its twelve kinds of fruit, yielding its fruit each month. And the leaves of the Tree were for the healing of the nations."

Revelations 22: 1-2

The Eternal

There is only One Life, eternal and everlasting; the same today, tomorrow, and forever. (4:1)[137]

It is the same because it is a shared process: creative, evolving, transforming, undergoing the psychic and spiritual initiations of continued cycles of growth, development, decline and further becoming. Amid these creative processes, we seek to know the qualities that make these transformations possible, the ground that cannot be measured, the substance that has no form. The One Life is a life dedicated to spiritual growth and inner transformations expressed in relationships that flourish with love, beauty, and the creative tensions of our mutual self-other discovery. Awakening to Spirit, we must each follow the call that leads us toward an inner opening, an unfolding of closed perceptions, a shaking out of our wings, a moistening to new birth and light. The One Life is the life of Spirit as it manifests in billions of life-forms, as it flows out into community, drawing us together with like-minded others in order to create visionary worlds whose contents intersect creatively with the visionary worlds of others. The One Life, the unitary ground, requires us to lay down our dogmatic bias, our exclusivity, our denial of differences, and inspires us to cultivate a deep and abiding receptivity to the creative, non-harmful worlds of others. If those worlds are harmful, prejudicial, violent, discriminatory, then we must learn to embody the principles of a spiritual path that can sustain life in the face of disagreement and coarse censure. These principles are rooted in creative nonviolence, branch out into many diverse teachings, and their fruit is a non-exclusive wisdom whose virtues cannot be shaken by aggressive or discriminatory denials.

What we must do is affirm life, its value, its uniqueness, its spiritual origins, its causal intentions that give rise to cooperative, mutually respectful ways of living. The "one true life" has little to do with doctrines or systems of belief, but much to do with the quality of life we live and the spiritual values we embody in our relationships with others. To live truly means to live honestly, with a deep reverence for all living creatures, and a respect for the mutual differences that make co-evolution possible. Without differences, there is no development, no search for authenticity, no stimulus to move beyond the stasis of a particular realization. Spirit acts in us constantly to make us more responsive, more sensitive to those differences in defining our own perspectives, our own unique evolute within being. If we follow a particular path, the way of the Hermetic Christ, this is not an absolute, nor a restrictive "one-way" see-

---

137. John 4: 13-14.

ing or knowing, but a principled way of life that seeks to embody and manifest the Christ-spirit, the Christ-heart, the presence of the divine Sophia, the Holy Wisdom. And this wisdom is non-exclusive, respectful of differences, valuing the integrity and subtly of other spiritual paths, teachings, and illuminations. This is the "joyful wisdom" that finds its deepest resonance in Mystery, in the initiatic presence of the most holy light, in the overflowing abundance of all spirit-centered teachings and pathways.

The Christ heart is not narrow or exclusive, but open, loving, self-emptying, embracing difference with undiminished desire for the transformation of all. The path of the Hermetic Christ is one that leads to the center of the Hermetic World Mandala, to the great Sun-Christ, the radiant luminous being whose energies and qualities pour forth without resistance to all beings, all created worlds. When we follow that path inwardly, toward the center, through the eye of wisdom into the matrix of light, we pass through that light into the holy immeasurable Mystery, then we see that forms and outward appearances, external teachings, differences, are not the measure by which we recognize the value of another path. We must look to the heart, to the inner luminescence of soul, to the dissolving currents of Spirit purifying awareness and conjoining it within the communion of all holy saints. The communion of saints is not a communion of only one faith or path or teaching, it is a communion within Spirit that unites each person with the illumined teachers of every faith, every path, every holy tradition of self-surrendered beings. These teachers and illumined ones may come from any path, traditional or non-traditional, orthodox, pagan, indigenous, simple or complex, male, female, or child. Or they may represent the ethereal worlds, the subtle planes, the non-embodied forms of the archetypal teachers, the masters, guides, nature spirits, and luminaries of the many layered visionary heavens. And what they share is currents of love, compassion, and wisdom within a greater Whole whose boundaries remain deep beyond fathoming.

This greater holy life is the "same today, tomorrow and forever" because the timely and lineal progressions of observable evolution and human "history" are only a slight part of much greater cycles of transformation that are being carried out on multiple worlds through the guidance and nurturance of Spirit. The "same" means "in the on-going processes of transformation," participant in the eons long evolutions of mind, heart, and soul, fully active and engaged in the exploration of inner potential. We are all inseparably part of the same becoming, the same shared, co-evolutionary life of Spirit working through diverse, visionary worlds in cultivating an inward turning out, an assimilation of the world through a blossoming forth of many radiant flowers.

The rich fragrances of these blossoms, their diverse colors and forms, however great or small, are all inseparable from the one life, the pervasive presence of Spirit. What is not the same is the structure and form, the actual pathways, the unique insights and the articulate teachings that sketch out a variety of spiritual directions. These are forms or patterns that emerge out of the unified warp and weft of all space and all time, out of the union of all that is inner with all that is outer, all that is above with all that is below. The blossoming forth of one tiny, unique flower, of one small roseate circle of integrated petals, is the rare, the precious individual expression of the one great life.

This life is also "eternal and ever-lasting" because it cannot be reduced to any particular manifestation, nor to any specific individual, time, or place. If Spirit fills the vessel, if the cup overflows, and the joy manifests its particular abundance or qualities, still Spirit's depths cannot be plumbed. The boundaries of Mystery are the one we create in giving articulation to inspiration, in expressing the illumined horizon whose measure exceeds our grasp. Thus, words that are written, spoken, or silently given, ride the edge of an immeasurable wave whose magnetic energies carry those words, give them depth, and then, pass them on into the vaster, inexpressible life. What a joy it is to know that words can never contain the reality that gives those words their inspiration! How wonderful to ride the wave and know, even for a moment, its greater, undeniable fullness. Thus in the context of relative expression, we can see the limitless, the depthless deep, Bythos, whose active creations are a woven net in the midst of Mystery.[138] The eternal within these relative processes of world making and unmaking, in the soulful life of creatures, is a qualitative presence, a felt reality whose enduring characteristic is to open a horizon within time without limits. All times are relative, all spaces are relative, all beings are relative, all teachings are relative, all holy manifestations relative in the face of enduring presence, in the face of a vaster, greater Mystery.

The holiness of Mystery lies in its capacity to evoke awe as we awaken to our relative, dependent, conditional life; to evoke ecstasy as we shed the outer layers of socialized learning, shed the garments of denial and doubt, rid ourselves of fear, of anger, lust, and greed; to evoke joy as we fully awaken to a presence whose alchemical action is to dissolve all structure, form and clinging; and to evoke peace as we realize our place, our union with others, our wholeness in the Whole.[139] The Christ-spirit in this process is a focal image, a radiant heart within a body that no longer acts as an impediment but becomes a center of awakening. The golden-white light of Spirit illumines the Christ-heart, filling it with a presence whose action in the world is a miraculous gift

---
138. 1 Corinthians 2: 9-10.
139. Bhagavad Gita 16: 21-23.

seeking only to open the hearts of others. Eternal life is not found after death, nor in heaven, nor in rewards for those whose goodness outweighs their faults, mistakes, or inadequacies. The true eternal life is all around us, right here, this moment, utterly present, completely part of the process by which we become true sons and daughters of divinity, true vessels of light. It is the source which gives us life, breath, understanding, and awe in the face of our collective encounters. Eternal life is the ever-living presence that makes this life possible and which abides deep within each of us, only awaiting the ascent of our will to guide us toward its actualization. Eternal life is the transcendent horizon that dissolves individual consciousness, absorbs the soul, transfixes awareness, and opens the visionary medium to its fullest, most expressive expanse.

This life is "ever-lasting" because it is not determined by time, nor the movements of worlds, the orbits of planets, stars, galactic cycles, macrocosmic movements, nor the backward flowing particles of times long ago or yet to come. It is ever-lasting because the temporal orders are only lesser cycles within its own timeless present. Teachings may come and go, teachers and paths as well, but Spirit endures, Mystery abides, and eternity is the immeasurable mark of its presence. Yet, these manifestations are works of Spirit; these worlds, jewels most valuable and rare; life, the unimaginable inner joy of creation. We do not seek to escape time or to become eternal. But we do seek to know the Mystery, to experience directly the ever-lasting, to dissolve the structure and form into its pure matrices of being, into its essential qualities within Spirit. This is the wonder of the Christ-spirit, descending into the embodiment of everything living, becoming fully human, breathing, feelings, thinking, desiring, contemplating the limits and possibilities of flesh and then awakening in metamorphosis, in transformation, flowering in an inner alchemy of luminous wisdom. Opening our minds, hearts, and souls, we can see the eternal now, within us, within the grain of sand, within the eye of a suffering other, within the most transient, momentary phenomena. We cross over, through the temporal barriers of an imposed order, into the timeless and enduring *Pleroma*, a surrounding atemporal Fullness of quickening insight, a knowing born of love through fading timeliness.[140]

In this open, unhindered view, in the Pleroma of the first fullness, the enduring ever-present fullness, space expands into infinite depths, and time dissolves into momentary expressions. Yet, in the creative processes the timely manifestation endures, implicated and implicit within the continuity of the All, within the Wholeness that preserves its own activities as seeds for future sowing. We are not eternal, we are not ever-lasting, but we are inseparable

---

140. Ephesians 3: 19.

from eternal and ever-lasting Spirit within which all becoming is retained, remembered, preserved as intrinsic to the greater activities of creation. There is no separation between time and timelessness, between the perishable and the eternal; those are distinction made before the visionary horizon opens its wonders. In the ordinary contracted state, we live surrounded by death images, the fear of dying, the isolated state of material doctrines whose authors cannot see beyond the physical contours of bodily life. But when the eyes of the soul are opened, when the heart receives the grace of Spirit, when the mind attains illumination, then the death images are dissolved, the contracted mental universe opens, and the wings of the heart are no longer broken. Then, it is possible to fly forth into a supra-cosmos of emergent becoming, absorbed into the expansive horizon of the timeless life, into the eternal, into the ever-lasting. This is call, a sounding of the waters whose bottom cannot be seen but whose depths can be known. Through cycles of death and rebirth, through multiple incarnations, the soul grows, learns, contracts, relearns and passes through the In-Between to better comprehend the complexity of the Whole. Reincarnation is an inseparable, natural feature of this process.

What is the same today, tomorrow, and forever, is the undying activity of Spirit in the making and unmaking of this world. The One Life is the life of every living creature, the shared reality of living within a plenticosm of diverse life forms, each with unique histories and trajectories on the cyclical paths of becoming. The true life is the life dedicated to realizing the gifts of Spirit in exploring life and its possibilities for maintaining a healthy, balanced world of mutually respectful beings. Whatever path a seeker follows, whatever truths they hold as real and enduring, are born of Spirit and nurtured in the depths of Mystery as yet one more possibility in the woven fabric of creation. Follow the vibrant strands that link you to others, that open you to love, to sharing, to healing, compassion, goodness, and creative self-expression. Honor those gifts in others, and encourage them, nurture them, inspire them to do the same. Live as one who bears a gift, a precious, valuable, life preserving gift, one that can only be given by not hanging on, by not grasping or demanding, by not pushing forward and by not holding back. Give that gift freely to all who receive it, honor its return, and nourish the consequence of its actions on the souls of every seeker. Such is the pearl of great value, the gift of life, life rich in Spirit, overflowing, and abundant with the grace of presence.[141]

---

141. Matthew 13: 45.

Unbound

To know there is Eternal Life, now, in the present, in the past and in the future; life unbound by space, time, matter, or form. (4:2)

Eternal life is an overflowing fountain, a spring whose pure water is lucid, transparent, subtle, and life-giving. The cup we hold to drink this water, neither blood nor wine, is a vessel of pure silver-white rimmed with gold. The silver is the softer, shaded lunar element, gold, the solar light by which all worlds are lit, illumined at the edge, in dawn and twilight. In the cup, the "waters of life" shimmer with the energies of Spirit consecrated by the prayers and blessing we offer from the heart, opening to Spirit, as a channel of transformation, as a receptacle of creative love. This water is immeasurable, flowing through the currents of the World-Soul, distilled from the pure solar and lunar light, itself a vehicle for unseen energies meant to guide and inspire. We accept this offering with graceful surrender to its purifying presence, we absorb it into our bodies as a revivification of our spiritual intent to become vessels of healing love, we pass it on to others without expectations or demands. May the blessings of that cup reveal to us the full measure of our depths; may the emptiness of the cup be a sign of our own receptivity to Spirit; may the touch of that golden rim be a taste of light. May we receive that grace which teaches us the round dance of interconnected feelings and beliefs; may we walk in that grace as in the medium of Spirit's cleansing. May that Eternal Life open to us the holy vistas of its unending depths and fullness and may our hearts, minds, and souls be capable of sustaining that vision for the benefit of others.

That life, eternal, is now and always, in every place and every time, and requires only an inward aspiration to call forth its gifts to the willing heart of a seeker on the path. Eternal life is not a reward for living according to religious doctrines; it is not "only for the elect" but is an intrinsic gift for each and every created being without exception, for every living soul. It is an inner horizon whose dimensions are immeasurable but whose joy and fulfillment surpass all visionary images and predictions. The Eternal Life cannot be contracted to material visions of heaven nor to subtle configurations of astral afterlife; it is not bound by conception, visionary myth, nor religious encounters. It is an affirmation of the boundless character, the illumined qualities of Spirit that make and unmake all these worlds, all these planes, dimensions, holograms, and reflections. The images, the metaphors, the holy places, celestial cities, alternative worlds, are all reflections vastly contracted, providing human reference to a reality that is the very universe itself. All the hell-worlds, realms of suffering, after death planes, "lower and higher" conditions, are visionary worlds whose co-created contents are perishable but whose life-source is everlasting. This is because Spirit as the creative matrix of made images and places, embodies an infinite variety of possible worlds whose relative conditions reflect the mental, emotional and spiritual predispositions of the beings that inhabit those worlds.

The mind goes to that reality which it contemplates, to the visionary world that the soul marks as real and necessary as the intended goal of a spiritual process. But Spirit is not mind, nor is it a consequence of mind; Spirit is the origin of mind and the underlying stimulus for the creation of every particular world. Mind after mind, heart after heart, soul after soul, these worlds are generated, believed in, aspired toward, and become the inhabited realm of an intended faith. But these worlds are all relative, all built on the inner mental-emotive conditionality of a faith constructed way of thinking or acting. These worlds can be dissolved, subside into their origins, be unmade, abandoned, forgotten or denied and still retain impressionable, existent structures within Spirit attracting yet new births and inhabitation. The soul goes to that world which it desires to inhabit, often driven by habit, unexamined prejudice, beliefs, fixed attitudes and age-old memories, passions or needs. On the Hermetic path, we seek to dissolve worlds, to transit the labyrinths of faith, dogma, and rationality in order to arrive at a fresh vista, an open horizon unbound, creative, and luminous. We seek to find the way that leads to Eternal Life now, in the present moment, in the embodied time of the seeker, in the inhabitation of any and every world without denying the possibility for life in other worlds, planes, or dimensions. It is not a simple universe, but a complex multiverse whose interconnected intentionalities and soulful bonds can unite us with innumerable other worlds.

The "one Eternal Life" cannot be reduced to any one world, to any one way, or any one faith, path, or teaching. Eternal life is a miracle, a wonder in the depths of creation that allows us to marvel at the gift of life given throughout all space and time. Such life is not "a reward" but a "gift" that makes all present awareness possible, that provides the circumstances for gaining an individual perspective on that which surpasses all individual expression. This gift, this precious and subtle matrix of energies that we inhabit and which inhabit us, is giving its fullness to us every moment, every heartbeat, throughout the entire history of every world that exists in whatever gross or subtle plane. Therefore, we celebrate Eternal Life as it is now, in the present, in taking the cup, in drinking the pure waters of life, in sharing that blessing with others. If we cannot awaken to its full scope and range, nevertheless, it is fully present in and through us, sustaining the heartbeat and nourishing mind and soul.

That life has always been here, always been part of who we are, in the most ancient past and in the farthest future, that life abides, the "same today, tomorrow, and forever." We may construct endless images of its form, enduring potential, causal impact and consequential result, but in none of these cases can we actually delimit its effects and capacities. What is limited is our own conceptualizations, what is delimited is the range of our individual mental horizons, what is ineffectual is our mental picture, our image, of what we call "eternal". That image is simple a lens, as in a telescope, that draws the reality closer, magnifies the view and for a moment reveals a new detail.

But the image is not the reality, and like the moon seen in water, we must not mistake the image for the lunar source of light. Hidden in the night sky, the solar energies rebound and create a shadowed world, like the mental world of human beings mistaking their images as the primal source of wisdom or illumination. But it is not the image we seek, it is the light, the primal source by which all images are made bright and infused with life. This is the inherent "essence of mind" or the spontaneity of the "illumined intuitions" of the heart, whose flash is rooted in a divine source, holy Spirit residing in soul. This life is not bound by matter, nor brain, nor nerves, nor flesh nor bone but sings in the body as a sacred presence just beneath the threshold of ordinary thought and memory. The ancient teaching that we must "remember" in order to reclaim the higher light is true, but what we remember is not past lives, or previous incarnation. What we "remember" is the indwelling presence of Spirit that has always been with us, that is inseparably part of every life, every incarnation, every visionary world. Yet that presence is masked by a thousand images, and ten thousand "masks of god" which then become icons substituting for an inner presence whose reality cannot be contained in form and mask. Spirit as the activity of Mystery shapes those forms in such a way as to press them beyond the boundaries of fixed forms and into the metamorphosis of yet another stage of manifestation.

There are forms that act as a radical focus, a summary image, an archetypal constellation that maintains the balance between personal incarnate appearance and a transpersonal presence, as in the images of the Enlightened Buddha, the Green and White Taras, the Crucified Christ, the Divine Sophia, Prajñāparamita, and all the celestial forms of multiple traditions representing higher powers. These forms are radical condensations of tradition and teachings whose symbolic contents are rich in multiple associations and meaning. In this context, "eternal life" may be seen as images in archetypal form and yet, no form is adequate to give us the full and complete depths of that life. The image is a vehicle, a means for the attainment of a more illumined view based in direct experience, in an inner opening to a spiritual horizon that exceeds the maximum that form can contain. All images of "heaven" are similar vehicles, as a symbol of transformation, as the fulfillment of a promise yet to come, as a sign like a rose or lotus, foretelling the dissolution of all images, signs, and forms. This is not death, but rebirth; not an end, but on-going creation; not sleep, but awakening. Sacred images, like sand paintings and mandalas can be made, contemplated, used for spiritual practice, healing, empowerment, but then they are dismantled, scraped up, and carefully deposited back into the holy earth from which the sands came. We return to the imageless source, the horizons of Spirit that imbue form with power but which is an unending source, a primal ground, inexhaustible.

All angelic forms, like the Sun Christ at the center of the World Mandala, are a means for the elevation of mind to the point at which the forms dissolve into uncreated light, into the vaster energies of Spirit. The form is relative, helpful as a means of the transformation, but there are many such images and every tradition contains symbols of inner eternal life. However this life is evaluated, it is radically present in even the simple sign or word because Spirit permeates all reality, all beings, all creation. It is not life apart, life in the past or future, but life now, in a present that dissolves the temporal horizon and is coextensive with the visible universe. And yet, it is the Mother of that creation, the fostered, dynamic, loving Spirit that while nourishing life, is not reduced to any one form nor to only the visible world. That life is the gift of Mystery, the outpouring of immense potential into uncountable vessels of that cannot contain the vital spark, the overflowing fullness. That life adapts to the most minute processes of procreation and sustains balance within the macrocosm. It compels us to seek a deeper, more mature wisdom and draws us towards the full capacity that life gives us, breaking us out of our habits, laziness, fears, and buffered way of living. Eternal life is the inner compelling presence that encourages us to become more fully alive, more fully aware, and more complete—to overcome alienation and move beyond complacent self-satisfaction. Eternal life is a powerful, propelling, nurturing presence just below the threshold of everyday awareness, urging us toward spiritual awakenings.

To attain this life eternal, we need only affirm its presence, open heart and mind, and live as though life fully mattered, that every living being is a sacred sign of its presence. The Christ sign of Eternal Life is seen on the slopes of Mount Tabor, in the transfiguration, not simply in the resurrection.[142] This transfiguration is a record of a holy moment in which the power of Spirit flows forth and the horizon of the visionary world opens to reveal the wonder and

---

142. Mark 9: 2-3.

depths of its presence. Each of us has within the capacity for transfiguration, for the uplifting sweep of Spirit to reveal its fullness and vaster capacity. And when we open our hearts, allow Spirit to move within and through us, then we taste Eternal Life, then we see through the glass more clearly, we behold the holiness of all creation. The gift of this life is always with us, it never departs, even in our darkest hour, in the midst of suffering, lost, pain, death and confusion, that life is there, brimming over, asking us to drink from the cup, to celebrate its presence. The waters of life are the source for sweat and tears, from joy, sorrow, friendship, and love. We drink from that cup daily in feeling the world and all its inner turmoil, all its intermixing energies, relationships and beings thirsting for life. To live fully, we must embody fully the life presence within us, opening our hearts to the Christ-spirit, to share that cup, to drink deeply and to constantly renew within our heart, the pledge we make to live a spiritual life. And Spirit is there to help us, to give us the strength and inspiration we need to meet all forms of challenge. Only open your heart and receive the gift, hold nothing back, make your heart an altar, an empty vessel, that you might be filled to overflowing.

Salvation

To know that the Light of Christ, in Mystery, lifts us above all heavens and hells; for the benefit of all beings, granting salvation to all. (4:3)

Heaven and hell are not mere imaginary places; they are visionary worlds whose existence has been created by the mental and psychic activities of millions upon millions of human beings. Both Christianity and Islam have taught the reality of hell and heaven and the imagery and novel descriptions of those places have circulated within the World-Soul for thousands of years among a majority of countries and nations. This is something more than mere imagination and something less than the evolutionary creative activities of Spirit. The creation of visionary worlds is a process of energizing social, emotional, and intellective world-constructs as places within which the dramas of human life are played out in a cosmic framework.[143] In the case of heaven and hell (as compared to the Buddhist six divisions of the Wheel of Life or *Bhavachakra*), there is an inherent dualism at work, a polarity that has no significant middle ground. This polarity reflects an archaic mental attitude, a reductive tendency that sees only the contrasts between opposites, a stark mental discontinuity

---

143. Lee Irwin, *Visionary Worlds* (1996) discusses this in greater detail.

between types, events, or persons organized in sharply incongruent categories. This is largely the creation of men and rooted in a male dialectic tendency that obscures shades of difference and tends to deny the relevance of overlap, ambiguity, shared relations, and subtle nuance. The rhetoric of punishment and reward is an extension of this oppositional worldview and also reflects a male punitive attitude rooted in authority, and often unjust control and social power over life and death.

Associated with certain forms of speculative thought, the dialectic of heaven and hell has been tied to often rigid moral and behavioral codes whose infractions threaten community members with terrifying promises of "eternal" punishment and condemnation. Sanctified in the name of an ultimate high god and a rigidly structured static cosmos, the terrifying promise is far more emphasized than the possible rewards. Punishment is used as a goad to maintain a certain prejudicial social and cosmic order in which only the conforming, obedient members of the hierarchy (dominated inevitably by men) can expect the promised rewards. Yet these visionary realms are more than mere reflections of social imbalance and polarized aggression, they are also populated by a vast panorama of spiritual beings east and west, demons and angels, devas, asuras and djinn, whose agency also works through the hierarchic structures of a visionary cosmos. These cosmic beings have manifested to a sensitive minority of visionaries whose reports and psychic experiences have added to the complexity and diversity of the invisible afterworlds. A multitude of after death visionaries have opened the doors on a complexity that far exceeds the simpler dialectic dualism of only two realms. The visionary cosmos of heaven and hell, the old order Mundus Imaginalis, is in a process of collapse, undergoing a fractal dissolution into its component structures, under the influences and inner promptings of Spirit, leading to new visionary cosmoi whose constructions are far more complex, nuanced, and overlapping.

The death of the archaic, polarized visionary worlds is a traumatic process, rooted in male prejudice, and bound by the desire for control and dominance. Those worlds are archaic because they have deep roots in dogmatic assertions that contrast perfection with imperfection, good with evil, love with lust, and selflessness with selfishness. The dialectic mode of thought is bound by its own predisposition to polarize, to simplify in the name of "higher" authority, the actual complexity of nature, society, and human relations. As a creative step toward wisdom, the dialectic serves a rudimentary need for simple organization and categorical definition; the binary structure has a creative role, but it is reductive and reflects only a minimal understanding of threshold experience. Experience at the threshold may polarize as a binary choice but it does not reflect the complexity and interactive dynamics of actual, long-term evolutionary maturation influenced by an increasingly complex participatory vision of the whole. Spirit moves beyond the dialectic; it is fractal, working through seemingly chaotic diversities to emergent creative expressions and synthesis, new stabilities, and then, future transformations. The visible and energetic cosmos is a multidimensional construct of alternative, branching worlds whose overlapping domains represent a variety of evolutionary pathways. The worlds we envision as native to our spiritual practices are the visionary worlds that act to energize human potential along a certain gradient of development. The image of the afterworld is a powerful context for determining actions in the present, therefore we must choose carefully, the world we would inhabit.

The activities of Spirit have been long energizing multiple worlds, worlds that are increasingly intersecting, influencing, and impacting the thoughts and beliefs of worlds once more isolated and alienated from each other. It is not a matter of superior or inferior (thus dialectic) teachings, but of on-going respectful dialogues which seek to benefit all participants. In this process the feminine voice is of great importance, the integrative principle is the embodiment of Wisdom in the form of a loving, clear minded teacher who has fully integrated feminine and masculine perspectives into a transpersonal view of the past and future. The feminization of male traditions is of utmost importance and the ferment of change in metaphysical and ethereal thinking will be vastly enhanced by outstanding women teachers. The future will rest in those persons most capable of riding the tiger and directing a multitude of energies toward deep and profound awakenings. The reinstatement of the feminine as divine models of full enlightenment is a Hermetic sign that the works of Spirit, of the Divine Sophia, are lifting the veil to reveal a more tolerant, interactive, and creative perspective in teachings of life after death. Life beyond the body is not a phantom life, but an exceedingly real, vivid and dynamic existence whose psychic and subtle correlates have yet to be fully delineated. Understanding those correlates requires a receptive, open, psychically sensitive predisposition free of dogmatic, authoritarian male ideals. It requires a feminized receptivity to diversity and difference, to the rich pluralism of all traditions and teachings.

This process of understanding is energized by a capacity to continue life-experience through a multitude of lives, through processes of embodiment that are not limited to only one incarnate experience. We have lived other lives and will live more lives after this one; the paradigm of one life and one end is a visionary creation based in an authoritative denial of the rich, multidimensional capacities of life beyond a single bodily incarnation. The denial of multiple lives has a function insofar as it teaches us to value with full effort and commitment, the life we have now, in the present. And this is correct, we should recognize that the veiled condition of our present incarnation is not an accidental quality, but an imperative of Spirit which asks us to fully and deeply commit to actualizing this life, in the present, with no certainty of what it yet to come. Theories of reincarnation should not seek to justify an acceptance of any social order nor a lack of effort by spiritual seekers, but sometimes the burdens we carry from the past must be fully worked through and neutralized in the hard, demanding conditions of a resistant present. The process of spiritual development is not a static burden, nor is it an inflexible debt. The fractal dynamics of Spirit, working through agencies of many subtle types, can, and often does, relieve an individual quite suddenly of burdens and past consequences. This is the healing miracle of Spirit, the transformative touch of the Christ light, that can unburden the heart and free us from past suffering and trauma.

On the Hermetic pathway, we are not seeking either heaven or hell; we are not participating in the dialectic polarities of oppositional logic, but training the mind and heart to function in a more holistic, nuanced manner fully congruent with the actual complexity of an emergent cosmos. Our goal is knowledge, *gnosis* of the Metacosm, a hyper-reality that sustains the full branching of diverse ways and embodied worlds, an illumination that leads to direct mystical experience of the transpersonal horizons within which all worlds, forms, or individual mental structures are unified. I call the active energy of this illumination the "Christ-light" insofar as it is stimulated by a heart-centered knowledge dedicated to the preservation of species and a compassionate love for all created life.[144] That light is an inner light, an opening of the heart and mind to the full expansive vistas of Mystery, to the inspired illuminations of a unitary cosmos replete with multiple visionary worlds and interwoven with many diverse stratum and subtle planes through which a multitude of agencies work for the awakening of each and every species. There is salvation in the sense that each individual seeks to realize the fullness of the gifts of Spirit through soul illumination; it is a shared knowledge, one that links us with every tradition and every being who works for the preservation of life. In following the Hermetic path, we learn to work with symbolic forms, metaphors of light, shade, dark, twilight and dawn, without losing a sense of the reality of each, without reducing the complexity to limited opposing logical sets.

In this way, we open the doors of perception to fully appreciate the won-

---

[144]. Matthew 5: 8; Mark 12: 29-31; Luke 6: 45; John 7: 38-39.

ders of creation in all their nuanced and interpenetrating domains. The visionary worlds of the Hermetic pathway are indeterminate, that is, they are in process, emergent and forthcoming, moving through cycles of actualization that lead to new possibilities. In this process, serial incarnations are a distinctive feature of continuity that links not only the past and future through the present, but also establishes a metaperspective in which those lives (along with the lives of beloved others) are simultaneously active and evolving. From the Hermetic point of view, the temporal horizon is not limited to lineal progressions, but opens to an illumined state of simultaneity, a relative and conditional awareness that expands into multiple lives and incarnations. I say this based on direct personal experience; I have seen my own incarnational past and future as connected and interactive within an eons long process of evolutionary commitments to species development. In this sense, I am by no means unique; many hundreds of thousands of aware others are simultaneously engaged in this very project, now, in the present. Most human beings are engaged in this project, not knowing the metaperspective, but nevertheless, motivated inwardly, through the urgency of Spirit, to maximize potential and to enact alternate pathways to wisdom and understanding. The Hermetic perspective accepts this diversity and works creatively, through the Christ light, to realize a compassionate, loving expression that heals past traumas and facilitates dialogue and greater cooperation.

In the Christ light we may see other forms and expressions of illumination, such as buddhas and bodhisattvas, Chinese immortals, the devas and asuras, yogis, saints, sufis, hasidim, archangels, goddesses and gods, and a multitude of spirit forms, guides, helpers, sprites and elementals. The Christ light is a radiance that stems from the roots of creation and embodies the compassionate, healing energies of love.[145] It does not restrain itself to the "elect or chosen" but pours itself forth like the sun, on all living creatures, physical, psychic, or subtle, nourishing them with the divine joys of Spirit through the inexhaustible potentials of deep, unfathomable Mystery. In that Mystery, there are a vast multitude of revelatory forms, agencies, spirits, presences, dominions, and powers, all engaged in the fractal dissolution and recreation of all that is Above, Between, and Below. In the ferment of this eons long process, worlds are made and unmade, heavens and hells constructed and deconstructed, not dialectically, but through interactive, conditional relations that enfold polarities into the greater creative matrices and expansive potentials of Mystery. From Mystery we came, and unto Mystery we return; from the deep we were created and in the deep we are reabsorbed and illumined. On the Hermetic

---

145. 2 Corinthians 4: 6.

way, the Christ light pours itself out granting salvation to all; offering the gifts of love, compassion, and wisdom freely. We are not compelled to accept these gifts, but if we open our hearts, we will see that the "new heaven and new earth" is right here, right now, without boundary, border, or closed doors.

Redemption

To recognize our faults and errors, to not judge others, in youth or in old age; to seek redemption through faith, knowledge, and truth; through kindness and reconsiderations. (4:4)

Self-knowledge begins in seeing our limits as well as in recognizing our potential for growth and change. Life is not static, nor is it a function of simple conformity to existing cultural norms; nor do we grow in isolation from the complexity of the world we inhabit. In exploring potential, it is inevitable that we make choices that are not always best, not always growth oriented, not always directed toward the most positive ends. And many times our choices are difficult and uncertain, the way is not clear, the outcome is hidden in a shroud of conflicting possibilities. Who benefits from our actions? Who suffers from our inactions? How can we best attains a realization of goals without harming another? How do the actions of others impede or aid us in growing beyond a certain level of insight or understanding? We best come to know ourselves through our relationships with others, through our successes and our failures, through responsible caring, and often mediocre efforts, and even through lapses into indifference or angry, resentful rejection. The wide range of our human emotions is a strength, not a weakness, and our ability to engage and enact from an emotional center is of great importance. The power of life, of Spirit, of love, is not a mental construct, but a lived reality, a powerful influx of emotional connectedness, an intense willingness to open to others as they are and not as we might want them to be. This love and connectedness is increased and enhanced when we open to Spirit and allow Spirit to love and act through us as vessels of transformation.

When we see our limits within Spirit, we are seeing beyond the boundary of self and opening to a greater wholeness in which all others are loved as well. The stages of self- knowledge lead from early self-preoccupations, to the opening energies of love and care, to sharing and learning with and through others while also maintaining integrity and self-affirmation. As Spirit flows into our lives, in community or as individuals, we begin to see beyond the veils of everyday concerns, we begin to open to a vaster, more expansive horizon of love. This love is not born of the human heart but it is carried in the heart as a sacred sign of a more energized way of living. This love flows forth out of Mystery and through Spirit actualizes our deeper capacities for relation and understanding. As Spirit carries us deeper into the transformative matrix, into the web of life linking us with all living creatures, with the World-Soul, with the Metacosm, then we see the potential for our full humanity. Our personal limitations, which are many, are nevertheless based in a state of contraction, a state of holding onto the lesser, everyday reality, to common prejudice, clinging to the ordinary as a raft of security in the midst of creative turbulence and a vaster, more expansive whole. And love flows into us as we open, walking the Hermetic pathways, loving the Christ-spirit as it cuts through our bonds and liberates us from a contracted, bound way of seeing. We do not lose our limitations, but we do transform, do expand into a wider visionary reality, do attain new balance and wisdom, Spirit given, Spirit blessed.

If we fall back into a less illumined state, we still carry the impress of Spirit as a seal now broken, opening us to deeper love and a remembrance of inner connectivity. But to sustain that connection, that flowing forth of love in Spirit, we must forgive those that have hurt and harmed us, we must forgive them fully that we too can be forgiven by others for the hurt and harm we have given them. The fearful circle must be broken, the circle of hurt, blame, rejection, sorrow, and lashing out for no purpose other than uncontrolled expression of passion or anger.[146] And we must forgive our self, having come to the realization of our own limits and selfish or unthinking acts, intentional or not, whose consequences have created a counter wave, a resurgent energy of dislike, shame, sorrow and pain. We do not move on the spiritual path away from these emotions and perceptions but through them to a deeper, calmer water, clearer, with less sorrow, less guilt, less blame, to a lucid, receptive opening in Spirit that heals our wounds and soothes all sorrow and blame. The will is not free, but conditioned by ten thousand influences acting on us over years and generations. To be free from these chains of accusation, guilt, and suffering, we must cut through conventional thought, unthinking collective attitudes, through the violence and hate, and liberate our bound souls in order to walk more freely, unburdened by past actions, humbled and purified. So we offer this cup, this healing water, this sharing in love without guilt or blame, this holy gift of Spirit.

We must learn to see and accept our faults and errors; who can live without some foolish, selfish, or immature, unthinking acts? We also learn to evaluate our development in relationship to a spiritual ideal. Without spiritual ideals

---

146. Luke 6: 37-38.

we have no measure, no way to index the relative strengths and weaknesses of our struggle toward a more illumined and spiritual life. There is no one ideal, no fixed and predetermine type that represents the spiritual path for all souls and incarnate beings. There are many ideals, models or examples, male, female, or child, all as illumined human beings, acquiring wisdom, attaining joy, ecstasy, and profound, holy intuitions. This awakening carries us across the boundaries of ordinary life, into an open horizon of possibility in which our faults and errors can be dissolved and our souls liberated from conditional, contracted living. As we open to Spirit, to the influx of new creative energy, we can let go of our feelings of blame and judgment made against others. When we carry guilt, self-blame, and feelings of inadequacy, we also project those feeling outward, critical of the imperfections and faults of others. In moving through our own imperfections, Spirit gives us the full energy of love to infuse into the world of all our relationships. When we are free, others are free from us; when we liberate our guilt, fear and anger, then those qualities are also liberated in our relationships. Spirit teaches us to let go of the heavy, burdensome sorrow, the old wounds, the nurtured injuries, the irritable disagreements, the agitations of different values and beliefs.

Spirit gives us a profound and holy gift, a capacity to truly release all our inner pain and discontent. The further we enter into the depths of Spirit, the more Spirit pours herself into the healing of soul and through soul, into the hearts and minds of those whose souls we touch. I praise Spirit, I rejoice in her bounty and gifts, I celebrate the wonder of her deep and unending compassion for all beings. Holy, holy, Mother of All Healing, Gracious Bounty, Radiant Inner Light, Overflowing Fountain, Pure Water and Grace, Hail to Thee! Spirit works through all pathways to heal us, to broaden our understanding, and to leads us to discover the image of divinity within us, the spark of presence, a Christ-Light. How can we blame others? In the end, we are responsible for our actions, for every deed, thought, feeling, and response, no one else, no blame can be assigned to others. Forgiving others does not mean they are right, or what they did or said or thought, was acceptable. Forgiveness is not about accepting the transgressions of those who may well have harmed or injured others; it is about letting go of hate and anger within, it is about releasing judgments, about opening the heart and purging the soul. Forgiveness does not happen once or twice, but flows forth continually from the heart in a state of illumination. This is why Christ could forgive even while on the cross—because his heart was open and Spirit was with him pouring love and transformative energies into the contracted world of his persecutors.[147] So we

---

147. Luke 23: 34.

learn forgiveness as an on-going discipline rooted in Spirit and exemplified by a spiritual ideal.

Thus we come to redemption, faith with knowledge, attaining a taste of truth like honey on the tongue when the seal of love is broken. Redemption in faith does not mean simple conformity to an external teaching, to a communal creed, or to any dogmatic formulations. Redemption in faith means believing deeply and profoundly, in the capacity of Spirit to act in your life as a guiding presence. Simply put, faith means believing in your deep potential for spiritual transformation. This is the Hermetic axiom: to believe in our human capacity, our individual potential, for radical transformation and illumined awareness. Whatever path you may follow, whatever teachings, or techniques you practice, grounding and foundational faith is a deep affirmation of inner potential united with a longing for spiritual fulfillment. Such faith is based not in will but in aspiration, in desire for a fuller, more complete, integrated life. The intentional structure of faith is created in adherence to guiding principles, to living sensitively with courage, in facing the challenges of living authentically, existentially committed to a path of transformation. One of these principles is the principle of love and forgiveness, an inward turning over that frees the heart from its contractions and gives birth to a more expansive, soulful being. We must believe in the transformative value of love, in the power of Spirit to act in and through us as a means to healing of others. We need only open our hearts to Spirit, to receive her grace through inner receptivity, and to be a luminous center of Spirit's gifts.

Knowledge, that is spiritual knowledge not just worldly learning, comes through Spirit as the impress of creative presences opening mind to its deepest noetic contents.[148] These noetic contents are images of the world and of our being-in the world, in the primal Ur-Space, in the Metacosm, where silence, meditation, and truth reveal the depthless deep beyond which mind cannot go. Temporal dissolution of mind is a form of such knowledge, not its destruction or denial, not a suppression or repression of mind's contents, but a transformation of mental horizons such that the individual mind is dissolved into Light, absorbed into the higher noetic world, illumined in flashes and immersed in the oceanic continuum of splendor, in the ten thousand veils over the face of the Divine Mother, in the infinite depths of the Forefather carrying all creation, the transcendent all-luminous All Conscious Mind without a center, without a boundary, the Unfathomable Most Holy Mystery. We grow into this knowledge as we open our minds and hearts to the action of Mystery in our lives, through Spirit, through the Christ-light, in dreams, visions, illumi-

---

148. Bhagavad Gita 13: 11.

nations and through study, reflection, thought, and mental discipline. There is redemption in knowledge of this mystical kind, not in a swollen pride or through inflations in learning, but through inner surrender to the holy depths of mind concealed in the noetic images and seed forms. Those images and seeds are dissolved, bursting into the Metacosm where they are absorbed and transmuted into the vaster energies and pluses of a living universe whose depths and dimensions are beyond measure.

The truth is found not simply in ideas, but in the direct experience of Mystery, in the actions of Spirit and in the subtle and pervasive intensity of an unquenchable love. In youth and in old age, in-between, in all the middle years, we struggle to overcome our petty judgments, our overly critical attitudes and our prideful clinging to particulars and to facts that we think define who we are. But in Spirit, we are vessels of transformation, overflowing into Mystery, and pouring ourselves out into the world in the co-creation of better, more loving worlds. So let us give up our harsh judgments and come up from the valley of revelation with a new teaching, one that values differences, admires complexity, does not seek to impose codes or laws, but like Christ returning from the desert, offers healing, love, and deep dedication to world transformations. And these transformations will occur best when we act with deep consideration for the feelings of others, act with genuine unshakable kindness, bring our words and actions into accord, and speak only of what we can actually give knowing our limits and boundaries. Consideration, kindness, respect, reciprocity, an ethic of positive, supportive aid, without blame or censure, is a profound gift, a spiritual blessing. It flows forth out of the heart of creation and into each of us in accordance with our ability to receive inwardly, the inspirations that abound around us. Our redemption is a matter of opening to that presence, to Spirit, to Mystery, to the Boundless Deep, so that the world can continue to undergo its powerful, remarkable awakening in all the populations of all species of all imaginable realms. So might it be!

Virtues

To practice five virtues: honesty, non-violence, self-discipline, patience, and generosity; to avoid lying, theft, injury to others, impatience, greed, and slander. (4:5)

Virtues are not ideas or abstractions, they are practices that we engage everyday as a testimony of our dedication to a spiritual path. Such practices are not limited to these five but incorporate many other mental, emotive, and physical habits as a basis for acting in a virtuous manner. As long as we think of virtues in an abstract or intellective sense, we will be divorcing ourselves from the ethical ground of actual human (and other) relationships. The real test of our ethical concerns, our belief in ideal values, is found in our daily relationships, in our capacities to relate to others through considerate, sensitive concern. This does not mean that we must sacrifice our integrity, beliefs, or commitments to a valued way of life; but it does mean that we must work to maintain balance and harmony without violating the integrity and values of others. Our relationships are dynamic and interactive, not fixed according to routine or mere habit; the action of Spirit is to enliven, to foster growth and responsibility in all our relationships. Therefore, our understanding of ethical values and virtues must also be dynamic and transformative, such that we continue to grow into an increasingly mature understanding of each and every virtue through years of dedicated practice and inner transformation.

The goal is living creatively through the cultivation of virtue as a means to illumination and not simply as an action required by a formulaic code. This is a matter of internalization. As long as a person wears his or her virtues outwardly, as a matter of social conformity or obedience, they only attain an external recognition. But when we take into ourselves the virtues as necessary for our spiritual development, as a means toward the realization of the inmost goals, then we can begin to find the luminous qualities that virtues give. Just as Christ criticized the hypocrisy of the teachers of the law because they were like whitewashed tombs, "outwardly beautiful but inwardly full of the bones of the dead," so too must we avoid practicing virtues because we seek affirmations only from the collective.[149] When we internalize virtues, practicing them as an act of free will, not forced upon us by others, then we begin to feel directly the effects of our practices in the changing quality of our life experiences. The embodiment of spiritual virtues is, at the deepest level, a transformation of self, a soulful refining of qualities, an expansion of subtle influences born and harbored in Spirit. Virtue is like a light lit in a smoky lamp that as it burns, purifies the wick, cleanses the glass, and in its most luminous expressions, provides light and guidance for others. But first we must strike the spark that will ignite the flame, our inner commitment to live virtuously, in accord with Spirit.

There are certain mental, emotive, and physical habits that provide nourishment for the growth of virtues. In a way, the naming of virtues is simply a means of verbalizing processes of refinement and receptivity to a more positive, qualitative way of life. Physically, proper health habits in bodily care,

---

149. Matthew 23: 27-28.

diet, exercise, maintaining flexibly, strength, and well-toned internal organs, is a matter of continual adaptation that recognizes the bodily changes of natural maturation cycles. The bodily habits of youth are not the habits of middle age, nor are either the same for later aging; every stage has its appropriate disciplines and practices. But the crucial factor is a careful attentiveness to bodily needs in a context of maintaining optimal health and respect for embodied life. The body is a temple, not a carnal house.[150] And these needs are not the same for men as for women; nor is there a strict gender difference, every individual is unique and each must work to find the optimal balance and health. Emotionally, the preparation for virtuous refinement requires an inner release of emotional energies (often stored in the body at a cellular level) that allows the psyche to freely feel and react without repressive or excessive reverberations. The free flow of feeling is of utmost importance because it establishes the strongest links with others in a natural context of personal interaction. Excessive emotional reactions may overwhelm self and others while repressive emotive internalization may obscure genuine feelings. Emotions must flow like the tides, moving forth and back in balance with the seasons, the rhythms of bodily life, the balancing intensity or release of the moment.

Mentally, a calm and centered attention is imperative. Mental training, like emotive training, should focus the energies of bodily, glandular, and psychic life to provide a central tranquility from which reactions may flow forth spontaneously, in a balanced, fluid response. Mental clutter, hyper-mental activity, constant mental chewing on ideas or thoughts or worries, leads to a state of imbalance because there is no center, no calm stillness within, no stability from which to evaluate the turbulences of the world. Meditation and inner centering prayer is highly valuable because it provides a momentary pause which, in more mature practice, can be carried over into active, everyday life. Like emotions, it is helpful to overcome reactionary energies, to integrate responses into a larger pattern of mental and emotive rootedness in stability. On the Hermetic pathway, this centering is symbolized by the Christ-spirit imbued with receptivity to the world and others in a state of empowerment to act through the guidance of Spirit. The heart is the center, not the head, deep perceptions of Spirit and the "still quiet voice" within, the gentle whisper, is what guides us toward light and illumination.[151] Therefore, mind must be quieted, brought into a concentrated stillness, open, receptive, unagitated, calm, clear, deep and luminous. Concentration sinks to the heart and opens there into the vaster depth whose creative energies can flow into us by virtue of our intentions and aspirations. And these intentions are formed and shaped by the

---
150. John 2: 21.
151. 1 Kings 19: 12.

virtues we practice, not simply by the ideas we think.

The cultivation of virtue begins in honesty, first self-honesty and then, honesty with others. This means dropping the deceptive, artificial pose of outward conformity and cultivating an individuated sense of personal beliefs and values. These values can only be effective if they develop through a radical self-honesty, an honesty willing to give up the buffers and pretenses that cushion us from knowing our true feelings and reactions. Only if we know ourselves thoroughly, deeply, through careful self-examination, can we hope to raise the threshold of our understanding to more illumined states. Persons who seek illumination without self-knowledge build on sand, not on rock. Experiences, dreams, visions, illuminations come and go, but the learning and integration remains insofar as we can take in the experiences as a means to deepen self-knowledge, and not simply as an external adornment meant to captivate or mesmerize through mere appearance. How often did Christ reprimand the disciples, those who lived and traveled with him, because of their lack of self-knowledge, their resistant unwillingness to strip away the externals and open to the greater depths of his teachings.[152] So too must we courageously seek to remove inner blinders, old order thinking, static values, inherited teachings and ideas, in order to move, live, and breath in Spirit, honestly, without self-deceptions. Only as we dive more deeply into the foundations of our personhood can we begin to be truly honest with others; only as we know ourselves, do we begin to fathom the complexity and struggles of the other.

Lying is a great barrier to spiritual development because it reflects an inward tendency toward self-exaggeration or self-diminishment or confusion that cannot honestly be authentic in all circumstances. This is not a matter of confrontations or resistant strategies to maintain a belief or concern. It is rather an inner measure of integrity, a capacity to evaluate and react to experience from a personal center open to but not determined by the actions, beliefs, or attitudes of others.[153] One can be honest and also gentle, deflecting the energies away without combating them directly or without letting them overwhelm sensitivity. Honesty is extremely helpful because it provides a base line for understanding our individual limits; recognizing these limits is the dynamic border at which we are challenged to grow. The Hermetic principle here is the synthesis of love and integrity, the alchemical sublimation that allows for the emergence of strong, positive attitudes and actions.[154] Action rooted in non-violence support honesty by offering alternatives grounded in positive human relationships, not through conflict, opposition or struggle, but through

---

152. Matthew 16: 9-11.
153. Colossians 3: 9-10.
154. Lee Irwin, *The Alchemy of Soul* (WA: Lorian Press, 2007).

clear, principled negotiation. Non-violence is also an attitude of mind, by no means passive, very active and engaged with issues of personal, communal, and global justice. Greed, theft, disrespect, assault, and aggression all stem from unchecked assertions of will; the balancing factor is respect for the rights of others and a willing cooperation meant to maintain virtuous relations under all circumstances.

In turn, this requires self-discipline. If we are honest, respect the rights of others, choose non-violence over violence, then we must learn self-discipline. We can choose to act with awareness of the impact of our actions on others; this means learning self-restraint based in respect for differences and alternative ways of life. This does not mean accepting violence or oppression as an acceptable norm because others refuse to abandon their own violent, disrespectful, and aggressive tendencies. Such tendencies must be met with resistance and confronted when they threaten the well-being of others. But the standard for that confrontation should be non-violence, rooted in self-discipline. Honesty, non-violence, and self-discipline must work together with patience and generosity (or love). Together, these virtues form a complex of values whose enactment requires each of them to be fully developed in order to fully actualize the spiritual potential of any given situation, however imbalanced and/or violent. Self-discipline is actualized on the level of our physical, emotional, and mental habits; it is not simply indexed by particular external practices, ascetic norms, or technical abilities. Self-discipline is a process of refinement, a smoothing out of all roughness, a shaping that remains natural and fluid, like water shaping stone. The currents of Spirit roll us forward toward the sea, the hard corners are softened, the pockets gently shaped, the contours made into curves.

If we are patient and generous, in a deep foundational way, then we know that giving to others is a form of fulfillment.[155] Not in giving away energy or exhausting self, not through diminishment but through a fullness of Spirit that flows out into others as a gift and a joy. Patience comes through years of practice, such that the surface may be ruffled, but the depths are ever calm. Generosity is like a deep well whose flood waters cannot be exhausted in giving but whose gift may require only a cup be shared. It is not the well that matters but what we raise up in the bucket through our own efforts and how willing we are to give what is, after all, not our own. This means being a channel, not for teachings or instructions, but for pure Spirit whose gifts overflow the vessel and connect through the Da'ath (pathways) linking us to others. Generosity is a form of love and love is the heart of the Christ-spirit, the cup that we offer

---

155. James 5: 9-10.

whose waters are life. We do not fill it with our own energies, but our energies determine the quality and purity that fills the cup. If we are impatient, greedy, speak ill of others, gossip and slander, lie, cheat or steal, then our energies will be blocked, unable to attune to the open, expansive fullness of Spirit. To walk the Hermetic path means to walk the path of healing; it means to walk in humility as a vessel of Spirit, as a lamp whose wick does not smoke, is well-trimmed, and ready to celebrate the holy marriage.[156]

Virtue is an adornment, a grace that transforms our efforts into something greater than ourselves. If we wish to walk a spiritual path, to follow the Christ-spirit or any other great teacher, then we must walk with those virtues radiant, celebrating the joy and healthy vitality of our path. We do not hide our light under a basket, we do not exclaim it from the hilltop; we simply let it burn as brightly as possible by living spiritually dedicated lives. That brightness is Spirit given, the purity of body, emotion, and mind leads to purity of soul and purity of action in Spirit, supported and nourished by all the life giving lights. In the wonder of creation, in the fullness of the Metacosm, a vast multitude of beings seek to be ever more virtuous that they may shine ever more brightly for the celebrations of life. The marks of your virtues are impressed on your souls, like the marks of prayer made by those who bow daily, seen on the brightness of their foreheads. These marks are energetic and subtle, but they manifest clearly to those whose eyes are open. The celebration of virtue is in the living, in the practice, in the realizations of the effects and in the reciprocal energies created flowing back into Spirit. The currents of virtue are ever-flowing forth and returning to their source through every virtuous action we take. Therefore, let us act intentionally, with great determination to live a virtuous, exemplary lives, however simple, however unpolished. In this way, the world is transformed and our lives become a sweeter, more resonant song harmonizing with the songs and the music of the Spheres.

Vice

To propagate the Way through example, not words or teachings; simply, without vice or addiction; to be a firmly planted tree, deep rooted, mature, with good fruit. (4:6)

In order to grow roots, we must learn to absorb the nutrients from the soil as well as from the energy of the sun and moon. This is the Hermetic way, the way that seeks to transform the body, heart, mind, and soul into an ever more

---

156. Matthew 25: 1-13.

luminous example of embodied light. Mediating between the under-currents that draw us into the turbulent streams of horizontal life, life lived through engagements with immediate gain and loss, with shared social life and interactions, and the over-currents of multidimensional life, life lived in visions, lucid dreams, aware of the extraordinary and miraculous, is the Hermetic norm. On the boundaries between all that is above and all that is below, the aspirant, the initiate, seeks to live in balance, harmonizing all that is inner with all that is outer. Bringing light into material form is the great challenge; regarding the body as temple, as a microcosm of the Whole, we seek to initiate a process of spiritual transformation that will endure as a sign of what is yet to come. The earthy, physical energies, sexuality, passion, feeling, the connection between *eros* and *psyche*, the rooted energies are as deeply important, equally divine, as the lunar and solar, astral energies that act to open us to the cosmic expanse. The Hermetic *gnosis* is to behold the heavenly light within, and through a consecrated will, to act as a vessel that once purified, becomes a source of inspiration for others.

The body is the Cup, and the Waters of Life are the solar-lunar, astral energies, drawn into the heart with every breath, and shared through love in the Hermetic circle. This circle is capable of infinite reproduction, linking as it does, with many other circles, each adding its own nuance, emphasis, or spiritual qualities. These waters also nourish the Tree of Life, which is the tree of the linked teachers and initiates of the Hermetic-Alchemical traditions. The roots of this tree descend into the deep soil of the Holy Ground, the Mystery, the pervasive teachings of evolutionary Hermetic spirituality. This is the olive tree of "neither east nor west" which produces the clearest oil and whose flame within the glass is "a glittering star, a light within light".[157] The fruit of this tree, the olive whose oil is pure, luminous and alive, is pressed by the divine presence and ignites in the heart as a glowing ember, and then becomes, by stages, a radiance whose illumination has no measure or end. The roots extend into every esoteric tradition, east and west, north and south, extracting the golden-white energies, the particles of plasmic-light concealed in the heart of embodied matter. Like material concentrates, astral particles flung down from the stars, these buried energies await refinement, a calling up of their sublime, transformative capacities. In walking a spiritual path, these concealed energies can be released, the heart opened to the Great Work, and mind and soul ripened, as an olive on the Tree of Life. The oil pressed from such a heart is fragrant, and provides another lamp on the tree, a tree on whose leaves is inscribed the name of each illumined soul.

---

157. Qur'an 24: 35.

The lunar energies that bathe the tree, in the depths of night, provide us with the dreams and visions that are initiatic, in which guides, teachers, and illumined beings reveal the lesser and greater mysteries. There too, we meet the Christ-spirit, and the holy Bride, the Divine Sophia, who each give initiation in their own special ways. There we encounter the angelic presences, the reflected images of the Logos Self whose refracted forms take on a personal and individual character, becoming a mirror to the evolutions of an individual soul. There too we can meet and interact with all those who have lived before, crossed over into the diverse realms of the Mundus Imaginalis, and learn from them, the lessons of afterlife teaching. In the solar lights that bathe the tree, we encounter the transcendental form of the "sun that is more than sun" — the Logos illumination of the Highest Light, the all-absorbing, transformative ecstasy of utter absorption into the All Absorbing. Here, all images dissolve, the 70,000 veils of light are rendered invisible, and the country of the soul is discovered to be infinite and without a center. The trunk and branches of this tree are sturdy, old, ancient beyond measure, firm and support every kind of winged life, yet it is not massive or overbearing but has a certain adaptive and elegant beauty. Drawing energies from above and below, lunar, solar, and earthy mineral infusions, it thrives in the quiet solitude of inward reflections and offers its fruit for the propagation and harvests of the future.

The soul of the individual is an image of this tree. Firmly rooted in spiritual practice, growing through the absorption of various teachings and instructions, spreading limbs through a reaching out to light, growing in cycles of expansion and contraction, standing firm in storm and turbulence, uniting earthy life with astral energies, it grows over the years, and only after a long period of development, does it begin to fruit. And it does this through example, not simply through ideas or mental excitement or emotional agitations. To become a deeply rooted tree, to become fruitful, requires much effort and a certain pruning and trimming of excesses and imbalances. A teacher may undertake to make these corrections, but in the deepest sense, we are each fully responsible for our individual growth and development. Much can be said about where we draw our nutrients, where we put down our roots, which soils we choose to root in, what waters feed our thirsts and appetites. Sometimes it is necessary to uproot and reroot, to transplant from one spiritual environment to another, from one place to a better place, even though, if the roots go deep enough, they can penetrate the hardest, driest, rockiest soil and find water and sustenance. To flourish, it is best to find the optimal setting for sinking deep roots, a place of quiet, with pure clean water, fresh air, sunshine, an expansive horizon and an open sky. And then, to live in a way that is consistent with your deepest spiritual ideals, your most dearly held willingness to become something other, something more than you presently are, something that will challenge your deep assumption and open new vistas of awareness in Spirit.

To live by example does not mean to disavow the value of words and teachings, but it also mean not to take words and teachings as a substitute for actual practice. Too many words, too many ideas, these can mislead and confuse. Too few words, fewer ideas, can produce a stunted growth. There is always the search for balance, for the right economy of what is enough and what is too much or too little. We are not all the same, and we do not all follow a similar pattern; what is too much for one is not enough for another. Therefore, let each individual seek to find the balance and adaptation that best suits capacities while also challenging preconceived notions. This is the meaning of shaking down and pressing together the measure we are given—as we give so are we given.[158] Therefore, let us rigorously press down and settle what we have to offer, shake it and separate out the chaff, purify our habits, attitudes, self-expression, and actions with others. Let us learn to love, be generous, patient and honest to an uncommon degree, to live peacefully, as the olive branch symbolizes, creative, vibrant with life, slowly growing and developing our understanding and wisdom. These are practices, not ideas; these are qualities we can cultivate in every situation, not just in mediation or prayer. The Hermetic challenge is to bring that light into the world, to link with others, with all creatures, not to hide it under a basket, but to bring it out in a gentle, loving, admirable fashion.[159]

Some of our roots form around habits of body, mind, emotion, and relationships that can impede and hold back the flow of energy and life that makes the tree fully healthy and fruitful. The problems of "vice and addiction" are that they corrupt the soul in the name of individual habits and attitudes of mind or relationship. All actions have consequences; all mental and emotive attitudes, all physical routines, produce patterns and these patterns, when unhealthy, become constrictive and blinding. The nature of "spiritual freedom" is not based in self-indulgence nor in living a highly buffered life that constantly justifies habits and attitudes in the name of personal preferences. Spiritual transformation IS a shaking down, a paring away, a getting rid of habits, attitudes, and practices that deform and contract soulful potential. Traditionally, this is the *"purgatorio"* or the purification process that sets up the conditions for deeper insight; this is the aspect of self-discipline that proceeds to dissolve excess, to get rid of the unnecessary weight, the heaviness of

---

158. Luke 6: 38.
159. Matthew 5: 15-16.

being that holds the aspirant in an old pattern, constricting life energies, not allowing the tree to blossom. Thus "vice" is the practice of habits — mental, emotional or physical — that impede, harm, or in some subtle way, undermine the spiritual development of self or of others. And "addiction" is the enacting of habits that are not under the immediate, conscious control of the individual; habits whose psychic energies function through conditioned automisms unregulated by mature spiritual values or ideals.

Cycles of anger, depression, or fear; implicit hostility in relationships, or timidity and capitulation; an incapacity to control sexual behavior; indulgence in eating, drinking, or physical laziness; mental skepticism, aggressive criticism, constant ambiguity, a lack of center, excessive violent fantasy, self-inflation or repressive self-denial, are only a few such habits that tend to mislead and act as buffers in the formation of spiritual health. We need to constantly work at setting up a life-style, a spiritual practice, that will progressively eliminate, or purge (*purgatorio*) the psyche of its acquire, unhealthy tendencies. This requires courage and self-honesty; courage to change habits, and to enact new patterns of behavior as well as the honesty to evaluate what really impedes lasting spiritual health. These tendencies are mostly inward, external public behavior is not the main arena for their notice; the real arena is inwardly, the real struggle, the inner work of transformation to a more loving, luminous, open, rooted, grounded being whose light is pressed from the clearest oil. The perceptions of others, particularly those of a beloved partner, can be very insightful, depending on their degree of spiritual development. Our role is not to criticize others, but to subject the self to clear and continual observation. What needs refined, what can be developed, what must we give up in order to become more aware, centered, open to the depths? These are the necessary questions that balance intellectual curiosity and study; intellectual sophistication is no substitute for spiritual maturity, such maturity comes from the depths of a well-integrated life, lived day-by-day.

In this process, one foundational guideline is the role and centrality of simplicity. In many ways, the spiritual process is one of constant refinement and simplification. True spirituality has a directness, a simplicity of response, and an uncomplicated rapport with the struggles and sorrows or joys of others. Such spirituality is not caught in constant internal fantasy, is not immersed in the circularity of unresolved attitudes or half-formed beliefs. It becomes increasingly clear, direct, simple, expressively lucid without denying the complexity or fullness of the whole. Focus and attention is not embedded in a single worldview, but moves through the diversity of worlds and perspectives with grace and clarity because it is rooted, has a center, and truly knows the value of differences without surrendering integrity or honesty about personal limits. This is because the seeker in order to master the path, must discard all the internal trappings that would impede an inner flowering of potential. This stripping away does not limit our freedom, but in fact, opens us to participation in a far more wonderful and visionary fullness in which "freedom" is defined by capacity and spiritual knowledge, not by personal addictions or acquired mental habits. The image of the Hermetic Christ rises here, as an image of one who makes deep and full commitment to a spiritual way of life, gets rid of excess and unnecessary tendencies, and embraces the inspirations of Spirit as the deep inner guide to a more miraculous way of life. Uniting heaven and earth, the soul of the spiritual practitioner is purified, the oil pressed and heated, and the flame lit through genuine presence. That light shines, even now, in the heart of every soul; only follow the inspiration, and Spirit will guide.

Healing

To work for the healing of self, others, the nations, the world; to reconcile conflict, to mediate, to act with integrity; to not abandon Christ, to never wave our own banners. (4:7)

The healing of self is not simply a search for the healing of old wounds, injuries, or mistreatment. Health is the discovery of the radiant, the blessed, the very roots of the word are traceable to good omen and holiness. To work for healing means to find the pivotal balance, the lower center of gravity from which we can take root deep in the earth and to draw upward the flowing energies that help us to branch and blossom, to open to light and sky, to be abundant with energy and grace. To be healthy means to be fruitful, rich with creative energies, active and responsive to the energies and lives of others. It also means to turn inward, to seek silence and solitude in cycles of renewal, to become the silent evergreen that sits deep rooted in tranquility, feeling the fall of rain or snow, hearing the bird's cry, the sound of wind in branch and grass.[160] It means moving in times of motion and yet, being completely at ease, resting in the action, moving without effort into the current of the moment, into the very eye of the turbulence where there is stillness. It means freeing the body, the emotions, the mind, of all undeveloped energy; it means not over extending, not losing balance, staying centered, protecting the heart while still being open to the world, the needs of others, the needs of self. True health is a radiance, a glow whose source is Spirit, infused and pervasive, subtly connect-

---

160. Luke 12: 27-28.

ed with the greater energies of co-creation and mutual well-being. Together, we create the Hermetic circle, linked with like-minded others, to focus and build the creative energies necessary for world transformation.

We start with self but know that it is a paradox to assume that self alone can be known without others. Inevitably, our search for health is traceable to our relationships with those we have known, lived with, suffered and struggled with, and at times, lost some aspect of knowing the "I" because it was overshadowed by the "other". Those painful relationships may break off, remain incomplete, unresolved in terms of unrealized possibilities of growth and transformation through more mature interactions and understanding. But we as individuals continue, we do not stop growing because a root has been cut or a branch broken. To survive such storms, we must be deep rooted, connected in our depths to Spirit, to the inner reality of presence as the grounding, healing, protective energy of creation. The spark of Spirit's presence, her deep radiant beauty, her joy and fullness, is always with us, the inseparable golden vein that runs throughout the rocky contours of our search for self transformation. This presence is a most profound source of healing, an inner reality of intense but subtle joy sustained in every breath we take. Spirit is that breath, that life-gift, that primal source from which all healing comes. And she encompasses us with her beauty, her divinity, her holiness in making us aware of how much she surpasses our human needs and how much more she has to offer. To embrace Spirit is to be embraced, and to be embraced is, through Spirit's guidance, to be healed. This is the union of knowledge (Gnosis) with faith (Pistis) that leads to wisdom (Sophia) and purity in sustaining the life of others.[161]

The healing of self and others comes through the intelligent combination of three crucial elements: loving kindness, honesty, and receptivity. The leading principle is a genuine love that is not obsessed or attached to its own satisfactions or needs over the satisfactions and needs of others. The Christ principle is to love, in Spirit and Mystery, even as you would have yourself be loved; to love not only those that love you, but even those that hate and reject you.[162] Such love is difficult, it turns us toward the inner reality of our utmost capacities and challenges us to love without discrimination those who are not only similar, but those who are also alien, different, and even dangerous. Yet loving them does not mean submitting to those alien or dangerous others; it means having strong roots and an inner strength and purpose that works for healing. Such love is by no means submissive nor passive; it is active, engaged, challenging, seeking to instill a vivid example of love through dedication to

---

161. Luke 7: 34-35; Romans 11: 33.
162. Matthew 5: 46-48.

spiritual ideals. The necessity of love is found in transformative Christ energy, heart-centered, whose effects are more than an act of will or human effort. When the heart-center opens, it transmits the creative energies of Spirit into the world as an impartial, deep-centered presence that awakens those same energies in others. Love is a flowing forth and a flowing back, in continuously circulating currents, that deepens and expands our awareness of Spirit as ever-active and present in all human relationships.

Healing in this sense means opening to that flow while maintaining the integrity of an expanding spiritual vision, one that is inclusive and yet, has its own center. The healing of the nations can only come about because we learn to love and respect the values we share in a non-aggressive context of respect and mutual honesty. Is this any different than a love relation between two adults? Honesty is crucial for the development of maturity in relating to others; it requires us to set aside our masks and to reveal our true faces, without shame or guilt, but with humility and receptivity to the perceptions of others. It means knowing the nature of integrity, of holding clear values and cultivating foundational virtues that do not oppress or harm others and which act as an inspiration for greater sharing and openness. We all have limits, boundaries that must be respected, but which, in the context of love, can be questioned, challenged, brought to the surface for reflection and dialogue. To love others as we love our self means to respect our inner capacities without denying the possibility of inner change and new attitudes and actions inspired by the insights and loving concerns of others. This means being receptive, flexible, capable of bending without breaking, of knowing how to redirect the energies of criticism to a positive learning without harboring anger or resentment. This is true for nations as well, the collective attitudes of majority representation must also be capable of bending, knowing how to redirect the energies of conflict into non-violent strategies aimed at rebalancing the excessive and extreme reaction.

Majority responsibility can only be sound when the members of that majority are themselves healthy, mature, and centered in the virtues of non-aggressive relationships. Violence is not a solution but a deep and profound social illness; the use of force to inhibit the actions of others contributes to the imbalance, to a contraction of soul that closes the mind to the transformative benefits of dialogue and self-restraint. Nor is it acceptable to become victims of that violence; such violence must be resisted and the integrity of a loving way of life maintained. We do not "render unto Caesar that which is Caesar's" if what is asked breaks the covenant of the spiritual path we follow.[163] The

---

163. Luke 20: 25.

challenge is to sustain that spiritual covenant that we make within the heart, in Spirit, with others, even when it means resisting the mandates of collective law or public demands. On the path of the Hermetic Christ, love and honesty, non-violence and compassion, are at the center, fidelity to spiritual commitments has greater precedence than unjust laws or immoral demands of states or nations. The Hermetic transformation is not under the authority or determination of any state or nation, nor is it under the strict control of any legislative body, nor can it be determined by vote, collective assent, or those who are leaders within the spiritual community. Each individual has an obligation to determine for him or herself, the exact nature of the vows, commitments, and values that would act as guiding principles for the unfolding of a genuine, lasting spiritual maturity.

Guidance can be sought, teachers consulted, confessions made, but we are each responsible to enact the path we freely choose. The guiding principle is a compassionate, enduring love for life and all creatures that is free from petty desires for dominance and no longer seeks to justify its own practice through holding it above others as somehow better or best. The false and unhealthy arrogance that most betrays Spirit in the act of love is a shallow sense of superiority, a greedy willingness to condemn others, a tendency to secretly believe in the artificial security of superficial collective attitudes as though such attitudes were a means to justify the denial of others. There are great limits in collective belief, a multitude can be wrong and misguided, regardless of their numbers. We hold to Christ as an example of willing commitment to a spiritual path that where it must confront the boundaries of harmful, cruel, oppressive or indifferent actions, it does so without an arrogant pride of place. There is no special promise for those who follow their spiritual path other than the reward given to every soul — we go to that which most reflects how we each lived and how we loved. Our fate in following a spiritual path is not predetermined, is not fixed or free of the overall influences of the full workings of Spirit. The limited scope of the present must be gently stripped away to reveal a much vaster horizon within which there is no "one way" and no "best path" but only a multitude of ways, each with their own benefits and values.

To reach out to the world as a whole is good insofar as we are able to do so through humility and appreciation of the multitude of pathways and spiritual teachings. To act with integrity means to have a path, to follow it consistently with a clear knowledge of its values and teachings, and to be an example to others of a chosen way. It does not mean to force that way on others, to hold our path above the paths of others, or to deny the relative value of our own committed and faithfully followed way. What may be absolutely true for us may be only relative to others and what is absolutely true for them, may only be relative to us. This is the nexus around which global harmony spins and the music it creates is multidimensional, vast and harmonic unto the ninth sphere — but beyond that it blends into an even vaster music whose voices are beyond counting. Thus to walk the path of the Hermetic Christ means to walk with humility, integrity, commitment, as one who seeks to reconcile and mediate conflict, tension, and disagreement. It means having a voice, speaking clearly with focused intent, being able to engage and debate the values of this path, kindly, without seeking to undermine the ways of others. Hold to your path, but be receptive to the teachings and insights of other paths, learn from them, allow Spirit to guide you in learning to deeply respect the ways and paths of others. In Christ, we find an example, in the Divine Sophia, another image of divinity, in the Holy Marriage, a uniting of the male and female perspectives, each valuing the vision of the other.

The Christ-heart embraces all ways, all paths, yet has a center from which to see the differences and similarities. The path becomes a reality because we choose as individuals to embrace its teachings and to enact them as guidelines for the evolution of new consciousness, to taste new wine in new bottles.[164] The amber of that liquid is from the sun, from the earth, from the elements that grow a vine whose fruit is sweet and potent. Therefore, we take it in small portions, ingesting it to make it part of us, over a lifetime of conscious living, dedicated to the highest ideals. The inner warmth is Spirit given and Spirit made, infusing awareness with the gifts of spiritual maturity that lead to health, balance, the perfect fruit. We must filter out inner impurities, transform the volatile tendencies, and integrate the vital and spiritual aspects in alchemical synthesis. Such transformation is healing and such healing is a means toward world-awakening; in the illumination of Spirit, we all benefit, we all share the positive release of creative energies. The only boundary is our own limits, accepted, recognized as creative limitations on possible future growth. We are not perfect, not ideal beings, but fallible, human, creative, aspiring to unfurl our wings, to feel the light, to be lifted in the transformation to new wisdom and understanding. To attain that goal, we must heal ourselves, those we love, those who love us, and all humanity through the integrity by which we live.

---

164. Mark 2: 22.

Peace
To know that all races and religions are one in Mystery, each to be honored in their contributions to peace; Christ is a way, but there are other equally good ways, difference is Creation; the Source, Infinite. (4:8)

The underlying unity and oneness is not simply additive or cumulative. It is not a function of the integration of diverse traditions, nor it is a consequence of a certain way of thinking nor is it a result of altering human awareness. This oneness preexists, it is an intrinsic feature of the whole, an infused presence inseparable from the initial conditions of creation in whatever mythos, science, or symbol system we may wish to express it. The altering of awareness, our opening to new horizons of perception is an opening to the greater unity that lies intrinsic not only to the human mind, but extends throughout the subtle multi-dimensionality of an evolving, transforming universe. The limits of our concept of "universe" do not allow us to reach the full realization of the magnitude of the whole. It's most intrinsic feature is awareness, not impersonal electro-magnetic energies or gravity or strong, weak, or counter forces. Such concepts circumscribe the actual nature of the instilled presence of life. No matter how impersonal the forces of creation may appear, no matter how awesome the titanic energies, without life, mind, awareness and understanding, it will remain incomprehensible, ungraspable, and forever enigmatic. But with life, with mind, awareness, living reflection and deep investigation of its life-enhancing and life-sustaining qualities, we can and will discover ever increasing dimensions of unity within the whole—as we spiral out and as we spiral in. Unity is inseparable from conscious being, inseparable from the emotional and noetic perspectives through which Spirit acts to lead us to greater wisdom and maturity.

To say "difference is creation" means that we grow toward spiritual health and maturity through a process of individuation, a process that does not sacrifice the importance of community or love. To become spiritually individuated means to know and celebrate our differences, it means to make the ascent into the light, to attain the gift of illumination, and to bring that gift as a sharing into the circle of beloved others. This Hermetic circle, whose sign is an image of wholeness and unity, holds at its center a precious gift. The enlightened individual, the illumined soul as another affirmation of the spiritual potential, reveals an inner capacity realized in radiant love and wisdom. This individual does not stand above others within the circle, but freely exchanges the center for a constant sharing of energies — from all members, each able to take the center and hold the pivot for the turning dance. Illumination is shared, enlightenment intrinsic to mind, soul, and heart and therefore, uncontainable in any one vessel. The degree of purity, the inner work done to liberate the currents of joy, the free flowing upward ascent of light joined with the downward fire of Spirit meets in a Witness-consciousness and absorbs "all that is above with all that is below". This is the true light at the center, to stand as a harmonious sign of the Hermetic union of earth and heaven, and to be an axis, a pivot, around which the immense energies of creation can circulate the requisite degrees of holy inspiration.

This is true individuation, one that carries the illumined soul far beyond mental health and balance into the mystical heart of creation. But it is more than a "flight of the one to the One" — it is a reunion of the soul with its deepest, most inward identity. The process of spiritual training and purification is like the grinding of a lens of purest crystal; the shaping will determine the way in which it will focus light. Being shaped and polished, it becomes a translucent lens that will bring light into a focal radiance. Yet, in itself it is transparent, a disk whose purity and beauty is so refined and distilled, that it is able to allow that light to pass through it with greater or lesser degrees of intensity. Some are polished in ways to refract the light, to reveal its various mediums of color and the subtle theosophies of radiance; others offer a sharp, focal intensity, transcendent wisdom; and others diffuse that light, sharing its joy and love with everyone whom they have contact, in the flesh, in dreams, in spiritual relations. Individuation is not a matter of simply having personal preferences and individual needs and desires; the trajectory of spiritual growth takes us into Spirit and into the depths and holy mysteries that radically transforms our very being. We become spiritually unique and yet, spiritually transparent, focal gems, radiant with unique color and hues born of Spirit and shaped by grace, personal choice, and inward surrender. True individuation requires inner surrender as much as it does a willing recognition and development of individual gifts and abilities.

Our paths diverge, but meet in a deep spiritual center; we find our freedom in transformation into angelic states whose potentials manifest in unique ways, the center. The center is everywhere but it is not the same for all beings, nor is it manifested in identical ways or paths or teachings. It is like this: the soul begins its journey toward the Throne, setting aside the heaviness of material life and external concerns. The soul hears a music most alluring, feels a current of the heart, most exquisite in sorrow and joy, sees the transparency of lights and aspires to journey through the many veils over the Face of Mystery. As the soul proceeds, each veil removed is a veil removed inwardly, each revelation, a revelation of inner potential. The further the soul journeys, overcoming fear and amazement, the more she comes to realize the infinite universe within, the depthless bottom that has no measure. As further veils are removed, an ever greater horizon expands and opens, revealing the most holy and profound intensities of depth and fullness.[165] The soul slows in its inner movement of self-will and is taken over by a current that now draws it toward its full capacity of perception and understanding. Spirit grasps this soul, opens the heart, reveals a true *gnosis*, a true knowing of the heart, of Spirit, of Mystery. The soul comes to an ecstatic halt, suspended within the full energies of mystical illumination, its own center transparent to a full spectrum of radiant manifestations. It acquires the Witness-consciousness, that is, it sees and knows Spirit in the direct manifestation of full mystical illumination. And there are still 60,000 veils of light between this illumined soul and the Holy One whose radiance sustains life in all forms, in all worlds, forever.

Always, whatever degree of illumination we attain, there are yet more degrees, more veils we can remove, even after we reach the full and complete ecstasy that extends our soul awareness to its ultimate degree and opens the noetic, transcendent horizon to its full scope and immensity. How can there not be different paths, different teachings, different spiritual ideals or goals? In a universe of infinite magnitude, veiled beyond human comprehension, how can there not be relative truths whose wisdom reflects multi-generations of seekers striving to slowly grow into the full stature of what it means to be fully aware, fully mature, fully conscious? This is our challenge, to grow beyond the limits and shadows of our relative truths and into the full integration, the individuated realization, that will contribute to the process of awakening an entire race and world. We do this not by embracing one path as higher or best, but rather by embracing our chosen path as best for us, as one way among others for attaining the goal. If we stand at the center, as a pivot, even for a moment, it is only so another can take our place and keep the circle moving, keep the energies flowing into the patterns and dances of spiritual growth and shared joy. All races and religions are one, not because they form a single synthesis, but because they offer their unique perspectives to the unfolding of human potential. And we honor them in their contributions to peace, to cooperation, to mutual growth and reciprocal respect.

This means that we can also choose not to follow a path and we can resist a path that would claim superiority or use violence as a means to further its own ends. I do not affirm the condemnation of others; I do not accept their condemnation based on spiritual claims; and I believe in the necessity of spiri-

---

165. 2 Corinthians 3: 16-17.

tual freedom. Our freedom is to choose between ways that promote and enhance life, and ways that threaten and deny life. Between the poles, there are many ambiguous choices, but these choices must be made based on spiritual principles that value life and peaceful co-creation. The life we value is not just human life, but all life, in all forms. The spiritual path we choose walks a way that seeks to promote and preserve life, to live in peace with fellow human beings as well as with other life forms, and to share spiritual perspectives without condemnation or denial of the positive life-affirming values of others. We honor all those ways whose adherents contribute to peace and to global well-being and we resist those whose goals would subordinate the lives of others to their own aggressive ideologies, policies, or dominance. The Hermetic ideal is transformative, that is, it seeks to promote growth and change; its greatest area of effort and concern is education, instruction in all fields of human endeavor, the promotion of balanced communal and ecological life, and the cultivation of individual gifts and abilities. Its processes are synesthetic, alchemical, and illuminative. Its goals are to contribute to world understanding through personal internalization of spiritual values and the actualizing of deep potential through *gnosis* and shared communal responsibilities.

The sign of this process in the image of the Hermetic Christ is represented under many different forms and teachings. With the *Regina Angelicum*, the Queen of Angels, it is the Christ child as the luminous spirit of uninhibited, spontaneous innocence still overflowing with the joy at magnitude of the creation under the guardianship of the Holy Mother Spirit surrounded by the protective guardians of the Throne, the Archangels of the Host. As the baptized teacher, it is the image of the spiritual seeker who journeys into the desert and seeks to confront the deepest fears and successfully subdues temptations and self-serving impulses. As the healer and spiritual teacher, it is the sign of an individual who resists the authority of tradition and offers new guidance and direction, confronting the static boundaries that inhibit growth and development. As the transfigured Christ of the mountain, it is the mystic guide, the illumined master who reveals understanding to a circle of devotees, followers, and those whose devotion and insight carries them beyond "inner" and "outer" teachings. The Christ of the crucifixion is the image of the surrendered soul, willing to give his or her life and dedication in order to preserve the dignity and integrity of a chosen spiritual path. What is required is an ethic of inner strength and devotion that does not lead to external confrontation, but works with those energies in a creative, non-violent manner. The Christ of the resurrection is the image of the ethereal teacher, the dream and visionary encounters that lead us, step by step, into the plurality of the heavenly realms and acts as a guide of souls, Hermes-Christ-Sophia.

There are other paths, other ways, other teachers, guides, and models. Many are great, some are truly profound and without peer, many of whom are hardly recognized within the orthodoxy of traditional teachings. Many masters, teachers, guides, shamans, and spiritual teachers of tradition, great or small, contribute to the Hermetic way. The distillation, the purification and subtle integration, is the task of the individual—to draw on the core teachings and to expand through personal study, application, and inner work. The Source is infinite, and the ways are open to individuation and difference; the unity is inseparable from any practice. But some practices are more effective and consequential than others and they differ in this through individual application and not through some greater scheme of hierarchical rank or progressive staging. Each must seek to find the peaceful way, the integration of feminine and masculine perspectives, the incorporation of Hermetic principles, and their actualization in a way of life that leads to illumination. Illumination is a necessary part of the path, there is no substitute in ritual, faithful vows, communal disciplines, social action, beliefs or studies, that can substitute for actual, direct knowing. And yet, genuine *gnosis* is no substitute for study, integration, and practice of communal values and a spiritual way of life. There must be balance, harmony, a full circle of connected relations that support and nourish the evolution of the whole. Each must find his or her place, each find what is real in the way of life lived and in the quality of love shared. And in all this, Spirit is there, guiding, present, abundant in grace.

The Waters
To give the Waters of Life freely, with compassion, love, mercy, and forgiveness; to not condemn nor judge those who walk in unknowing, nor deny the unheeding. (4:9)

The Waters of Life are given to each of us as a gift of greatest value: to live, breathe, sense, feel, and to be aware of all that passes within and without us. These waters are poured out as a clear, luminous stream of the most minute and subtle particles, as energetic manifestations of Spirit, on all the mountains of the world. They flow down off these mountains, forming into pure streams, rivers, waterways and wells forming oceans, rains, seas, and the living presence of moisture, dews, and swelling, cyclic clouds. This water world is thus gifted with life in all its water based forms, filling our own bodies with its fluids and flowing hydrate molecules. And these are living waters, not just compounded from molecular form, but also infused with the very presence of even more subtle energies, energies whose life giving qualities descend from the very stars that light the heavens. These are healing waters, life-giving moisture, fluid, liquid life, the amniotic, Hermetic carriers of Love, Spirit, and Mystery.[166] There is nothing sterile about the Waters of Life, they brim over with an intensity of spiritual presence so subtle and inseparable from the whole that they constantly renew and revive our flagging, diminished potentials. These Waters offer us renewal and rebirth, a reconstitution of our aspiration to become vessels of Spirit, a receptacle within which animate life is transformed into a holy, luminous, self-aware being.

Without these waters, there would be no life, no joy, no tears, no sweat, no renewal, no effort to embody the Infinite in specific forms, in the compressed heat and sensitivity of new born children. In the subtle world, these waters are converted into energies, into an exchange and sharing of feeling, thoughts, beliefs, and desires. When Yeshu'a, the Anointed, raised his cup and made his vows of remembrance, binding those who loved him with his love, then the wine became water, flowing through human tissues to the heart and there, was transformed into divine love. That same love flows through all human relations, liberated from historical circumstances, and merged with the compassionate teachings of all paths that seek a spiritual transformation of humanity. These currents of love, like ever-flowing and regenerating streams of water, draw us toward a more heart-centered way of life, a more conscious loving that does not inhibit but stimulates our capacity to truly rejoice in the diverse loves of others. When we love freely, without resistance to an inward opening outward, without attachment or demands, without possessive attachment or clinging needs, then we open to that Christ love, to compassion that carries us beyond the historical past or present into a reborn future. In the present moment, love is an Infinite capacity inseparable from its expressive actualizations, yet irreducible to any one instance. It is a matrix of relations extending into depths we hardly recognize and including a vast multitude of souls.

This giving and sharing of the waters is not simply an act of charity or generosity. It is much more; it is a form of sacredness, a participation in Mystery, a fullness that cannot be bound to discreet motives or self-serving ends. It is not a head-centered giving, nor a consciously constructed rational for ethical or shared human responsibility. It is a giving that flows spontaneously out of the heart, into the world, overflowing the boundaries of human self, connecting with the sorrow, joy, and struggles of others, effortlessly, and yet, remains centered in the depths from which that love flows. This is what it means to

---

166. Revelations 21: 6.

give "freely" those waters, to have no attachments to what is required of others to receive the gift; for nothing is required, only that you give fully to the best of your ability. We are each a channel for these waters, each a fountain and a well, each a spring whose depths and clarity vary in accordance with our inner work and self-development. It is not an ideational giving, but an emotional, heart-centered opening to mystical depths through which flows a life-renewing presence original to the creation of life. When we love deeply and truly without effort and with our whole being, then life is renewed and restored. And when we love in Spirit, through Spirit, then love becomes a revelation, an unveiling of hidden depths, an encounter that transforms.

In this encounter we discover the qualitative necessity of mercy and forgiveness, a capacity that does not reject the rejections of others. This is a great challenge on the plane of everyday relations as long as we hold acceptance and rejection as central to a sense of self-definition. But when we learn to let go of our narrowly defined sense of self, when we are able to open to Spirit, to allow for an inward expansion of the heart, to experience the immediacy and power of love as a transformative medium, then we begin to experience love in the Infinite sense. Such love flows into all the cracks and crevices of a more fragmentary, limited self, lifts it toward greater health, and reveals an expanse within which self is utterly transformed. In that transformation, in each small step and in each opening, the qualities of forgiveness and mercy become ever more active, ever more inseparable from loving without censure or blame. It is rarely difficult to see the imperfections of others, this requires no special ability; but it can be difficult to see the perfectibility of others masked by those imperfections. We are all imperfect beings, without exception, Yeshu'a ben Miriam included. We are not all-powerful, all knowing, perfect, ideal beings but limited, fragile, temporally conditioned, and incomplete in the realization of our full potentials. In such a circumstance, mercy and forgiveness is truly necessary at all levels of interaction, from the most external to the most intimate.

Our capacity to love is a measure of our inner willingness to not internalize the differences and disagreements, the conflicts we may have with others. There is disagreement, there is non-congruence, misalignment, missed connection, and out-and-out differences. But those differences are not the determining characteristics for actualizing genuine spiritual love, compassion, and forgiveness. Nor is it a matter of sameness, in values, in a spiritual path, in community, or in any group membership. Many are the ways of the world and all its inhabitants, and the majority is fully worthy of genuine love and nurturance, the remaining minority needs only to give up attachments to violence, pride, aggression and fear to join the diverse spiritual circles of the multitudes. But even in the case of the most disturbed, most violent, the most unconscious or self-aggrandized, the most narrowly denying, self-serving individual, there is still a need for love and forgiveness. Otherwise, there will be no healing, no redemption, and no end to suffering and isolation, no exit from a self-created hell. There is no reason to assume that all or even most others will find in the Hermetic Christ a helpful sign of guidance, a useful archetype of awakened spirituality. Plurality is creation, diversity is a holy work of drawing out potentials and capacities. Many are the holy works and many are the paths; each must follow the path they are called to and each can find the means for a more illumined life.

Where our paths intersect with those of others is in wisdom and love, in compassion, in healing, in forgiveness and mercy, in not judging but seeking to ecstatically transform the ordinary into the celestial garden of positive human relations. Not in dominating, not in the name of a greater truth, but in the act of loving the healthy-minded and in healing those whose illnesses diminish us all. There are many who would deny the value of a spiritual life, who constantly pass judgment on the insufficiency of spiritual practices, or on any religious beliefs, or inner aspirations that contest their own bias. On the path of the Hermetic Christ, we do not judge those who so judge others; we seek instead to transform our own behavior in such a way as to exemplify the luminous truths of the path we walk. The compelling evidence of a spiritual path is the quality of life lived, the depths of human relationships, the passionate commitment to a transformed awareness, actualized in luminous insights. This "knowing" is a spiritual experience, and like Christ on the mount of transfiguration, it is realized in the heart of those who truly love and participate fully in Spirit. Do not deny those who would deny you, and do not serve their passions or goals if they contradict your spiritual path. We each must chose, and in choosing, commit ourselves to the chosen way, still loving those others that we may not have as companions and co-travelers on the path.

Many are the unheeding, many those who would deny their own potential and who claim they cannot see illumination in their own hearts. Caught in the world of immediacy, in family, in physical-emotive life, in the intellective labyrinths of social, economic, and scientific institutions, they would deny all relevance to religious and spiritual aspiration. We each walk our own path, no one can walk it for us; but at the very least, we can respect the rights of others to follow a non-violent, ethically mature way, religious or not. Many of the unheeding are caught in the labyrinths of soul and self, in the socially constructed realities of an intellective, material, rationalized world devoid of belief in Spirit or Mystery. They do not remember dreams, do not credit the invisible world, do not accept the intuitive, symbolic, or felt impressions of a subtle and energetic nature. Their ideas about religion are often very immature, undeveloped, hardly recognizable as a viable spiritual outlook. Instead, having rejected religious thinking at a very young age, they no longer think in those childish terms and they no longer develop a more mature inquiry into the nature of religious experience, revelation, or spiritually motivated ethical concerns. In many ways, the issues at the heart of this matter revolve around the insufficiency of much religious thought, its narrowness and in more contemporary or popular guise, its superficialities. But such a response only looks at the glassy surface, sees only an appearance, a crude externalism, and reacts only to an outer form.

To go within, to penetrate to the moist, warm center of life, to arouse an inner feeling of longing and aspiration toward a full realization of potential takes much, much more than just a critical reaction. The challenge is to live in such a way that our qualitative life speaks for us, that there is presence and illumination as a visible witness to an inward journey. It is not form that matters, but awakening to Spirit, to the creative energies of transformation. In so doing, we can only enact the visionary worlds we inhabit as a sign of a future possibility, of a becoming, whose realization is at most only a possibility in the minds of the unheeding or unbelieving. We must choose peace and coexistence over conflict, war and reprisals; differences in religion and spirituality should contribute to the richness of soul we all inherit, not diminish it for a material substitute. We hardly know our full potential, hardly recognize our capacities in a living universe of multiple worlds, visions, and luminescent journeys. Take up the Cup, fill it with love, compassion and forgiveness, and share it with another, pass it on to them quietly through example, not by words and promises. Enact the path, make it inseparable from every doing, every condition that confronts us with a choice: to be more or to be less. Mind, heart, soul, all function to support a capacity for expansion, an ability to incorporate more reality and deeper seeing and understanding. Receive that Cup in humility, take it and drink the waters deeply, into the very marrow of thy soul, and then, pass it on without clinging, without grasping at its essence.

Bread

To share the Bread of Life, in communion, in fellowship, with friends and strangers; giving when you are asked, receiving when you are given, simply, with sincere feeling. (4:10)

This bread is the Bread of Life, a mixture of grains, all healthy and nutritious, not over refined or stripped of its fiber and wholeness. It is a flat bread, unleavened, a bread whose value lies in its freshness, its warmth from the oven, its fragrant healthiness and simplicity.[167] It is a bread made in many homes throughout the world wherever there is love, joy in family, communion in the many names of Spirit, a sharing that springs from the heart when we value those we love and who love us. This bread is not manufactured by industry, nor created for the masses in palatable but sterile forms, nor engendered for profit or personal gain. It is not harvested and winnowed in mass quantity, nor propagandized in the name of a collective image or belief. It is not "life" as a consequence of superficial living or a hurried consumption, ill digested in the name of convenience or addictive habits. This is a bread that must be carefully prepared, skillfully baked, finely chewed, and fully absorbed to benefit from its life giving qualities. It is bread that gives life because we accept it as a sign of the simplicity by which we choose to live. And it must be shared in order to be blessed with the qualitative nuances of communal beliefs and spiritual ideals. It is not a matter of mass belief, of numbers, of the five thousand fed with only seven loaves, but of the quality and power of a surplus that overflows the limited boundaries of individual concern and opens to the immensity of Spirit in giving us all life, healthy, and prosperity.

The sharing of this bread comes from a depth of sincerity when we embrace our spiritual path and seek to foster the heart of creation. The heart is overflowing with a multitude of possible expressions whose uniqueness can only be known in the sharing, in coming to know the other as a testimony of an alternative truth resonant with our own. This resonance, this receptivity to the other in warmth and caring, this genuineness of feeling that overflows from a compassionate attitude toward creation, is nourishment. When the Christos said, "This is the bread that came down from heaven, the manna, and whoever eats it will live forever," he speaks of the gift of Spirit that is poured out on all those whose generosity and love is not bound by only common beliefs or concerns.[168] He speaks of a love that is able to cross the boundary and to reach out to the stranger and the alienated, to the lost, confused, and unhealthy, to those in need of bread with substance and nourishment. The fiber in this

---
167. Mark 14: 22; 1 Corinthians 5: 8.
168. John 6: 58.

bread is not dyed an artificial white, nor is it bleached by common processes meant only to appeal to superficial taste and external appearances. This fiber has resistance, has an inner strength and fortitude that can stand up to the demanding needs of physical life and personal interactions. It has color from its multigrain sources, it's capacity to blend spiritual qualities from numerous grains while still maintaining the integrity of its taste and texture. It is not a stale, tasteless bread, but one rich in favor, subtle, life-giving.

It is a manna that comes down and in the dawn light can be gathered like particles of dew from the spiny thorns, later dissolving in light, and reconstituting itself yet again in the new born day.[169] Manna is a spiritual, alchemical sign, a hermetic substance whose preparation requires a pure heart and a non-possessive mind. To absorb manna is to eat the bread of the presence, to see it as a sign of the promise fulfilled as it sustains us, day to day, in loving and serving others.[170] The dawn light is its manifestation in your own heart of the tenderness and sorrow that causes to you to reach out to others in their needs, for the benefit of their renewal through love. It is a quality seen in loving your children, your mates and family, animals, any who suffer or are unjustly subject to the bias and prejudices of neglect, discrimination, and indifference. The blind and unseeing as well as the ill and impoverished are all worthy of that bread, all capable of being sustained and renewed by it. The new born day is the day of the arising of that light within, the illumination of the heart through generosity, loving, and kind regard directed toward the well-being of others. The dissolving of that light is its reabsorption into the very blood and bone, its assimilation into the heart-mind where it acts to liberate our fears and open our boundaries. To act with love requires courage, an inner strength that seeks to recognize how as individuals we can each assist the growth and development of others. And our greatest assistance is not in words or ideas or in beliefs, but in acts of kindness motivated by genuine compassion.

It is also a sharing that occurs with friends and those within the fellowship of a multitude of Hermetic circles. In the name of the Christ, we can remember the Bread of Life as a sign of the teaching and heart of Christ that asks us to share with others through the anointments of Spirit. Through a quickening of the heart, we can receive inwardly the joyful gift of spiritual communion, of shared reverence, of an inner harmony of thought, mind, and deeds. The bread we share is the reverential gift of giving to others what we can honestly give without false promises or empty forms. This is not a matter of simple empathy or identity through a vicarious similarity of circumstances. It is much more a transformative love that does not seek to impose in any way, the differ-

---
169. Psalm 78: 23-25.
170. Matthew 12:4.

ences masked by momentary needs or painful, shattering events. It is a bread we share on a daily basis, not just in times of need or crisis or in unexpected turbulence and chaos. On the basis of this every day sharing, the day of turbulence and chaos is no different than any other day, it only demands more of our strength, rootedness, grounded, stable seeds of presence. This is why that bread must nourish us in our daily rounds, as a staple in our diet, as a constant nourishment that provides us with the strength and capacity we need in all times, in peace, war or chaos, to not contract or deny, but to remain open to Spirit even in the midst of the most tremendous suffering. Our daily communion strengthens the bond between the heart and the world, it creates a pattern of shared joy that can endure the severe trial of unexpected crisis or the emotional demands of others. Our concern, on the path of Christ, is to meet those needs in centered calm, in the ground of a more permanent, enduring being that cannot be shaken by the transient instabilities of social chaos or imbalance.

On an individual basis, we practice the art of giving and receiving in the name of Spirit, the Christ love, the Sophianic compassion, in all circumstances, as a spiritual norm. In a collective circumstance this individual practice is not annulled or surpassed by communal events or collective decisions. Under all circumstances, the practice of the individual as a vessel of Spirit cannot be annulled and will not be annulled as long as each gives freely the bread of life to others. The union of those who share that bread is more than a corporate act of collective ascent or communal identity, it is a spiritual correspondence that requires a sincere and developed integrity born in the heart of each person. It is not a matter of conformity or obedience to collective norms; it rather a willing communion in Spirit to purify the heart and to practice generosity through the promptings of Spirit. We are not all prompted in the same way nor are we all called to the same tasks or service. Each must find the norm of their practice within the visionary contents of a faithful and purified heart, one free of egoism and vanities of station or collective membership. This does not mean that the community has no rule or standards that apply equally to all members, but it does mean that these standards are not binding on the kind of service the heart chooses. Our fellowship is not found in a closed community but in the wholeness of the world and in all communities whose circles link with generous service to the needs of the many and not simply the desires of the few. Love is not bound by law or rule, but like Spirit, overflows and follows its own courses.

There is a discipline in receiving as well as in giving. For in giving we may set aside the feeling of our own importance in order for the work of Spirit of flow forth for its own ends. And so it is with receiving. We must set aside our own feeling of either worth or unworth, in order for that giving to expand into the fullness that the promise teaches. And what is the promise? It is the gift of the Holy Spirit, of the influx of the Divine Sophia, of the pouring out of the fullness, the qualitative inspirations best adapted to those who truly give and to those who truly receive. In receiving, we must also be empty vessels, appreciative of the gift but not clinging to it, knowing that it is an act of Spirit whose instrument is a particular need made visible. In this act of receiving, there need only be a simplicity of feeling that does not attach itself to the gift but fully values the giver as a momentary actualization of a deeper, sometime concealed, love. What the mind may think is not the key, it is what the heart feels beneath the superficial thoughts or motivations of the moment. The act of giving can be transformative if we do not cling to the gift but only exchange with one another, the creative energies of Spirit that make gifting possible. The heart is a gate whose door is hinged in both directions—it opens inwardly as we receive from without and outwardly as we receive from within. Within, the well-oiled hinge is a pin and pivot around which the hinge swings, and this pivot is our deep commitment to our spiritual path, to Spirit and the Christ Heart. In opening forth and back, it follows our breath, our breathing in and breathing out, in the calm, deep seated energies that giving and receiving actualize.

We give when we are asked, but only insofar as we can give in accordance with our state, conditions, and circumstances. There are those who would ask much and give little, who would demand more and give less, who would resist and insist. Our task is not to simply meet the demands or needs of others, for such demands and needs have no end. Our task, in following a spiritual path, is to understand the nature of compassion and love, and then to give and receive that love in a healthy and balanced way. It is not to exhaust inner resources through a compulsive giving-in to the unjust demands or heedless passions and appetites or unhealthy needs of others. The spiritual path is a test of balance, of inner clarity and purposeful action that shapes inner capacity in terms of spiritual goals. One of those goals on the Hermetic path is the practice of compassionate concern and generosity in relating to others, to all others, as a living example of dedicated kindness. The bread of life is to be shared with all those whose hunger is genuine and whose appetite is for spiritual knowledge; and if others taste it out of curiosity or through the influence of another, so much the better. But not everyone will eat it, and some will find it hard and lacking in flavor, while others may reject it because it does not satisfy their needs. Let them go their own ways, let them eat the bread of their own choosing, and understand that even the dogs can eat crumbs from under the table and be nourished.[171] We give to all what we can give, however much or however little, and we receive in the same manner, being guided by the principles of our path and following where Spirit leads. Thus, each seeker finds his or her own norm, and in so doing, defines the nature of their gifts and the extent of their rewards.

The Cup
To drink from the Cup that gives Life, the Grail of pure living and dedicated intent; to quest for spiritual rebirth, to overcome boundaries, to awaken the soul. (4:11)

This Cup is a crucible, a feminine vessel, whose contents are poured forth from Spirit in the name of the Divine trinity of Isis-Sophia-Mary. This is her vessel, her silver sign of transforming joy that gives life, the golden rim a token of illumination. Engraved on the cup is he Ankh symbol, the *Crux Ansara*, which signifies the properties of life and hallowed breath, a pure blessing that anoints head, heart, and soul. I hold this cup out to you, clasped in two hands, extended from my heart, asking you to receive it with joy and deep faith in its transforming powers.[172] This Cup or Bowl is a Hermetic vessel, a symbol of ceremonial communion, a nurturing of holy life in the depths of the womb.[173] There is ecstasy in this cup, there is sorrow and pain; there is joy, love, desire, passion, and a profound *eros* whose union of *psyche* with *nous* or holy mind in the Hieros Gamos signifies both temporal and spiritual fullness, ever-deepening through tests of integrity and devotion. This sacred cup harmonizes and also grants visionary revelations; it is the Kykeon of the ancient Eleusinian Mysteries filled with the eternal ambrosia of Demeter. It holds the wine of the blessings of the Christos now transformed into purest water, carrying within it the sacred energies of Spirit, poured out for the many and not just the few. The emanations of this cup are boundless, uncontainable, filled with merit, and vibrant with compassion, wisdom, and intuitive understanding. Take it with care, drink it clear minded, free of guilt or shame, pass it on to another, enhanced with your own devotion and aspiration. Do not refuse it, even to the stubborn or denying, for only in shared peace can the emptiness be filled.

This cup gives life because it is not only filled with visible liquid but also with invisible Spirit whose energies are absorbed by the thirsty soul. These

---
171. Mark 7: 28.
172. Mark 9: 41.
173 Corpus Hermeticum 4: 4.

energies act to awaken that desiring soul by feeding the depths of a great thirst for God-in-Truth, for the immanence of Mystery, for the transcendent ecstasies of true *gnosis*, for true awakening, true joy and union. The presence of Spirit is not uniform, nor equivalent with self-similar extensions in symmetrical space. Spirit is not an extension at all, it does not expand into emptiness nor contract into presence; its activities are multidimensional and give shape and content to all manifest forms—spatial, energetic, material, organic, and living. This occurs through intentional formations and enfolded orders built over eons and focalized through symbols and hieroglyphic signs as access points to depthless interconnection. All of nature is a hieroglyphic sign and humanity is inseparable from the on-going process of transitive becoming; the cup is a focal point, a symbol and sign, to link intentional harmonies in the process of creating a more loving and well-balanced humanity. The soul of the cup flows from the soul of the one that holds it, but that soul flows from living Spirit and is a gift taking specific form, filled with aspirations which blend within the cup and give it qualitative life. Soul itself is a cup, a subtle vessel of dynamic qualities, capable of great transformation in the full satisfaction of knowing its primal origin and cause. Spirit harbors soul just as soul harbors the cup, which is itself a hieroglyph of love passed on in the sharing.

This cup is also a Grail, a holy token of the quest for true wisdom and understanding. It represents the longed for sign that can only be found if the seeker is willing to give up attachments to collective denials or to habits and comforts that reinforce material pleasures to the detriment of self-understanding. This is why those who seek the Grail must take a vow of simplicity and non-possession; not to reinforce asceticism, but to resist attachments to worldly comforts that distract or mislead from the quest. Similar attachments to poverty and radical denials of flesh are equally distracting and do not guarantee a successful realization of the goal. The goal lies between extremes, in balance and harmony with the unique sensitivities and capacities of the individual. The quest has no set pattern, nor predetermined stages or determinable end. Each person sets out with only the naked capacities of birth and circumstances, adversity and adventure is spun from the looms of Spirit according to the aspirations and qualities of the individual soul. The pattern that emerges is a reflection of the integrity and depths of the quest, more complex for some and less rigorous for others. The realization extends into the patterns of those who have also quested and will quest in future aspirations. The greater convergence lies in the ways in which the patterns overlap and interconnect; the Grail quest is not a single quest but a convergent union of individuals centered on honorable love, devotion, and creative peace.

The qualifications for this quest, this search for the Cup of Life, for the gifts of Spirit and the shared joy of communion, are rooted in primal values. The aspirant must be dedicated to pure living, continual development, and the realization in direct experience of the varying stages of illumination. He or she must be willing to give the whole will to actualizing a spiritual path in all stages of life, as lover, mother, father, caretaker, worker, friend, adviser or teacher. The quest is not separate from responsibility in relationships and maturity in worldly actions. The cup is not a physical object but a communion in Spirit symbolized by the rites of shared concerns and the deep devotions of the heart. In giving we receive, in passing the cup on, we are nourished. These words are also a cup, transmitting inner intent and dedicated seeking. Pure living does not require renouncing family or children, nor does it mean taking vows of chastity or poverty. Pure living means acting without selfishness, opening the heart, being compassionate and clear-minded, resisting alienation and reaching out to others without grasping or seeking rewards. It is more than altruism and more than tolerance; it stems from deep spiritual roots that draw inspiration and sustenance from Spirit and flowers through spontaneous joy and beauty of soul. Pure living is an ideal whose realization takes effort, refinement, and a casting off of self-centeredness that takes pride in being numbered among the elect. There are no elect but only a multitude of souls seeking to realize the fullness that transcends their limited capacities. Those that wish to be esteemed for their spiritual accomplishments are still standing at the threshold; those that cross over stand below, not above.

The search for the cup leads us to rebirth but this also requires death and renunciation. What we renounce is our poor habits of mind, our addictions, habits and attachments to negative emotion, blame, censure, denial, defensive rationalizations and self-justifications. What we seek is balance, inner honesty, sincere outward expression, a deep integrity of purpose and a harmony between thoughts, words, and actions. Finding the cup means entering the circle, clasping the hands of others, purifying motives and relations, and learning to act with deep reverence and generosity. To reach this we must often give up attachments to former states, attitudes, old beliefs, and habits of denial. This is painful but necessary—in exile we seek conversion, in conversion we seek purification, in purification we seek illumination, and in illumination we seek reintegration. Many are in exile, lost and cut off from Spirit, living in self-preoccupation and in shadowed confusion; but it is not Spirit that separates them from their own ground. We each chose our ground, our place where our roots are deep or shallow, where the soil is fertile or rocky and barren. Like the seeds scattered among thistles, we must go into the earth, be willing to die to the old forms and beliefs, and be reborn in thrusting roots down to nourishment and leaf and stem toward light.[174] Where two or three are gathered together, Spirit is present; even where one seeks alone, spiritual companions are found. The angels of death and rebirth are always with us, the transformation, always a living possibility, even among the most fallen and confused. Coming out of exile means taking up the quest, determining deep within the possibility for utter transformation.

Always we are struggling against boundaries that are self-created or passed on in family, culture, or inherited modes of belief or denial. In following the Hermetic Christ, we take an example from his willingness to confront those boundaries, to go into the desert, into the unknown lands of the not-yet-awakened soul and there, to confront inmost temptations and grasping after personal satisfactions or conformity to unheeding prejudices. If we overcome these temptations within, progressively refining and deepening our roots, still we must also confront those boundaries in the worlds of others, even in those we love most dearly. Thus the strategy of the quest, grounded in nonaggression and peaceful ideals, moves forward into the world with an inner determination to live as an example of ideals realized inwardly. This is not a matter of abstract thoughts or esoteric models of reality; it is a matter of love, inner luster, and heart-felt expressions of spiritual joy. These expressions may be seen in small things—in how we greet others, how we treat friends and strangers alike, how we bend but do not break, how we stand firm in the face of ignorance, and how we reach out through example rather than through words and empty talk. It is the being of the soul that must emanate, penetrating the external forms, and touching the hearts of others. Physician heal thy self; let the light of Spirit be thy guide; presence, thy teacher.[175] Cut your bonds, unwrap the winding cloth of death, and be reborn into light and new life. Take the cup and drink deeply, be refreshed and nourished.

To awaken the soul, we must purge it of its attachments and bindings that blind us to a deeper, more profound beauty. Christ taught the blind to see and the deaf to hear; this mean that every person can be awakened to Spirit if they believe deeply enough in the hidden powers of the soul.[176] Many are bound, few are free. Most live in the shadowed world of half-belief, half-denial, confusion, uncertainty, or swing toward some absolute whose limits are an obvious barrier against inner unknowing. Many are proud, thinking themselves in possession of knowledge or understanding, their pride hidden behind a mask of false humility or detached superiority. But spiritual knowledge requires a

---
174. Mark 4: 7-8.
175. Luke 4: 23-24.
176. John 9:39.

melting of the heart, a dissolving of the ossified remnants of old order thinking, a grinding up of inner self-acclaim. To truly see or hear means to open the inner eye and the inner ear, to dissolve into light, into beauty, into wholeness in which there is no need for resistance.[177] Then we receive the cup, then we slake a thirst that desires refreshment, and join with others, to celebrate in mutuality our shared rebirth. For this cup gives knowledge of the whole, of the greater life beyond individual concern and enfolded with Mystery and Holy Wisdom. To receive the cup, the heart must be emptied of pride and free of guilt or shame; the heart, like the cup, being empty, is then filled with Spirit, ennobled, and sanctified beyond the norms of conventional understanding. This is the cup of ecstasy and joy, given, shared, passed on, and returned; the circle is unending and the illumination, without limits. Blessed are those that receive the cup, but more blessed are those that pass it on without attachment or self-concern.

Reborn

To follow Christ, even unto Death; to die and to be reborn; to live again, in this world, the worlds between, to go beyond, and still to embody flesh. (4:12)

The cycles of death and rebirth are part of the greater cycles of creation and dissolution which themselves reflect innumerable stages of cosmological transformation. All is in motion and inwardly still; all is inwardly contained and outwardly expressed through the energies of Spirit in innumerable manifestation. Spirit is the great Mother Wisdom that works to embody the unfathomable depths of Mystery, to make visible the invisible reality, to bring into existence, the yet-to-be. In this process of interlinked cycles, in the movement of the greater macrocosm and the responsive adaptations of the lesser microcosm, the creative energies flow both outward into the great expanse and inward into the incarnate depths of each individual. The creative life is found in making real the possibility that enhances the Whole, that gives nuance and depth through foreshadowing, that brings a pattern into focus and integrates it into emergent revelation. The goal is to crystallize in each life, the archetypal energies that lead to on-going transformation and expression of Spirit. The expression is not merely a transitive utterance, a song lost in the void, but a contribution to the music of the spheres, to collective harmonies that are enhanced by even a single note. The melody is the quality of life we

---

177. Bhagavad Gita 18: 56-58.

live in contributing to the harmony of others and in sustaining an inspiration that encourages others to join the greater creative work. Spirit sustains the creative harmony and carries within it, the deep memory of all that ever was or will be. And Mystery is the all-containing, inexhaustible matrix, the ocean of all-being in which there is nothing that is not sustained.

Certainly we live after the death of the body, this is a fundamental aspect of Mystery and Being. However, we do not yet comprehend the subtle interconnected and layered relations and identities that contribute to the awareness of any one individual. We are not simply a construct of material body and immaterial soul, but a layered complex of energetic processes that penetrate deep into the physical structures of matter, even to the micro-level, and expand far into the subtle body structures of the layered etheric worlds, seen in dreams and visions. The energies of the material world are by no means isolated to only material form, but also contribute in subtle ways to the energetic forms of consciousness in superordinate states of awareness. Even at the level of a molecular structure, there is "soul" and those energetic structures can be modified and shaped by conscious intent. We are far more fluid and transformative than a strictly material physics can describe; consciousness is far more creative and adaptive than a chemical, behavioral or cybernetic description can capture. Our soulful life is a mediation between the energetic processes of the body down to the substructures of the particle and the energetic processes of mind or awareness up to the most comprehensive mystical union. In this opening to Spirit, the boundaries are dissolved and the mental constructs are seen to be only distant reflections of a living, luminous, integral reality.

The wholeness of this existent cosmos is not measurable by external instruments nor fully knowable by external observation. It must be penetrated through the human heart and known through a soulful life of harmonic relations and subtle perception. We must grow into the wholeness, must learn to incorporate into our understanding a visionary basis for knowledge that far exceeds the rational or perceptible norms of the everyday mind. And yet, that everyday mind is an inseparable feature of the whole which, like the caterpillar, must undergo an inner transformation in order to have the necessary wings for flight and new explorations. Further, the metaphysical complexity of this whole, as seen from the Hermetic point of view, is far more than any one individual can fully comprehend. Therefore, we each contribute according to our gifts and offer our insights as a contribution to an emergent understanding that exceeds individual prowess or insight. Spiritual life is not about greatness or competition or some vast wisdom that exists on an inflated scale of human omniscience. It is rather a search for authenticity, maturity, and relative illumination that leads to inner peace and a genuine influence that contributes to our collective understanding. This means we each must seek within the correspondent truths which seem most valuable in living an authentic spiritual life, one committed to inner transformation and communal well-being. The visionary basis of that understanding is found in direct spiritual experience, in an awakening to Spirit that brings the soul fully to life and gives it the requisite sensitivity to perceive more fully, the wonder and beatitude of the visible world.

Death is a natural part of this process. We all die, we all undergo the transformations of death and in that dying, those transformations reflect the quality of life we have lived. Our deaths are impermanent, transitive, soulful encounters with our own inner qualitative being; they are also an new opening toward life, a new reception of understanding, a prelude to rebirth. As it is written, "Of those living in the shadow of death, a great light has dawned,"[178] that is, the light of recognition and remembrance of lives past, of the invisible world which is the parent of our existence, of previous life in the subtle planes, and of Spirit that guides us inwardly to primal *gnosis*. Our death is a process of continuing transformation that leads us in stages through the depths of our own preconceptions, expectations, guilt, fears, anxieties, and hopes. Christ sais, "If anyone keeps my word, he will never see death."[179] This means that when we follow a spiritual teaching, trusting in its truthfulness and direction, it will lead us to the expected goal. Not to see death means to discover the inner truth of creation that it is on-going, transformative life in all modes and conditions. There is life after death, that is, there is continuity and inner causal relations that sustain psychic continuity between incarnations. But we not simply a soul carrying the past, we are, in death and rebirth, reformed, reconstituted, transformed through radical processes that recreates our newness and innocence. Stripped of memory, drawn down into the womb, we are no longer that old *persona*, that past external life, but now become a naked reconstitution of potential bringing new qualities to fruition through emergent, creative endeavors.

But this is not the fate of every soul, for some are able to retain a necessary awareness that observes the processes by which the subtle layers of consciousness are subject to confrontations with the *archons* of dying. These *archons* are deep patterns of subjective formation, fully capable of manifesting as living entities and confronting the soul with choices and possibilities in the process of determining its future conditions. Advanced practitioners of the Hermetic path can face these encounters with an inner knowledge born through vision-

---
178. Matthew 4: 16.
179. John 8: 51.

ary experience allowing them to move through the stages that lead to a desired rebirth or to an a post-incarnate existence within the invisible worlds. They may chose, through deep conscious intent, to seek the Christos in an afterlife of ecstatic revelation or they may chose a faithful rebirth in order to serve the processes of collective, incarnate evolution. To die and be reborn is no simple thing, it may happen in a multitude of ways dependent on the attitudes and emotional maturity of the individual or on their faithful adherence to a spiritual path, or their deep inner convictions. We each serve in ways that best express our needs and personal history; we must each seek the norm and balance that will best sustain us through a multitude of possible experiences. In the worlds between, there are unlimited possible alternatives, constructed by inner intentions and outward actions leading to inevitable consequences. The "many rooms" of the invisible worlds are all conditional, relative, and subject to the formative, casual influences of actual life choices.[180]

The wheel turns and we turn with it in accordance to our desires, hopes, and fears. On the Hermetic path, we follow Christ in the promise of eternal life, but not fixated on a particular place or on some visionary heaven. The Kingdom of Heaven is within, and that means that we are each a subjective axis of creation, each responsible to bear within our soul, the image of the Kingdom most appropriate to our full potential.[181] For me, that image does not resolve itself into a place, but into a spiritual illumination whose center is everywhere and whose content is indescribable in its fullness and beauty. There is death in that image and rebirth, there is a dissolution of person and a reconstitution in a multitude of alternative forms, there is light and darkness, activity and rest, fullness and utter emptiness, a no-thing-ness whose attributes are ineffable and wondrous. All worlds, planes, levels, visionary conditions, and the vast multitude of all beings dissolve into that realization, into the unconditional surrender that leads to soul's absorption into the Unity of All. This is peace, this is rest, this is holy and unspeakable joy. What follows is only the stimulus that arises as an creative desire to enact again the drama and explorations of Spirit, prompted by the teeming life of creation and its multitude of forms. The significance is to embody Spirit, to be a living example of the creative life, manifesting the joy of *gnosis* in the actions of the everyday. True illumination is rebirth and the influence of that illumination spreads through many worlds and is not bound by local space or time.

To follow Christ means to climb into the high hills of the transfiguration, to behold the opening of the doors of the past and future, to share the vision of a reborn world no longer subject to the greed, ignorance, and despair of hope-

---
180. John 14: 2-3.
181. Luke 17: 20-21.

lessness or selfish envy. It means to cast off the rags and tatters of fragmented living, of unclear values, confused ideals, and uncertain longing. In following Christ, in aspiring toward Holy Wisdom, we seek a new life, a path leading to illumination that is trustworthy and adaptable, flexible in allowing for difference and fully supportive of individual ability and aspiration. In following this path, we accept death, the inevitable transformation, both physically and psychically, as inseparable from the inner awakening. We seek this transformation and take love as the guiding inner impulse, to be more loving, more able to allow Spirit to act and work through us, for the good and healing of others. In entering more deeply into the ocean of illumination, we go beyond form and afterlife, we go beyond physical incarnations, and enter the most holy Mystery as the ultimate source of rebirth. Coming back, we accept the necessity of incarnate life as contributing to the creative processes of Spirit in the manifestations of immeasurable depths. Without these worlds how could we ever be, ever know, ever understand the fullness from which we come? This means that we are each a vessel of transformation and that our death and rebirth is a means for the creation of the cosmos as a whole. Let us therefore, embrace that challenge and seek to become co-creators and illumined signs for the well-being of all. So be it, now and always.

Anabathmos

THE EVERLASTING: ONE RECITATION

"And when I heard and saw these things, I fell down to worship at the feet of the Angel who showed them to me, but he said to me, "You must not do that! I am a fellow servant with you and your brothers the prophets and with all those who keep the words of this book. Worship God!"

Revelations 22: 8-9

Everlasting
There is only One Christ, One Spirit, One God; only One True Life, eternal and everlasting. (5:1)

This is the heart of the recitation, the One Christ, One Spirit, One God; a God "above all and in all" whose bounty and magnitude exceeds our capacity to understand and yet gives us the grace and life to seek an increase in our understanding.[182] We find that increase not only in the pursuit of knowledge, but also in the opening of the heart to Spirit. In that opening we discover a new horizon of faith, a faith that does not depend on the dogmas and creeds of men, but on an inner transformation and awakening. Faith is more than simple belief, we may believe in God or soul or Spirit, or believe in certain teachings, stories, or the truth of parables and signs. But this is the faith of childhood, not the mature faith of deep commitments and adult understanding. To have faith does not mean to believe in certain ideas or to hold certain writings as true or to think that such belief is itself a guarantee of spiritual rewards. There is a magnitude to faith that goes far beyond the written word, far beyond a coded belief, far beyond a communal assent. In mature faith, in deep rooted devotion, there is an opening to Mystery, to the living presence of Spirit, to the inflowing wisdom of an uplifted heart filled with the joy and illumination.[183] To believe in Christ, in Spirit, in God and Mystery, is to truly surrender inwardly to the immensity of the creative light that illumines all souls and all creatures, great and small. This is the spark that lights the fire that illumines the world that we may all see the light and spark in others.

Faith is a prelude to knowledge, and knowledge fulfills faith by giving it a basis in direct experience. But such knowledge does not end faith, it only enhances and enriches the substance of faith that it may become more full and complete within us. Faith that is rooted in knowledge, in *gnosis*, is what leads us to maturity and to "attaining to the whole measure of the fullness of Christ."[184] For the goal is to embody the Christ-spirit and to experience an anointment of the heart, the warmth and spiritual fullness of the inspired love that flows through Spirit and into the receptive vessel of a loving soul. This requires more than belief, it requires a deep faith in the abiding and creative activity of Spirit at work within others throughout the world. This is not a matter of one faith or one creed or one path, but an overflowing fullness that fills the lives, hearts, and minds of a multitude of others whose paths are guided by a unifying presence. The One Christ is a power and presence whose image is dif-

---
182. Ephesians 4: 6.
183. Daniel 2: 19-23, *Chokmah*, Jewish feminine wisdom tradition.
184. Ephesians 4: 13; 2 Corinthians 4: 6.

ferent for every soul, but whose Spirit is a preservation of life in all its unique and different forms. This Christ-spirit gathers together and harmonizes, does not condemn or deny; this Christ is an embodiment of forgiveness and inner peace seeking creative and peaceful coexistence. This Christ is joined with the Divine Sophia, the feminine wisdom that redeems him from intolerance and gives him a sanctified heart able to accept and embody the world in the fullness of its creative differences.

Faith grows deeper as knowledge increases and the soul becomes more self-aware and receptive to the working of Spirit in all its diversities of form and expression. Faith overturns narrow doctrines, overturns blind acceptance, and challenges every soul to divest itself of all its externally acquired learning. And such knowledge and wisdom brings that soul to a center in which it can discover the depths of its own limitations and the partiality of its reach and comprehension.[185] Faith is not a bridge, but a river; not a path, but a mountain. We must plunge in and swim with the currents that guide us toward the ocean of our being; we must climb above our self and out of the cloudy lower lands that restrict our view in order to attain a height from which to revere the infinite heavens. Faith is the net that holds all our desires for truth and all our aspirations for spiritual instruction; we must spread it wide in the waters of life in order to bring up our inmost dreams and inspirations. Faith is like a small seed that becomes a resting place for winged creatures, for the eagle in that tree is an image of Spirit calling us beyond all visible form and function.[186] Faith is an intensity of feeling that allows the heart to accept its finite ground in the face of an immeasurably holy expanse filled with life and potential of every kind, species, and being. The unending joy is the current of the river, the pure etheric air of the mountain, the beautiful creatures created as inspired signs whose enigma is their embodiment of Mystery. The veils are many and to remove them, one by one, we must deepen our faith and let go of defensive skepticism, doubt, and fear.

In acquiring a deeper faith, we must be willing to give up our less fertile ideas, must be willing to surrender what we may once have held dear. This is the nature of the process, to draw us in and then, to bestow upon us the insight and illumination that allows us to grow beyond a former insight or understanding. We shed our skin, outgrow our less mature understanding, move beyond the horizon of what we comprehend, and seek knowledge that leads us to a new vista, a vaster heaven of possible visionary realizations. There is also quiet and stillness as well. In inner deepening, a settling of mind,

---

185. 2 Peter 1: 5-7, Gnosis or experiential feminine knowledge, illumination; Luke 11: 52, must enter into one's self for such knowledge; Romans 11: 33, gnosis and sophia.
186. Mark 4: 31-32.

a cleansing of the heart, a release of troubled thoughts, a letting go of anxieties, an unburdening, a flow of tears that washes away our sorrows and leads us to the warmth of an inner insight. There are many paths to this experience, and many ways that enhance and strengthen our practice and devotion. Of all these, a simple inner determination is to love and to be loved, to give and to receive without clinging or demand, to take only those responsibilities we can fully realize, and not to over reach or to lie or deceive in despair or selfish expectations. Cleansing of heart is an act of constant practice, a "prayer without ceasing" that works toward an inner calm and receptivity no longer guarded against selfish and unwholesome thoughts or desires.[187] This is because the practice must go deep to integrate and transform the heart so that it does not generate unwholesome desires or impure thoughts. A pure heart requires faith and genuine effort to purify motives and to clarify ideals and goals; when we walk a spiritual path, we practice continually, every day, every place, without exception.

The One Christ has many faces, many forms, many teachings, but only one heart, one love, and one source—the holy depths of Spirit and Mystery. Spirit enwraps the Christos and gives a heart of love so deep and powerful that such love cannot be contained in any one form, or in any manifestation or human vessel. The love it gives is ecstasy, a union so deep and full that in the moment of merging there is no difference, no second, no other, only the one true being that is boundless and whose center is all pervasive. Spirit gathers together the multiple strands of the Christos, its manifest incarnations, all its minute expressions, all the tears and laughter and holy shouts of joy and makes of them a continuous weaving of spirit-related communities. There is no one perfect teaching, only an overflowing variation of words and expressions pointing toward the fullness of Spirit in acts of anointment, in the blessings given to the loving soul united in joyful love with the entirety of all that IS. In this union of Spirit, with Christos utterly absorbed into Mystery, the soul is transformed into a purity of light whose radiance takes the form of a boundless love for all creation. In such a state, all "lower or higher" worlds dissolve, there is no differences in "planes or levels" and no distinction between self and others. This state is a mirror within which the image of self vanishes into an image of cosmos dissolved into an imageless fullness whose imagery creates and uncreates all worlds, planes, dimensions, or divisions. In that union, there is no "heaven or hell" and no afterlife or reincarnation; there is only a holiness of light that overwhelms and transforms, uplifts, dissolves, and utterly unites.

From the One Spirit, as the dissolving medium of all creative energies, we

---

187. 1 Thessalonians 5: 16-17.

arrive at the One God whose nature is Mystery and whose being and becoming is known only in the ongoing actions of creation, sustenance, revelation, and reabsorption. That which lies within the cycles of the making and unmaking, the potential for life, awareness, and understanding is an ungraspable magnitude of potential whose inner reality is only glimpsed in the outward forms of all created life. It is not the created form but its inner transformation that gives us the key to unlock the secret of its power and intention. Life is not stillness. It is a process, a becoming that may retreat into static resistance for the preservation of a valued way of life, or it may break out of the shell, shed the skin of its past attachments, and expose itself to new life and becoming. This inner urge toward newness and expansive being is the creative work of Spirit, drawing on the fullness of Mystery to embody yet a more self-aware and creative manifestation. We are each a manifestation, each a carrier of Spirit, each a unique expression of Mystery in the process of becoming. The value of our spiritual commitments is found in the ways they enhance our understanding of our communal relations, our shared loves, and in how they contribute to a peaceful, creative unfolding of inner potentials. Such understanding is a divine activity, a bubbling up from within of the effervescent presence, the creative urgency of Spirit acting to lift us toward our highest possibilities in wisdom, compassion, and shared responsibilities.

The One True Life is the life dedicated to a fulfillment of our inner potential through a creative, non-violent life of exploration and discovery meant to enhance and contribute to the well-being of all species life. Humanity is not first, even though human beings wish to see themselves as in every way superior to other species. No one species is superior and the very concept of superiority is a falsification of the human situation. All species coexist by necessity, we live in a shared world of concerns in which the health and well-being of any one species reflects the health and well-being of all other species. The preservation of life and diversity is the greater good, it best reflects the activities of Spirit as constantly supporting emergence and awareness for each and every being. And the emergence of awareness in every being contributes to our own self-understanding in a complex universe of multiply worlds and possible other life forms. We are not alone and we are naturally akin to all the creatures of our world, all those in seas and on lands and in skies, and to all the plants, trees, organic forms, to the very minerals, rocks, mud and sand. There is no reality to the arbitrary distinctions made between "man and animal" or between "humanity and nature"—such distinctions no longer serve to enhance our understanding. The One True Life is life lived in the fullness of the continuum that joins us with all creatures, visible and invisible, as companions in the exploration of life and its potentials. The One True Life is not a creed or doctrine or a written teaching; it is a living experience in which each person seeks to enhance his or her awareness of the value, beauty, and necessity of life in all its wondrous variation and variety.

The seed in the human heart that represents gnosis and illumination is the seed of life, the gift of Spirit, given to us as an inspiration to move beyond the limits of our inherited ideas, beliefs, and forms. It is a divine ember, a spark, an eternal presence within, whose contents can be opened to a vast and profound Mystery and embodied in the symbols and signs of an anointed life. The Hermetic Christ is such a sign, the arising of which is a light whose promise is found in a transformation of the inner and outer world. In Christ is the seed of Life, placed there by Wisdom as a light of Spirit, who embraces him, unites with him, and in ecstasy, leads him to the depths and heights of Mystery, bestowing upon him visionary forms for the enlightenment of others. And this Christ descends into our heart, like a dove at the River Jordan, and gives us the greatest of all gifts, the gift of spiritual awakening, the gift of the illumined soul.[188] There is no condemnation in that gift, blessed and enhanced by Wisdom; it comes freely to us, following the inward devotions of the heart, responding to prayer and song, filling us with joy and opening our hearts to Mystery. Spirit, how my heart longs for Thy presence, how it fills me in its moments of fullness and how it leaves me longing when it departs! Let us open our souls and seek the One True Life, lived in Spirit, Spirit-filled with joy and wisdom, kind, compassionate, giving, not selfish or demanding, rich with abundant energies, and filled to overflowing with all the unique qualities of an inspired soul. May we attain to such a life, may we be worthy of it, may we find the grace that is meant for each and very soul, surrendered in its depths and made whole in rebirth. Amen.

Faith

To start with the "i" in faith and to develop the "i" in Christ, that you may see clearly what you only now believe, that you may realize the "i" in Infinity and the "i" in Absolute. (5:2)

Faith as mystery is an opening of inner magnitude, an awakening to deep reverence, and a call to realize our inmost potentials. It is not a criteria that determines the fate of others. This is a crucial point. What we believe in following a spiritual path does not determine the fate of others, nor does it qualify the

---

188. Matthew 3: 16; Luke 3: 22; John 1: 32.

believer as having a special perspective on the determined end of individual or collective efforts in striving to realize spiritual goals. The goal is to actualize potential, to find balance and compassion through respect and appreciation for differences. Belief in a dogma that predicts the suffering of others is shallow and cruel; such belief only serves to inflate the self-importance of the believer, only acts to continue the imbalance, injustice, and inhumanity of those who consider themselves above the laws of retribution. I tell you truthfully, retribution is a whip and a goad that strikes the user far more deeply and destructively than those at whom it is aimed. Retribution falls heavily on those who would most use it as a means to justify their own beliefs; suffering is not determined by doctrines rooted in denouncing and denying others. What determines suffering is the inner attitude, the pride and abuse that denounces, the contracted visionary world of those enclosed within a bound duality, right and wrong, heaven and hell. Their fate is determined by unreflective belief in the authority of men to make laws concerning the eternal and everlasting.

In this condemnation, all such laws act to serve only the interests and compulsions of the unexamined soul. These laws become, in such a context, a means for the elevation of the few over the many at the price of denying the full working of Spirit in the human heart. Spirit does not work for the few, but for all; does not privilege some, but celebrates the value of each and every creature. The Christos comes for the many not the few, for the sick at heart, for the confused, uncertain, exiled, and longing, unbelieving, doubtful and lost, not for the certain or proud or narrow-minded. He challenges certitude, he confronts inflexibility, he overturns the tables of those that would exchange a predetermined material world for an emergent spiritual awakening. And he says, "Blessed are the pure in heart, for they shall see God."[189] This purity of the heart, this willingness to not deny, but to affirm through principled living, is found in the value and scope of love. And "Blessed are the peacemakers, for they are the sons and daughters of God" means, those who sow peace will reap the rewards of peace in emulating the very heart of divinity.[190] But those who deny and condemn will surely reap the rewards of condemnation and denial. The peacemakers are not quarrelsome nor vain in the practice of their committed path, they know the value of respect and the importance of diversity and difference. Thus we must create a new understanding, a new faithful commitment to spiritual values that fully recognizes the works of Spirit. For Spirit infuses our faith with understanding and elevates our perspective above condemnation and carries us toward a peak of illumined insight in which all paths are celebrated and no path is privileged above others.

---
189. Matthew 5: 8.
190. Matthew 5: 9.

When I say we must start with the "i" in faith, I mean that each person must determine within his or her own heart the most appropriate way to live. We must seek this understanding not in terms of simple adaptation, not through conformity to the beliefs of others, not in surrendering responsibility to an external authority. The "i" in faith is the "i" in individual, that is, the "i" that finds its own center and recognizes that the iota over the "i", the dot, is the divine spark, the presence that illuminates. This "i" has an inner component, an iota of Spirit, a sparkling atom of the heart, a touch of presence, that is also the "i" of insight and the "i" of wisdom. This "i" is not a capital, individual "I" for in that isolated capital I, the iota has been lost, obscured by an increase of self-concern and pretensions that conceals what is hidden in the heart. The "i" of faith is deep and is by no means limited nor isolated; it is the "i" of union that becomes I-Thou, the spiritual maturity that finds its fullness in opening to its interconnectedness with the divine source, its root of all becoming. Only in fully opening to Spirit, in finding the I-Thou as a living relationship that includes all beings and all worlds, does faith finds its full acclimation. But the "I" severed from the Thou, standing either alone or in community, remains isolated, a rigid capital, supported only by the plural "i" in imitation, that is by a copy of the beliefs of others. The living "i" in faith, the unique "I" (eye) is a constant opening to the Thou, through love, through human relationships, through healing, protective nurturance, through respect and acceptance.

On the Hermetic path, if we seek a model for this "i" in faith, we need turn only to the "i" in Christ. We see immediately that the "i" in Christ is not his own, but an "i" that is found in the double "i" of Spirit. This union of two into one, this joining of twin spirits, this double harmonizing of right and left, of inner and outer, of above and below, male and female, is the very work of the Hermetic seeker. The divisions and fragments of self must be gathered together, brought into harmony, and made whole in the remaking of self as a vessel of Spirit. Paul writes that the "Spirit of life set me free from the law of sin and death," and this means that laws of condemnation and denial are overturned and through Spirit the aspiring soul is reborn into a new faith that no longer condemns or denies.[191] The angel of inner potential must join with the soul of the seeker, in Spirit, opening the heart to a sacred marriage, the union of I and Thou. For the Christos is with us, part of our opening to Spirit, found in the "i" of radiance, through love, compassion, and kindness. And in Christ, the "i" becomes transformed, it lifts faith toward a transfiguration, it leads it toward knowledge, to the "i" of gnosis, illumination, and inner unity. The "i" in this unity is the same as the "i" in Christ, the same as the twin "i" of

---

191. Romans 8: 2.

Spirit, the "i" of faith that becomes known in the I-Thou. Faith is not rudimentary, nor is it simple or childlike, though in its fullness, it retains an innocence whose beauty is an expression of its inner source. Faith is a process, a path of maturation that leads toward awakening and then, continues to affirm the value of walking the path.

What we see through a glass darkly (enigmatically) can be made clear and luminous in this life, can become a lens that magnifies the beauty of creation.[192] When we place the "i" of faith in the "i" of Christ and that "i" awakens to Spirit and is united with the one source, in all its infinite names and qualities, then we discover the "i" in Infinite. The "i" in Infinite is smaller than the iota over the "i" of the heart and yet it includes a universe. The "i" of universe is not one "i" but a multitude of souls united in a visionary illumination in which the "i" in Infinity becomes the "i" in Absolute. There is no "i" in Absolute. And so it is in the fully awakened horizon of faith when the I of I-Thou has become the "O" of Absolute, the Alpha-Omega, the serpent that swallows its own tail and dissolves into the Hen-to-Pan, the All-In-One. This is Mystery, the holiness of divine, creative energies dissolved into the boundless expanse yet flowing wave after wave, in and through every created life. In this expanse there is no "i"—it has become "essence of essence"— the immensity from which the world was first created, rich in primal capacity and boundless in expression. This does not mean the "i" is lost or denied or negated by the ineffable infusions of such glory; it only means that it becomes suspended, transformed in ecstasy, and led toward a new wisdom, a new understanding. And in that understanding, faith is also reborn with a new depth whose bottomless deep only stirs the heart to remember and reflect on the lesser "i" as a gift of most holy proportion. As the lesser to the greater, as the feather to the wing, as the moon to the sun, and as the star to the cosmos, so too the "i" of faith is to the "i" of the illumined heart.

When we think of faith we must not compare it to creeds that have been set up as external barriers between the saved and the condemned. Such barriers are false and spring from a false hope, a hope that only one path with fulfill the fully intensity of all that resides in Spirit. But even an entire world, in all cultures and all times, cannot fulfill this hope. Yes, every seeker of the path who sets aside exclusivity and who walks with humility and grace, can reach redemption and salvation through faith and knowledge. But, this redemption does not guarantee the redemption of others nor does it inhibit the practice of other paths to salvation and fulfillment. What is guaranteed is nothing less than a direct consequence based on personal choice and commit-

---

192. 1 Corinthians 13: 12.

ment, therefore, be careful what you chose! Choose a faith that is open, loving, non-condemning, receptive to alternative, and rich is possibility. Choose what will encourage growth, nurture the seeds of hope in sustaining a peaceful and non-violent way of life. There is no true condemnation other than the ways in which we each shape our self though the courage or cowardice of our choices. In this process of choosing, faith can provide an enduring context for spiritual growth, one that illumines a path through inner conviction free from the taint and corruption that claims authority over the paths of others. It is sheer ignorance to make such a claim, one rooted in habits of mind and soul, bound by fear and anger and an unhealthy lust for power or control. The power of faith is not found in its application to others, but in its application to self, to your practice, your ideals, your goals and hopes.

The judgment to come is happening even now, at this very moment and in every moment since the creation of the world. It is not a consequence of an external judge removed from the processes of everyday choice, need, desire, and fear. It is a consequence of an inner determination by which the quality of the life we have lived is judged through utmost clarity and inner seeing that removes all veils and blind beliefs. In following a spiritual path, the removing of veils is natural and necessary, we must reach our goal naked, stripped of illusions, and free from the burdens of the faiths of others. The judgment is a consequence of our own choosing, our own confusion or lack of concern, our denials, affirmations, or our generosity and kindnesses, our willingness to forgive and to work for mutual healing and receptivity to differences. There is no grand climatic end, only an on-going rhythm punctuated by collective moments of transformation, an opening of horizons in which our faith (or shame) will act to send us forward or back, which will compel us toward the visionary worlds we choose. As in dying, the soul goes toward that which it contemplates, becomes an image of that very place it claims as its own, wrapped in illusions and yet sent toward the unraveling of its inmost guilt, shame, or fear. Therefore, we take the inner journey, in good faith, to unravel in advance, the labyrinths of soul and self, to bring to light the hidden imbalance and to use the precious life-gift as an opportunity for increasing our wisdom and awareness. We seek integration, wholeness, spiritual illumination, and this has nothing to do with affirming or condemning the paths of others. It has only to do with a judgment of our own soul, laid bare in light and healed in Spirit through honesty, love, and inner surrender.

For those who can understand the mystery of faith, it is endless and has no limits nor end. The "i" in faith is like the three "i" of Infinite—the last is the "i" that is uncertain and stands alone desiring direction in the visible world, seeking guidance, and a path to walk. That "i" awakens to the second "i" which is a path found, in the midst, in the visionary world of the *'alam al-mithhal* or the Mundus Imaginalis, an image of the perfected self, an angel whose image is a reflection of our own inner potential for illumination. And as we move toward the union of these two, the actual and the spiritual ideal, the outer and the inner, the real and the supra-real, we become aware of the third I, the mature I of gnosis that discovers its lasting unity within Mystery and Spirit, as the I that has always been there from the very beginning, the I that is Thou, the first I of Infinite. So we come back to faith, to the humble "i" that carries us beyond the "i" of belief into knowledge, into *gnosis* through committed living, through faithful adherence to values and qualities of life that we seek to embody fully. An embodied faith is a living faith manifest in the body, the behavior, the emotional and mental attitudes, and the spontaneity with which Spirit acts to guide and direct that life. This lesser "i" is the heart and the iota, the spark that burns at this very moment in your heart, in your soul, in your longing aspirations toward full wisdom and understanding. Therefore, open your heart, believe in your path, live it day by day, with every breath you take and every thought you think and every act you make. That is how you express your faith, it burns a pattern into the world and creates an image of soul whose resonance lingers and endures even after the body dissolves. Blessed are those whose faith is enduring, rich and full but more blessed are those who live simply, and through faith, find knowledge. So may it be.

Education
To seek knowledge, learning, and education in all that is knowable, but to never neglect the heart, nor to act to harm others; to love deeply, to know Spirit-in-Christ. (5:3)

The education of the mind is not the same as the education of the soul or heart, for the heart is the spiritual-center of soul. The education of mind proceeds through acquired learning, that is knowledge learned and absorbed through the cultural media of a current historical circumstance. But knowledge of soul comes through relationships with others, through heartfelt relations that inform our sense of identity as relative to the qualitative good we cultivate through love. Love is not simply feeling or passion, it is a spiritual characteristic that requires us to cultivate an inner discipline of honesty, genuine sincerity, deep loyalty, and a willingness to give and to receive through shared feelings of mutual support and kindness. It may require confession and forgiveness; overcoming guilt or shame; finding stability in the midst of doubt. Love requires depth and fullness of soul, a feeling sensitivity for the value and worth of others, a deep sense of empathy, compassion, and interest in the creative vitality of human relationships. And these relationships are not easy! A lasting love of humanity must undergo transformations of soul necessary for the recognition that human beings do not always act on worthy motives, do not always value their relationships, do not always seek what is mutually beneficial. Selfish brutalities, repressions, and denials of others, vanities that believe only in self-serving perspectives, the characteristics that represent a contracted, alienated soul, are pervasive in all cultural environments and eras. This is why education of the soul is crucial to human survival, why we must restructure our learning practices to include a heart-centered approach that complements and enhances education of mind.

The education of mind becomes a burden when it is simply an enforced learning that strives to distill complex forms of knowledge into recurrent patterns of instruction. Learning cannot succeed as a stereotyped methodology, as a redundant and reiterative distillation of abstract ideas applied in a strictly mental arena. Learning, to be effective, needs to engage imagination, creative activity, artistry, emotional commitment, and depths of feeling. It needs to move beyond rote learning, abstract formula and rational methodologies that decenter and deny the human actor a role in the process of engaged living. We are not passive and empty, but each full, vital, bringing with us the character and unique abilities that we each embody as feeling, thinking beings. No one is a "blank slate" and educators have a spiritual obligation to recognize the uniqueness of the individual as an intrinsic and central feature of the educational process. And the educators are also unique and distinctive, having a variety of styles and methods for sharing their knowledge and insights. Education should act to elicit the full capacity of the individual, to bring into light the hidden potential and the unrecognized capacities, for both teachers and students. This is certainly true on the spiritual path: the teacher's role is not to force his or her own personal interpretation on the student, but to guide and direct the student to formulate his or her own interpretations, to come to an understanding that is suited to an inmost potential and capacity. The relationship is one of mutual respect and sharing, a relationship in which knowledge of the heart provides a foundational context for learning.

Knowledge, learning and education express three distinctive aspects of the process by which we become more mature. Knowledge is boundless and has an ever-increasing fractal structure, its constantly intersects with a multitude of alternative areas of specialization and simultaneously can be deconstructed into ever-more specialized learning. And there are many types of knowledge, knowledge based on the study of ideas, or people, or cultures, or times, or techniques, or on the analysis of nature, space, time, history, philosophy, religion, or science or any of the thousands of activities that human beings enact either now or in the past or future. There is also an inner knowledge, a more personalized learning, a knowledge based in personal intuition, pragmatic actions, introspection, discovered in dreams, imagination, in artistic expression or through personal realizations that become a basis for growth and new insights. There is also third kind of knowledge, a knowledge grounded in a transpersonal media of existential, participatory encounter that leads to the profound spiritual awakening and illumination. These three, which I characterize as outer, inner, and transpersonal, are all important aspects of soulful education. And all three should be part of the educational process through which a human being acquires a genuine, direct sense of individual (and collective) potential. Learning, in this process, refers to the ways in which we internalize the various kinds of knowledge and make it a consistent feature of our interpretation of human experience. This includes the necessity of learning from inner experience, that is, bringing our inner knowledge into the context of our daily life, into our relationships, and integrating that knowledge as a consistent expression of our real identity.

Education is a processes of continual discovery, through outward study and experience, through inward study and experience, and through our encounter with the transpersonal, transformational aspects of a living and Holy Cosmos. In this process, the heart is the center, not the brain or the mind. Mind too easily becomes over-stimulated, over-active and filled with a superficiality of external apprehended ideas whose reality is far from integral to the actual life and capacity of the individual. Over-development of mind leads to imbalance. Excess in learning creates a false wisdom, one often based in externally "acquired" knowledge, a pride of learning, a purely mental vision of the value and worth of the full range of human experiences. Many intellectuals are misled by the brevity of their engagement with life experience and substitute a purely mental learning for actual full embodied life experience. A sheltered intellectual life cannot give a person the depth and seasoning he or she needs to fully comprehend the diversity of human experience. Alternatively, external experience, travel, or exploration without any depth of learning or study can quickly result in a superficial sense of being experienced while actually being quite immature. The challenge is to fully embrace the complexity, to experience life deeply, and to do it with a sense of direction and purpose aimed at maturity and spiritual illumination. All things knowable are infinite, but human capacity is finite and qualitatively unique. Therefore each person must seek the synthesis that best serves his or her needs to move forward on their spiritual path.

In this process the heart takes precedence as the organ of soul that best guides an individual toward their utmost in realizing inner potential. The development of soul is a primary goal on the spiritual path and must not be confused with external processes of learning. Outer knowledge and inner knowledge must combine in the heart as the Hermetic vessel of transformation while mind serves as a creative knower through inner maturity. We are all engaged in a developmental process insofar as we seek to actualize unrealized potential, insofar as we find the courage to attempt new modes of expression and to enhance our expertise in a multitude of areas. In developing soul, we can chose to walk a spiritual path, perhaps one best suited to our personal needs and aspirations, but one also that includes and values the insights of others. Others, our relationships, are crucial and basic to spiritual development and isolating oneself from others is a denial of the challenges and demands of creative spiritual life. We might chose a period for retreat or have regular times for privacy and introspection and this is good and necessary. But we also need meaningful, long-term, loving relations that help us to have perspective and a relative sense of who we are in terms of the capacities and spiritual qualities of others. The heart is a sensitive organ of perception, a center of empathy and feeling whose cultivation requires a constant attention to our relations with others. To open the heart means to love, to love each and every person with whom we interact in a kind, Christ-centered, compassionate way.

The love we cultivate does not just include human beings but in a spiritual sense, it includes all living creatures, the plant world, the earth, the planets and moons, and all created forms and subtle worlds. We should strive not to be ethnocentric in loving, but work to break the bonds of our own ignorant attachments to human accomplishments and our patterns of social interaction. Relatively, human beings have only modest accomplishments, and they have a great legacy of waste, destruction, aggression and oppression of others, degrading the environment, and the world at large. To love deeply means to truly revere the creation, the world, in all its nuances and subtle graces, its power, intensity, and brilliance. It means to be thankful for the opportunities of embodiment and to see incarnate life as one of the most profound expressions of divinity. The Spirit-in-Christ knows this and constantly works to open the hearts and minds of human beings to the reality of the greatness of the entire creation and not just the human aspects of it. The Spirit-in-Christ is an expression of inner surrender and reverence for the creation as capable of redemption, as capable of being transformed through human virtue and compassion, as inspired by the inner fires of spiritual maturation. The source of this inspiration is a love of creation, a love of the world and all the beings in it, a love so deep and powerful that it becomes a means for that transformation, the very medium through which it is accomplished. Such a love must be learned through an inward dedication of the heart to true education and instruction. The education of the soul is a millennial process of cyclical learning, a process of constantly learning and relearning the valuable lessons, the teachings, that lead to a more loving way of life.

The real education lies in awakening the inner fires that lead the loving heart to a deep knowledge of divinity. In that Mystery lies all knowledge, all learning, all capacity for understanding and wisdom. And Spirit acts, in the Christ-heart, to enlighten and illumine the soul, to open it to love and grace, and to give it the substance of things seen and known, not just dreamed or imagined. The precious gifts of Spirit are an enhancement of our outer learning and those gifts act to illumine everything we study and every knowable aspect of existence. There is nothing outside of Spirit, nothing that does not proceed out of Mystery for the illumination of the heart. And the deep truth of this learning is to respect life, to not harm others, to love creation, and to act with kindness and respect. This is the simple, direct wisdom; from it, everything else proceeds and overflows into the diversity of the world, down to the most minute particle and up to the greatest macrostructure. From the golden atom of the heart to the light in the eyes of another, we can see a reflection of spiritual virtue that has no boundary in enhancing the felt reality of the world.[193] This is the wonder of creation, that it has no boundary in its capacity to unfold hidden depths that illumine the soul. To see this, to experience it directly, we need only seek the appropriate learning and knowledge. Then we must embody that knowledge in all our acts of coming and going, in stillness and motion, in silence and word, in fire and ashes, so that every aspect of life becomes a teaching. Then we can say we have acquired an education and we can express it in the thankfulness we feel deep in our hearts and through our love of others.

---

193. Luke 11: 34.

Good Thoughts
To speak good thoughts with love, neither from fear nor hope of rewards; to open the hearts of others through the openness of your own. (5:4)

To speak good thoughts means to cultivate the good mind, good thoughts, good words; to cultivate the good mind requires a heart that is not envious, jealous, divided, or closed to the depths of Spirit. Good thoughts reflect an inner centering of mind on the positive value and worth of each and every created being, a centering that spreads out into the wholeness of the world and seeks an inner harmony. It is a predisposition that is cultivated for a purpose, that is, to become a mirror, a *speculum arcanum*, that reflects accurately the images and appearances that turn the wheels of becoming. Yet, this mirror does more than simply reflect, it also enhances and adds its own luster, its own character of light, focalized and directed toward an inner penetration in which the body of the image is pure light, reflected and enhanced. Thus the mirror of the heart, polished in prayer and inner meditation, becomes a medium for the enhancement of the image, an enhancement or radiance we call love. For the heart to attain this, it is necessary for mind to enter into silence, into the deep, into the unspoken word and there, to surrender to the very quintessence of our inner ideations. This requires us to strip the intellect of its acquired forms, to cast off the husks of words, to suspend reflective thought, and to allow mind to reach a subsiding stillness, a deep sinking into essence and awareness. The good mind is clear, deep, lucid, calm, integrated, illumined by the creative energies of Spirit and able to reflect deeply the multilayered signs of mental life. Such a mind is free, spontaneous, and not bound by the linguistic norms of common thought and rationality.

Good thoughts arise spontaneously because we choose to live a good life, one that does not cause harm or shame to others, one that seeks to assist in the birthing of an expansive awareness in ever diversifying forms. The fractal energies of mind are focused and directed toward the realization of spiritual goals; a path is recognized, one that intersects with the paths of others and seeks dialogue and shared discourses. But the speaking of those discourses does not come from mind alone, does not arise from the necessity of defending or promoting a mental world, does not rest upon a substrata of resistance or denial. Good thoughts arise from good-hearted, loving kindness settled upon the bedrock of compassion, a foundation of steadfast faith in the healing power of mutual, caring relations.[194] How can such compassion arise if we do not

---
194. Qur'an 19: 96.

dedicate the heart to being a center of loving concern? "Love and be loved" is a first principle. Love is an energy of exchange whose deepest source is Spirit. It does not simply flow out but circulates, reflected in the mirror of the heart as an illumined image of what may yet become. Spirit is the primal source of love and compassion, the deep well from which we draw the purest waters of life, the cup we share in confidence and communion.[195] Good thoughts are a reflection of the purity of the heart; this means that insofar as we are able to cultivate a loving heart, the depths of that love will inform our thinking. It is love, not thought, that is the basis of world peace and non-violence; it is love, not words and ideas, that will establish the lasting community and the enduring forms of the future.

Where ideas arise, where good thoughts are cultivated, where the mental life is active, we must always ask how those thoughts are informed by or help to inform a loving heart, a deeply caring soulful concern for the well-being of others. But these others are not simply those who think or believe in a similar path, but all others, including those who walk in shadows and anger, in fear, denial, violence or in unhealthy preoccupations. The good mind is not closed to the fear, anger or despair of the uncertain, lost, or denying. The good mind, drawing on the compassion of a loving heart, generates good thoughts for the purpose of generating insight, for the cultivation of a more mindful way of life, in order to establish a bridge of communication and caring. On the path of the Hermetic Christ, we do not reject or deny those who might reject or deny a spiritual path or practice. The path of the Hermetic Christ is a path of loving kindness and good thoughts directed toward an inner harmony of all paths and ways.[196] To speak good thoughts with love is the way, the Hermetic path embodied in the heartfelt image of the Christ-spirit and the well-spoken Bride. This image of the heart may take many diverse forms, in the *speculum arcanum*, it can transmute and transform—it may become the bride, the divine Sophia, Maria Mater, the Regina Angelicum, or an image of an archetypal angel of the fourfold creation. The Christ image takes many forms, in any race, any age, any time or place. There is no one image and no final form, all are subject to the creative workings of the heart inspired by Spirit under the mantle of the most holy Mystery.

When we speak of love in thoughtful reflection, infuse our thinking with compassion, we no longer seek reward nor recognition. The experience of love, the actual opening of the loving heart, the flow of the creative energies of Spirit, brings with it a connectedness and interpenetration that is joyful and profound. When love infuses thought, it becomes a radiance and stimulus to

---
195. Mark 9: 41.
196. Galatians 5: 22-23.

the thoughts and awareness of others. And it flows back, is reflected in the arising of love and compassion in the thoughts of those with whom we engage. If there is resistance or denial of this loving energy, then it may become a stimulus towards contraction, a drawing back, a fear that clings to its own center or a rejection of what is other or alien. But where love thrives, as a genuine way of life, as a pathwork of sincere effort founded in the purification of the heart, then love is a stimulus to more creative thinking. Love flows out of itself into the world as a creative energy whose purpose and desire is to find underlying harmony and correspondence, without denying differences. Such love seeks a rapport that will establish meaningful connection and relation. Love seeks to preserve the difference by finding the correspondences that place that difference into its relationship with the Whole. The center of this activity is not the individual, not the ego-identity of a particular soul but a network of relations in which the individual heart is a node of correspondence, an reflection of the creative energies of Spirit. The reward of these loving, thoughtful relations is a creative, interactive flow of love that sustains an increasingly illumined mind. This has nothing to do with the "fear or hope of reward" at the level of the personal one-to-one relationship.

To love is to participate in a network of creative, loving energies that sustain awareness and lead mind toward illumination. Whatever we are given, we pass it on by purifying our attachments and letting go of ego-satisfactions, self-inflating pride, that might hinder the gift and subvert its intention or joy. To be a mirror means to reflect back what we are given with a minimum of self-distortion, to add and not subtract to the luster of the gift. To bring more light to the gift means to draw on Spirit as the medium through which all love flows, to allow Spirit to inform the love of others through a pure reflection of its inner contents, motives, and aspirations. Where these motives are contracted or centered around selfish needs, Spirit becomes the means for penetrating resistance through a subtle inner pressure to open the heart more fully, to release fear, contraction, and anxiety. The loving heart acts without blame, without censure, criticism, or harsh words and cruel or indifferent thoughts. A spiritual love, a Christ-love, proceeds through a process of self-transformation, through an inner awakening, an inner opening of the heart to Spirit, in the image of the Christos-Sophia, the holy angel of illumined self-awareness. It is a process of purgation, of acquiring an inner detachment from selfish preoccupations, grasping needs, or unhealthy appetites. In blaming others we only drive them away from the workings of love and the good mind, we only create dissatisfaction and discomfort. This does not mean that we should abandon honesty nor fear to confront the boundaries within self or in those we love, yet we must learn to act from love and through love to make love the condition in which good change can be fostered.

To open the heart to another means there must be an inner grounding, an inner connection with the up-swelling sources of love through Spirit. I am not speaking of romantic love, nor of love grounded only in feeling for others, but of a deep spiritual love grounded in the depths of Mystery. The Urground of love is not simply emotional attachment or dependency on others; it is an opening of the heart to Spirit in complete surrender, that is, without concealing or repressing in any way the deepest activities of mind and soul that all may be transformed and made new. Opening to Spirit is a form of death, a willing surrender of any demands or stipulations, a renouncing of predeterminations, a letting go of all expectations, ideals, or hopes. It is nakedness before the fire, an inner humility and renouncing of all claims and hidden or self-inflated dreams. It is a stripping away of artifice, an unclothing of soul, a showing forth of wounds and contractions for the purpose of healing and rebirth. It is making the heart into an altar and mind into an Urground of silence that Spirit may guide, inform, and awaken the deep potentials of self and soul. On that altar burns the flame of devotion whose brightness increases as we renounce and let go of all blaming, all grasping, all clinging. As love begins to transform awareness, we discover the creative energies that flow into the world through and about us. This is a working of Spirit acting to enhance and increase the manifold activities of creation. As the heart opens to these creative energies, they act to enhance the experience of love, act to open the hearts of others. Such a heart becomes a lamp, a way in a dark place, a light for the feet to follow a path toward illumination and knowledge.[197]

The hearts of others are each a reflected image of Spirit, however contracted or closed the heart may seem. Deep within each of us is the spark and activity of Spirit; in the good mind, in the tranquil and calm repose of reflected images, in the feelings stimulated by a clear, crisp morning sunrise. That same sun rises also in the heart as we progressively learn to love ever more deeply the works of Spirit through the creative actions of others. In the Christ heart, this love is a source of healing, of new life, and of rebirth into a more luminous world of good thoughts, good words, and good actions. On the Hermetic paths, the images and symbols, the metaphors and analogies, the signs and wonders, are all only outward appearances leading toward Spirit. And Spirit works through all, not through some or only a few, but through all and in all, for all, for the transformation of the world and all beings, for the good of the many and the most. As we love so do others love us. As this love grows so also

---

197. 2 Corinthians 4: 6, *Photismos*, illumination, light of knowledge (*gnosis*) in the heart.

grows the possibility of a loving and harmonious world. We can only attain a world in the ground of love through personal commitment to the realizations of love in actual daily living. This means to constantly work at cultivating Spirit in all coming and going, in action and inaction. Even in the midst of chaos and confusion, Spirit is there, awaiting the receptive heart, an opening of the moment. In that moment it flows forth into the heart, into the world, through others, and reflects back in accordance with the purity of our motives. Therefore let us cultivate the purest motives, the most sincere intentions, for the transformation of the world and for a living presence that values all life and all differences sustainable in and through love.

Marriage

To treat one another with deepest respect and reverence, hearing what the other needs, giving where possible; to never raise male or female over the other, to live in mutuality with equal justice. (5:5)

According to a Hadith of the prophet Muhammad (praise be to all prophets whose words lead to peace), marriage is half of the spiritual path. With this I must agree as there is nothing more worthy of our humanity than a lasting love between a man and woman that deepens over the years and leads each toward spiritual understanding. It is not always an easy path! But who has been discriminated against more than women? And who has born the burdens of male bias and prejudice for the fact of her gender in every spiritual tradition? I have no respect for spiritual teachings that demote women because they are women; no spiritual teaching is worthy of its name unless it promotes a genuine spiritual equality between men and women. And children as well must be held as equals, not less or in any way inferior to the status and realizations of adults. These observations are central to the Christ-spirit and a loving heart is earned only through the practice of love in our most familial human relationships. Let a man learn from his wife and daughters, let a woman advance in wisdom through her love of husband and sons—this is the path of the heart. On this path, the painful lessons of love are born in the depths of the soul, the sorrows felt are like hot irons that leave their marks as memories of love lost and betrayed. This is because love, at the level of partnership is the greatest challenge we face in creating a truly co-equal and loving world of just and sincere relations. How many have suffered! How many are incapable of sustaining a genuine partnership, how it grieves me to see the imbalance and friction that erodes so many relations!

There is a deep sorrow in Spirit for all these failed relations, a deep wound whose healing must come, moving us beyond pain and sorrow into a more creative, shared life. Of all the burdens I feel in this world, the failure of men and women to live loving relations is the greatest, second only to the abuse suffered by so many children. This harm to children is the wound of God, the torn fabric of the pattern that must be mended, the rupture that creates an opening for healing. There is a prayer of the world that asks "to be struck deep in order to be healed," and it is this prayer which is now being enacted in male and female relations.[198] And there is cause for this separation because the wounds are deep and not simply forgivable, not simply reconciled by abstract promises or by brief acknowledgement of past injustice. The way toward healing requires a deeper, more penetrating honesty, a more committed will that seeks far more than token gestures or verbal promises. The healing must come from a deep commitment to equality, mutuality, and co-creation in all aspects of human endeavor and life. There is no area of life from which women should be excluded, least of all as spiritual teachers and leaders. If a man or woman choose not to engage in an area, let it be because of voluntary not enforced decisions. Spirit overflows into every aspect of life and fills the heart with a capacity that exceeds gender. This does not mean that gender has no significance, gender is a quality to be respected, honored and revered. We can move beyond gender, beyond sexual definition and character, beyond the structural capacities of body. We do this, on the Hermetic path, not by ignoring gender, but by recognizing its unique, sacred characteristics and its distinctive contributions to spiritual life.

A woman's body is a temple, a man's body is a light; when light is in the temple, both are illumined. Marriage is a way toward such an illumination; it is a ground of committed life together in which two ways intermingle and join in creative relation. This does not mean, however, that such a union requires subordination on the part of either individual; do not raise one over the other. One may have more ability in one area, the other, more ability in ways the first does not. It is not a matter of strengths or weaknesses, it is a matter of mutuality and common decision making leading to responsible actions that are sustained over the entire life of the relationship. Many human being are not mature enough for this kind of conscious, committed, spiritual relationship; many are not yet able to accept the mutuality and responsibility of the relation. Many are not willing to engage in co-equal, genuinely shared decisions guided by spiritual principles. Are spiritual principles necessary

---

198. Isaiah 30: 26.

for a marriage to endure? Yes, on this I have no doubts. Marriages that work as a ground for healing the soul, for healing the world of sorrows, are truly spiritual relations. They share far more than an emotional *eros* of body and soul. They also share a commitment to spiritual ideals and values which each partner undertakes to actualize on a day to day basis. The Hermetic path is a path of transformation; it is not static, not fixed or bound by laws, dogmas or the rules of men. It is an emergent, inner awakening that leads to a continual reformulation of life practices, an alchemical making and unmaking that seeks to perfect potential and personal qualities. It seeks to enhance the quality of life through establishing a heart-centered love, a Christos, at the center of all thoughts, words, and co-relation.

To develop this inner purity of soul, a purity whose radiance is a lucid, warm, humorous, compassionate love, requires that respect for the other be an expression of spiritual devotion. It is not devotion to the other but devotion to the divinity within every created being, a devotion to the fruitful blossoming of the other through love, through awakening to the ideal, through a becoming that illumines the other just as their love illumines us. The light that you give me, I give back; the light I give you, you give back; this light is a gift of Spirit. It's radiance is love, its purity is respect and trust, its colors are all the unique qualities that make us each distinct. At the heart of every spiritual marriage is the I-Thou, the "I" of faith, Christ, Spirit, Sophia, the Infinite, and the "Thou" of divinity seen and known in the other, in their love, struggle, desires and dreams. Respect and reverence proceed through a careful listening, a willingness not to block the other, not to deny them their right to be different, unique, motivated by alternative desires and dreams. When I love I do not seek an image of myself, but the image of the other as he or she might most want to be. In loving the other, I want to love her or him with utmost sincerity, by respecting the differences that make us each unique. In this love, there is no need to sacrifice the qualities that make each soul an individual expression of creation. What we do through our relationships is bring to the surface all the hidden and undeveloped areas where we need to work. So we learn to listen first and foremost, we learn to hear what the other says and we do not override that speaking with our own inner dialogues. In this love, we support all forms of gender relations in which mutuality, kindness, respect, and non-violence prevail.

When we learn, through spiritual practice, to silence the inner dialogue then we can begin to hear the speaking of the other. But we must go much further. Having heard the speaking, we must now take that speaking into ourselves, weight it in terms of love (not selfish needs), and ask if the speaking is just, honest, true for the other. And if this speaking is just, true, and honest, then we must realize that however difficult the task, the other needs and wants love to support the fulfillment of his or her speaking. And perhaps those needs require change, new patterns of interaction, ways that impact the deeper self. This is the challenge of love! Do you think you can walk a spiritual path without changing the way you live? Love requires change and transformation, a willing partnership of adaptation, an equal justice in which change flows in both directions, in accommodation to the other and in his or her accommodations to you, in mutual adaptations and a deepening appreciation of what the other needs in a unique and special sense. This means we cannot raise one gender or person over the other nor subordinate one to the other; there must be equality and co-adaptation, there must be a willingness to accept the responsibilities of creative change as on-going. Spiritual growth requires constant attunement to the subtle world and this, in turn requires establishing an ever more articulate expression of need balanced against the needs of others. In marriage, these needs are in rhythm with each other when partners are well-attuned; the rhythms are shifting and counter punctual because there is deeper harmony, a complementation evolves that express the creative ground through which the relationship can flourish.

The sorrow at the heart of the world is the mistreatment of women and children by insensitive men directed toward outer appearance and external social control, toward male dominant patterns of social life that do not respect or love the intrinsic feminine. These patterns are falling and will not stand. The future of human relations lies in the empowerment of women to acquire through the creative energies of their own wisdom, works, and words, a new voice and presence in determining a co-equal world. The spiritual basis of that empowerment lies in loving relationships that endure and have a heart whose radiance is an example to others. Love is the greatest gift of Spirit, the heart, the brightest temple in which its flame gives light and purpose. Spirit pours Her creative energies into the dedicated heart, gives the flame its brightness, and lights a way toward a more just, reverent world. But we must open inwardly to that Presence in order for this transformation to effect the necessary change. It is not a matter of personal will directed against injustice and irreverence, though at times this is necessary. It is more a matter of cultivating a loving heart in which the radiance of Spirit can act to facilitate the inner transformation that leads to new actions and goals. Men must take this path as well, must open their hearts to love, must acquire the inner radiance to exemplify the holiness that is soul-born and soul-illumined. In marriage, the path is to work together to affirm the spiritual values you share and to enhance the capacity for each to give in his or her own way to the other. Marriage is half the spiritual path because it is the most profound testing ground of all that we hold dear. Marriage tests our ability to choose well the partner with whom we would seek a spiritual illumination.[199]

Therefore, let us love each other deeply without reservation because we know that we each seek an illumined heart. In this way, the world is reborn and we share a light that has no end. If we desire an equal justice, then we must live in a just manner and be directed by angels of grace and good will toward mutual, and not just individual, growth. No creative relationship can escape crisis, two creative souls do not avoid the necessity of struggle simply because they hold spiritual ideals. We do struggle, engage in debate and disagree, sometimes fiercely; but we must learn not to go to the extreme of denying the other their right to a different way of life or diverse values that do no harm. Every person is free to choose their relationships and every relationship is subject to the stress and strain of worldly life. Without a spiritual center, this stress will destroy many relationships; a multitude of disconnected loves will not heal a wounded soul. What is necessary is rootedness, a grounded and loyal trust that works through the upheaval and challenges of personal growth and then, grows more loyal, more willing to engage and sustain the value of love. There must be a connection of hearts, a union that illumines through dedicated receptivity to the needs of both self and other. There must be balance, respect, and a necessary degree of individual autonomy in order to pursue the actualizations of a creative self-expressive life. This is what love seeks to preserve, the unique distinctiveness of the other, their value as a work of divinity. In giving respect for the autonomy of the other, we also receive an equal respect from the other for self-autonomy. This is a central feature of mature love; it is not a merging that dissolves differences, it is a merging that takes joy in differences.

When we hear what the other needs, we give what we can toward the fulfillment of that need, even making sacrifices when necessary for the well-being of the other. This is natural and good. But if we give in a way that perverts or distorts our own gifts or represses the good that is in us, then we have lost the center. At the center, we give what we can without emptying our hearts; we give more because Spirit gives through us, the gifts we have to share. Perhaps, we give less than what the other desires. Yet, we are not here simply to fulfill the needs of others; the purpose of love is to share and to grow, not to sacrifice vitality and health through the immodest demands of others. There must be balance in giving and receiving, there must be a spiritual harmony that does

---

199. The Gospel offers no guidance for marriage or coequal marital relations.

not ask too much of the other. This is why autonomy is important, because it sustains spiritual life without dependency and artificial, grasping needs. But this autonomy must not become a wall or a barrier to intimacy; it must remain open and receptive, fluid and sensitive to the other. This is the call in enduring love, to be an individual following his or her spiritual path and to be a lover, wife or husband to another who also follows a spiritual path. We rejoice when our paths cross and we celebrate together, the joys of Spirit as it intersects and enriches our lives together. And we have our times apart and our own disciplines and practices respectfully supporting the same in our partner. Together we create a greater wholeness, and apart we each radiate the loving energies of our union. In this way others enter into the circle of love, and their energies are renewed and renew us. Love is the center and in the Christos, becomes a radiant light whose lamp is a mutual harmony of light, co-created.

Sexuality
To know that sexuality is sacred, a joy and natural pleasure, a celebration of life, a part of Christ and the Bride; to avoid excess, abuse and manipulation; to be gentle, willing to learn. (5:6)

What can be more sacred than the procreation of life? The union of the male and female is a divine symbol of totality that requires more than the part to make a whole. The Hermetic sign is the union of the feminine and masculine principles, the Christ-Sophia ecstasy of the *Hieros Gamos*, the sacred marriage in which male and female find their complementary other. From such a union the One becomes many and the many become One; bodies join and liquid life vibrates with all the potencies of Spirit. Sexuality opens the heart to the life energies of Spirit and those energies flow through the body as healing and arousing sensations whose purpose is a celebration of the joy and delight in creation. Sexual experience is by no means simply physical, it is a deeply emotional and psychic event whose intentions are rooted in the soul's capacity for joining with another to share a mutual opening of the heart. Sexuality is a wonder, a taste of the higher life of illumination embodied in the hearts of those we most cherish and made available to us through every sense and sensitivity. Sexual experience is a Ground of Being, a Hermetic activity whose goal is to unite the higher and lower, the above and below, the inner and outer, the soft and hard, with perfect mutual correspondence. Sexual energies are a miracle of life, awakening dormancy and allowing the awareness of each partner to flow into a mutually ecstatic moment that is no longer bound by time or temporal space. It is a core experience of embodied life whose lack can lead to sorrow, confusion, and a disturbed alienation for the beauty and holiness of the body.

A woman's body is a temple, a man's is a light, their union is an illumination of souls that release in mutual joy, the deeper feelings and sensations of orgasmic union. This is profound, a sacred event whose depths are thoroughly visionary and transformative. In bringing light to the temple, approach with pure thoughts and clear motives: to honor the divinity within the other, to purify the heart of selfish attachments, and to give fully without reserve, a complete and genuine love. In the Hermetic teachings, the sexual experience is thoroughly natural and suprasensual; it recognizes the creation as physically inscribed, as signs living through embodiments which reflect divine mysteries. Sexuality stripped of these qualities of divinity becomes a form of entrapment, a pattern or habit of momentary action that does not satisfy or fulfill its deeper potential. It is not only a matter of respect and timing, but of love, reverence, and a deeper opening that enlivens the soul in a joyful way. To receive light in the temple, receive the beloved with gracious intentions earned through trust and mutual reverence, based in a mutual honoring of the divinity within. This divinity does not come from either partner, nor is it a gift that one gives to the other. This divinity is holy unto the depths of creation, where it is born of Spirit and where it transmits the life-force in all its subtle, psychic energies through the joyful moment of union. It is a spiritual and Hermetic illumination to awaken to the holiness of sexual union, to see within the joyful, playful interpenetration, the arousing perception of the Infinite.

The "joy and natural pleasure" of sexual intimacy is a sign of the joy and pleasure in creation. It is a powerful reminder of the ecstasy of conceiving a cosmos, of creating life, worlds, suns, moons, and stars. There is a whole cosmos in making love, just as there is a whole cosmos in giving birth. It requires a beginning, middle, and end (but not always in that order!) that moves through the stages of arousal in order to maximize the experience and to fully arouse the deepest and most potent energies. The sacred in the sexual is knowable through the appropriate processes of arousing all the senses, allowing each sense to open to its deepest love energy, in order for the eye to truly see, the flesh to fully feel, and the tongue to truly taste. On the Hermetic path, we can celebrate sexuality in all its non-harmful variations as a means of spiritual sharing and fulfillment without violating in any way, the genuineness of a path leading to illumination. The symbol of the Sophia-Christ union, the sacred marriage, is an index of the heights that such a union may attain. A deep moment of genuine love, of truly heart-felt connection, of a passionate desire shared and fulfilled together in sexual union can manifest transcendence and states of ecstatic awareness. The path is diverse and sexuality may or may not be a part of the practice, but under whatever circumstances sexuality may occur, it should be an act of reverence whose goal is something other than the momentary sensation. The practice is always a means toward *gnosis*, and therefore, requires an inner purity of love whose expression carries the practitioner toward the goal.

Love in sexual expression may be long and drawn out in successive stages, timed with moon cycles, and coordinated with seasons; or it may be brief and intense with great passion that lifts both to new awareness. There is a rhythm and variety to sexual relations that cannot be measured by any external system or count; it requires an inner knowing, a deep intimacy with one's own body, a knowledge based on careful attention to the health, well-being, and vitality of physical-emotive partnership. Every couple must find their own rhythms and moments, their periods of intimacy and of privacy, their times together and times apart. The flow of energies is a matter of a certain developed sensitivity that is fully attentive to the other in both matters of sharing and in matters of separation. In sexuality, there should be no coercive pressure, no demands or insistent grasping after the energies and sexual gifts of the other. Sharing, in the Hermetic sense, must be mutual and by mutual consent, proceed through the appropriate rhythms to break the mold of habit, to deconstruct routine relations, and to open the gates for the energies of Spirit to animate soulful awareness with renewed energies of connection. This requires attention and focus. It is not a matter of habit taking over, in fact, attention is a means for the breaking of habitual response but only if the attention is guided by spiritual attunement. There is a necessary adjustment, a bringing of energies into synchronic relation, a harmonizing of body-soul with body-soul, such that one feels the attraction and desire for the other.

The *eros* of love is its capacity to energize a desire for union, to awaken the sleeping potential of sexual identity through an energy of arousal. Coming into attunement means bringing the emotional and psychic qualities of each partner into a clear resonance, into a vibrancy that circulates from the heart through the entire body. We make love with our entire being, all senses, open emotions, receptive to the energies of the other when the energies of the other are loving, kind, trustful. Just as we give so are we given, just as we open, so is there opening; but this requires a relationship of trust and mutual sensitivity developed over time and through experience. To maximize the experience is to raise it to a spiritual encounter whose goal is a deep flowing experience of bodily energies enhancing soulful feeling. A lover cannot always easily move from the contracted space of daily life and its demands, into this openness of soul that meets the soulful other in spiritual receptivity. That is why there must be attunement, no rushing forward, but a soulful awakening of desire and an opening to shared feelings of attraction and desire. Those who push ahead without this attunement can easily become a threat or create anxiety because the inner feeling, the capacity of open, is buried beneath immediacy and insensitive demands. We must each learn from the other, learn of their needs and rhythms, learn how to reach past the barriers and self-defense, through a genuineness of love whose spiritual foundations rest on deep respect and care.

Only the truly foolish imagine that because of many sexual encounters he or she understands love and sexuality. This kind of pride stems from shallow physical and emotional attitudes toward sexual encounter, from a kind of statistical arrogance, an attitude not born from genuinely shared love. This is because each person is different and each relationship requires the utmost attention to love in order to succeed in attaining a spiritual union sexually. This can only be found in a soulful meeting that places that relationship in the center of the circle, in a recovery of innocence that no longer judges a partner based on experience with others. We must be willing to learn from each other, experience in life through love is the best teacher, not many sexual partners. Indiscriminate sexuality leads to a loss of vitality and an obscuring and masking of the primacy of the spiritual qualities of loving union. Love to succeed must be deep, sexuality to last as a source of spiritual renewal must arise on a basis of on-going creative life, in shared, mutual exploration and experience. Richness in life means to engage the creative process at a deep level that infuses both partners and allows each to develop as individuals while yet sharing love and affection. There must be kindness, consideration, respect, an equality of decision making, a mutuality of efforts that supports the sexual expression of each. There must be times of withdrawal, solitude, inner focus, silence, and privacy that is not invaded by impetuous demands and the quick satisfaction of physical urges.

The Hermetic path requires discipline and a channeling of creative energies so as not to impinge on the other; yet, there must also be an honesty that allows the expression of needs without censure or blame. This means avoiding excess, abuse, and manipulation of the other. One person's measure of satisfaction may not fulfill the needs of another, therefore there is compromise; over time this compromise can be made into an energy of delight. On the other hand, it is sometimes necessary to give because the need of the other is genuine and deep. This requires significant knowledge of the other, enough that it is possible to see through habits and states into the actual needs the other carries. Many are wounded sexually, therefore their needs are greater and more difficult to meet. Sexual healing does not always lie in sexual activity; what is needful is to find the deeper cause of suffering and to heal that cause so sexuality can be reclaimed in a new light. Sexuality has a shadow side and can become an arena of powerful disturbances and contestations of will, dominance, passivity, and grasping after the other. Abuse in sexuality is one of the worst violations, and the violation of children is a crime of great magnitude, as is rape and all forced sexual actions. Healing these wounds is a profound challenge, for they lie at the very center of life, at the very heart of the most sensitive response to love. On the Hermetic path there is no violence, no abuse, and no manipulation of others sexually. To violate another sexually is a fall of the most serious sort from the path; restitution can only come through long efforts of self-reformation and dedicated service in serving needful others.

The sign of the Hermetic union is a healthy, glowing love whose accomplishment is born of many years of devoted work and effort to unravel all the misunderstanding, misdeeds, misspoken words that may have hurt or harmed. Such love is born of letting go of the other to be the person he or she might best become while also being a steady partner in sharing all the unexpected twists and demands of the path. Each must walk the path in their own way, and sexuality is part of that path, not always and for everyone, but for a majority, it is an inevitable feature of love. Therefore we seek an expression and integration of sexuality as part of the path, with a loving partner also committed to spiritual transformation. Sexuality is a beacon of life, a joy of shared fire whose light is a celebration of Spirit and whose consequence is a deep, more heartfelt love. The Christ-Sophia is the sign of incarnate wisdom growing from a virtuous life of kindness and respect, shared in emotional maturity and bodily joy, without which we are poorer and less rich in Spirit. The holy mysteries of love are seen in the emblem of two bodies joined in love for the purpose of celebrating life as a gift to be reverenced. In acting on the impulses of Spirit, through sexual relations, we touch the heart of creation, celebrate life, and acquire a brief moment of illumined grace. From that touch, that taste, we can move more deeply into loving relations and acquire a fully spiritual view of sexuality as a blessing on our humanity in the face of creation. The Mother-Father sign is the image of the androgynous union, the alchemical image of King and Queen united in one body for the propagation of the children of light. When we read the signs of love in this fashion, we awaken a deeper center in Spirit and she flow to us, enhancing and celebrating our mutual joy.

Children

To raise children with a genuine sense of freedom and with the autonomy to choose and to act with integrity; to not oppress them with a parent's faith, nor turn from them in theirs. (5:7)

The raising of children is without doubt a great task and for the committed parents, a great challenge and spiritual obligation. Such a task is part of a life-long relationship whose strengths depend on a lasting, genuine mutual respect and positive love. Love is a foundational quality whose depths and fullness are a matter of individual development and maturity. Love between parents and children can go no deeper than the awareness of each individual in the relationship. In this sense, there is a clear difference between what each parent brings to the relationship and how each parent allows the relationship to foster a continuing maturation. There is a Hermetic circle in all parenting relationships that includes a basic triad of mother, father, and child, further extended through siblings and extended family relationships. But at the heart of this complex of familial relations is the central triad, the fundamental symbol of the tripart relation between mother-father-child. No matter how many brothers and sisters a child may have, or how many children a couple may have, each child is an obligation and each child has his or her own obligations that must be balanced first within the context of the parental relationship and secondly within the family as a whole. What sustains these obligations is love, a very deep and genuine affection that is shared and communicated with consistency and heartfelt sincerity. Love is the manifest Spirit in a wholesome relationship that seeks the mutual development of each member of the triad. And mutual respect is the working dynamic ground of a lasting lifetime of love between family members.

The image of the Christ Child is one of dependency on the love and affection of the parents, on the mother and the father. As maturation occurs, this dependency is transformed into mutual obligations, and, at an even later stage, parents may well become dependent on their children. This is the cycle of life in the normative sense, and every stage can be a spiritual challenge. Children are a most precious heritage, a true gift of Spirit, born through the processes of life evolution and affinity rooted in intergenerational patterns of development. Not all such patterns are developmental; some are regressive and ancillary to the real needs of the soul. Children are not simply extensions of the will and desires of the parents, such an attitude is one of immature thinking and self-centered, grasping needs. Children are a gift of life that requires utmost attention to foster their inner sense of healthy well-being. An individual or a couple seeking to follow a spiritual life might choose to have no children. This is a natural choice for those who feel so inclined, not one forced or required for spiritual development. Children can be part of any spiritual path, can be a central focus for active development by which a parent learns to serve, to guide, to exemplify a spiritual way of life. Those without children may choose to work with children in a wide variety of circumstances in ways that fulfill the need for a parenting experience. There is no one pattern that is best; each person must decide on what role parenting and children will play in personal development and spiritual growth. It is a decision in relationships that should be made mutually and without coercion or emotional pressure on one another.

Integrity in raising children stems best from a deep commitment that springs from the heart of each partner, though mutual desire, not from external conformity or social expectations. Love is at the heart of child rearing because when a child is genuinely wanted and loved, he or she has the best ground for future health and development. But the parents must be able to sustain that love and support through the turmoil of their own spiritual growth and through the stress and strain of social and personal struggles. It is better to have children after a certain degree of social and spiritual maturity is reached. Maturity in child-rearing is crucial and however much one may love another, however much a couple may want children, their obligations to those children require them to consider the long term commitment involved in child rearing. Even in a communal setting in which child rearing is shared among multiple community members, there is still a primary obligation between parents and child. Such relationships are more than biological. The relationship between individual members of the biological triad are rooted in life processes and spiritual patterns that often extend into alternative life experiences, into the psychic world of former lives and future directions. The soulful life of the child is often deeply linked to the soulful life of a parent, sometimes, to the soulful life of both or to other related members of the family. Some of these patterns are multigenerational and reflect relationships that have very long term interactions and carry with them obligations and deeply attached emotional energies.

In order for the child to realize her or his potential, to excel in a positive, balanced way, there must be a sustained commitment, a continuity that supports the child's spiritual growth.[200] This does not mean imposing upon the child the parent's spiritual or religious orientation. Children are not simply extensions of parental will or parental emotional commitments. Every child

---

200. Matthew 18: 2-4, 10.

is unique and every child has a right to freely chose his or her own spiritual path and way of life. The parent's obligation is to exemplify their spiritual path through a dedicated example in excellence in living.[201] Core values of any spiritual path are only as valid as the actual lifeway they produce in real life experience. Love is only an idea until it becomes embodied in real acts of deep emotional expression and enduring, mutual sensitivity. And spiritual love, a deep felt and realized presence in Spirit, is a living manifestation of graceful care and compassion. Such a love flows out of Spirit, through the heart of the beloved, and into the world as a healing and unifying presence. On the Hermetic path it is the light of the Christos, the brightness of the divine Sophia, the joyful harmony of soul that gives birth to an inner purity that sees in every child, a divine image. That image of divinity is in every child and it acts as the spiritual center of an evolution whose goal is to fully actualize that inner potential through careful and supportive cultivation. Like a young plant, the soul of a child is growing into the world, seeking embodiment in order to realize an inner image of possibility. In order to grow into the world in a healthy, positive sense, what is needed is a supportive and loving community, intelligent guidance, a respectful family, loving parents. A child is a blessing and should thus be blessed by loving parents and by all brothers and sisters.[202]

To teach a child autonomy, each parent must have developed those qualities necessary to function through independence in thought, action, and belief. But not at the cost of denying that same freedom to others, particularly not by refusing children the right to decide for themselves, what is necessary and needful for their own development. This does not mean we should allow children to be willfully harmful or disrespectful to others, nor does it mean allowing patterns of selfish concern to dominate an emerging identity. Freedom of thought requires an inner ability to think intelligently and to judge compassionately. What children need is direction and guidance in forming core values that will serve them in developing a respect for others and motivate them in exploring alternatives without denying their own inner needs or aspirations. These core values are part of every creative spiritual path that escapes the limitations and narrow mindedness of making judgments about others strictly in terms of one's own inherited beliefs. We all make judgments, and we all hold a variety of hierarchical values; but what is the core and what determines our ability to make judgments for or against others? On the Hermetic path, the core values are love, devotion, dedication to disciplined spiritual activities, and a continual process of education, intellectual development, mutual explorations, and creative synthesis. The symbols of that path are the

---
201 Matthew 7: 9-11.
202. Matthew 19: 13-15; Mark 10: 14; Luke 18: 16-17.

illumined heart, the light at the center of the world, and that light's manifestation in a variety of alternative spiritual paths. And the core of education is respect, sensitivity, and a deep commitment to cultural equality in rights, freedom, creativity, and social justice.

Thus children should be loved and taught a respectful sense of autonomy so they can act with integrity in their encounters with others.[203] This means they must understand and encounter integrity from an early age. They must be exposed to the core values of exemplary love and respect from the very beginning. And if a couple is unable to manifest the necessary stability and inner qualitative life, they should wait and not subject their children to unintegrated and undisciplined parental emotion, to unclear mental lives. Some parents make the profound mistake of thinking that because they live busy engaged external lives, in their work and social efforts, that such activity is an indication of a disciplined life. Such activity may be an applied, externalized example of one narrow type of discipline but it is far from the inner discipline necessary for living a directed inner life established on the basis of spiritual values and a significant degree of self-knowledge. Many are the parents I have met whose outer lives were a constant whirl of activity but whose inner lives were immature, completely lacking in introspection, and devoid of any strong sense of integrity or spiritual values. External activity is no substitute for inner knowledge; and unexamined social norms are no substitute for carefully chosen and enacted spiritual values. To teach integrity, a parent must live with integrity and there must be an integrity between a parent's word and his or her actions. The more a parent exemplifies his or her own spiritual values, the more they respect the right of their child to think for him or herself, and the more likely a parent is to provide a model for that child's development.

When parents lack spiritual values, when they do not pursue a spiritual path and take the easy road of conventional, unexamined social lifeways, the more likely they will offer little or nothing to the spiritual life of their child. Then a separation occurs as the child begins to realize that there are better ways to live, that conventional social rules can be questioned, and that normative expectations are often founded on shallow and superficial goals. Conventional religious indoctrination is even worse. Because the child is taught not to question the spiritual values they learn, they create a false consciousness. Spiritual life cannot proceed through mere imitation, not if the goal is the actual spiritual illumination of the soul. Only a questioning approach can activate the necessary inner motivation to cross the barriers of social convention and unexamined prejudices. All religions should be questioned, all spiritual

---

203. Colossians 3: 20 tells children to obey parents; but this requires parents to fully respect their children and to give guidance based on respect, love, and empathy.

paths should be subject to critical examination. But this should be done in a respectful and compassionate manner, not simply through an embodiment of cultural arrogance and rational pride. There is nothing wrong in questioning the history, teachings, values, disciplines, organizations, or goals of any religious or spiritual tradition. On the Hermetic path, all ways are subject to study and examination, all paths are resources for education and enlightenment. But no path, least of all the Hermetic path, is to be taken as final or the only way. On the path of the Hermetic Christ, all paths intersect and they meet in the heart of the faithful adherent and lead to a loving and compassionate understanding.

If a child chooses a different path, so be it. If one parent chose one way and the other another way, so be it. But let the intersection of those differences meet in the heart of loving one another and supporting each person's spiritual growth. One of the great Hermetic secrets is that a path freely walked can lead to a heart in which all paths meet. The best way to create the necessary opening of the heart is to act with integrity in loving others while also encouraging them through example. Therefore, let no parents oppress their children in the name of either their belief or disbelief and let no child deny his or her parents because they follow another path. And let single parents work to foster a love for both genders in the child and not let their own experiences blind them to the value of each gender in a more loving world. Single parents have a great burden, as do their children because they have broken the bonds of the alchemical union through which the child was conceived. I do not censure those relationships nor relationships of same gendered parents. But I do caution such parents to foster in their children a loving attitude, that the children form no negative mental habits toward opposite gendered others. Parents cannot live for their children and if they do, they only perpetuate the errors of all parents in creating a world of stereotypes and shadows where children are masked by unauthentic emotional needs. It is not a world of shadows, of images of our own image, that represent the goal, but rather relationships fully alive in Spirit and overflowing with creative abundance and joy. In such a world, freedom of belief is a crucial balance in learning love and honor in all relationships.

Work

To work at honest labor or profession for the good of others and not to the detriment of self; to be considerate, creative, and concerned for the well-being of all humanity. (5:8)

Work is not the center of life, and labor is not an activity that makes men wise nor women worthy of admiration in their elder years. Work is all too often a process that serves a collective tendency, or an institutional activity whose aims do not foster or promote the development of the individual. Work is not the primary basis of personal development; it can easily become an enslavement to needs and necessities which only maintain a façade without depth or fulfillment. Work itself is not enough, it must be meaningful work, work that serves the processes of human development in the most positive sense. Work can easily be a form of entrapment, a round of effort and attention that serves no interests beyond impersonal goals, profits, and limited benefits. Work can be a primary form of activity by which social injustice is strengthened and selfish and narrowly collective goals are served. Work can reinforce the stereotypes of social class and create a false and artificial division between the wealthy and the poor or it can serve the interests of the few through the exploitation of the many. The point of work is not for profit or wealth or power, it is for the value that it gives in enhancing and deepening positive human relations through cooperative efforts and shared benefits. The value of work is found in the ways in which it enhances the qualitative experiences of life and not in how it contributes to quantitative benefits for a privileged minority. Work is a means by which we connect with other human beings through positive efforts, not a matter of gaining advantages to serve our own interests.

On the Hermetic path, a practitioner should choose work that does no harm to others, either directly or indirectly, and results in activity that benefits others through an ethic of positive spiritual values. This is not a matter of formulating a rigid code or inflexible standards. Every situation must be developed individually in terms of the inner clarity and coherence of the practitioner. The consequences of any work should be evaluated in terms of the impact not only on other human beings but also on the environment and on other living creatures. Further, the profits gained through non-harmful work should not be invested in any other form of activity that leads to harm or injury for other living creatures. Work, as a spiritual activity, is best cultivated as a means for the development of lasting positive relations that seek to preserve and value natural, social, and cultural worlds. No such world should be developed through a diminishment or denial of another. Work in such a plural context requires an ethic of respect for differences that is basic to Hermetic practices because difference is an important basis for growth. Worldviews that arise on the basis of excessive power concentrated in the hands of the few, supported by military strength, follow an aggressive ethic of dominance over others resulting in violence, imbalance, and suffering. Work that supports such a dominant worldview only contributes to the illness and imbalance. An aggressive worldview that denies the value of differences, that seeks to dominate through violence and the imposition of unilateral values, exaggerates its own cultural importance and is unhealthy, immature and destructive.

Work in such a culture has diminishing value insofar as the output of labor is a means for the aggression of that cultural world against worlds of others or against its own non-conforming members. An anxious self-defense is no better as it creates a climate of hostility and basic non-cooperation in the name of self-interests and an ethos of isolation and intolerance. On the Hermetic path, work is a means for transformation that does not isolate itself from the larger concerns of the world. The Hermetic path is rooted in globally shared spiritual traditions that seek to integrate cultural diversity in the development of meaningful activities that support world peace, diversity, and cooperation. Such a path has a multitude of forms, expressions, and activities aimed at not only personal transformation but also communally linked, shared transformations. These transformations are not reducible to any single pattern or narrow philosophy. They arise on the efforts and work of many different individuals who share an ethic of cultural preservation and a creative and open attitude toward the future. The relationship between cultures and their institutions, from the Hermetic perspective, is one best defined as co-creative. Work, in this context is aimed at serving the process of cooperation between diverse groups and by developing an inner sensitivity toward spiritual values that can be enacted in an appropriate social environment. The Christ-spirit in this context is to cultivate a loving attitude that is able to confront the boundaries at which changes can be instituted for the benefit of others. It means to seek social justice and to act from a center of positive regard to what each individual, community, or nation can contribute to the process of creating a harmonious, enduring global plurality of cultures.

By "honest labor" I mean work that may be physical and grounded in a pragmatic approach to learning and serving others. Physical skills are certainly necessary for development and work must not be limited to only intellectual or aesthetic activities. Working with the whole body is a crucial part of serving the physical transformation of the world; a garden is not simply thought but made by hand, with tools, through direct physical activity. Many tasks require physical labor and there is no reason to regard such labor as less valuable or meaningful in comparison to more intellective tasks. The pride of education is the downfall of many intellectuals who cannot see beyond the horizon of their specialty and into the world of physical work that utterly supports their own intellective activities. Physical work, the sweat of hard won tasks in handling the physical processes, is crucial and by no means secondary to the necessary work that supports all of us. The basic tasks of labor are all valuable, and every task can be carried out with spiritual integrity, at every level of effort. But such labor should not serve to benefit others through an exploitation of the laborer. An ethic of social justice requires that genuine efforts made in the most basic services receive a full and adequate reward. An imbalanced society exploits basic labor and those who benefit suffer from an imbalanced mental outlook: the beneficiary fails to enact the necessary reforms and transformations that would create a more just and balanced benefit for all.

This failure is a form of denial and isolation from the human situation, one that proceeds through supposing that more privilege does not have more responsibility. But those who benefit from the labors of others have a spiritual obligation to work for the mutual benefit of all. The spiritual responsibility of management is that it must seek to instrumentalize reforms and transformations that will fully recognize and recompense the labors of those from whom they benefit. This means that surplus and profit must be reinvested into the welfare of the laborers, profits shared and not accumulated only for the few. The more one benefits from the profitable activities of others, from their honest labors, the more responsibility those beneficiaries have to work for the welfare, health, and happiness of those that support them. There must be reciprocity, a sharing that benefits all, and not simply empty gestures that create a pretense of giving only to hide an underlying contempt or selfish greed. There is no need for trumpets when we give the widow's pence, better to give it silently and with humility based on an appreciation of how we are each served by the labors of others.[204] In the Christ-spirit, this giving is not simply a requirement but, like the rich man passing through the eye of a needle, it is a spiritual virtue that flows through a deep generosity of human concern and care for the well-being of others.[205] We must purify our motives in giving as well as in receiving; to give in Spirit requires no recognition from others. Responsibility in work is not just a matter of meeting external criteria, but of living up to internalized spiritual values that must be enacted to be made real.

Nor should work result in a diminishing of the worker. Work in the best sense, is creative, challenging, demanding, and yet, fulfilling and beneficial.

---

204. Luke 21: 1-4; Mark 12: 41-44.
205. Matthew 19: 23-24.

Professional labor is the same, it should rise on positive educational experience and proceed through stages to a sense of accomplishment based on inner values and not just on external expectations. The reflexive aspect of all work is to ask: How does this work benefit others? How does it benefit me? Are these two benefits in balance and expressive of my spiritual values? If each of these questions can be answered positively, then the path of work can be made into a spiritual path. But if any one of them is negative, then the path is impeded until that negativity can be rectified. These questions must be asked continually, at every stage of development and challenge, particularly the question of spiritual values. On the Hermetic path, these values are constantly under study and observation in the daily activities of living. The test of the Hermetic transformation is the continual efforts put into manifesting and exemplifying spiritual values in visible forms and expressions. But then, to draw back, reflect, and refine the inner quality of the spiritual work. The mirror of the heart must be polished to allow the purity of Spirit to reflect into the world as a creative source of honest, heart-felt change. This requires sincerity, truthfulness, sensitivity for the feelings of others, clarity of thought, and a willingness to act from motives of compassion. Work should be a positive source for spiritual growth, a medium in which the soulful making of self and others is drawn out mutually with respectful appreciation of differences.

Being considerate and thoughtful of others is a basic practice that leads to inner growth when it cuts through the conventions of outward form. Our considerations for others should not proceed from social habits adopted without reflection or through external social expectation. The value of polite consideration has a spiritual ground in basic human respect and concern for maintaining healthy relationships. It is not a matter of outward forms, but of inner intentions. Creativity is part of the means by which we find ways to open the hearts and minds of others through a respectful and caring presentation of self. The self-other relationship is a creative ground for spiritual growth in every situation where we can find the words of our heart to speak an inner truth that harms no one but also brings to light unspoken concerns that go beyond mere convention and social form. The guideline is not convention but an inner honesty that proceeds through compassion and sensitivity to articulate and to enact the spiritual arts of transformation. Every work situation has these opportunities, that moment when we might act or speak in such a way as to bring to awareness a nuance or a concern that might encourage authenticity by not avoiding necessary issues of development. The Hermetic path is one of transformation, a spiritual art, whose expression and enactment is not isolated to a private realm of inner practices but also functions in the public arena of work and play. Our considerations must move beyond the merely polite and obvious and into the more shadowy realms of development and confrontation with barriers and resistance to spiritual growth.

We are each called to work in accord with our abilities and spiritual gifts. Those callings are diverse in extremes and can range from the most simple to the most complex forms of labor. But this work is necessary for the maintenance of the world, even in the context of spiritual retreat and communal withdrawal. The challenge is to find that work which most benefits the processes of spiritual transformation and serves as an instrumental means for the betterment of communal life. This does not mean that all work must be communal; some workers are best able to serve in tasks more isolated and individual than collective or social. Each must find his or her own path and ground that work in a way of life whose core values are rooted in positive spiritual transformations, in an on-going synthesis of work, play, love, community, and world service. One can accomplish this through art as well as through science, through physical labor as well as through entertainment or providing services for others. My own path has been the path of son, brother, carpenter, home-maker, cook, student, educator, husband, scholar, friend, poet, musician, writer, and spiritual teacher. In every role, I strive for an inner spiritual clarity that will make that work into a valuable experience for others. I see my work as no better or more important than the work of tens of thousands of hundreds of thousands of others. We are all called to epitomize our spiritual values in the work we do and to actualize our potential in serving the actualizations of others. In that process, the Hermetic Christ shines forth as a source of visionary inspiration whose inner presence acts to transform work into a spiritual path. When we walk that path with sincerity, love, and creative integrity, it then becomes a continual source of inspiration and a means for true illuminations.

Play
To rest, play, enjoy life, to laugh, smile and not live in shadows; to reject ascetic extremes, the denial of pleasure, and oppressions of flesh; to celebrate life but to avoid excess. (5:9)

The Hermetic path is not a path of ascetic renunciation and Yeshu'a, the exemplary incarnation of that path, ate and drank and took his leisure with friends and foes alike.[206] At the wedding festival Yeshu'a turned water into wine. While teaching, he called for fish and bread for the hungry who "ate and were satisfied." And he ate and drank with those who witnessed his resurrec-

---
206. Matthew 11: 19.

tion and was "full of joy in the Holy Spirit."[207] Be joyful and love one another, and the joy of Christ will be in you; this is the promise he gave to those who lived with him and who did not fast or deny themselves the natural satisfactions of the body.[208] On the Hermetic path, work is not the only way; there must be relaxation and a letting go of worry, concerns, and obligations. The path of transformation is one requiring inner balance and a rhythmic flow between work and rest, between effort and release, between inner calm and outer activity. The turning pivot at the center of the turning world balances these diverse energies and makes them into a creative resources for the restoration of mind, body, and soul. Communities that thrive must also dance, must welcome the joy of celebration, festival, rites of passage, times of remembering, all with a joyful depth of feeling. Development on the spiritual path must move beyond the sobriety of critical discontent and denial, must acquire the luster of an illumined heart that take joy in life and willingly admires the beauty and diversity of creation. The path of joy is intrinsic to the loving heart, it is open and not closed or overly concerned for its own dignity or status.

Too many have fastened onto the belief that the denial of flesh and natural impulse is an effective means to attain spiritual ideals and many paths are constructed around principles of ascetic denial. On the Hermetic path, affirmation is the way and loving support recognizes the necessity of satisfying healthy appetites to foster growth and a sense of well-being. I am not an ascetic nor do I believe that vows of asceticism are necessary or good for the soul's life and evolution. Some may be drawn to such a path and to those I say walk with care in the way of ascetic vows, never let those vows blind you to the natural needs of incarnate life. The Hermetic center is to live in balance and to choose modes of life that are simple but healthy and that celebrate the natural being of family, love, sexuality, and good habits in eating, rest, work, and play.[209] The formation of ascetic communities that act to repress bodily needs and to deny the value of family, marriage, or children are moving toward an extreme whose methods can easily mislead and produce a remarkably naive immaturity in those who have lived many years under such a system. In this life I have met many monks and nuns who I have found to be quite sincere, open, loving and yet, immature and astonishingly unaware of all of the ordinary struggles of persons who work in the everyday world and who must constantly face the challenges of adaptation and survival. They are particularly remote from the problems of family life, child rearing, and the emotional aspects of sincere sexual love.

---

207. Romans 14: 17.
208. John 15: 10-11.
209. Romans 14: 3.

I do not say that an ascetic way of life cannot produce good, only that such denial will not guarantee maturity or insight into the spiritual conditions in which most humanity lives. There can be ascetic practices that are effective in refining sensitivity and maintaining optimal health and clarity of mind, but these practices do not require special vows, nor rigid codes to actualize their benefits. On the Hermetic path, each individual must determine the nature and extent of their needs in relationship to their goals. And a life of exclusive sobriety and seriousness is not a balanced life, the joy of the path must overflow into activities and natural rhythms that correspond to healthy physical life. There can be play, exercise, games, dances, art and music, festivals and celebrations; times of letting go and times of sharing pleasures. What makes these activities viable on the spiritual path is that they stem from a healthy conception of balance and that they avoid extremes and self-indulgences that harm or injure self or others. Excess is not the way and extremes are not the basis for healthy development; there may be times when we push to the very edge of an ability but then, we draw back and rest. When we move toward the extreme, then we heighten the danger that such an extreme will foster our pride, or establish our abilities strictly in terms of our capacity to surpass others. Competition can be good and it can sharpen our skills and inner potential, but only if it is carried out in a balanced, healthy manner that foster respect for the abilities and concerns of others. Joy is in the sharing and in the mutual benefits, as well as in the inner satisfaction that we have done our utmost without crossing the boundary into extremity.

Balance in pleasure means engaging in activities that enhance the quality of life, that makes the moment full and enjoyable and opens the mind and heart to the value of the present. Spirituality is not simply a postponed realization or a concern for a future that has not yet come. It is much more a concern for a present in which we live in fullness and potential; the spiritual path is the means to make life more enjoyable and valuable now, today. Play is a form of release that is favorable because it allows us to feel and sense our humanity in a light and joyful flow of exchange and inner excitement. If we avoid excess and extremes, healthy pleasures are a means for strengthening life energies. They encourage freedom of expression, balance, and new extensions of self through spontaneity and release from habitual routine and often entrenched patterns of action.[210] In this process of release, laughter and humor are of great importance and a lack of humor is a good indication of burdens unreleased. Humor is a spiritual gift and laughter is a means for expressing our sense of the limits and comedy of human life, it's absurd conditions and

---

210. Bhagavad Gita 6: 17.

often ridiculous poses. On the Hermetic path, joy, laughter, and humor form a lasting complex of relations that touch the very heart of creation. Humor is a function of freeing spiritual energies to express, in a non-harmful way, the convolutions and contradictions of human behavior and beliefs. But in avoiding extremes, such humor is best founded on principles of recognizing one's own limits rather than the limits of others. I take humor as being a crucial aspect of sound spiritual teaching because the teacher can laugh at his or her own limits and boundaries.

A smile is better than a frown and laughter is better than disgruntled complaints and grumbling criticism, not laughter at others, but laughter with others. Those who wish to make others the butt of their humor suffer from a kind of prideful blindness because they fail to see the very shortcomings in themselves that makes them a caricature of their own critical humor. Humor in the healthy sense does not victimize others, does not celebrate an in-group by castigating an out-group, and does not seek status by confirming through humor the bias, prejudice, or disdain of one's own group. Humor in the healthy sense is based in an ability to see the ironic, disproportioned, and strangely mutated contours of the gap between the ideal and the actual. This certainly includes our own behavior and shortcomings. In a more positive sense, a genuine smile is a form of friendly communication and non-harmful humor can create a warmth and sharing that rational analysis cannot reach. Humor can also be superficial and offensive as well as self-serving and demeaning of others; this type is actually not humor but prejudice masked as levity, usually at the expense of others. Sometimes humor can be effective as a means to move people along their path without being offensive but by challenging them with irony that reveals a misdirection of energy. Overall, goodwill and warmth of heart, a lightness of spirit capable of descending to profound depths, can be the best means for reaching out to others and for hearing what they truly want to say. A smile in this context is a means for establishing a non-judgmental link with another, one that expresses love rather than criticism.

In spiritual work, there is a tendency to sink into shadows where humor and play often are absent or incapable of lifting the heaviness that shrouds a deeply serious intent. In such a circumstance, the seeker must examine more carefully the role of joy in celebrating the risings and manifestations of life. Pleasure in sexual experience is certainly a Hermetic sign that creation is an act of joy and even ecstasy. The spiritual arts best unfold their inner potential through a joyful context of inspired expression fired by the imagination and energized through experimentation and exploration. The Hermetic path is not constructed from the past or by precedent of what has been; it unlocks its secrets by moving into an unknown future where play and exploration are central. Joy is at the heart of creation and there is a playfulness in Spirit that seeks to find newness in expressions of subtle truth. There are moments of effervescence, of a bubbling up of laughter and light, that savors the pleasure of the moment and the intensity of the insight. This bursting of light erases shadows and offers a brightness of feeling and thankfulness that expands from the heart and penetrates to the core. In that joy we penetrate and are penetrated and the joy is an *eros* in Spirit, a pleasurable ecstasy that rides a wave of mutual becoming that celebrates life and new insight. Becoming trapped in shadows is a danger; caught in sobriety, seriousness, moody immobility, we lose our way and find only the roots of our fears, tangled and twisted in lacking light. Joy is a transformation. When we open our hearts to the inner joy of Spirit, to its play and humor, we can find our way through the darkest thicket and brambles.

Our celebration is a celebration of life, in all its incarnate forms, in all the fleshly limits and possibilities. We celebrate these possibilities without injuring others and by rejoicing in the multitude and variety of combinations. Life is rich beyond imagining and complex beyond computation. In joy we can see the limits and still laugh together as we search for alternatives to carry us over a boundary or divide. Humor is a healing force, and laughter and play, a healing energy. On the Hermetic path, we seek the laughter of the Christ-spirit, the joy of that laugher joined in the round dance of communal celebration and harmony in Spirit.[211] The Christ smile is one of great humility and pleasure in the accomplishments of others, and in the joy that fills the heart from the light at the center of the world. That smile can ignite the smiles of others and the sparkle in the Christ eye is a laughter filled with tears and joy. And this is good! Our laughter is a benefit and a gift, it serves to lighten our aspirations and to give us the inner expansion that helps us connect with all those who share the laughter. We avoid extremes, but we do not hold back in enjoying what is healthy and pleasurable; we can work, but we can also play and enjoy the play of others. Without this humor and play we will lose our lightness and make our spiritual path ponderous and dark, a way of shadows, not lights. So let play and humor be part of the path, an uplifting inner joy that comes through Spirit as a purification of sorrow and suffering. And our smile can be quiet, subtle, full of life and a source of joy to others, without effort and without forethought. Spontaneity is best and Spirit is the mother of spontaneity; who know this, has understanding and smiles!

---

211. Luke 6: 21; Ecclesiastes 3: 4.

Old Age
To grow old gracefully, to acquire wisdom, learning, a bright clarity in Spirit; to exemplify a life dedicated to Christ; to shine with the radiance of mature age. (5:10)

Growing old gracefully means lessening our demands on others and allowing them the freedom of their choices. On the Hermetic path, growing old means growing into a more aware sense of the value of individual differences and the spiritual importance of diversity within the creative evolutions of Spirit. It means being accepting and not judging the differences in terms of the experiences of only one lifetime. It means opening the heart to the value of diversity and encouraging and fostering the exploration of potential and individual self-worth. It also means pursuing a spiritual path to its completion in such a way that the fruit of this effort is still sweet and lustrous at the very end and not shriveled, hard, or bitter. There is often too much resentment in old age, resentment based on poor choices, on living defensively, on the consequences of efforts directed outwardly to the detriment of the soul's growth. There is a danger of hardening, of pulling into a shell created by a life time of habits whose energies were not directed toward the fruitful nourishing of soul. To grow old gracefully we must each live a graceful life, not just at the end, but as a consequence of a life time of effort to transform mind, body, and soul through positive, loving relationships, in a life dedicated to the fulfillment of spiritual ideals. This requires an inner resistance to normative values propagated as "necessary" or "good" which only serve to reinforce an outer ethic of conformity and obedience to social norms neither reflexive nor dedicated to personally transformative goals. Growing old gracefully means having integrity that has evolved over a lifetime of dedication to Spirit and whose consequence is a gentleness and strength which cuts through the miasma of external, collective norms, and sees into the depths of creation.

To acquire wisdom means something much more than reading and studying many books, or attending many group events, or intellectualizing the contents of a spiritual path. The pursuit of wisdom is inseparable from every aspect of life and its core development springs from the quality of our human relationships. To fail in maintaining a high quality of creative love, a Christ-centered, Sophia-centered dedication to fostering the human spirit through positive regard and strong emotional support will result in a state of isolation, discontent, and a lack of fellow-feeling for others. Empathy is an important part of the spiritual path, and giving to others is a necessary virtue. But this empathy and giving must be balanced with an inner calm and maturation that is not dependent on others for its growth and development. Wisdom is learning this balance: to love and to give, and to go within and find inner strength and guidance that no human being can supplant. The presence of Spirit is a boundless resource whose energies can guide and direct the evolution of soul through a heart-centered living that neither exhausts or depletes itself in the giving. A surplus of Spirit overflows into our lives as an inspiration to reach out and share the bounty with those who are receptive and willing to receive. It does not mean forcing our way of life on others nor does it mean devaluing those who choose another path, another manifestation of Spirit. Our evaluations of others arise from the depths of our feeling and empathy, but our judgments require more than a rationale to justify our feelings. Our judgments, in wisdom, require a lifetime of experience dedicated to the pursuit of spiritual values and their actualization in a realized way of life.

This means our judgments will always reflect our degree of spiritual maturity, and constantly reveal our degree of inner balance and integration. To live in balance means to find the center from which life flourishes and from which the critical mind is released from its bound and limited perceptions. This center is found in Spirit, in the heart of a living cosmos whose inner coherence connects us through deepening awareness, in waking and sleeping states, with an outer world of rich, complex becoming. This becoming is not bound by local social or cultural patterns nor is it determined by the limited experience of the individual or the community. This becoming is a deep and profound spiritual Mystery whose purposes and capacities exceed the comprehension of humanity. Growing old gracefully means recognizing this Mystery as a living presence in the heart, an abiding energy of transformation in all human events, and as an energizing inspiration for the awakening of a complex, global and noetic consciousness. To live in balance means to live with a full awareness of the multidimensional evolutions of Spirit and to embody an integrated perspective on the processes of the Whole. In the Christ-spirit, we can see this in the powerful manifestations of Spirit as miraculous visions, dreams, callings, prophetic words, healing capacities, and the deep wisdom of genuine spiritual maturity. If we live a balanced life, deeply dedicated to spiritual ideals, consistently practice the Hermetic disciplines, and live according to sound ethical values guided by love and empathy, we will arrive at old age with a keen sense of judgment and appreciation for the full workings of Spirit.

Otherwise, if we live contracted, self-serving lives, or lives dedicated to serving others in ways that do not foster inner growth but result only in exhaustion and depletion, we will arrive at old age as caricatures of wisdom— bellicose, quarrelsome, self-indulgent, filled with complaints, blindly demanding of others, withdrawn, locked in a shell of poor habits and constant self-justifications. This is not wisdom, but ignorance; it is not understanding but impoverishment and contraction, a descent into a second childhood which is shallow, confused, and increasingly unaware. Death in this state is fearful but in a state of wisdom it is welcomed and celebrated. The quality of our life and quality of our human relationships bear fruit; what matters is not what we have studied or done, but what we have learned and taken in to share with others. What matters is love, compassion, forgiveness, honesty, insight, purity of motives, and a deep determination to realize our utmost in potential through living respectfully and in generous reciprocity with others. Those who fail in learning these truly important virtues through many years of practice and refinement, will not understand old age as joyful and celebratory. But those whose hearts are pure and receptive to Spirit, who live generously and graciously accept the gifts of others in giving their own, will dance the dance with great joy and ceremony. They will not be stiff and immobile from lack of exercise and passively surrender to their own inner laziness; they will be active, engaged, creatively pursuing, in quiet ways, the wisdom they have earned through inner transformation. They will be sweet not bitter; calm, not anxious; attentive, not distracted; full, not empty.

To exemplify a life dedicated to the Christ-Spirit, in old age, is a matter of interpretation; there is not one way nor fixed criteria by which such dedication can be judged. Sometimes we move away from the center in order to gain a better perspective on it, so that when we return, we bring with us a wealth of understanding of other ways. Such has been my own path; I have studied many religious traditions and many indigenous and folk ways as well. And in all this I have learned much that has enhanced my appreciation for the human capacity for spiritual knowledge. The way of Christ is broad, not narrow, and the realization of the Christ-spirit is a Mystery, not a measurable fact or a matter of obedience to fixed rules or inflexible theologies. Living Spirit is a teacher of great complexity and power whose inner promptings and vivid presentation is beyond codifying and predetermination. To live in Christ means to follow the devotions of the heart in co-creating a world of love and compassion for all living creatures. It means to respect all religious and spiritual teachings that contribute to a more compassionate and just world and to embody within one's own life, the living Spirit of the Christ-Sophia union. To exemplify does not mean to proselytize, to embody does not mean to preach or to evangelize; it means to live as an example of the teachings, not by words of the mouth but by acts of the heart. To exemplify means to live quietly, peacefully, dedicated to principles of spiritual growth through the evolution of the Christ-heart in everyday service and devotion. It means to seek illumination and *gnosis* without external signs or demands; it means to go within and to find the dwelling place of Spirit.[212]

Dedication to Christ requires a dedication to a spiritual path that goes far beyond collective social organizations. It may function through such organizations but that is only an outer form, not the necessary up-swelling of Spirit in the inner heart of the devotee. Like the descent of the Spirit as a morning dove, this dedication falls gently onto the heart of the pure minded, descends gracefully into the spiritual center and reveals there the incredible immensity of the Christ-spirit. The Christ-heart, the golden white lotus of its unfolding rays, reveals an inner *gnosis* whose mature realization is a deep inner harmonizing with outer events. Here one encounters the Hen-to-Pan, the great Mystery of the divine unity, the One That Is All, as experienced through mystical joy and ecstatic realizations. This is what leads to maturity. How many years it takes to integrate and balance such a realization within the soul! How difficult it is to penetrate the masks of our humanity, the layered boundaries which mark the stages by which we each exhaust a lower potential in order to ascend to yet another layer of creative vision. Finally, we break through the veils and behold the Infinite Oceans of the All Becoming Mystery where the multidimensional Metacosm transforms into its deepest essential Unity, where the All is truly One. The symbol of that transformation is the enlightened Christ-Heart, the dedicated rebirth and resurrection of the soul to its higher capacity for spiritual union symbolized of the Christ-Sophia relation. In this union of all that is male with all that is female, lies the path of maturity, lies the way of the Christ as a realized, illumined teacher whose old age is a testimony to a life well lived.

The radiance of this spiritual realization, this attainment of illumined union and spiritual ecstasy, is a path without end. There is no final goal and no necessary consequence that cannot be transcended; there is no collective realization that cannot be surpassed. When we mount upward, we find wider horizons, more space, not less. When we penetrate the depths we find an unending ecstasy, not a blind determinism nor a capricious chaos. What is relative to our wisdom is the degree of our illumination; insofar as we attain genuine insight and an awakened heart in Christ, we also find a deepening maturity boundlessly aware of its innocence and lack of knowledge. This is the paradox of wisdom, that we acquire greater innocence as we open to the infinite within, seeing in that light, the relativity and limits of our own experience, learning, and accomplishments. How great it is! How wonderful! Who

---

212. Bhagavad Gita 7: 1-3.

can fathom it?[213] The radiance of maturity is born of this spiritual realization, it is fostered in its inner integration, and comes to fruition through dedicated humility and practice.

At each stage of development, new horizons of possibility are opened and the potential of Spirit overflows the vessel and fills it with a surplus whose depths are immeasurable. The radiance of mature age is a radiance whose intensity and invisibility is a subtle function of the actual attainments of soulful life and inner spiritual realizations. Its manifest capacity is often unprovoked and occurs spontaneously, effortlessly, to benefit others as an act of Spirit, an act that follows the heart. Love another, desire their healing and behold, such a desire becomes actual and such love has its own immediate, subtle manifestations. This is the luster of old age, this is the miracle of the Christ-spirit, working through the speculum of the heart to reflect its rays on all those who would most benefit from its brightness.

Death

To make death as natural and as unprolonged as possible; to die with friends and family, lovingly; to reduce suffering but not to sacrifice clarity of mind. (5:11)

Death is natural and dying should be natural as well. In the Christ-spirit, death is an unavoidable climax whose experience leads to transformation and new life. This is clearly symbolized by the empty tomb after the crucifixion; the resurrection motif in Hermetic spirituality is inseparable from the transfigured, arisen Christ. As Paul writes, "the natural body sown perishable is resurrected in the spiritual body (*pneumatikón*), imperishable."[214] This spiritual body is the continued life, the on-going essential identity, now transformed according to inner strengths and merits into new, soulful forms of being. These merits are the fruitful consequences of positive, intentional actions strengthened through attentive living and compassionate sharing. In dying, these actions, and those less meritable, come forth in the form of individual visions of suffering and joy. At such a time, the love of family and friends, of those whose love is a sign of transformation given through Spirit, can act as mediums for the souls transition through death to new life and resurrection. Death is not to be feared but faced with inner calm and deep acceptance of the transformative moment, guided by love, through living a loving life. What we bring to our deaths is not simply the habits of a lifetime, but the consequences of our rela-

---
213. Romans 11: 33.
214. 1 Corinthians 15: 42.

tionships with others and the network of energies that have acted to sustain life shared and enjoyed together. Death does not occur simply on the physical plane nor is it a simple consequence of bodily failure, illness, or disease. Death is a transition whose action is rooted in the will and desire of the dying who, in letting go, surrender to a greater process of becoming.

Death is not an end, such a belief is a material illusion, a consequence of thinking only in physical terms. Life is not physical in any strict sense and death is more than a material event. Life is also a psychic, emotive, visionary, spiritual experience that relates us through various sensitive perceptions to a larger, living cosmos of unlimited subtle causes. These causes are spiritual as well as material, soulful as well as energetic, creative as well as reactive. In that greater cosmos of becoming and evolutionary transformation, death is a powerful necessity whose purpose is to shift our awareness out of the rooted, material life and into a new openness to alternative existence. Many people deny death, but at the coming of their own death, rediscover a new meaning and significance through Spirit. The reality of Spirit, in the Hermetic Christ, is the affirmation of life beyond death and beyond a strictly material conception of physical identity.[215] The body is a matrix, a construct of ensouled intelligence and feeling, made visible and material as a medium of experience through an eons long process of adaptation and development. But this development precedes birth and continues far beyond death; birth and death only mark the transitional boundaries between alternative conditions. These alternatives are not the same for each person and differ according to the understanding and maturity of each soul, contingent upon continued growth and integration. The consequences of dying are not the same for every person, they differ significantly according to the willful and compassionate dimensions of personal action and behavior.

In the Hermetic teachings, the life of soulful being is not based on a promised of a distant eternal life, but on the actual on-going present of personal spiritual realization. What occurs after death is not prefigured according to a mythic account of after life, but reflects the actual spiritual and psychic predispositions, intentions, and deep seated attitudes of the dying. Death is a transition to a more viable encounter with these predispositions and intentions, a greater dramatization of soulful being no longer limited by the material boundaries of ordinary aging and death. Released from material bonds, the soulful being enacts its own dramatic construction of its inner psychic world. Its inner predispositions to see and experience a visionary reality is heightened and empowered by the conditional aspects of its new life circumstance in the

---

215. Romans 7: 4.

disincarnate state. The soulful being experiences its own inner predispositions now enhanced and expanded through a liberation from material constraints. It interacts with other soulful beings and inhabits a correspondent psychic-noetic world, best suited to its own soulful condition. This may be regressive as well as developmental; it may mean higher or lower consciousness; greater or lesser awareness; greater of lesser interactive relationships, from joyful reunion and community to a fearful isolation and enclosed alienation. There is no one way, nor one afterlife, nor any set pattern to which all souls must submit. Such teachings are fantasies rooted in the desire to control, manipulate, and punish which reflect the violent and condemnatory attitudes of such a teaching. And those who follow such teachings go to their rewards unaware of the destiny they are co-creating.

Dying should be natural and easy and respected. And expectations should be lowered and not raised, for death is an encounter with limits and boundaries. The moment of dying is surrender, in the most positive sense, when the soulful being releases its hold on one life in order to embrace another without sacrificing love or commitments or ties. Such ties are resolved but not lost, and such love is a continuous fabric in the knitting of new becoming into reborn patterns and relations.[216] If we wish to move from light into Light, then we must also live by the degree of light we embody in each and every condition. What we take into our dying is the consequences of how we have lived in the deepest and most committed sense. Our strengths and weaknesses are not as significant as our deep seated habits, inner attitudes, and consistent patterns of thought, feeling, and reaction. Death is a stripping away, a surrender of flesh, a giving up of embodiment for a more fluid, sensitive awareness in deliberate, soulful perception. As such, we are each a living consciousness whose essential nature cannot be grasped and possessed but only opened to a greater reality of being and awareness. Or we can contract, draw in, be fearful, angry, confused, lost or deliberately divided, fragmented and scattered. Soulful being can be sundered, that is, split and divided into multiple expressions and these aspects can acquire autonomy and independence. Or we can draw together with others, merge and find a collective identity in mass conversion to a certain order and perception within a variety of alternative spiritual worlds. But none of these consequences are predetermined by anything other than the intentions, predispositions and conscious actions in soulful, existential life.

Because this is a transition of great importance, not only for self but for others, we should strive to create the most supportive, relaxed, and personal circumstances possible. Death should not be hidden away nor be imperson-

---

216. Luke 1: 79.

alized or treated as though it were simply an end or termination. It is an ongoing, a new awakening after sleep, a rising up from the body of death into possible light and renewed energies. Death is a personal choice and dying is a personal choice as well; we should choose carefully our circumstances and time. While this is not always possible, it is a Hermetic teaching that choosing your death is possible and desirable. The place, time, and moment can all be chosen in an act of surrender and transition. Sometimes we surrender to outside forces and events, sometimes according to introjected diseases, both individual and collective, and sometimes we can choose a natural, brief transition. There is no one ideal nor is there one preferable pattern. Each must follow the necessity and inclinations of his or her heart; but dying is a personal choice and should not be given over to the will or control of others. No medical professional has the right to determine if a person should continue to live or to die; to make such a decision is to abuse the rights and privileges of the dying. The right of the individual to choose the nature and time of their death far exceeds the rights of either the state or any medical profession to make such determinations. To prolong life is not a goal of the Hermetic spiritual path; just as Christ faced his death, even in the prime of his life, so too, we must each chose, where possible, the time and place of our dying without surrendering that right to others.

Not all will choose an independent death, most will elect to follow the norms of their social circumstances and the communal practices of their spiritual group. That too is a choice and should be accepted as long as it does not result in the violation of the person in terms of their right to refuse treatment or medical applications. No one has a right to force treatment on another and any medical professional or healer who assumes the right to make such a decision violates the spiritual integrity of the individual. Nor on the Hermetic path should we choose to anesthetize, dull, or surrender consciousness to experimental pharmacology or drugs, herbs, and other mentally inhibiting treatments. To relieve pain, some substances may be used, or to effect cures, pharmacology may be useful and necessary. But in approaching death, there should be clarity of mind and heart; a lucidity that is not masked by drugs or psychotropic substances. Death should be natural and dying should be in a clear, luminous, natural state of release and surrender. Perhaps someone dies in sleep, quietly and in a deeply relaxed state; this is excellent and valuable. Another suffers and must face prolonged dying based in the nature of an illness or disease; treatment is necessary to ease this person through the stages of their illness, medication might be necessary or advisable. But in dying, in the approach of death, clarity is more desirable than a masked condition of forgetful, disoriented, hazy awareness only vaguely aware of its imminent end. While it is not a permanent end, such a death can prolong the suffering and confusion of the dying after their death and can, in fact, lead to a serious impairment of their understanding in the after-death state.

To die with friends and family, surrounded by their love and concern is certainly a most desirable end. It allows for leave taking and farewells, and opens the reality of death to the living who witness the end of another in the positive light of giving emotional support and strength. In losing another, we must learn not to cling to their departed life, must not overly grasp at holding them in the embodied form. There must be a willing release, a positive loving letting go of the living to help the transition into another stage of life. As a mother must not hold onto her child but let it come forth and be born, so too the living must not inhibit the dying but allow them the dignity to die in their own way without clinging and holding them back. Death is a crisis only when it is impeded, postponed, or denied to those willing to let go; in those unwilling to die or let go, it becomes a crisis based in fear and denial. But fear and denial will not stop death. On the Hermetic path, death is faced many times, and dying is the art of transformation; it requires courage, inner purity of mind, and willing surrender to processes greater than the individual will. Without appropriate living, dying is hard; without a spiritual practice, dying in an unknown journey without guides or directions. On the spiritual path, death is a constant aspect of meditation and reflection; we all live on the boundary of death every day. This fact should be brought to mind regularly and attended to with depth and focus. In considering death, we also face the importance of living fully in the practice of our inmost values. To embody a good death requires living a good life, one naturally grounded in health, joy, positive relations and a loving heart toward others. The good death is a mirror for the good life, and even in tragic circumstances, to die well is an ideal worthy of pursuit.

The World

To live in the world and through the world according to the dictates of the heart; a heart surrendered to Christ, resurrected in Spirit, and redeemed in Mystery through unending Grace. (5:12)

To live in the world means to see and understand the world as a creative ground for transformation. The Hermetic path does not seek escape or denial of the world and the Hermetic Christ is a presence in this world that facilitates transformation through love and healing. The *prima materia* is Spirit and the place of its manifestation is the entirety of the creation including all physical and material worlds. These material worlds are by no means lower; they represent the place of highest synthesis where all material, psychic, and spiritual energies coincide. From here, in this world, we may attain the full realization of our deepest capacities for spiritual illumination and understanding. We accomplish this through a series of alchemical-hermetic processes that purify, sublimate, and integrate soulful being with the fullness of the created worlds. We unite "all that above with all that is below" and synthesize our understanding into a creative resource for further awakenings. This process is on-going and has no final end; it proceeds through stages toward maturity by opening ever wider vistas for exploration. In the multilevel cosmos, there is a continuum of experience that far exceeds ordinary human awareness and unveils a Metacosm in which a great multitude of worlds link through the essential teachings of a great variety of illumined teachers. It is not the teachers that matter, nor even the teachings or revelations; what matters is the transformation and spiritual awakening of the many to the One.

The One that is All, *Hen to Pan*, has no boundaries or limits, no adequate descriptions, and no one teaching that best represents its manifestations. As an unbound totality, the living depth of Great Mystery, the Unknown Deep, it is beyond the capacity of language to access because it is truly translingual and transrational. It does not function in and through thought or language but through revelatory states and higher perception in which the cognitive functions are suspended in an enstatic, transpersonal illumination. Yet the consequences of that enstatic realization, that deep *gnosis*, acts as a creative and moving presence in the world to bring about a continual stimulation of awareness and insight. Such an illumination is like a cup from which others may drink and be sustained in living life in the direct, natural sense, like a staff that supports us or a sword that cuts through ignorance and shadows, like the cornerstone of a foundation. Its purpose is not simply the ecstasy of the moment or the inner transformation of the individual, both necessary and good, but also to instrumentalize Spirit. The path of *gnosis*, in the rebirthed Hermetic teachings, is to become a vessel overflowing for the awakening of others. As Yeshu'a was a living manifestation of the Christ principle, so too are each and every follower of the path; the degree of their influence, a reflection of the communal and collective needs of their times. It is not influence that matters, but the living presence of the Christ-Sophia union in the heart of the seeker. From this union, the effects emanate into the world giving creative support to a world-transforming affirmation, through love, through healing, through deep and shared respect.

The world is our challenge; our social and cultural milieu, the place where the transformation is most needed. We can change our location, build better communities, and reorient the cultural and social norms to a more illumined way of action. Or we can live in stasis, caught in the webs and energies of older and less aware ways of thought and behavior. The choice to follow the Hermetic path, the Hermetic Christ, is a choice for transformation, for an decisive way to move though boundaries with inner humility. It is not a choice for aggressive self-assertion, nor for passive acceptance of collective norms; it is an inner way between extremes, one that choose creativity and inner development over conformity and obedience to external norms. The Hermetic path unlocks a creative determination to move through the static and archaic energies of past errors and into a more fluid, adaptive, and alchemical spirituality based in compassion and respect. The new wine is not a wine of intoxication but of deep sobriety whose luminous effects purify and expand awareness into dimensions of joyful understanding. Whatever our location, in new communities or old, as individuals or as a collective, the challenge is the same, to live in accord with the Christ-spirit, a heart-centered life of caring relations and exemplary, trustworthy, and mature behaviors.[217] This means living a committed life based in commonly shared values that redirect human energies toward an informed, life-preserving, creative mentality. It means knowing and acting according to clear spiritual goals that orient the soulful being to a heart-centered way of life. It means valuing the world and all the beings in it as reflections of Spirit, as sparks in search of insight and understanding.

To live according to the dictates of the heart means that we must first purify the heart, purify our mental and emotive life, and discipline the undisciplined habits of socially diverse, distracted, and confused collective tendencies. By collective tendencies I mean something more than commonly held popular attitudes or large scale, unreflective collective notions. I also mean the collective tendencies of the small scale community, any community, however small, that seeks to impress members with conformity to communal sanctioned values, behaviors, or mental perspectives. To purify the heart means to discover an inner freedom that cannot be bound by socially constructed rules or shared mental configurations. The journey toward illumination is a journey toward freedom from external determination or control; it also is a journey toward inner surrender to the up-flowing, unitary energies of Spirit as it shapes and forms the inner landscape. It is a journey that deeply values relationships but also maintains integrity. The consequences of this transformation extend far

---

217. John 7: 38.

beyond the mental horizon of the individual being and yet, that transformation seeks to individuate and actualize a maximum in spiritual potential. The "dictates of the heart" are only as pure and deep as the soulful intelligence of the individual, an intelligence subject to continual development and integration. Often in the process we may reach a plateau, a period, sometimes lasting years, in which we seek to actualize earlier insights and experiences. The danger is to imagine the plateau as the desired goal or end. There is no end or final goal, only the on-going processes of spiritual transformation in an expansive universe of infinite magnitude and scope.

Therefore, every plateau is a place of reintegration and reflection, a temporal expansion that suggests a need for reassessment and self-examination. It is not a place from which to judge the accomplishments, strengths, or weakness of others, but a place to evaluate self-limits and potential. It is a time of reflection and reconsideration, an opportunity to honor all the debts of the past and to reformulate perspectives on the future. It is a momentary pause that is meant for healing and a shaking of the foundations; a time to let go of all attainments, successes or failures, for a revaluing of primary intentions. Always, there is room for new development and greater maturity in understanding the processes that sustain our many correspondent relationships, with others, with self, with the Metacosm. In this time of self-reflection, the Christ-spirit must also be reassessed, revalued, and the luminous energy opened to the deeper unknowable core. The truth is greater than Christ, greater than the image or the presence, and far surpasses the static tendencies of older age to concretize and hypostatize. Dissolve the images! Let go of the forms and figures, release all angelic manifestations, surrender all spiritual experiences, and empty the heart-mind to the unfathomable core of the Deep. Dissolve the patterns, the plateaus, all movement, all comings and goings, all stillness and action, all being and being-in. There, the Christ-spirit dissolves, the Sophia vanishes, the self-reflective mirror, the speculum of the heart, disappears and the reflexive intellect finds its highest resolution in the vastness of the All-Pervading Deep. There, there are no boundaries, no coming in or going out, no movement and no stillness, only the ever-living eternal One.

To be resurrected in Spirit means to be rebirthed into and through the mystical world of visionary experience, again and again, until the process of refinement and sublimation is no longer visible in demarcated stages or states. This is not simply a matter of will or intentions, it takes more than will or intention to fully accomplish the process, to fully realize the depths and fullness of *gnosis*. All is *gnosis*, there is nothing that is not *gnosis* and no being or being-in can recognize the limits or ends. What has limits, boundaries, and conditions is the actual being, the specific vehicle of the manifestation, the particular being or vessel within which Spirit works. Resurrected in Spirit means realized to the utmost of those boundaries, accomplished to the fullness of our individual capacity, matured to the depths where we are surpassed and transcended. Even the greatest spiritual teacher, prophet, reveler, or enlightened being has these limits, has a boundary that reflects an era of awakening and transition. We can climb the mountain, some climb higher, some lower, but those lower down may see more and those higher up may completely miss a view that would complement and enhance their understanding. Every teaching is limited and conditional and the Hermetic path is no different; it too has its boundaries, limits and relative value. The worth is in the individual application and in the capacity stimulated toward a realization of inner potential. To fully realize this capacity, death and rebirth must occur, however subtle or slow, however rapid or sudden; and then the realizations must be integrated into a lifetime of living in an embodied, value-centered way.

There are no shortcuts to spiritual maturity, and no technique or belief will engender a predetermined end. Every person who undertakes the spiritual journey will discover that it branches, again and again, in accordance with their needs and inner capacities. A path that does not branch and that does not engender further choices and decisions is bound by its collective norms. On the Hermetic path, the life of the individual is highly valued as a unique manifestation of Spirit, one whose realization requires responsible choices, meaningful relations, and personal decisions. It is not a path of self-sacrifice as much as a path of self-realization, one receptive to the needs and concerns of others, but not determined by those needs and concerns. Freedom in Spirit is a realization of the Hermetic principle that we all live in correspondence to one another and that the strong center is magnetized by its individuated development. That magnetic current is an increasingly strong center for Spirit to actualize the realizations of others and in the reciprocity between beings, in correspondence, a multitude can be transformed. On the Hermetic path, this center is subtle and magnetic but non-coercive; attractive, but not controlling or consensually over-determined; energetic, but neither compulsive nor dogmatic. The inner values of its full realization are love, compassion, and understanding shared with others in a non-competitive and receptive manner. Shared perspectives take precedence over authoritative, individual claims while individual development takes precedent over communal expectations.

Reciprocity between followers of a Hermetic perspective is experimental, exploratory, interactive, and grounded in loving respect. Conformity is not the issue, personal development proceeds through exploration and testing, not through simple obedience or a rote affirmation of beliefs or values. Every step must be lived, particularly the capacity to love through the Christ-spirit, to heal the wounds of others, and to energize the necessary transformative awareness that leads to rebirth and illumination. Belief in illumination is by no means sufficient or adequate; only the actual quest and search for illumination, only its actual attainment can produce the desired impact. And this search must pass through a life-time of stages and states to fully realize its depths and capacity and limits. No one experience is adequate and no one burst of light sufficient for the understanding the fullness of the Hermetic transformation. In the Christ-spirit we find an image of the awakened soul that no longer clings to the external form or tradition, that no longer exhibits a proud exterior and an inner emptiness. Everything must be ground to dust, shifted, shaken down, tested, and refined until we can fully recognize the boundaries of our own illumined experience in the face of the Deep. Then we can work for the transformation of humanity without effort, can be a living example of the Christ light, can illumine the dark fears and heal the divisions and fractures of global humanity without pushing forward our own worth or value. Then we can live in peace and in peace, we can love one another because we have discover the secret of our common humanity, born of Spirit and realized through an infinite variety of holy paths. This is the Christ Blessed Raa-Nub. Amen, and again, Amen.

Raa-Nub

The Sixty Aphorisms

I. THE WAY: ONE CHRIST

The Christ: There is only One Christ, eternal and everlasting; the same today, tomorrow and forever. (1:1)

The Way: To seek Christ in both self and others as a true source of guidance and inspiration, as a key to the deepest mysteries of the heart. (1:2)

Faith: To distinguish the Christ of faith from the Christ of flesh, to know that Christ is infinite in every manifestation. (1:3)

The Gate: To know that Christ is a Gate by which we enter the depths of eternal Creation, a way without end, a light without limit. (1:4)

The Four Faces: To know the four faces of Christ: the literal, the metaphorical, the mythic, and the mystical; four cornerstones of mature faith. (1:5)

The Fifth Face: To behold within one's self, the fifth face of Christ, with joy and humility resolved and reconciled in a healing love. (1:6)

The Church: To revere Christ and not the church in substitution to Christ; to follow inner Light beyond the ideologies of dogma or tradition. (1:7)

Authority: To invest no fixed authority in priest, minister, teacher, or guide; to follow the intuitions of the heart through devotion to Christ. (1:8)

Robes: To keep the robes and garments of Christ clean, pure, undefiled; to wash from them, all martyr's blood, all stains of sacrifice. (1:9)

Diadems: To know that the diadems of Christ are persons of humble faith who manifest Presence in a smile, in a touch, a word or caress. (1:10)

Grace: To open the heart in healing self and others; to give where there are wounds or sorrow; to share in Christ all joys and grace. (1:11)

Illumination: To seek full and complete knowledge through illumination and higher awareness; to see in Christ, the ascents and descents of Spirit. (1:12)

II. THE TRUTH: ONE SPIRIT

Spirit: There is only One Spirit, eternal and everlasting; the same today, tomorrow and forever. (2:1)

Truth: To know that truth is never too high nor too deep to be fathomed; beyond prejudice, perception and sense, in outflowing depths of Spirit. (2:2)

Below: To learn from all teachings, not to worship Christ above others; to know a Way within Spirit that puts self below, not above. (2:3)

Resurrection: To rejoice in resurrection and new life; to seek the manifestations of Christ in the gifts of Spirit, celebrating life, not death, nor the cross, nor crucifixion. (2:4)

Communion: To join in communion of Spirit with all faiths, all ways; to not deny differences, to value diversity, to share and celebrate, to see the Christ of others. (2:5)

Devotion: To love as the Bride loves, purely, with deep devotion, without attachment or sentimentality; calmly, in Spirit's deep Wisdom, forgiving, open, full of good fruits. (2:6)

Blessings: To know the union of the Bride and Bridegroom through the blessings of Spirit; to behold the New Heaven and the New Earth, the unity of all Above with all Below. (2:7)

The Veils: To know Spirit as the Mother of many Mysteries; that the heart is veiled, to remove the veils, gently, with loving care, to see the Child reborn (2:8)

Gifts: To know the City of Peace as Spirit dwelling within all humanity; to enter the Gates of the City with gifts of thanksgiving. (2:9)

Humanity: To receive the gifts of Spirit in a fullness of humanity; to live in harmony with all species, to reverence all life, to serve rather than to be served. (2:10)

Comfort: To give comfort to those in need without distinctions of class, position, race, color, gender, or age; trusting the power and humility of Spirit, of Christ. (2:11)

Divinity: To see and honor the divinity of others as they are honored in Spirit; to let go, to not cling nor build barriers, but to open a Way and make it a guided path. (2:12)

III. THE LIGHT: ONE GOD

God: There is only One God, eternal and everlasting; the same today, tomorrow and forever. (3:1)

The Light: To seek with humility, patience, devotion, and courage, the Mysteries of Light; a knowledge that surpasses ideas, images and intuitions. (3:2)

Unknowing: To seek God in Mystery, in all stages, in the depths of Unknowing; to discern that all stations are Christ created and all stages, Spirit born. (3:3)

Prayer: To know that prayer is a ladder and meditation an Infinite well; to draw deeply, to extend fully without fears, attachments, or sorrows. (3:4)

Attributes: To know God as veiled in attributes, images, forms, qualities, inwardly, outwardly and in Christ; to pass beyond and yet, to honor each manifestation. (3:5)

The Footstool: To know that the Footstool of the Throne is in your own heart; may you be strong enough to receive It, even an atom of its dust! (3:6)

Wisdom: To be utterly One in the Mystery, with God, in essence and manifestations; by Wisdom inspired, by Light uplifted, illumined, alive. (3:7)

Mystery: To enter the Mystery of God with an empty heart; in unity and accord, to surrender to fullness without measure; Immersed, overflowing, utterly dissolved. (3:8)

Unity: To maintain the unity of Spirit in the bonds of peace; to diversify, individuate, recombine, create, explore and expand with ever greater honor to the Whole. (3:9)

Revelations: To seek revelations in what is small as well as what is large, in the subtle, correspondent, Above, Below, and In-Between; in what gives life and in what takes it away. (3:10)

Beyond: To never say "I am God" for God's Mystery is within every being and comes on "clouds of glory" infinite with beauty, grace, and that which is Beyond knowing. (3:11)

The Return: To know God-in-Christ is a great gift and grace; but only if that knowledge returns to the world sure, serene, dedicated to lasting harmony and peace. (3:12)

IV. THE ETERNAL: ONE TRUE LIFE

The Eternal: There is only One Life, eternal and everlasting; the same today, tomorrow, and forever. (4:1)

Unbound: To know there is Eternal Life, now, in the present, in the past and in the future; life unbound by space, time, matter or form. (4:2)

Salvation: To know that the Light of Christ, in Mystery, lifts us above all heavens and hells; for the benefit of all beings, granting salvation to all. (4:3)

Redemption: To recognize our faults and errors, to not judge others, in youth or in old age; to seek redemption through faith, knowledge, and truth; through kindness and reconsiderations. (4:4)

Virtues: To practice the five virtues: honesty, non-violence, self-discipline, patience, and generosity; to avoid lying, theft, injury to others, impatience, greed, and slander. (4:5)

Vice: To propagate the Way through example, not words or teachings; simply, without vice or addiction; to be a firmly planted tree, deep rooted, mature, with good fruit. (4:6)

Healing: To work for the healing of self, others, the nations, the world; to reconcile conflict, to mediate, to act with integrity; to not abandon Christ, to never wave our own banners. (4:7)

Peace: To know that all races and religions are one in Mystery, each to be honored in their contributions to peace; Christ is a way, but there are other equally good ways, difference is Creation; the Source, Infinite. (4:8)

The Waters: To give the Waters of Life freely, with compassion, love, mercy, and forgiveness; to not condemn nor judge those who walk in unknowing, nor deny the unheeding. (4:9)

Bread: To share the Bread of Life, in communion, fellowship, with friends and strangers; giving when you are asked, receiving when you are given, simply, with sincere feeling. (4:10)

The Cup: To drink from the Cup that gives Life, the Grail of pure living and dedicated intent; to quest for spiritual rebirth, to overcome boundaries, to awaken the soul. (4:11)

Reborn: To follow Christ, even unto Death; to die and to be reborn; to live again, in this world, the worlds between, to go beyond, and still embodied flesh. (4:12)

V. THE EVERLASTING: THE RECITATION

Everlasting: There is only One Christ, One Spirit, One God; only One True Life, eternal and everlasting. (5:1)

Faith: To start with the "i" in faith and to develop the "i" in Christ, that you may See clearly what you only now believe, that you may realize the "i" in Infinity and the "i" in Absolute. (5:2)

Education: To seek knowledge, learning, and education in all that is knowable, but to never neglect the heart, nor to act to harm others; to love deeply, to know Spirit-in-Christ. (5:3)

Good Thoughts: To speak good thoughts with love, neither from fear nor hope of rewards; to open the hearts of others through the openness of your own. (5:4)

Marriage: To treat one another with deepest respect and reverence, hearing what the other needs, giving where possible; to never raise male or female over the other, to live in mutuality with equal justice. (5:5)

Sexuality: To know that sexuality is sacred, a joy and natural pleasure, a celebration of life, a part of Christ and the Bride; to avoid excess, abuse and manipulation; to be gentle, willing to learn. (5:6)

Children: To raise children with a genuine sense of freedom and with the autonomy to choose and to act with integrity; to not oppress them with a parent's faith, nor turn from them in theirs. (5:7)

Work: To work at honest labor or profession for the good of others and not to the detriment of self; to be considerate, creative, and concerned for the well-being of all humanity. (5:8)

Play: To rest, play, enjoy life, to laugh, smile and not live in shadows; to reject ascetic extremes, the denial of pleasure, and oppressions of flesh; to celebrate life but to avoid excess. (5:9)

Old Age: To grow old gracefully, to acquire wisdom, learning, a bright clarity in Spirit; to exemplify a life dedicated to Christ; to shine with the radiance of mature age. (5:10)

Death: To make death as natural and as unprolonged as possible; to die with friends and family, lovingly; to reduce suffering but not to sacrifice clarity of mind. (5:11)

The World: To live in the world and through the world according to the dictates of the heart; a heart surrendered to Christ, resurrected in Spirit, and redeemed in Mystery through unending Grace. (5:12)

Bibliography

Biblical Texts:

There are many translations and on-line resources for all biblical texts; my own preference is for the RSV (Revised Standard Version) as most commonly read, also the New International Version; for references, Michael D. Coogan et. al, editors, *The New Oxford Annotated Bible with Apocrypha* (NY: Oxford University Press, 2001, Third Edition). For the actual Greek text, see Alfred Marshall, *The RSV Interlinear Greek-English New Testament* (MI: Zondervan, 1978). Many other Greek and Hebrew biblical interlinear text translations are available on-line, including various Concordances, for example see: http://biblehub.com/interlinear/ and http://www.biblestudytools.com/ and for the Qur'an see http://www.altafsir.com/Quran_Search_Eng.asp .

Additional References:

Ali, Abdullah Yusuf. Translator. *The Holy Qur'an*. Kitab Bhavan, New Delphi, 2001.

Irwin, Lee. *Visionary Worlds: The Making and Unmaking of Reality*. NY: State University of New York Press, 1996.

_____. *Awakening to Spirit: On Life, Illumination and Being*. NY: State University of New York Press, 1999.

_____. *Alchemy of Soul: The Art of Spiritual Transformation*. WA: Lorian Press, 2007.

Radhakrishnan, S. Translator. *The Bhagavadgītā*. Harper Collins Publishers, India, 2010.

Salaman, Clement. Et al. *The Way of Hermes: New Translations of the Corpus Hermeticum (with Hermetic Definitions)*. VT: Inner Traditions, 2000. For a more thorough analysis of these texts, see Brian Copenhaver, *Hermetica* (Cambridge University Press, 1998).

About the Author

Lee Irwin is a Professor in the Religious Studies Department at the College of Charleston (SC) where he teaches comparative world religions with an emphasis on Native American traditions, western esotericism, hermeticism, contemporary spirituality, mystical cosmology, and transpersonal religious experience as related to dreams, visions and paranormal perception. He is the Vice President of the Association for the Study of Esotericism (ASE) and a Guiding Voice for the Seven Pillars House of Wisdom. He has been a workshop leader, guest speaker, and group facilitator for over twenty-five years, particularly in the areas of visionary cosmology and the development of the sacred human. He can be reached at: Irwinl@cofc.edu.

About the Publisher

Lorian Press is a private, for profit business which publishes works approved by the Lorian Association. Current titles can be found on the Lorian website www.lorian.org.

The Lorian Association is a not-for-profit educational organization. Its work is to help people bring the joy, healing, and blessing of their personal spirituality into their everyday lives. This spirituality unfolds out of their unique lives and relationships to Spirit, by whatever name or in whatever form that Spirit is recognized.

For more information, go to www.lorian.org.

www.ingramcontent.com/pod-product-compliance
Lightning Source LLC
Chambersburg PA
CBHW020049170426
43199CB00009B/216